CW01163281

The Media and Inequality

This book brings together a vast range of pre-eminent experts, academics, and practitioners to interrogate the role of media in representing economic inequality. It explores and deconstructs the concept of economic inequality by examining the different dimensions of inequality and how it has evolved historically; how it has been represented and portrayed in the media; and how, in turn, those representations have informed the public's knowledge of and attitudes towards poverty, class and welfare, and political discourse.

Taking a multi-disciplinary, comparative, and historical approach, and using a variety of new and original data sets to inform the research, studies herein examine the relationship between media and inequality in the UK, Western Europe, and the USA. In addition to generating new knowledge and research agendas, the book generates suggestions of ways to improve news coverage on this topic and raise the level of the debate and will improve understanding about economic inequality, as it has evolved, and as it continues to develop in academic, political, and media discourses.

This book will be of interest to academics and practitioners alike in the areas of journalism, media studies, economics, and the social sciences as well as political commentators and those interested more broadly in social policy.

Steve Schifferes is currently Honorary Research Fellow at City, University London's Political Economy Research Centre (CityPERC) in the UK, where he was the Marjorie Deane Professor of Financial Journalism from 2009 to 2017. He has lectured widely on the global financial crisis and is the co-editor of two volumes, *The Media and Financial Crises* (2015) and *The Media and Austerity* (Routledge, 2018). He reported on economics and business for BBC News from 1989 to 2009.

Sophie Knowles is Senior Lecturer in Journalism at Middlesex University. She has written widely on the media's role in the global financial crisis. She co-edited *The Media and Austerity: Comparative Perspectives* (Routledge, 2018). Her new book, *The Mediation of Financial Crises: Watchdogs, Lapdogs or Canaries in the Coal Mine*, was published in 2020.

Routledge Research in Journalism

34 Journalists and Job Loss
Edited by *Timothy Marjoribanks, Lawrie Zion, Penny O'Donnell and Merryn Sherwood*

35 Global Media Ethics and the Digital Revolution
Edited by *Noureddine Miladi*

36 The Future of the Presidency, Journalism, and Democracy
After Trump
Edited by *Robert E. Gutsche, Jr.*

37 Journalistic Practices in Restrictive Contexts
A Sociological Approach to the Case of Iran
Banafsheh Ranji

38 The Media and Inequality
Edited by *Steve Schifferes and Sophie Knowles*

39 Newspaper Building Design and Journalism Cultures in Australia and the UK, 1855–2010
Dr Carole O'Reilly and Dr Josie Vine

40 Emerging Practices in the Age of Automated Digital Journalism
Models, Languages, and Storytelling
Edited by *Berta García-Orosa, Sara Pérez-Seijo and Ángel Vizoso'*

41 Global Pandemics and Media Ethics
Issues and Perspectives
Edited by *Tendai Chari and Martin N. Ndlela*

For more information about this series, please visit: https://www.routledge.com/Routledge-Research-in-Journalism/book-series/RRJ

The Media and Inequality

Edited by
Steve Schifferes and Sophie Knowles

Routledge
Taylor & Francis Group
LONDON AND NEW YORK

First published 2023
by Routledge
4 Park Square, Milton Park, Abingdon, Oxon OX14 4RN

and by Routledge
605 Third Avenue, New York, NY 10158

Routledge is an imprint of the Taylor & Francis Group, an informa business

© 2023 selection and editorial matter, **Steve Schifferes** and **Sophie Knowles**; individual chapters, the contributors

The right of **Steve Schifferes** and **Sophie Knowles** to be identified as the authors of the editorial material, and of the authors for their individual chapters, has been asserted in accordance with sections 77 and 78 of the Copyright, Designs and Patents Act 1988.

All rights reserved. No part of this book may be reprinted or reproduced or utilised in any form or by any electronic, mechanical, or other means, now known or hereafter invented, including photocopying and recording, or in any information storage or retrieval system, without permission in writing from the publishers.

Trademark notice: Product or corporate names may be trademarks or registered trademarks, and are used only for identification and explanation without intent to infringe.

British Library Cataloguing-in-Publication Data
A catalogue record for this book is available from the British Library

ISBN: 9780367611729 (hbk)
ISBN: 9780367611750 (pbk)
ISBN: 9781003104476 (ebk)

DOI: 10.4324/9781003104476

Typeset in Baskerville
by codeMantra

We dedicate this volume to the memory of Professor John Hills

Contents

List of figures — xi
List of tables — xiii
Notes on contributors — xv
Acknowledgements — xix
Preface — xxi

Introduction: The media and inequality — 1
STEVE SCHIFFERES AND SOPHIE KNOWLES

I
Understanding inequality — 9

1 **Flat-lining or seething beneath the surface? Two decades of changing economic inequality in the UK** — 11
POLINA OBOLENSKAYA AND JOHN HILLS

2 **Wealth inequality in the UK** — 29
CARYS ROBERTS

3 **Social Mobility** — 42
DUNCAN EXLEY

4 **Racial economic inequality: The visible tip of an inequality iceberg?** — 54
KURT BARLING

5 **Homeownership: The key to wealth inequality?** — 68
PIRMIN FESSLER AND MARTIN SCHÜRZ

II
Framing poverty and inequality 83

6 Poverty and the media: Poverty myths and exclusion in the information society 85
PETER GOLDING

7 The rhetoric of recessions: How British Newspapers Talk About the Poor When Unemployment Rises 1896–2000 98
DANIEL McARTHUR AND AARON REEVES

8 Factual television in the UK: The rich, the poor and inequality 117
JOANNA MACK

9 The Attention Cycle of Income Inequality in the UK and US Print Media, 1990–2015 135
MARTIN W. BAUER, PATRICK McGOVERN AND SANDRA OBRADOVIC

10 Comparative trends in the portrayal of poverty and inequality 150
JAIRO LUGO-OCANDO AND BRENDON LAWSON

III
Public opinion, inequality, and the media 163

11 Public attitudes to poverty and inequality 165
ELIZABETH CLERY

12 Debating inequality: The case of Piketty's capital in the 21st century 176
ANDREA GRISOLD AND HENDRIK THEINE

13 The media and austerity 192
MIKE BERRY

14 Covid-19, inequality and the media 211
STEVE SCHIFFERES AND SOPHIE KNOWLES

15 **Stuck in a feedback loop: Why more inequality leads to lower levels of concern** 226
JONATHAN J.B. MIJS

Index 239

Figures

1.1	Percentage change in full-time hourly pay by gender, 1995 to 2015 (adjusted by CPIH)	14
1.2	Levels of net household income after housing costs at different parts of the distribution, 1995–6 to 2015–16 (2015–16 prices)	15
1.3	Change in median incomes after housing costs by age group, 1995–6 to 2015–16 (2015–16 prices)	18
1.4	Income after housing costs at the 10th percentile for selected regions (£/week, 2015–16 prices)	21
1.5	Change in incomes after housing costs by housing tenure, 1995–6 to 2015–16 (2015–16 prices)	22
2.1	Aggregate total wealth (net) (£million), 2016–18	30
2.2	Median household wealth by region or nation of Great Britain, 2016–18	32
5.1	Functions of Wealth. Illustration authors' own	70
5.2	Renters, owners, and capitalists in the US, the UK and continental European countries	73
5.3	Shares of income in relation to the population share of renters, owners, and capitalists for all countries	76
5.4	Shares of wealth in relation to the population share of renters, owners, and capitalists for all countries	77
5.5	Wealth-to-income ratios for renters, owners and capitalists in the US, the UK and continental European countries	78
7.1	Unemployment rates and stigmatising rhetoric about the poor in Britain, 1896–2000	104
7.2	Increases in unemployment and stigmatising rhetoric	106
7.3	Association between unemployment and the frequency of stigmatising words or phrases, 1896–2000	109
7.4	Trends in the frequency of stigmatising rhetoric and welfare attitudes in the UK	112
9.1a	Public discourse in relation to academic publications, with the three phases of 'sounding the alarm', 'calming down', and 'sorting the problem'	139

xii *Figures*

9.1b	The growth of scholarly economic literature on 'income inequality' and combined UK and US salience of 'income inequality' relative to newshole	140
9.2	Topic salience of 'income inequality' as percentage of all inequality items in any one year and for all newspapers	143
9.3	The surge of inequality news in the US and in the UK, indexed to the peak year	144
9.4	The surge of income inequality news in the US and the US, comparing business news outlets (WSJ, FT, on the left) with general news outlets (NYT, GUA, on the right) indexed to peak year	144
10.1	Nodes present in article by news outlet	155
10.2	Percentage of nodes present in The Guardian over three years: 2002 (n = 27), 2009 (n = 46) and 2019 (n = 197)	159
11.1	View that there is "quite a lot" of poverty, by HBAI absolute poverty measures, 1994/95–2018/19.	167
11.2	Proportions agreeing there is "quite a lot" of poverty in Britain, by type of media consumed, 2006–18	171
12.1	Number of newspaper articles by stance towards redistribution policies, 2014–2015	185
14.1	Percentage that think poverty and inequality will increase as a consequence of the pandemic	215
14.2	Percentage who want to see more equal distribution of wealth	217
14.3	Frequency of accessing economic news, 2005–20	219
14.4	Public satisfaction with media coverage of economy during the pandemic, 2011 vs 2020	220
14.5	How well did journalists do covering the following? 2011–20	221
15.1	Belief in meritocracy across countries over time	227
15.2	Citizens' inequality beliefs by social class and country-level income inequality	231
15.3	Citizens' inequality beliefs by change in income inequality experienced	233
15.4	Citizens' concerns about inequality by social class and popular inequality beliefs	234

Tables

1.1	Levels and changes in household wealth, 2006–8 and 2014–16 (nominal)	16
1.2	Overall inequality measured by 90:10 ratios, 1995–6, 2005–6, and 2015–16	17
1.3	Levels and changes in household non-pension wealth by housing tenure, 2006–8 and 2014–16 (nominal, £000s, GB)	23
1.4	Changes in median hourly pay incomes after housing costs, and wealth by ethnicity, selected groups, 2005–15	24
1.5	Levels and changes in median and 10th percentile hourly wages, incomes, and wealth by disability status, 2005 to 2015	25
5.1	Class shares in percentage of total income and wealth	75
6.1	Percentage of households owning selected communication goods, UK 2019	94
6.2	Household expenditure on communications, UK 2018/19	95
7.1	Descriptive statistics for words measuring stigmatising rhetoric about the poor	103
7.2	Association between unemployment rate and stigmatising rhetoric adjusting for covariates, 1896–2000	107
7.3	Association between unemployment rate and placebo words adjusting for covariates, 1896–2000	108
7.4	Examples of newspaper word usage by relevance and sentiment	110
9.1	Research corpus of print media, 1990–2015	138
9.2	Compares peak levels of media salience for different issues since 1990	142
10.1	Frequency and percentage of news stories that feature poverty	156
10.2	Most cited source by news outlet	157
12.1	List of selected news outlets	178
12.2	Number of newspaper articles with a stance towards economic inequality	180

Notes on contributors

Martin W. Bauer is Professor of Social Psychology and Research Methodology at the London School of Economics, UK. He investigates 'common sense' in a comparative perspective and in relation to emerging technologies. His international project-network, MACAS, designs and analyses public attitude surveys, mass media mapping and qualitative enquires on controversial topics of science across the world.

Kurt Barling is Professor of Journalism at Middlesex University, UK. He is a former special correspondent for BBC News, where he spent 25 years reporting on British social, cultural and economic affairs, and won several awards for his work on reporting race. His book, *The 'R' Word*, on racism, was published in 2015.

Mike Berry is Senior Lecturer in the Cardiff University School of Journalism, Media and Cultural Studies, Wales. His research focuses on how the mass media affects public understanding of social, political and economic issues. His book, *The Media, the Public and the Great Financial Crisis*, was published in 2019.

Elizabeth Clery is a freelance social researcher, who has previously worked for NatCen Social Research, the Government Social Research Service and in the voluntary sector. She has a particular interest in poverty, inequality and welfare, and in ensuring that social research fully informs policy development and evaluation in these areas.

Duncan Exley is Former Director of the Equality Trust and now trains and advises voluntary-sector organisations on reaching and involving a wider demographic. His book, The *End of Aspiration? Social Mobility and our Children's Fading Prospects* was published in 2019.

Pirmin Fessler is a senior economist at the Austrian Central Bank. His current research focuses on wealth inequality, intergenerational transfers and private households' portfolio choice and financial vulnerability. He is a member of the ECB's Household Finance and Consumption Network, and an Advisory Board member on the Luxembourg Income Study.

Peter Golding is Emeritus Professor at Northumbria University, UK, where, until retirement, he was Pro Vice Chancellor for Research and Innovation. He was head of the Department of Social Sciences at Loughborough University, UK, from 1990 to 2006, and then Pro Vice Chancellor for Research there. His classic study, *Images of Welfare: Press and Public Attitudes to Poverty*, was first published in 1982. His latest book is *Unpacking Digital Divides* and he is currently completing a book on communications and inequality.

Howard Glennerster is Emeritus Professor of Social Policy at the London School of Economics.

Andrea Grisold is Professor of Economics and Director of the Institute for Heterodox Economics, Vienna University of Economics and Business, Austria. Her latest book, *Economic Inequality and News Media: Discourse, Power and Redistribution* (with Paschal Preston), was published in 2020.

Sir John Hills was the Richard Titmuss Professor of Social Policy at the London School of Economics. He was Director of the Centre for the Analysis of Social Exclusion (CASE) from 1997 to 2016 and Co-Director of the International Inequalities Institute from 2015 to 2018. He published widely on poverty and inequality, both for academic and non-academic audiences, and was a government policy advisor on poverty, pensions and public housing. John died on 21 December 2020.

Sophie Knowles is Senior Lecturer in Journalism at Middlesex University. She has written widely on the media's role in the Global Financial Crisis. She co-edited *The Media and Austerity: Comparative Perspectives* (Routledge, 2018). Her new book, *The Mediation of Financial Crises: Watchdogs, Lapdogs or Canaries in the Coal Mine*, was published in 2020.

Brendon Lawson is University Teacher at Loughborough University. He specialises in the communication of data, especially during crises.

Jairo Lugo-Ocando is the Dean of the College of Communication at the University of Sharjah in the UAE.

He was previously Deputy Director of the School of Media and Communications at the University of Leeds, UK, and Head of the MA Global Journalism programme at the University of Sheffield, UK. His book, *Blaming the Victim: How Global Journalism Fails Those in Poverty*, was published in 2014.

Joanna Mack is Honorary Research Fellow in the School of Policy Studies at the University of Bristol, UK, and co-editor of the *Journal of Poverty and Social Justice*. She was Senior Producer, then Head of Video and Audio at the Open University, UK, from 2004 to 2016, having worked for many years in broadcast television. In 1983, she pioneered a new approach to measuring poverty as the director of the ITV series *Breadline Britain* and has continued to broadcast, write and lead research on this topic. Her most recent publication is *Breadline Britain: The Rise of Mass Poverty* (2015).

Daniel McArthur is Post-Doctoral Research Fellow in the Department of Politics and International Relations at Oxford University, UK. His research has focused on the relationship between economic inequality and the stigmatisation of people in poverty in public opinion.

Patrick McGovern is Reader in the Department of Sociology at the London School of Economics. He specialises in the sociology of work, international migration and labour market inequality, and is the co-author of *Markets, Class and Employment* (2007), an ESRC-funded longitudinal study of the conditions, attitudes and experiences of British workers.

Jonathan J.B. Mijs is Assistant Professor in Sociology at Boston University, USA, Veni Fellow at Erasmus University, Rotterdam, the Netherlands, and Visiting Fellow at the International Inequalities Institute, London School of Economics. He has researched and written widely on public attitudes towards inequality and meritocracy.

Polina Obolenskaya is a Visiting Fellow at the Centre for Analysis of Social Exclusion (CASE), London School of Economics and a Research Fellow in Sociology at City University of London. Her research interests are social and economic inequalities, poverty, and multidimensional disadvantage, as well as, more recently, violence and its impact on society.

Sandra Obradovic is Lecturer in Psychology at the Open University and an Associate Researcher at the Electoral Psychology Observatory, London School of Economics. Her research interests focus on exploring the connections between history, national identity and socio-political change.

Aaron Reeves is Associate Professor of Evidence-based Social Intervention and Policy Evaluation at Oxford University and Research Fellow at LSE's International Inequalities Institute. His research focuses on understanding the causes and consequences of social and economic inequality across countries.

Carys Roberts is Executive Director of the Institute for Public Policy Research, a leading UK think tank that focuses on economic and environmental justice. She was previously the Chief Economist and Head of the Centre for Economic Justice at IPPR.

Steve Schifferes was the Marjorie Deane Professor of Financial Journalism at City University of London, UK, from 2009 to 2017 and is currently Honorary Research Fellow at City's Political Economy Research Centre (CityPERC). He has lectured widely on the global financial crisis and is the co-editor of two volumes, *The Media and Financial Crises* (2015) and *The Media and Austerity*

(Routledge, 2018). He reported on economics and business for BBC News from 1989 to 2009.

Martin Schürz is Head of the Monetary Unit at the Austrian Central Bank and project leader of the Austrian Household Finance and Consumption Survey. In 2017, he was the Albert Hirschman Research Fellow at the Institute of Human Sciences (IWM) in Vienna. His research focuses on the wealth inequality and emotions.

Hendrik Theine is Post-Doctoral Researcher at the Institute for Heterodox Economics, Vienna University of Economics and Business, Austria.

Acknowledgements

We are grateful for the support of Middlesex University in hosting the Media and Inequality Conference in December 2019, which was the origin of this volume, as well as providing continuing support for this project. We are also grateful for the additional financial support for the conference provided by the Institute for New Economic Thinking (INET) and its research director, Thomas Ferguson. Among other things, this enabled us to invite international participants to take part, including our keynote speaker, Nobel Laureate Joseph Stiglitz. Steve would also like to thank his colleagues at City University of London's Political Economy Research Unit where has been an Honorary Fellow during the preparation of this volume.

We would like to pay a special tribute to Sir John Hills, the Richard Titmuss Professor of Social Policy at the London School of Economics, who was both an inspiration and the lead speaker at our conference. He sadly passed away during the preparation of this volume, and we are dedicating it to him. John was one of the world's leading scholars on inequality and poverty. He was not only an outstanding academic but also a superb communicator, who believed it was important to improve public understanding of inequality. We have included an appreciation of John's work by his predecessor at LSE, Professor Howard Glennerster.

We would like to thank our publishers, Routledge, for their understanding of the difficulties caused by the pandemic while this volume was under preparation, and all our contributors who persevered under these conditions.

We are grateful to the Oxford University Press and Sage Publications for permissions to republish the articles by John Hills and Polina Obolenskaya; Aaron Reeves and Daniel McArthur, and Jonathan J.B. Mijs, respectively.

This volume could not be completed without the love and support of our partners who believed in us and understood the importance of this project. Steve would like to thank his wife Caroline for her love and support. Sophie would like to thank Ryan for his continued and unwavering support of her work.

Preface

Remembering John Hills
Howard Glennerster

John Hills' untimely death in December 2020 was a great personal loss to those of us who knew him well and an even greater loss to the community of scholars who have sought to understand inequalities in society and the barriers to advancement that threaten the lives of so many.

John was recruited to the LSE by Tony Atkinson in the late 1980s to join and co-direct, with Julian LeGrand and Atkinson, a programme of work on the economics of social policy called the 'Welfare State Programme'. What was the economic and distributional impact of the Welfare State? Since it took a quarter of our National Income, these were important questions. They were either largely neglected by economists or presumed to be harmful. Economics needed to take distributional issues seriously, Atkinson argued. That is what John Hills did for the rest of his career.

He remained at the LSE until his death shortly before what would have been his 'retirement'. John brought statistical rigor, hard economic analysis and a passion to put things right. This meant he never thought it enough to write papers in the top journals, though he did that. Your findings had to be simplified and communicated to a wide audience, he argued. You had to be prepared to spend time working for and sitting on independent committees and government working parties.

His work for the *Rowntree Inquiry into Income and Wealth* (1995) raised public appreciation of the sheer scale of economic inequality that had grown since 1980 in the run up to the 1997 General Election. That it became a significant political issue at that election was in no small part the result of his work for that Inquiry.

The Turner Commission (2005) on pension policy, on which he was a key member, achieved a political consensus that had been absent for half a century. For those trying to plan for their retirement, the repeated changes of political direction in the post-war years could not have been more destructive. Fuel poverty policy was also reshaped as a result of a report by him. His public service and this body of work were deservedly recognised in his Knighthood in 2013. But

John knew that report writing was not enough. You had to be prepared to get up early in the morning and appear on the BBC's Today Programme or take part in the Jeremy Vine Show. You had to challenge critiques, misunderstandings or the sheer misrepresentations of a committee's work and do so quickly. A report was not done and dusted once it was published. It had to remain in virtual unofficial existence and challenge critics. It was something he and Adair Turner did successfully with their pensions report.

It was not enough merely to convince academic colleagues. You had to boil things down to the key arguments and come up with simple illustrations. Perhaps the classic example of this was the work he did with Julian Le Grand in 1989 and 1991 for Granada Television's *World in Action*. They took two families – the Ackroyds and the Osbornes – a working class and a better off middle class family – and tracked their fictional but realistic lives. What did they contribute in taxes to pay for welfare services and what did they draw out over a lifetime? To a large extent, people drew out what they paid in. The welfare state was a lifetime savings bank at work, not a set of handouts to layabouts. Later, he brought this analysis up to date and elaborated on it in detail in *Good Times Bad Times: The Welfare Myth of Them and Us* (2015). It was perhaps his most powerful popular contribution.

The work of the 'Welfare State Programme' and that of its successor (the Centre for the Study of Social Exclusion), which he led for so many years, are lasting tributes to his team building and leadership. As I recalled earlier, they grew from an initiative by one of the country's, indeed the world's, leading economists – Tony Atkinson. He, too, died before his time taken by cancer. As indeed, did Richard Titmuss, after whom John's Chair was named. But great work and great personalities live on. That is true of them and will be true of John.

References

Hills, John (2015) *Good Times Bad Times: The Welfare Myth of Them and Us*, Bristol: Policy Press.

Pensions Commission (2005) *A New Pensions Settlement for the Twenty-First Century: The Second Report of the Pensions Commission*, London: The Stationery Office.

Rowntree Foundation (1995) *Rowntree Inquiry into Income and Wealth* Volume 1 *Report* Volume 2 *Evidence* by John Hills, York: Joseph Rowntree Foundation

Introduction

The media and inequality

Steve Schifferes and Sophie Knowles

Inequality has become the defining economic issue of our time. In the last few years, there has been increasing recognition by key international organisations such as the World Bank (2020), the IMF (2020) and the OECD (2020a) that growing inequality is a key factor in stifling growth. National governments increasingly recognise that they must develop strategies which benefit the 'left-behinds'. Growing public concern about inequality has also led to populist revolts against political elites that have swept America, Britain and parts of Europe. The inequalities revealed during the coronavirus pandemic, and now the cost-of-living crisis, have rekindled the debate. The media will continue to play a crucial role in mediating our new understanding of inequality.

But the media's performance in covering inequality and poverty has been patchy. As a result, the public is not well informed about the extent or dimensions of inequality. There has been even less debate in the media about the causes of inequality and possible remedies. In contrast, inequality's twin, poverty, has attracted considerably more media attention and has been the subject of more academic research. However, much of the media coverage has portrayed the poor in highly negative terms, encouraging stereotypes which stigmatise those on benefits. Far less attention has been paid to potential remedies for poverty or its deeper causes. And while those in poverty are shamed, far too frequently the rich are portrayed as benefactors of society who live an affluent lifestyle we should all aspire to.

Our key aim in this book is to stimulate a debate on how journalists are covering inequality and how they could do better. Journalists face challenges in understanding the complex dimension of the problem, while academics are often unable or unwilling to use the media to communicate their views to the public. We want to encourage further academic research in this area and especially to encourage more inter-disciplinary and comparative work. Therefore, this volume includes contributions from journalists, economists, social policy experts and campaigners as well as media scholars. While our focus is on the UK, there are a number of comparative chapters span the globe, ranging from the US and Germany to Brazil, India and Australia.

DOI: 10.4324/9781003104476-1

Why inequality matters

In his popular book *Good Times, Bad Times: The Welfare Myth of Them and Us (2015)*, John Hills had a simple answer to this question. Measured over a lifetime, poverty, job insecurity and financial difficulties affect far more of us than we realise, so the policies that governments pursue towards inequality and poverty should be of interest to us all. He argues that poverty and inequality are inevitably linked together, so it is not possible to consider the one without the other.

The pioneering work of Tony Atkinson (Atkinson, 2015) is an indispensable guide which explores the many dimensions of inequality, both in the UK and internationally, and the best ways both to measure it and tackle it.

It is widely recognised that inequality has negative effects both on the economy and on overall well-being. The Nobel prize winning economist Joseph Stiglitz argues in *The Price of Inequality (2012)* that the growing inequality of income and wealth, with disproportionate gains at the top, weakens the economy and leads to slower GDP growth and more instability.

Richard Wilkinson and Kate Pickett (2010, 2018) show that less equal societies are more likely to suffer from a range of other social ills, including higher crime rates, more mental illness and poorer educational outcomes. Their evidence is that material possessions alone cannot compensate for the loss of community and solidarity. The shame of poverty also has a crippling effect on mental health as well as material well-being of those who are poor (Walker, 2014).

The pioneering work of Sir Douglas Black (1988) and Michael Marmot (2020) has demonstrated that economic inequality leads to huge disparities in health, with life expectancy 10 years higher in rich areas than poor ones.

The Covid-19 pandemic has cast an even harsher light on the issue of inequality in Britain and countries around the world. It has shown how inequalities of wealth and income, social class, education, housing, age and ethnicity all contribute to the differential health and economic impacts of the pandemic, and how important the media's role was as the filter through which the public receives the messages that politicians and scientists wish to convey.

The structure of the volume

Understanding the complex dimensions of inequality and the various ways it can be measured is a prerequisite for good reporting. Therefore, in the first section of the book, we consider the various dimensions of inequality, including income, wealth and social mobility and recent trends in these areas. Secondly, we look at the portrayal of poverty and inequality in comparative and historical perspective and in different media. In our third section, we look at the complex interaction between media coverage and public and political attitudes towards inequality. This includes new research on the public's view of the media coverage of the pandemic and its economic consequences.

This volume focuses mainly on *economic inequality in the UK*, although we are well aware of the need for further media research on its other dimensions (such as race, disability, gender and age). There is also a growing body of academic research that focuses on global poverty and inequality (Atkinson, 2019; Deaton, 2015; Picketty, 2014; Milanovic 2016; Chase and Banteby-Kyomuhendo, 2015). And in the UK, the policy debate on how to tackle inequality has intensified (Atkinson, 2015; Deaton Review, 2020; IPPR, 2018; Resolution Foundation, 2018).

Part I: the dimensions of inequality

As the chapters in the first section demonstrate, the complexities of measuring poverty and inequality should not be allowed to distract us from the central facts – the growing inequality and poverty in Britain in the last few decades, and the decline in social mobility, income and wealth for the next generation, compared to the relative success of the Baby-boomer generation.

John Hills' and Polina Obolesnskaya's opening chapter outlines the way inequality in its various dimensions have evolved over the past 20 years. They show that overall, inequality grew rapidly in the 1980s and 1990s and, since then, has levelled off at a much higher level. But there has been a marked change in the share of the top 1%, whose incomes increased sharply over the last decade while the living standards of the majority stagnated. Meanwhile, composition of the poor has changed, with the majority of the poor now in low-paid jobs. While the number of poor pensioners has declined sharply, the number of children living in poverty has also increased to one in three.

Wealth inequality has grown even faster than income inequality, as the chapter by Carys Roberts explains. The total value of wealth in the UK tripled in the last 20 years, with much of the growth associated with escalating house prices. That wealth is largely concentrated in the top 10% and especially the top 1% of society. The gap between the income of company bosses and the average worker in their firm has also grown exponentially. The tax system – which taxes income more heavily than wealth – also contributes to this disparity.

The structure of wealth in quite unique in Britain, as compared to other developed countries, as Martin Schürz and Pinmin Fessler illustrate in their comparative chapter. While residential property dominates wealth in the UK, financial wealth is much more important in the USA, while company ownership and ownership of rental property is more important in Continental Europe. This fact may explain the greater political challenges faced in the UK in taxing wealth.

From a long-term perspective, a key issue is social mobility. As Duncan Exley's chapter shows, social mobility in the UK has declined since the 1950s and 1960s when an increase in higher paid, white-collar jobs as a proportion of the labour market allowed more people to move up the ladder without increasing downward mobility (Goldthorpe, 1980). Education has been seen as the key to individual social mobility, but changes in the job market have stymied working-class mobility. Lack of access to the property market for the younger generation is also contributing to growing inter-generational inequality.

Finally, Kurt Barling's chapter on race and inequality shows that certain ethnic minority groups (but not all) have suffered disproportionally from poverty and falls in real income. He argues that we need to disaggregate the BAME category (Black and Minority Ethnic) used in Britain to better understand what is happening. He is concerned that the prominent portrayal of very successful black people in the media distracts from a proper understanding of the still difficult situation that the majority still face.

Part II: portrayals of Inequality and Poverty: stigmatising the poor?

This section reflects the fact that poverty rather than its structural roots in inequality has been the main focus of media attention and research. What is particularly striking is that the negative portrayal of poverty in the popular press has changed very little in the 40 years since the publication of Peter Golding's pioneering *Images of Welfare* in 1982. As he shows in his current chapter, the poor are still being stigmatised as scroungers who are too lazy to go to work. This category now also includes immigrants who are seen as taking advantage of the UK benefits system and is little changed despite recent cuts to the level of benefits.

As Golding points out, these attitudes have deep roots in English culture going back to hundreds of years. The historical link between unemployment and 'scroungers' in the press also goes back a long way, as the chapter by Aaron Reeves and Daniel McArthur demonstrates. Their work, using a data set that spans 100 years of UK newspaper coverage, shows that negative coverage of the poor rises during economic recessions, contradicting the notion that there would be more sympathy for the poor when their poverty could be attributed to the state of economy, not simply due to their own moral failings.

A negative view of the poor is increasing dominating factual television, as Joanna Mack's chapter outlines. Serious television documentaries on poverty and its causes have declined following changes in government regulation that reduced the public service obligations of broadcasters. In their place, there has been a rise in reality TV shows that stigmatise the poor. The result has been 'poverty porn', cheap to make, fly on the wall documentaries with such titles as *Benefits Cheats*, while other 'reality TV' celebrate the role of the rich. As a documentary film-maker for ITV in the 1980s, who produced a seminal series investigating poverty in Britain which she has regularly updated (Mack and Lansley, 1985; 2015), Joanna has had first-hand knowledge of this change.

Looking at comparative and international perspectives enriches this picture. Jairo Lugo-Ocando and Brendon Lawson examine the debate about poverty and inequality on a global scale, updating his earlier work (Harkin and Jairo Lugo-Ocando, 2018). He demonstrates how the emphasis on 'neo-Malthusian' principles, that the poor are a burden to society, and the parallel rise of neo-liberalism have taken root in media coverage around the world. Paradoxically, he shows that in many developing countries, which generally have a higher level of poverty and inequality than in richer countries, the media are now even stronger advocates of this position.

As well as the portrayal of poverty and inequality, a key issue is how much salience they have in the media. Are these issues given enough prominence to become part of public debate at all? Martin Bauer and colleagues provide a comparative view of the coverage of inequality in the US and the UK through analysing newspaper content over 20 years. They find major fluctuations in the degree to which the press follows these issues, but at no time has inequality 'broken through' with the public as, for example, climate change has done (which is now seen as a central problem of society). The up-and-down cycle of coverage does bear some relation both political and academic interest in inequality, but the relationship is not always clear. This brings us to the importance of the political debate in shaping media coverage and public attitudes to inequality, which is the focus of the next section.

Part III: the press, the public and inequality

Does the public share the view of much of the popular press about the poor?

In the first contribution to this section, research by Elizabeth Clery shows that coverage can change public perceptions of poverty in both directions. Using longitudinal data from the British Social Attitudes Survey, she argues that increased coverage of poverty in the last few years in the quality press (especially the Guardian) has led to a significant rise in those who think poverty is increasing, even though the official data showed a flatter trend. Although her data show that newspaper readership did correlate with attitudes to poverty, the overall change in public perceptions was largely accounted for by changes among Labour voters, suggesting that political views are also a key element in the equation.

But what about the role of politicians, and how much do their arguments influence the media and the public? Mike Berry has looked at the coverage of austerity after the election of the Coalition government in 2010. He used television news bulletins and focus groups to examine their impact on the perceptions of poverty, inequality and the role of state. He shows that government narrative that blamed austerity on Labour profligacy rather than the 2008 financial crisis – repeated over and over by the Chancellor George Osborne and given widespread media coverage – became dominant and remained the conventional wisdom for most of the decade. One consequence was a strengthening of the belief that those on benefits 'who kept the curtains drawn' were sponging off the state when its resources were being stretched.

Differences in political ideology in the different countries can also help explain how the same academic research on the rise of inequality can lead to very different conclusions. Andrea Grisold and Hendrik Theine use discourse analysis to examine the press reception given to Thomas Piketty's influential and extraordinarily popular book, *Capital in the Twenty-First Century (2014)*, which argues the root of inequality is the higher returns to capital compared to the returns to labour. As she explains, the reception of Piketty's book varied considerably in different countries, as did the lessons the press (and politicians) took from it. While Picketty was feted, not least in the US where he was invited to the White

House by President Obama, there is little evidence that this led to proposals for higher taxation of wealth. In fact, press scepticism about his argument was even higher in Germany, where despite a large welfare state, conservative economic ideology was dominant.

The chapter by Steve Schifferes and Sophie Knowles brings the story up to date by examining public attitudes towards the media coverage of the pandemic in the UK, using a specially commissioned opinion poll. It shows that the public has an intense interest in understanding the economic consequences of the pandemic but is highly critical of how well media has done its job. The polling also shows that public concerns around inequality and poverty are rising although there are still some divisions on how much the government should do to remedy the situation.

A deeper perspective on the limits of the media's ability to change attitudes on its own provided by Jonathan J.B. Mijs. His comparative study looks at the coverage on inequality in the press in four countries, two in the developing world. He shows that giving people more information about growing inequality has little effect on attitudes when they believe that the government is so corrupt that it will do nothing about it – and, indeed, when officials are themselves seizing much of the country's wealth for themselves. He also suggests that the growing residential and job segregation between rich and poor means that there is less sympathy for the plight of the less well-off.

Conclusions

The chapters in this book demonstrate the wide range of issues that arise from any discussion of the media and inequality and also provide some pointers for further research. Academic research on the media coverage of inequality is an early stage, compared to the amount of work on portrayals of poverty. Why is there so little coverage of inequality? And why have negative stereotypes of the poor persisted for so long? More comparative and historical research could help answer these questions.

There is also something of a disconnect between the outstanding research being done in the UK on the extent of poverty and inequality, the limited understanding of these issues by some journalists and editors, and the misperception of the public regarding the basic facts on the extent of poverty and inequality. One challenge in covering inequality for journalists is its complexity and the lack of one central measurement that captures what is going on. Another is the much more highly politically charged discourse, as any in-depth discussion is likely to throw up the controversial question of redistribution.

Further research is needed, both in terms of the level of knowledge journalists have and the sources they use when writing stories on this subject, as well as understanding the process of editorial selection of stories. Establishing closer working relationships between academic experts and journalists, and fostering greater understanding among editors, could help bridge this gap. Another important factor is how journalists approach and portray individuals who may be in very different social and economic circumstances from themselves.

We are living in a time of profound change when trust in many institutions – from the media to the government – has sharply declined and when new global problems – including the pandemic and the cost-of-living crisis – are emerging which may require very different ways of thinking. Inequality is one of those big issues whose time has come. The media must play its proper role in contributing to the debate, and as scholars must continue to examine how well the media is playing that role. We hope this volume has contributed to that process.

References

Atkinson, Anthony (2019), *Measuring Poverty around the World*. Princeton: Princeton University Press.

Atkinson, Anthony (2015), *Inequality*. Oxford: Oxford University Press.

Black, Sir Douglas (1988). *Inequalities in Health: The Black Report*. London: Penguin.

Chase, Elaine, and Grace Bantebya-Kyomuhendo, editors (2015), *Poverty and Shame: Global Experiences*. Oxford: Oxford University Press.

Deaton, Angus (2020), *Inequality: The IFS Deaton Review*, Institute for Fiscal Studies, accessed at https://www.ifs.org.uk/inequality/

Deaton, Angus, (2015), *The Great Escape: Health, Wealth and the Origins of Inequality*. Princeton: Princeton University Press.

Golding, Peter, and Sue Middleton (1982), *Images of Welfare: Press and Public Attitudes to Poverty*. Oxford: Martin Robinson.

Goldthorpe, John (1980), *Social Mobility and the Class Structure in Modern Britain*. Oxford: Clarendon Press

Harkin, Steven, and Jairo Lugo-Ocando (2018), *Poor News: Media Discourses on Poverty in Times of Austerity*. London: Rowman and Littlefield.

Hills, John (2015), *Good Times, Bad Times: The Welfare Myth of Them and US*. Bristol: Policy Press

International Monetary Fund (2020), *The IMF and Inequality*, accessed at https://www.imf.org/en/Topics/Inequality

Institute for Public Policy Research (IPPR), (2018), *The Commission on Economic Justice*, accessed at https://www.ippr.org/cej/about-cej/

Mack, Joanna, and Stewart Lansley (2015), *Breadline Britain: The Rise of Mass Poverty*. London: Oneworld Books.

Mack, Joanna, and Stewart Lansley (1985), *Poor Britain*. London: George Allen & Unwin.

Marmot, M (2020), *Health Equity in England: The Marmot Review Ten Years On*, accessed at https://www.health.org.uk/funding-and-partnerships/our-partnerships/health-equity-in-england-the-marmot-review-10-years-on

Milanovic, Branko (2016), *Global Inequality*, Cambridge, MA: Harvard University Press.

OECD (2020a), *In It Together: Why Less Inequality Benefits All*, accessed at http://www.oecd.org/social/in-it-together-why-less-inequality-benefits-all-9789264235120-en.htm

OECD (2020b), Building a Resilient Economy: How we can emerge stronger from the Covid-19 pandemic, accessed at https://www.oecd.org/coronavirus/en/

Piketty, Thomas, (2014), *Capital in the Twenty-First Century*. Cambridge, MA: Harvard University Press.

Resolution Foundation (2018), *A New Generational Contract: The Final Report of the Intergenerational Commission*, accessed at https://www.resolutionfoundation.org/advanced/a-new-generational-contract/

Stiglitz, J. (2012), *The Price of Inequality*. London: Allen Lane.

Walker, R (2014), *The Shame of Poverty*. Oxford: Oxford University Press.

Wilkinson, Richard, and Kate Pickett (2018), *The Inner Level: How More Equal Societies Reduce Stress, Restore Sanity, and Improve Everyone's Well-Being*. London: Allen Lane.

Wilkinson, Richard and Kate Pickett (2010), *The Spirit Level: Why Equality Is Good for Everyone*. London: Penguin.

World Bank (2020), *Poverty and Shared Prosperity 2020: Reversal of Fortunes*, accessed at https://www.worldbank.org/en/publication/poverty-and-shared-prosperity

I
Understanding inequality

1 Flat-lining or seething beneath the surface? Two decades of changing economic inequality in the UK*

Polina Obolenskaya and John Hills

Introduction

The United Kingdom (UK) is well known as one of the more economically unequal industrialised countries (OECD, 2015). It is commonly perceived that inequalities have increased in recent years. The economic and financial turmoil from 2008 is an obvious engine, as are the subsequent fall and then very slow recovery in real wages (Clarke and Gregg, 2018), the austerity policies of the 2010 Coalition and then Conservative governments, and rapid growth in the biggest fortunes after the initial impact of the crisis (*Sunday Times*, 2018). Assumed inequality growth and the ways some people and areas have, therefore, been 'left behind' have been blamed for recent political dramas, including the 2016 Brexit vote.

But even in aggregate, the picture is more nuanced. Trends since 1970 in four income inequality measures—the Gini coefficients and 90:10 household income ratios, measured both before and after allowing for housing costs remind us that the big changes in UK income inequality were a generation ago, mainly under Mrs. Thatcher in the 1980s.

In this chapter, we focus on the 20 years after 1995–6. The overall trends for this period are far less dramatic than the recent rise in the salience of inequality might suggest. The 90:10 ratio, whether before or after housing costs, ended in 2016–17 close to where it started in 1995–6—slightly up after allowing for housing costs, slightly down before allowing for them. Neither shows a dramatic rise after the crisis; if anything, there is a fall. The Gini coefficients reach high points around the time of the crisis, falling back sharply by 2010–11, with a rise afterwards that is reversed in the final year. As a general description, inequality has plateaued, rather than its increase continuing or reversing.

Other forms of UK economic inequality show contrasting trends. For instance, inequality in male hourly wages continued to grow between 1994 and 2014, with the 90:10 ratio rising from 4.1 to 4.5 (Belfield et al., 2017, using FRS data).

---

* This chapter is adapted from 'Flat-lining or seething beneath the surface? Two decades of changing economic inequality in the UK,' published in *Oxford Review of Economic Policy*, 35(3), pp. 467–489.

However, this was much slower inequality growth than in the preceding 20 years (e.g. see Machin 2011).

Wages are only one component of household income. One reason why income inequality narrowed immediately after the crisis was that policy at that stage continued to maintain the real value of the most important social security benefits. With real wages falling for those in work, generally higher up the income distribution than those for whom benefits are most important, this compressed some inequalities. The largest cuts in the real value of benefits came later in the life of the Coalition and under the current Conservative government.

More generally, changes in the overall structure of direct taxes and benefits affect the relationship between market incomes (earnings and investment income) and disposable incomes (after state benefits and direct taxes). Analysis of a separate survey by the Office for National Statistics (ONS) confirms that the big increases in both market (original) and disposable income inequality occurred between 1979 and the early 1990s (ONS, 2019, Table 11). Market income inequality in this series peaked in 1993. It fluctuated between the start of our period, 1995–96, and 2012–13 but then fell. As a result, the Gini coefficient for household market income was 1.7 percentage points lower in 2015–16 than in 1995–6 (falling to 46.6 per cent). Disposable income inequality also fluctuated between 1995–6 and 2005–6, dipping in the final year, giving a slightly smaller 20-year fall of 1.1 percentage points. Redistribution through direct taxes and benefits did a little less to moderate inequality at the end than at the start. These trends are again less dramatic than some might expect, in both cases, towards somewhat lower inequality in 2015 than in 1995.

Wealth inequalities also followed a distinct path. As we show below, household wealth inequality (as measured in the ONS Wealth and Assets Survey (WAS) increased slightly between 2006–8 and 2014–16 if private pension rights are included, but increased sharply, if they are excluded.

What has happened to overall economic inequalities in the UK in recent years, therefore, depends on the precise kinds of resources, time period, and parts of the distribution examined. This already suggests that developments below the surface may not have been uniform. In this chapter, we present the analysis of data from a variety of sources to examine how inequalities changed both between and within population groups defined in different ways, including by characteristics protected by equalities legislation. It builds on the approaches used by the National Equality Panel (Hills et al., 2010), which used data for years immediately before the crisis, and subsequent analysis (Hills et al., 2016). It extends the analysis to cover the two decades from 1995 to 2015, looking, in particular, at which groups emerged as winners and losers in each decade.

We begin this chapter by setting out our methods and the data sources used. We then describe the trends in overall inequality shown by these data, and the sharp contrasts between the two decades. The section that follows examines the most pervasive change that younger adults lost ground to older ones. We then examine what happened to the better- and less well-off within groups defined by family type, region, tenure, ethnicity, and disability status to see which, if any, were 'left behind'.

Sources and methods

We use three main data sources (see list of Data References at the end) chosen to allow disaggregation between and within population groups:

- Quarterly Labour Force Survey (LFS) individual data from all working-age adults on their hourly wages, weekly earnings, highest educational qualifications, and economic activity by characteristics from 1995 to 2015 (UK).
- FRS individual data from all adult household members matched to household level total net equivalised household income (as in the Department for Work and Pensions (DWP)'s Households Below Average Income, HBAI, dataset). We examine before and after housing costs incomes from 1995–6 to 2015–16 (GB to 2001–2; UK subsequently).
- ONS/CASE analysis of the Wealth and Asset Survey looking separately at (a) 'financial and physical wealth' (net financial assets and possessions excluding property such as housing); (b) net financial, physical, and property wealth ('total non-pension wealth', also including property such as housing net of mortgages); and (c) total wealth including the value of private and occupational pension rights. We examine these by household characteristics for the 2-year periods (starting in July) 2006–8 to 2014–16 (GB).

With ten potential classifications of population groups examined over a period of 20 years, we can only be selective in what we present here. We also concentrate on three of the outcomes covered by our wider analysis, chosen to capture some of the most important components of economic resources:

- Hourly wages for men and women working full-time (at 2015 prices, adjusted using the Consumer Price Index including owner–occupiers' housing costs and Council Tax, CPIH).
- Equivalised household income after housing costs allocated to each adult in the population (at 2015–16 prices, adjusted using DWP's bespoke variants of CPI, which exclude rents, maintenance repairs, and water charges for after-housing-costs analysis). Where relevant, we refer to changes before allowing for housing costs.
- Total non-pension wealth (in nominal terms, not adjusted for inflation).
  We concentrate on inequality within each group measured by changes at the 10th, 50th (median), and 90th percentiles for each group, and the 90:10 ratio between the first and last of these.

For the wage and income data, we contrast changes over equal length 10-year periods, the upswing period from 1995 to 2005 and the decade incorporating the 2008 economic crisis from 2005 to 2015. The WAS data start in 2006–8 and so changes in them are only available for 8 years within the second decade (and so start from a later point than the other series). We conduct the FRS and LFS analysis using the STATA 'Inequalities Programme' – a programme developed by Eleni Karagiannaki (2022) to undertake distributional analysis of continuous outcome variables.

Overall trends in UK inequality since 1995

Hourly wages

As a benchmark for the subsequent detailed analysis, this section looks at overall trends in the three outcomes. Figure 1.1 shows hourly wage changes across the distribution over the two decades. In the first decade, median pay grew by 20 per cent for men and nearly 30 per cent for women. Over the second decade, real pay fell at the 10th percentile for both men and women (but more for men) and at the median for men. At the 90th percentile, there was limited pay growth for men and women comparing 2015 with 2005. As a result, women's pay inequality remained roughly stable over the entire period, but increased for men, despite the slight narrowing for both genders in the first decade. The greater rise in women's wages than men's meant that the gender wage gap narrowed across the distribution (although less at the top). This also meant that overall pay inequality for men and women together ended the same in 2015 as it had been in 1995 (Table 1.2). But, the dominant feature in these figures is the contrast between the two decades, with healthy growth in real pay in the first, but stagnation in the second.

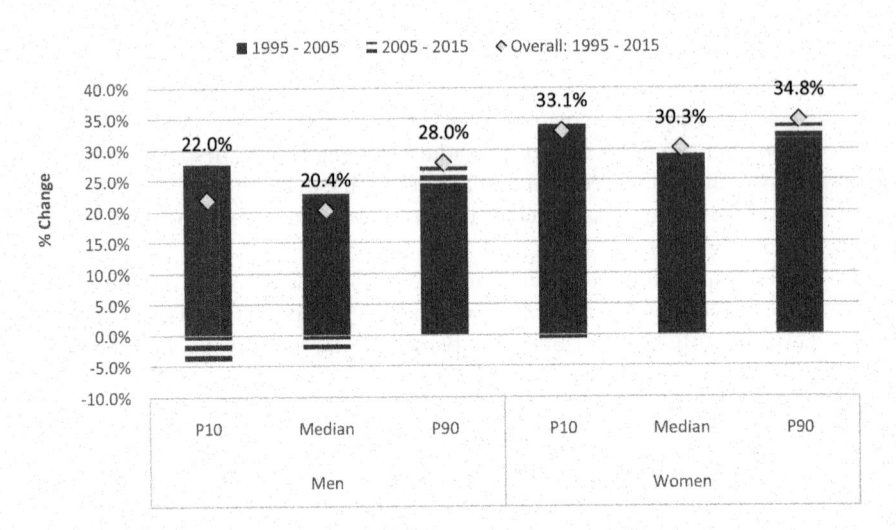

Figure 1.1 Percentage change in full-time hourly pay by gender, 1995 to 2015 (adjusted by CPIH).
Source: Authors' analysis of LFS.

Household incomes

Median household incomes before allowing for housing costs (BHC) grew by 39 per cent, more quickly than hourly pay. Falling housing costs meant that median after housing costs (AHC) income grew even faster—by 45 per cent. Overall household incomes grew faster than hourly pay (or weekly earnings) because pensioner households are included here. As we show in the next section, with rising private and state pensions, incomes of those aged over 64 grew much faster than working-age incomes (much of them from pay), particularly after allowing for housing costs

At the bottom, BHC incomes grew faster than at the top (although the 30th percentile grew fastest), so the 90:10 ratio fell slightly over the period. By contrast with the rest of the distribution, 10th percentile AHC incomes grew no faster than BHC, with no rise at all between 2005–6 and 2015–16. As a result, the 90:10 ratio for AHC income grew over both decades. But, the dominant feature is how little overall living standards improved in the second decade compared to the first, rather than the inequality changes.

Figure 1.2 shows levels of AHC income to which the changes described above correspond, year by year. This also emphasises the differences between the second and first decades, particularly at the 10th percentile, where income in 2015–16 was the same as in 2005–6, and shows how the precise years used to calculate changes can affect the picture. We use 2005–6 as the break-point in our analysis

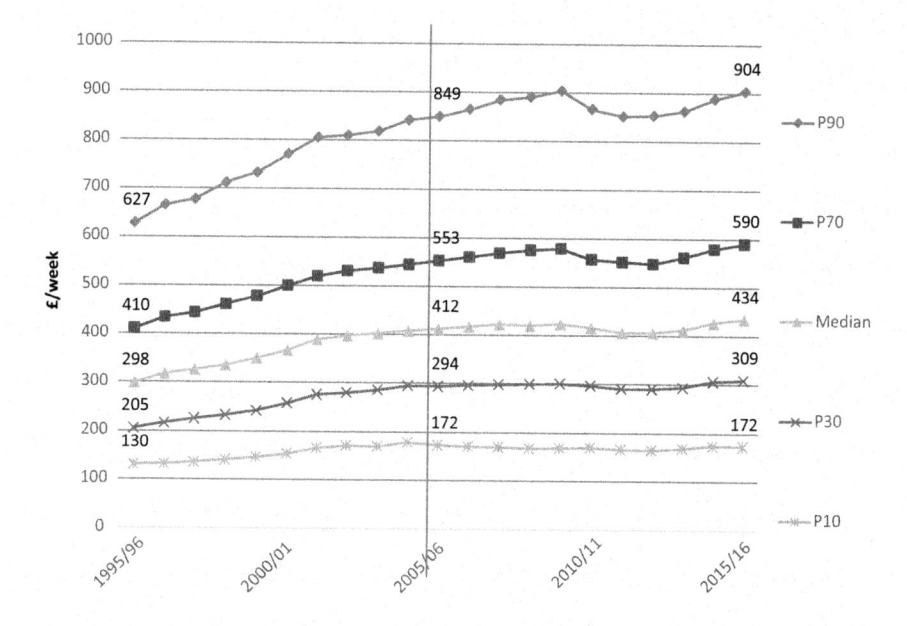

Figure 1.2 Levels of net household income after housing costs at different parts of the distribution, 1995–6 to 2015–16 (2015–16 prices).
Notes: £ per week; Incomes adjusted to equivalent for couple with no children.
Source: Authors' analysis of FRS/HBAI.

here to compare equal-length periods and avoid over-emphasis on the peak. If instead, 2007–8 were used as the break-point, changes since then would look even more dismal for most.

Household wealth

Nominal wealth totals grew over the eight years from 2006–8, contrasting with the slow growth in (real) wages and incomes. However, growth rates differed across the wealth distribution and for different types of wealth.

Growth in non-pension (physical, financial, and property) wealth was much lower for those in the middle and at the bottom of the wealth distribution than at the top, resulting in increased inequality (Table 1.1). The 90:10 ratio for non-pension wealth grew from 66 in 2006–8 to 77 in 2014–16. This reflected lack of growth in (net) property wealth away from the top of the distribution. When ONS's estimates of the value of private pension wealth are added in, total wealth grew by 32 per cent at the median, but by 53 per cent at the 10th, and 54 per cent at the 90th percentiles. The lower discount rates applied to promised future (defined benefit) pensions made their capitalised value much greater by the end of the period

Given the huge differences in levels of wealth across the distribution, percentage changes convey only a little of what changed over time. For instance, the 53 per cent rise in total wealth at the 10th percentile was only worth £4,800, while 54 per cent at the 90th percentile meant a rise of £427,000, 90 times as much. For many purposes, it is these absolute changes, and what they represent, for instance, in their equivalent in years of average income, that will be most important.

The WAS data, therefore, suggest that total wealth inequality (including private pension rights) across the bulk of the household wealth distribution, as measured by the 90:10 ratio, increased very slightly between 2006–8 and 2014–16.

Table 1.1 Levels and changes in household wealth, 2006–8 and 2014–16 (nominal)

	Percentile	2006–8	2014–16	Change 2006–8 to 2014–16 Nominal (£000s)	Percentage
Financial and physical wealth	10	6.0	7.5	1.5	25.0
	Median	42.9	50.4	7.5	17.5
	90	178.0	228.7	50.7	28.5
Financial, physical, and property wealth	10	7.5	8.2	0.7	9.3
	Median	146.6	156.1	9.5	6.5
	90	491.7	633.8	142.1	28.9
Total wealth (including pensions)	10	9.0	13.8	4.8	53.3
	Median	196.7	260.2	63.5	32.3
	90	786.3	1213.4	427.1	54.3

Source: ONS/CASE analysis of WAS.

Table 1.2 Overall inequality measured by 90:10 ratios, 1995–6, 2005–6, and 2015–16

	1995–6	2005–6	2015–16
Hourly wages[a]	3.8	3.7	3.8
Income BHC[b]	4.1	4.1	4
Income AHC[b]	4.8	4.9	5.3
Total non-pension wealth[c]	n.a.	66	77
Total wealth including pension wealth[c]	n.a.	87	88

Sources: Authors' analysis of LFS and FRS/HBAI; ONS/CASE analysis of WAS.

a Hourly wages for full-time employees.
b Total net equivalised household income for adults. The ratios are for GB up to 2001–2 and the UK thereafter. These results differ slightly from Figure 1.1 as that relates to all individuals, while these relate to adults only, as used in the following sections.
c Total non-pension wealth is financial, physical, and property wealth of households. The associated years for data collection for wealth are 2006–8 and 2014–16.

The Gini coefficient, taking account of the top and bottom, also changed little, rising from 61 to 62 per cent (ONS, 2018, Table 4). However, non-pension wealth became more clearly unequal, with the 90:10 ratio rising from 66 to 77. Gini coefficients for the property wealth and financial wealth components of non-pension wealth rose sharply, so the Gini coefficient for total wealth inequality excluding pensions increased from 59 to 63 per cent.

While the WAS data are very useful for the kinds of breakdown explored below, they are limited in coverage of the very wealthiest. Analyses that take account of other kinds of wealth data, including from estates, but also from newspaper data on the assets of the wealthiest, show greater inequality. Alvaredo et al. (2015, Figures 2 and 3) show that data of those kinds suggest significantly greater shares of the total for the top 1 per cent and top 10 per cent than the WAS data, with increases in them since the early 2000s.

In the detailed analysis below, for space reasons and simplicity, we concentrate on household wealth including financial assets and property but excluding estimated private pension rights. It should be remembered that overall inequality in this measure increased over the period, whereas it did not if pension rights were included.

This section emphasises two things: first, quite how good overall growth in real wages and incomes in the decade from 1995 look retrospectively, compared to the dismal picture for the decade from 2005; second, that, in several respects, changes in overall inequality were small. Table 1.2 summarises this and gives benchmarks for later sections. Over the whole 20 years, hourly wage inequality was unchanged, incomes before housing costs became slightly less unequal, but incomes after housing costs more unequal. Over the second decade household wealth became more unequal when pension wealth is excluded.

The steepening age gradient

The aggregate statistics presented above are often the focus of discussion but disguise much that is going on beneath what appears a calm surface. Over the

20-year period, real wages grew across the overall distribution by at least a fifth, and real incomes after housing costs by at least a third. However, some groups gained much less or even lost, particularly after 2005. Similarly, while overall non-pension wealth grew across the wealth distribution after 2006–8, albeit much less in the middle and bottom half, it fell for some groups. This section reports on the pervasive differences we find by age. The next section focuses on those who have done particularly poorly when analysed by other characteristics.

While hourly wages increased for all age groups in the first decade, there was a remarkable contrast over the second decade. Median hourly wages fell for men and women between 2005 and 2015 in the age groups up to 30–34 but continued to grow for men aged over 54 and women aged over 34. More detailed analysis shows that the first decade saw faster growth for younger men and women at the bottom of the wage distributions (P10) than at the median for their age groups, but their real losses in the second decade were greater than at the median. For the best-paid men and women, there was also a strong age-gradation over the whole 20-year period: the 90th percentile for men aged 25–29 rose by only 8 per cent and by 19 per cent for women, while the 90th percentiles for those aged 55–59 grew by 43 per cent for men and 36 per cent for women.

This age gradation of economic fortunes is accentuated, looking at net incomes (see Figure 1.3). AHC incomes of those aged over 64 rose by more than 80 per cent over the whole period, including continued growth after 2005. But for those in their 20s, growth was less than 30 per cent, all of that occurring in the first decade. Those aged 80 or more gained a little less than younger pensioners, but still substantially. At the tops and bottoms of the distributions within each age group, income gains to those aged 65 and over were also much greater than for

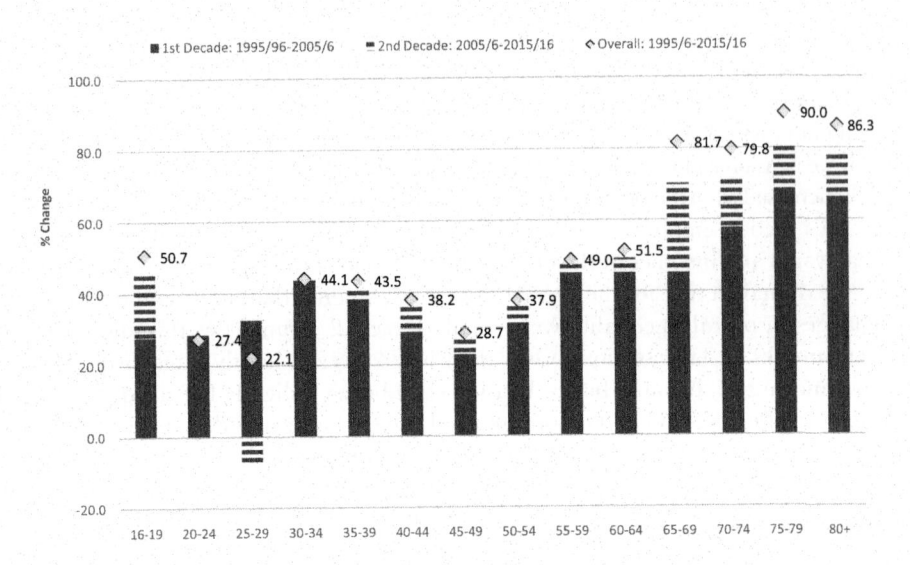

Figure 1.3 Change in median incomes after housing costs by age group, 1995–6 to 2015–16 (2015–16 prices).
Source: Authors' analysis of FRS/HBAI.

younger people although there was less gradation by age within the working-age population than at the median. One striking exception was that incomes at the 10th percentile of those aged 60 to 64 were nearly 20 per cent lower in real terms in 2015–16 than for their equivalents in 2005–6. All of this fall occurred between 2010–11 and 2015–16. This coincided with the rise in women's state pension age, which meant that the social security safety net became much less generous for some in this age group. In addition, the 10th percentile for the group aged 80 or over fell by 3 per cent after 2005–6, contrasting with 13 per cent growth for the poorest younger pensioners.

Changes in median non-pension wealth show an even more striking age difference: it fell by a sixth in nominal terms for the groups aged below 55 but grew by almost a third for those aged 65 or over. More detailed analysis shows that, away from the medians, at the 90th percentile of the older groups, increases of 30 per cent or more represented substantial amounts—a 51 per cent rise meant wealth grew by £290,000 for the richest 65–74s. But even the 90th percentile for 25–34s grew by only £5,000 or 2.4 per cent. As a result, 55–64s now have median non-pension wealth £217,000 higher than those 30 years younger—equivalent to £7,000 for each year of age difference, even excluding accumulation of pension rights.

Allowing for pension wealth makes the difference even larger. Median total wealth including pension wealth reached £547,000 for 55–64s in 2014–16 but was only £66,500 for 25–34s—£16,000 for each year of age difference. At the top, ONS's valuation of pension rights implies that a tenth of 55- to 64-year-old households had more than £1.9m in total wealth, up by £640,000 from 2006 to 2008, and six times the 90th percentile for 25–34s of £310,000.

To summarise, in the second decade, the fortunes of younger adults declined sharply in all the respects we examine. Median hourly pay fell in real terms (CPIH adjusted) for men and women in the age groups up to 30–34 between 2005 and 2015. However, pay continued to grow for men aged over 54 and women aged over 34. Over the whole 20 years, pay grew by more than a third for men and women aged 55 and over, but by less than 20 per cent for those in their 20s. Even for the best-paid men and women at each age, there was a strong age-gradation in growth.

This carried over into more complete measures of income, with those over state pension age gaining most. After allowing for housing costs, median incomes of those aged 65 or over rose by more than 80 per cent over the whole period, including continued growth after 2005. But for those in their 20s, growth in median incomes was less than 30 per cent, all coming in the first decade. One notable exception was that, as women's state pension age rose, affecting the value of their state safety net, real incomes at the 10th percentile for those aged 60–64 were nearly 20 per cent lower in real terms in 2015–16 than for their equivalents in 2005–6. And, incomes for the poorest over-80s fell after 2005–6, in contrast to the poorest younger pensioners. Already large wealth differences widened over the period: median non-pension wealth fell by a sixth in nominal terms for the groups aged below 55 but grew by almost a third for those aged 65 or over.

Who else was 'left behind' over two decades?

It was often the already poorest within particular groups who fell furthest behind even if the group as a whole fared reasonably well. We, therefore, concentrate in places on the 10th percentile of some groups. We look, in turn, at family type, region or nation, housing tenure, ethnicity, and disability status.

Family type

The age gradation in economic fortunes described above is reflected in differences between family types. Adults living in pensioner couple households and single pensioner adults saw the sharpest increases in their household incomes after housing costs across the distribution over the whole period from 1995–6 to 2015–16, with gains of 75 and 81 per cent at the median, respectively, including growth in the second decade. For lone parents, there were sharp differences between the poorest and others. While median lone parent incomes after housing costs were a substantial 65 per cent higher in 2015–16 than in 1995–6, the modest growth at the 10th percentile for lone parents in the first decade was almost reversed in the second, leaving the overall real income growth of only 3 per cent over 20 years, well behind the poorest of other family types.

Region

National figures for hourly wage growth shown earlier also mask substantial differences between regions and nations. For men, the first decade showed variation, from 17 per cent median wage growth in the East Midlands to nearly 40 per cent in Northern Ireland. For women, median wage growth was also fastest (35 per cent) in Northern Ireland as well as in the South West in the first decade, while it was slowest (23 per cent) in the South East. In the second decade, median wages fell in most regions, with women in London worst hit (falling 6 per cent), but median women's wages in Scotland rising most, by 9 per cent. However, what happened to wages in London was generally unexceptional, in contrast to what we show below for incomes and wealth.

Incomes before housing costs rose fastest in London in the first decade. Over the whole 20 years, London's income growth was behind only the North East, which grew much faster than elsewhere after 2005–6. Median AHC incomes rose much faster than hourly pay or BHC incomes—by nearly two-thirds over the 20 years in the North East and more than half in the South West. But, London's position changes dramatically, becoming one of the four slowest growth regions.

Rather little correspondence emerges here between regions that lagged in household income terms and those that are often perceived as having been 'left behind'. It is at a sub-regional scale that the contrasts between, for instance, cities such as Manchester and their surrounding towns emerge (Beatty and Fothergill, 2016)

But, the differences are starker away from median regional incomes after allowing for housing costs (see Figure 1.4). At the bottom (10th percentile), Londoners' incomes grew by 28 per cent in the first decade but fell by 14 per cent in

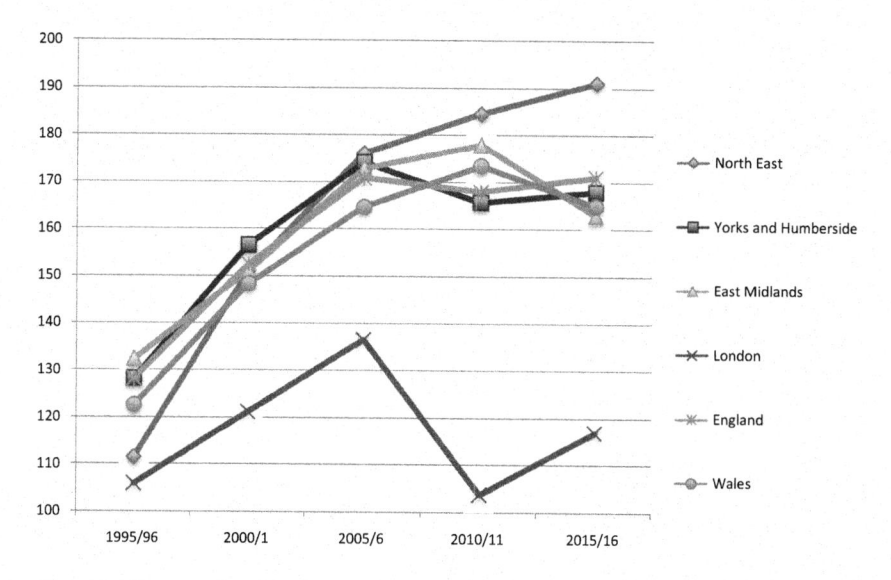

Figure 1.4 Income after housing costs at the 10th percentile for selected regions (£/week, 2015–16 prices).

Note: FRS figures are for GB only up to 2001–2.

Source: Authors' analysis of FRS/HBAI.

the second decade, meaning they only rose 10 per cent over the whole 20 years. The levels of the 10th percentile for selected regions that were below the 10th percentile for England as a whole in either 1995–6 or 2015–16. In 1995–6, the poorest Londoners were only slightly below the next poorest (in the North East). By 2015–16, the 10th percentile for Londoners had fallen to only 72 per cent of the poorest in the East Midlands (now the next lowest). The poorest Londoners lagged behind because of their rising housing costs: before housing costs, incomes for the poorest Londoners grew more than in most other regions.

Even at the 90th percentile, Londoners' AHC incomes fell after 2005, so despite having the largest growth in the first decade, the overall growth for the highest-income Londoners (41 per cent over 20 years) was a little less than growth at the 90th percentile nationally. The decline in AHC income after 2005–6 for the poorest Londoners meant that inequality in London measured by the 90:10 ratio—already 7 in 1995–6, compared to 4–5 in most other regions—was over 9 in 2015–16, compared to less than 6 in any other region. The poorest tenth of Londoners had less than £120 per week in 2015–16, while the richest tenth of Londoners had more than £1,080 per week.

Wealth inequalities between London and other regions and within London are even more dramatic. Median non-pension wealth of London households grew by 87 per cent (over £100,000) in 8 years within the second decade when wages and incomes rose so sluggishly. In several regions, median nominal wealth fell.

Median wealth in London and the North East was similar in 2006–8, but by the end, driven by house price increases, median Londoners were £138,000 wealthier. While wealth grew by 88 per cent at the 90th percentile in London, it only rose by 17 per cent at the 10th percentile, so the 90:10 ratio in the capital reached an extraordinary 320 in 2014–16, far higher than elsewhere, where it varied between 47 and 83.

Tenure

The composition of housing tenures changed considerably over the period, with access to both social housing and owner-occupation becoming more difficult for those in their 20s and 30s, more of whom, therefore, became private tenants (Intergenerational Commission, 2018, ch. 3). As a result, comparisons across tenures in 2015 and 1995 do not necessarily compare like-with-like, so need careful interpretation. For hourly wages, the main contrast was between owners with faster wage growth and tenants with slower growth (for both men and women). The exception was the lowest-paid social tenants, whose hourly wages rose by 32 per cent over 20 years for men and 35 per cent for women, following the introduction of the National Minimum Wage in 1999. Real wages grew by nearly half for the best-paid male outright owners.

Apart from social tenants at the 10th percentile (whose incomes fell after 2005) and private tenants at the 90th percentile (whose incomes were flat), there were increases in AHC incomes across the distributions by tenure (Figure 1.5).

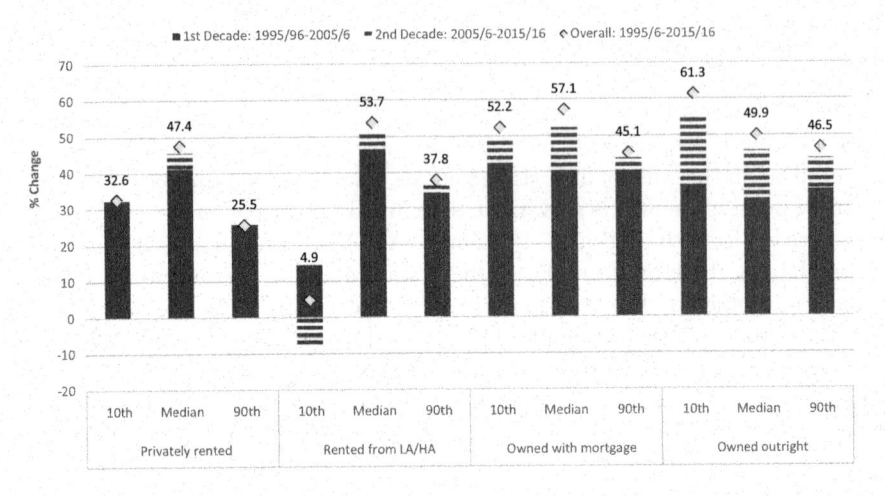

Figure 1.5 Change in incomes after housing costs by housing tenure, 1995–6 to 2015–16 (2015–16 prices).

Source: Authors' analysis of FRS/HBAI.

Incomes rose by more than 45 per cent overall for each of the owner–occupier groups shown (more than 60 per cent for poorer outright owners). By contrast, incomes after housing costs fell by 8 per cent for the poorest social tenants in the second decade. This meant that their incomes were only 5 per cent higher in 2015–16 than they had been 20 years before. The result is a stark difference between tenures in household income levels by 2015–16. Outright owners had median net weekly income AHC of £556, more than twice that of median social tenants with £270. At the top, a tenth of outright owners had weekly incomes over £1,000, while at the bottom, a tenth of private tenants had incomes below £100, after their housing costs, and a tenth of social tenants under £120.

Since the total wealth measure we are using here includes property, it is not surprising that households that were outright owner–occupiers had the highest levels of non-pension wealth in both years and also the largest growth over the period across the distribution (see Table 1.3). Median non-pension wealth for outright owners increased by 26 per cent (or £76,000), while that for social and private tenants only by 8 per cent (or £1,200) and 14 per cent (or £2,400), respectively. At the bottom of the wealth distribution, patterns are even more varied: 14 per cent (£19,000) growth in wealth for the outright owners, no change for social renters, but a fall of a tenth (£200) in the already low wealth of the poorest private renters. Faster growth in wealth at the top of the distribution for each tenure group—including by a third to £966,000 for the best-off outright owners—meant that inequality within tenures grew. The already high 90:10 ratio for wealth of private tenants grew from 51 to 63, while that for outright owners also grew from 5.4 to 6.2.

Table 1.3 Levels and changes in household non-pension wealth by housing tenure, 2006–8 and 2014–16 (nominal, £000s, GB)

	Tenure	2006–08	2014–16	Change 2006–8 to 2014–16 Nominal	Percentage
P10	Outright owner	135.5	154.5	19	14
	Mortgagor	56.6	59.7	3.1	5.5
	Social tenant	2.5	2.5	0	0
	Private tenant	1.9	1.7	−0.2	−10.5
Median	Outright owner	285.8	361.5	75.7	26.5
	Mortgagor	177	184.4	7.4	4.2
	Social tenant	14.8	16	1.2	8.1
	Private tenant	17	19.4	2.4	14.1
P90	Outright owner	728.7	965.6	236.9	32.5
	Mortgagor	481.8	569.6	87.8	18.2
	Social tenant	50.4	54.8	4.4	8.7
	Private tenant	97.2	107.6	10.4	10.7

Source: ONS/CASE analysis of WAS.

Ethnicity

What we can present by ethnicity on a consistent basis is restricted by data limitations, especially in the first decade. Table 1.4, therefore, summarises what the sources show for the second decade. The patterns are not straightforward, however:

- For white respondents, male wages fell more than for all men, but women's wages and household incomes and wealth grew more than for all women.
- The wealth of Indian households grew more rapidly, with median wealth exceeding the overall median and that of the White ethnic group by 2014–16.
- Pakistani male wages and household income and wealth grew more rapidly than for the whole population, but female wages fell by more than 10 per cent.
- Bangladeshi incomes grew by a third over the period, even though male hourly wages fell by more than most other groups.
- For income and wealth, Black Caribbean households had rapid growth, but by contrast, Black African households became poorer. Wages fell for both men and women for the two groups combined.
- Male wages and wealth grew rapidly for Chinese respondents, but household incomes fell.
- The most notable difference is between those with Pakistani and Black African ethnicities, with the latter showing most signs of being 'left behind' after 2005.

Table 1.4 Changes in median hourly pay incomes after housing costs, and wealth by ethnicity, selected groups, 2005–15

	Hourly wages Per cent change 2005–15 (2015 prices) Men	Hourly wages Per cent change 2005–15 (2015 prices) Women	Income after housing costs[a] Per cent change 2005–6 to 2015–16 (2015–16 prices)	Median non-pension wealth (nominal)[d] Per cent change 2006–8 to 2014–16	Median non-pension wealth (nominal)[d] Wealth level 2014–16 (£000s)
All	−2.1	0.8	5.7	6.5	156.1
White[b]	−2.6	1.4	6.5	6.72	166.52
Indian	1.8	2.9	9.5	22.3	187.4
Pakistani	13.7	−11.3	20.2	30.2	113.4
Bangladeshi	−7.2	Na[c]	33	5.3	15.8
Black Caribbean	−7.93	−6.03	23	19.5	45.8
Black African			−21.4	−13.5	15.4
Chinese	28	3.1	−0.7	106.6	119.4

Sources: Authors' analysis of LFS and FRS/HBAI; ONS/CASE analysis of WAS. Individual's own ethnicity in LFS and FRS and that of household reference person in WAS analysis.

a Income figures based on three years' pooled data centred in 2005-6 and 2015-16.
b Wealth figures are for White British.
c Hourly pay is for 'Black African', 'Black Caribbean' and 'Black Other' combined as these are not available for individual groups in LFS for 2015 data.
d LFS (wages) and FRS (incomes) figures are for the UK; WAS (wealth) figures are for GB.

Disability status

In all the comparisons shown, disabled people and households had lower levels of pay, income, and wealth (Table 1.5). For instance, median AHC incomes of adults reporting a disability in 2015 were only 77 per cent of those who did not. Median hourly pay fell by 7 per cent for disabled women. By contrast, median pay rose by 5 per cent for disabled men, while it fell slightly for non-disabled men. However, for the lowest-paid disabled men, pay fell by 8 per cent, while it fell only slightly for the lowest-paid other men.

While median incomes rose at the same rate for disabled and non-disabled individuals, incomes for the poorest disabled household fell by 7 per cent. Despite the more rapid growth in wealth for older households shown above, the median non-pension wealth of disabled households fell. In most respects, therefore, disabled individuals and households lost ground between 2005 and 2015, particularly those with the lowest incomes.

Summary

In contrast to the consistent patterns by age examined above, those we observe comparing population groups defined in other ways are much more complex,

Table 1.5 Levels and changes in median and 10th percentile hourly wages, incomes, and wealth by disability status, 2005 to 2015

	Not disabled			Disabled		
	2005	2015	% change	2005	2015	% change
Median hourly wages (£, 2015 prices)						
Men	12.9	12.6	−2	10.9	11.5	5
Women	11.2	11.3	1	10.3	9.6	−7
Tenth percentile hourly wages (£, 2015 prices)						
Men	7	6.7	−4	6.6	6.1	−8
Women	6.5	6.4	−0.8	6.1	6.1	−0.7
AHC income (£/week, 2015–16 prices)						
Median	437	465	6	339	360	6
P10	175	180	3	165	154	−7
Non-pension wealth (£000s, nominal)						
Median	155	173	12	126	118	−7
P10	8	11	37	6	7	19

Sources: Authors' analysis of LFS and FRS/HBAI; ONS/CASE analysis of WAS.

Notes: Definitions of 'disability' vary between the three surveys. 'Disabled' categories are hourly pay, 'Disability Discrimination Act' *and* 'Work Limiting Disabled ('not disabled' is *neither*); AHC income, 'disabled' are adults reporting a limiting long-standing illness or disability; non-pension wealth, 'disabled' are households with at least one individual with an activity limiting disability or long-standing illness. LFS and FRS figures are for the UK; WAS figures are for GB.

often with contrasts between the worst-off within each type and those with median or higher resources. We identify a number of groups who did particularly badly in different respects during the slow-growth decade from 2005 to 2015. These include:

- The incomes of the poorest lone parents.
- The incomes after housing costs of the poorest Londoners.
- Median household wealth in the East Midlands and North East.
- The incomes of the poorest social tenants.
- Median incomes and wealth of Black African households.
- Disabled individuals and households in general, especially the wages of disabled women and the incomes of the poorest disabled adults.

Conclusions

The two decades from 1995 to 2015 in the UK were marked by both economic and political drama. The first half had steady growth in living standards, but this broke down with the financial and economic crisis of 2007–8. A left-of-centre Labour government with redistributive policies from 1997 gave way in 2010 to a Conservative-led Coalition government which embarked on policies of retrenchment and 'austerity' in (selected) public services and working-age cash benefits (Hills et al., 2009; Hills et al., 2016). By the end, 'inequality' had become a more prominent public concern.

And, yet on the face of it, the two decades after 1995–6 had much greater stability in economic inequality across the bulk of the population than the preceding period from the late 1970s when income and earnings inequalities leapt dramatically. Although, at the very top, the income share of the top 1 per cent was much higher in 2015 than 20 years earlier, other measures of income inequality ended close to where they started (although with some year-to-year variation, notably in the years immediately after the economic crisis).

Why then did inequality become more salient? One reason was that there was such a contrast between the two decades in overall growth in wages and living standards. In retrospect, it is easy to forget how much they rose in the first and, therefore, how great the contrast was with the second decade of near-stagnation. It is one thing politically for there to be high (or even rising) inequality if accompanied by growth. It is quite another for inequality to be maintained on a historically high plateau while accompanied by stagnation.

The second aspect which we have dived into is that this apparently calm surface at the population level masks substantial change, looking more deeply at differences between groups defined in different ways. Some of those differences apply across groups, from their poorest to their best-off members, but others are more subtle, with particular parts of their distributions having done much worse than others, particularly after 2005. For those lagging behind what were very slow overall improvements, this meant absolute losses.

A major social change was the sharp decline in fortunes of younger people in pay, income, and wealth after 2005 compared to older people. This decline was pervasive, affecting better- and worse-off within younger age groups, and affected wages, incomes, and wealth (although the incomes of the poorest 60- to 64-year-olds and poorest over-80s fell after 2005–6). For groups defined in other ways, the pattern was more complex and does not correspond to simple ideas of who had been 'left behind' before the 2016 Brexit vote but reveals how some gained and others lost substantially.

The apparent 'stability' in income inequality, at least, over the period is, therefore, something of a mirage: the nature and depth of economic inequalities have changed markedly for some groups even if overall levels remained relatively stable.

References

Alvaredo, F., Atkinson, A. B., and Morelli, S. (2015), 'The Challenge of Measuring UK Wealth Inequality in the 2000s', III Working Paper 4, London, London School of Economics.

Beatty, C., and Fothergill, S. (2016), *The Contemporary Labour Market in Britain's Older Industrial Towns*, Sheffield, Centre for Regional and Economic Social Research, Sheffield Hallam University.

Belfield, C., Blundell, R., Cribb, J., and Joyce, R. (2017), 'Two Decades of Income Inequality in Britain: The Role of Wages', *Economica*, 84(334), 157–179.

Clarke, S., and Gregg, P. (2018), *Count the Pennies: Explaining a Decade of Lost Pay Growth*, London, Resolution Foundation.

DWP (2018), *Households below Average Income: An Analysis of the UK Income Distribution 1994/95 to 2016/17*, London, Department for Work and Pensions, available at https://assets.publishing.ser- vice.gov.uk/government/uploads/system/uploads/attachment_data/file/691917/households-below-average-income-1994-1995-2016-2017.pdf

Hills, J., Brewer, M., Jenkins, S., Lister, R., Lupton, R., Machin, S., Mills, C., Modood, T., Rees, T., and Riddell, S. (2010), *An Anatomy of Economic Inequality, Report of the National Equality Panel*, CASE Report 60, London, LSE.

Hills, J., De Agostini, P., and Sutherland, H. (2016), 'Benefits, Tax Credits and Pensions' in R. Lupton, T. Burchardt, J. Hills, K. Stewart, and P. Vizard (eds), *Social Policy in a Cold Climate: Policies and their Consequences since the Crisis*, Bristol, The Policy Press.

Hills, J., Cunliffe, J., Obolenskaya, P., and Karagiannaki, E. (2015), Falling Behind, Getting Ahead: The Changing Structure of Inequality in the UK, 2007–2013, Social Policy in a Cold Climate Research Report 5, CASE, LSE.

Hills, J., Sefton, T., and Stewart, K. (eds) (2009), *Towards a More Equal Society: Poverty, Inequality and Policy since 1979*, Bristol, The Policy Press.

Intergenerational Commission (2018), *A New Generational Contract: The Final Report of the Intergenerational Commission*, London, Resolution Foundation.

J. Wadsworth (eds), *The Labour Market in Winter: The State of Working Britain*, Oxford, Oxford University Press.

Karagiannaki, E. (2022), 'distout and svydistout: Help file to accompany Stata programmes for undertaking distributional analysis of continuous outcome variables. London, LSE. Accessed at: distout and svydistout: Help file to accompany Stata programmes for undertaking distributional analysis of continuous outcome variables (lse.ac.uk)

Machin, S. (2011), 'Changes in UK Wage Inequality over the Last Forty Years', in P. Gregg and OECD (2015), *In it Together: Why Less Inequality Benefits All*, Paris, Organization for Economic Cooperation and Development.

ONS (2018), *Wealth in Great Britain Wave 5: 2014 to 2016*, London, Office for National Statistics.

ONS (2019), 'Effects of Taxes and Benefits: Disposable', dataset released 26 February 2018, London, Office for National Statistics, available at https://www.ons.gov.uk/peoplepopulationandcommunity/personalandhouseholdfinances/incomeandwealth/datasets/householddisposableincomeandinequality

Sunday Times (2018), 'Rich List 2018', London, Sunday Times.

Data References

Department for Work and Pensions (2018), Households below Average Income, 1994/-95–2016/17. [data collection]. 11th Edition. UK Data Service. SN: 5828, http://doi.org/10.5255/UKDA-SN-5828-9

Department for Work and Pensions, National Centre for Social Research and Office for National Statistics. Social and Vital Statistics Division, Family Resources Survey series, 1993–2017 [computer file]. Colchester, Essex: UK Data Archive [distributor], 2019. SN: 200017. https://beta.ukdataservice.ac.uk/datacatalogue/series/series?id=200017

Office for National Statistics, Northern Ireland Statistics and Research Agency. Quarterly Labour Force Survey, 1992–2018. [data collection]. Colchester, Essex: UK Data Archive [distributor], 2019. SN: 2000026. https://beta.ukdataservice.ac.uk/datacatalogue/series/series?id=2000026

2 Wealth inequality in the UK

Carys Roberts

Assessments of government policy, and whether they are progressive, tend to focus on income inequality. Would a particular policy benefit people on lower incomes more than those on higher incomes? This is, of course, important. However, the political focus on income inequality alone has masked the true extent and nature of economic inequality in the UK. To understand economic inequality better, we need to look at wealth. Though the two concepts are often used interchangeably, wealth and income are distinct: wealth is a *stock* of assets, whereas income is a *flow* of economic resources. And, it is far less equally distributed than income.

The wealthiest 10 per cent of households in Great Britain hold on average £2,516,400 in wealth, compared to zero in the bottom decile, according to the latest wave of the Wealth and Assets Survey (ONS, 2019a). By comparison, average household income of the top decile in the UK in 2017/18 was £84,325, 20 times higher than in the bottom income decile (£4,199) (ONS, 2019b). In aggregate, the wealth held by the top 10 per cent of households (45 per cent) is more than five times greater than the wealth of the bottom half of all households combined (8 per cent).

In the long run, wealth inequality levels have changed quite dramatically. Wealth inequality in the UK declined substantially after the First World War, from a very high peak, and fell throughout most of the 20th century (World Inequality Database, 2020). This was largely due to the destruction and mobilisation of the assets of wealthy households during the two world wars and the Great Depression, along with the redistributive post-war settlement and a dramatic and deliberate expansion in home ownership (Atkinson, 2015).

Today, the Wealth and Assets Survey estimates that personal wealth stands at £14.6 trillion in Great Britain (ONS, 2019a). This personal wealth is held by individuals, in private pensions (42 per cent), property wealth (35 per cent), financial wealth such as stocks and shares (15 per cent) and physical wealth like cars and paintings (9 per cent). Over the past 15 years in which the survey has been collected, inequality has increased on several measures, though modestly (ONS, 2019a). The different components of wealth have fed into this in different ways. Automatic enrolment has expanded pension participation, reducing inequality of pension wealth. Property wealth has become less equal since the late 2000s as

DOI: 10.4324/9781003104476-4

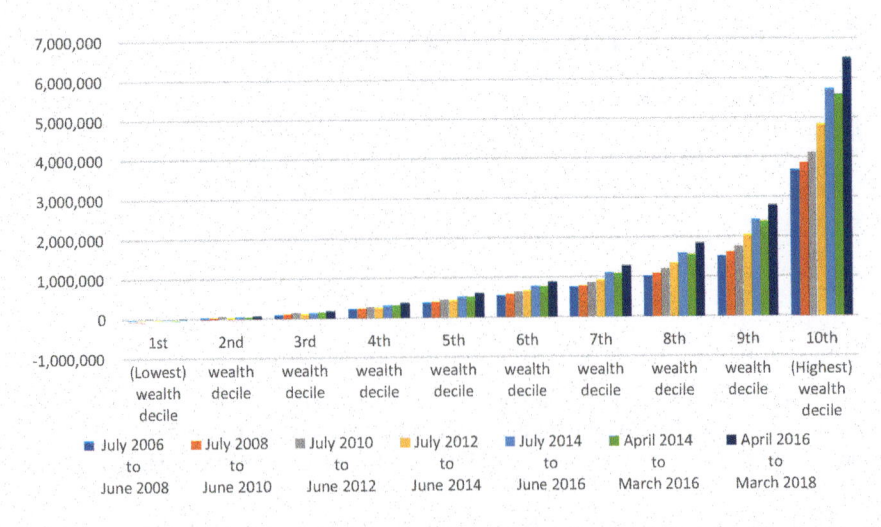

Figure 2.1 Aggregate total wealth (net) (£million), 2016–18.
Source: ONS (2019a).

house prices have risen, such that while housing was a great equaliser last century, now it is pushing in the opposite direction.

While changes in headline wealth inequality measures have changed modestly, there are two causes for concern. First, measuring *inequality* obscures an important point. Because the overall level of personal wealth has increased, from three times national income in the 1970s to more than seven times today, absolute levels of wealth amongst the wealthy have reached high multiples of average income, even as inequality measures have not changed so dramatically (Bangham and Leslie, 2020). The result is that it has become much harder for someone on a low or average median income to move up the distribution or to buy a house at all. This is illustrated in Figure 2.1, showing that aggregate wealth has increased in the highest deciles since the first wave of the survey in 2006–8, by substantially more in absolute terms than the increases in lower deciles.

Second, the Wealth and Assets Survey underreports wealth at the top because the wealthy are less likely to respond to surveys and more likely to keep wealth offshore. When offshore wealth is included, the top 0.01 per cent of households have doubled their share of wealth since 1980 to around 5 per cent, 30–40 per cent of which is now held offshore, enabling the avoidance of tax (Alstadsæter et al., 2017).

Why wealth inequality matters

The large discrepancies in wealth matter. They shape our well-being and chances in life, and who has agency and power.

While wealth is more unequally distributed than income, the two are correlated, with the wealthy also likely to have higher incomes. This relationship flows in both directions. Higher earnings from work allow individuals to save a greater amount and store this in savings or other assets, accumulating wealth. But, wealth also generates income in the form of rents, dividends and interest, and in the form of a financial uplift when assets are sold or realised. Wealth confers on its owners the ability to generate income outside of or alongside work.

Wealth, and, critically, our likelihood of inheriting it, strongly shapes our financial security, well-being, opportunity and power in the economy. Having enough savings to cover the cost of an appliance breaking means not worrying about that eventuality, or having to go into debt when it does. Not having a financial buffer means unexpected life events are threatening: it is associated with stress, relationship breakdown, a lack of choice (for instance, in leaving abusive relationships) and a lack of control over one's life (Bynner and Paxton, 2001). Larger savings can cushion the blow of being made redundant in a recession – especially important if living in a country where state benefits are well below average incomes. Pension wealth provides the certainty of a retirement with dignity and security.

Household wealth also has its inverse in household debt. Measures of wealth typically are measured in *net* terms, meaning it can be negative, as in the case of the overleveraged mortgage holder. Those with debt are twice as likely to develop serious depression, and once they have, experience half the recovery rate of those without debt (Acton, 2016).

Wealth confers opportunity. Studies controlling for background factors have shown an 'asset-effect' on life chances. Having some wealth at age 22 is associated with positive impacts at age 33, including participation in work, higher wages, good health, absence of depression and greater political agency (McKnight, 2011; Bynner and Paxton, 2001). Those with assets are better able to take risks and invest in new ventures: among successful entrepreneurs, the most commonly shared trait is not personality but access to financial capital, often through gifts and inheritance (Bahaj, Foulis and Pinter 2016; Blanchflower and Oswald, 1998). Entrepreneurs with access to more valuable collateral create larger firms and more value added, and are more likely to survive, even in the long run (Schmalz et al., 2017). Recent research has pointed to the role of wealth as an insurance mechanism for voters considering financially risky electoral behaviour, posited to have led to a greater likelihood to support Brexit (Green and Pahontu, 2021).

Wealth also provides its owners with power and control. Most simply, as described above, this could be the power to choose a different life or leave an abusive relationship. It could also mean the ability to influence decision-making. The All-Party Parliamentary Group on Inclusive Growth surveyed the UK public and found that 28 per cent think the wealthiest have greater ability to 'direct or influence the behaviour of others or the course of events' than any other actors, including the government (APPG, 2018). Ownership of capital grants is not just a right to income but to control how businesses are run (Lawrence and Mason, 2017).

The unequal distribution of wealth is particularly unjust when that wealth is not the result of saving, but instead has been inherited, or is the result of speculation and luck. Wealth in the UK is frequently gifted rather than earned, both between and within generations. The amount of gifted wealth has increased: between 1977 and 2006, the total wealth gifted each year, expressed as a proportion of national income, is estimated to have doubled from 4.7 per cent to 8.2 per cent (Atkinson, 2013). So too, asset values frequently rise, not because of investment skill or effort on the part of the asset holder, but simply because of external factors such as higher demand, rising interest rates, public investment and economic growth. Rising house prices, in particular, have been a major source of wealth increases for homeowners over recent decades. High house prices are, in part, a result of scarcity, and the inherently fixed quantity of land. If my house increases in value, it's because others want to buy it; in this zero-sum game, my wealth is down to your inability to access the security of a home (Ryan-Collins et al., 2017).

There are also important patterns to observe in terms of how inequalities fall. Indeed, wealth inequalities run along the same grooves as, and reinforce, economic inequalities more broadly.

One such example is in how wealth varies by region and nation. Figure 2.2 shows how the median household in the South East of England has almost three times the wealth of the median household in the North East. While much of this is driven by the large differentials in house prices, financial wealth is also highly unequally distributed across the country; both pension and physical wealth are also unequally distributed, though to a lesser degree.

Though auto-enrolment has dramatically improved pension scheme participation, women remain less likely to be contributing to a pension scheme than men and are likely to hold lower pension wealth, with particularly large gaps opening up at age 35 and above, when many women are combining work with childcare. While Indian households have similar household wealth to white British

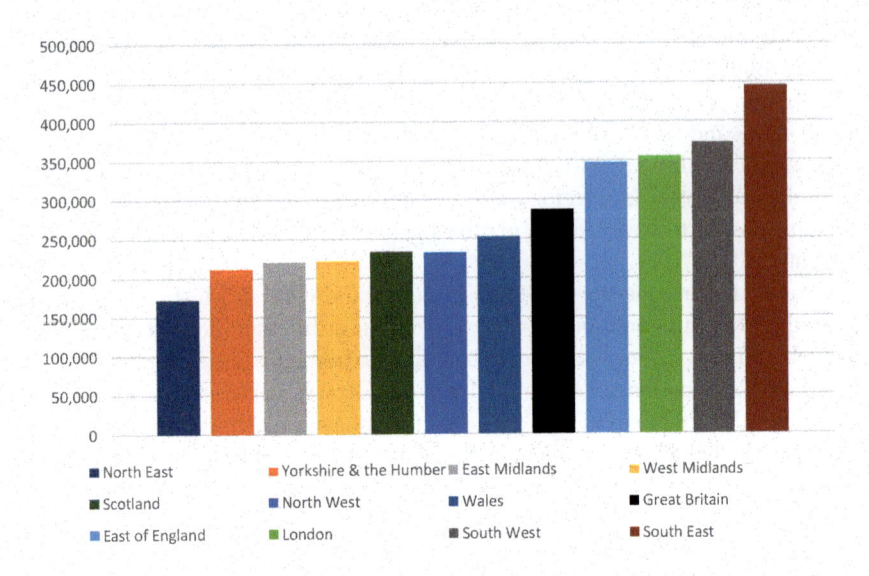

Figure 2.2 Median household wealth by region or nation of Great Britain, 2016–18.
Source: ONS (2019a).

households, other ethnic groups are likely to hold less; Bangladeshi and Black African households have less than a fifth of the wealth of white British households. This is the result of labour market outcomes but also housing tenure and a lower likelihood of recent migrants inheriting wealth (Khan, 2019).

People accumulate wealth throughout their lives, so we should expect older people to have more wealth than younger people. But, there are large intergenerational inequalities in wealth beyond what would be expected from age differences alone. In the first half of the 20th century, each generation had more wealth than the last. But, every generation since the post-war 'baby boomers' generation now has less wealth than the generation before them had at the same age. Much of this change is driven by property; people born in the 1980s had just a third of the property wealth at age 28 of those born in the 1970s (D'Arcy and Gardiner, 2017).

It is becoming increasingly hard for younger cohorts to share in the UK's wealth without substantial support from family, which not everyone has. In 2014, house prices were seven times higher than median earnings in England, compared to about four times in 1997, after controlling for changes in the quality and size of housing stock (Marsden, 2015). The solution for the lucky few is the 'bank of mum and dad', but access to help from family is skewed by social class: while 13 per cent of people in social classes AB had received a gift to help them buy or maintain property, only 3 per cent in classes DE had (Rowlingson, 2012). Rising house prices and declining home ownership have created inequality *between* generations today, but that will lead to increasing inequality *within* generations as those with wealthy, home-owning parents inherit that wealth.

Dynamics of divergence

In developed countries, the share of national income going to wages has fallen substantially since its peak in the late 1970s. In the UK, the labour share fell points from over 70 per cent in 1975 to almost 54 per cent in 1996. It has since recovered somewhat, but is currently stable at around 59–60 per cent, ten percentage points lower than its peak and long-term average in the mid-20th century (ONS, 2018a). One factor that can explain these changes in the shares of national income and wealth is the higher rate of return to capital. When the rate of return on capital after tax is higher than the rate of economic growth, wealth will become ever more concentrated, as those with capital (or very high earnings, which allows them to use their earnings to invest) accumulate wealth from capital income faster than those relying on ordinary labour income are able to save (Piketty, 2014).

While conditions in the 20th century – from global wars to productivity increases – temporarily halted this dynamic of divergence, in the 21st century, the rate of return to capital has returned to its pre-first world war trend of exceeding the rate of growth of the economy as a whole (Piketty, 2014). This is a problem not just for the first-order effects on wealth inequality, but for the macroeconomy as a whole. Wealthier households are less likely than poorer households to consume any extra income they receive. This might not be a problem if it was instead invested in the productive economy, but in our economy, increasing amounts are invested in speculative assets such as property or existing equities, generating high returns from economic rents rather than supporting productive growth.

For example, the rapid appreciation of housing wealth has diverted investment and lending away from more productive uses in the real economy towards the housing market. This is a problem for productivity, growth and prosperity, as the majority of real estate loans and mortgages do not increase the productive capacity of the economy nor contribute to GDP growth or higher wages. Instead, their primary effect is to drive up asset prices (Stirling and King, 2017). Rising house prices reduce consumers' spending power in the rest of the economy as higher proportions of income are spent on housing costs.

Alongside and, in part, resulting from this, dynamic has been the recent phenomenon of stagnant real wages since 2010 as productivity in the economy has flatlined. In real terms, average weekly earnings in the UK in July 2018 were the same as they were in July 2010 (ONS, 2018b). The wealthy have accumulated while those without wealth have stood still.

Are wealth taxes the answer?

As demonstrated by its rapid reduction through the last century, wealth inequality is not an immutable fact. Both inequality, and absolute levels of wealth, can and have changed over time, as a result of both global events and policy choices. There is a clear case for policy to redistribute wealth in order to spread its benefits to those without it. I would also help to prevent the capture of economic growth by those at the top, increasing direct investment to the productive economy and restraining the market and political power that large amounts of wealth generate. Yet despite the clear inequalities and problems posed for opportunity and prosperity, recent governments have done little to address wealth inequality and, in some cases, have exacerbated it.

Nowhere is this more apparent than in tax policy. Historically, wealth taxes – in the form of estate taxes and other property taxes – were a much more substantial portion of tax revenue in the UK than they are today. Indeed, income taxation was only introduced at the turn of the 18th century. In the 1930s, the largest estates were taxed at rates of up to 40 per cent; by 1945, this had risen to 65 per cent, and by 1949, 75 per cent (Glennerster, 2012). Today, however, taxes on income and consumption have become the dominant source of revenue in the UK and around the world (Lawton and Reed, 2013). Together, these forms of taxation raised revenue worth 23.4 per cent of GDP in 2019/20, whilst the main wealth taxes – capital gains tax, inheritance tax and the two stamp duties – raised tax worth just 1.4 per cent of GDP (OBR, 2020).

Our wealth tax system is inefficient from a purely economic perspective. Differential rates of tax on different types of asset, such as the exemption of owner–occupiers from paying capital gains tax, create economic distortions and encourage the direction of investment towards speculation over existing assets, driving up prices. Taxes on transactions, such as stamp duty, prevent sales and capture gains poorly. It is also regressive and exacerbates wealth inequality. Income from wealth is lightly taxed relative to income from labour, exacerbating the concentration of wealth and creating opportunities for owner–managers and executives to avoid tax by receiving pay in the form of capital gains and dividends rather than wages.

The IPPR Commission on Economic Justice, which was made up of leading figures from across the economic system, called in 2018 for an end to the preferential treatment of asset income by the tax system. The Commission proposed equalising tax rates on income from wealth and income from work, through raising capital gains tax and dividend income tax rates to match taxes on labour income (IPPR CEJ, 2018). Currently, if you had no employment earnings, you would pay 2 per cent tax on £20,000 of dividends, whereas if you were earning £100,000 from work, you would pay 29 per cent on that additional £20,000 (Nanda and Parkes, 2019). There are also numerous capital gains tax reliefs and allowances that allow asset owners, and those able to reclassify their income as capital income, to avoid paying tax. IPPR has also proposed reform of property taxation, to replace council tax and stamp duty with an annual property tax more closely related to the value of property. This would better capture gains made by owner–occupiers, who are exempt from capital gains tax on their homes (Blakeley, Roberts and Murphy, 2018).

As well as taxing *returns* to wealth, countering existing and entrenched inequalities would require reducing the capital that wealthy individuals already hold. Piketty proposes a global wealth tax; an alternative would be a wealth tax collected at the point when the asset is transferred through inheritance or sold. This would help to deconcentrate wealth between families and ensure unearned advantage cannot be passed from generation to generation.

The current UK system of inheritance tax contains many exemptions, is easy to avoid and favours the 'wealthy, healthy and well-advised'. Just 3.9 per cent of deaths in 2017/18 resulted in an inheritance tax charge (ONS, 2020). In 2018–19, someone could inherit £900,000 from their parents without paying tax, while someone working 40 hours a week on the National Living Wage from age 18 to 70 would only earn £753,000 in their entire life (in today's money) and would pay almost £100,000 in tax (Corlett, 2018). The IPPR Commission on Economic Justice proposed that inheritance tax be replaced with a donee-based lifetime gift tax, which above a lifetime allowance would tax not just inheritance upon death but also gifts – such as housing deposits from the 'bank of mum and dad' (Blakeley et al., 2018).

Beyond the tax system

The flipside to taxing wealth away is to grow the wealth of those who currently have little. This could include policies to raise wages, enable people to save and build pension wealth. Expanding ownership of financial wealth, both individually and collectively, could also bring the benefits of wealth to many more people. Pension wealth is the only type of household wealth to have become more equal in recent years, in large part due to the introduction of automatic enrolment in pension schemes (ONS, 2019a). Such an approach to spreading financial wealth was begun by New Labour with the introduction of Child Trust Funds, scrapped by the Coalition government at the beginning of their term.

The above approaches take an individual approach to broadening wealth. But wealth can also be, and is, held collectively. Collectively or publicly held wealth can confer many of the same advantages as private personal wealth. For example, financial returns can be used for the benefit of the collective or distributed to individuals. Collectively – most often publicly – held wealth such as land and housing stock can be used to provide security to successive generations in perpetuity, against dynamics of concentration found in markets. Public and collective ownership does not diminish total wealth but rather ensures that the benefits of wealth are shared through democratic means.

Policy aimed at building collective wealth could take the form of encouraging worker ownership models, or at a larger level, of establishing a citizens' wealth fund to ensure the gains of growth, including through technological innovation, are shared (Lawrence and Mason, 2017; Roberts and Lawrence, 2018). Returns could be used to fund expanded public services or distributed through a dividend or universal inheritance. Recent policy, however, has pushed in the opposite direction. In recent decades, the growth of private wealth has corresponded to a sell-off of public wealth into private hands. To take land as one example, two million hectares of public land, worth £400 billion and representing 10 per cent of British land mass, have been sold to the private sector in recent decades (Christophers, 2019). The subsidy gifted to social housing tenants purchasing their homes through Right to Buy by 2003 amounted to £200 billion in 2010/12 terms; while this initially expanded private wealth, it also accentuated inequalities between those able to buy and those without the right, or buying less valuable homes (Hills and Glennerster, 2013; Atkinson, 2015).

The advantages of private wealth are reduced when public, tax-funded provision of services is expanded, such that the state bears risks rather than the individual. In countries with less generous social security provision, private wealth is even more important as a source of financial security and to pay for life events (Domeij and Klein, 2002). In the UK, where there has been a shift from collective provision and risk pooling to individualisation of risk, this may have contributed to increased demand for housing and pensions (Quilter-Pinner et al., 2020; Atkinson, 2015). An alternative to growing private wealth is, therefore, to increase the provision of welfare payments and services such as social care.

Finally, government could pay greater attention to the effects of broader economic policy on the concentration of wealth. For example, the vast programme of quantitative easing embarked on by the Bank of England following the financial crash was shown to have driven up asset prices through a portfolio rebalancing effect (Stirling, 2018). An explicit mandate for the Bank of England to redress these dynamics could help; so too could make greater use of fiscal policy and public investment during recessions to better target spending where it is needed and counter the wealth inequality impacts of monetary policy.

What might the future hold for wealth inequality and policy to tackle it?

Wealth inequality, far from disappearing from the public conversation, is likely to grow in salience and importance over the coming decades.

Automation, in particular, risks increasing wealth inequality, in two ways. First, where labour is substituted for by machines, this shifts the distribution of income towards capital relative to labour (Lawrence, Roberts and King, 2017). In developed countries, an estimated 50 per cent of the fall in the labour share of national income since the 1980s has been driven by technological change (IMF, 2017). Second, automation is also likely to further polarise the labour market, with people working in either 'lovely or lousy' jobs (Goos and Manning, 2007). In the lovely jobs, people whose skills complement new technologies are likely to be increasingly highly rewarded, increasing their ability to save. By contrast, those whose skills can be replaced will bear the brunt of transition and compete with machines for low wages (Haldane, 2015).

The rise of digital platforms is already concentrating wealth, by facilitating the rise of 'superstar firms' in which a small number of highly profitable (and low labour share) firms command growing market share in a 'winner take most' market, producing significant wealth for their founders or owners (Autor et al., 2017; Furman and Orszag, 2015). As the scale of data produced and analysed grows, this is likely to generate ever-greater rewards for a small number of large digital monopolies. This dynamic occurs on the global, not national stage, with a few Silicon Valley bosses, and their global investors, capturing huge wealth as a result.

The Covid-19 pandemic has exacerbated wealth inequality rather than pushed against it (Berry, Macfarlane and Nanda, 2020). Households with higher income have saved money, as restrictions and concerns about the virus have caused a reduction in spending on retail and hospitality. Meanwhile, lower-income households are more likely to work in these sectors that have been affected and see their income fall or go entirely – pushing them into debt to cover just the essentials (Round, Nanda and Rankin, 2020). High-income households are almost twice as likely to have increased their savings compared to low-income households (Bank of England, 2020).

> Inequalities between the working poor and the asset-owning wealthy are likely to be exacerbated by second-round or long-term effects of the crisis. Some might point to the current plunge in stock prices and stuttering property markets as evidence that asset-owners will indeed share the pain. But this is only true for those who need to cash-in their assets in the short term – for instance, pensioners nearing retirement or homeowners who need

to sell. By contrast, those with excess liquidity will be able to buy assets at historically cheap prices and reap large rewards when they rebound in value. The long-term effects of rising indebtedness on the one hand, and a likely rebound in asset prices on the other, are likely to further widen inequalities between the working poor and the asset-owning wealthy.

(Berry et al., 2020)

In this context, taking steps to address wealth inequality is urgent. Yet, the technically feasible steps to tackle it are amongst the most challenging policy reforms for politicians to introduce. The expansion of collective wealth and, indeed, many of the policies to grow the number of good jobs have been limited by fiscal conservatism both in policy ideology and in the public narrative. Policies, including new taxes, can be held back by vested interests and sceptical bureaucrats (Glennerster, 2012). Meanwhile, politicians of both major parties in the UK have been derided and had their electoral fortunes damaged by wealth tax proposals: Ed Miliband, with the so-called 'mansion tax', and Theresa May with the 'dementia tax' (Elwes, 2014; The Guardian, 2017). Inheritance tax is spoken of as the UK's 'most hated tax' despite its very low incidence.

Opposition to these policies may, in part, stem from a lack of understanding of the true nature of wealth inequality in the UK, both in extent and in the nature of how that wealth was earned. In place of luck, 'hard work' is assumed to be the reason people are wealthy. But opposition to wealth taxes can also be attributed to strongly held values that reformers do not usually address, or at least their presentation has failed to speak to. The UK has an unusually high rate of home ownership following on from the reforms that initially expanded property wealth, and ownership is held up as British ideal. Taxes on wealth, and on the ability to pass on that wealth, are seen by some as an attack on values of aspiration and family – even if those opposing them would be unscathed by the taxes themselves. Loopholes in many existing wealth taxes contribute to a sense of unfairness (Corlett, 2018). Meanwhile, the norm of a strong and protective welfare state with public provision of service and collectively held wealth has been eroded over time.

However, the political tides may be changing. As Covid-19 has necessitated large government spending, attitudes to tax, and, in particular, the responsibility of those who have fared well through the pandemic to pay them, have shifted. Three-quarters of people now say they favour higher taxation of wealth, including 64 per cent of Conservative voters and 88 per cent of Labour voters, with broad support across a range of wealth tax measures (Tax Justice UK, 2020). A campaign to introduce a property tax has won the public support of multiple Conservative MPs, and in 2020 the Chancellor of the Exchequer commissioned a review of capital gains tax by the Office of Tax Simplification (Fairer Share, 2021; OTS, 2020). So far, any tax increases to pay for the costs of the pandemic have fallen on income, not wealth.

More broadly, the pandemic could mark an inflection point where attitudes to the role of the state and its contract with its citizens may change. Times of crisis have previously facilitated new forms of politics and shifts in responsibility from private household to collective provision. Wealth inequality runs on regional and generational lines; narrowing it can serve to address the growing group of voters currently locked out of sharing in the wealth.

Wealth inequality can feel intractable, but in reality, it is not an immutable fact. The policies to counter it are well-documented, and as policymakers look to move beyond the current crisis, the political tectonic plates for change may be grinding into place.

References

Acton, R. (2016). *The missing link*. London: Money and Mental Health Policy Institute.

Alstadsæter, A., Johannesen, N., and Zucman, G. (2017). Who owns the wealth in tax havens? Macro evidence and implications for global inequality, *National Bureau of Economic Research*, Working Paper 23805. http://www.nber.org/papers/23805

APPG [All-Party Parliamentary Group] on Inclusive Growth. (2018). Research suggests British people worried by growing political power of global super-rich. https://www.inclusivegrowth.co.uk/research-suggests-british-people-worried-growing-political-power-global-super-rich/

Asthana, A. and Elgot, J. (2017). Theresa May ditches manifesto plan with 'dementia tax' U-turn. *Guardian*. https://www.theguardian.com/society/2017/may/22/theresa-may-u-turn-on-dementia-tax-cap-social-care-conservative-manifesto

Atkinson, A. B. (2013). Wealth and inheritance in Britain from 1896 to the Present, *CASE paper 178*, London School of Economics.

Atkinson, A. B. (2015). *Inequality: what can be done?* Cambridge, Massachusetts and London: Harvard University Press.

Autor, D., Dorn, D., Katz, L., Patterson, C., and Van Reenen, J. (2017). The fall of the labor share and the rise of superstar firms'. Working Paper for The Centre for Economic Performance. http://cep.lse.ac.uk/pubs/download/dp1482.pdf

Bahaj, S., Foulis, A., and Pinter, G. (2016). The residential collateral channel, *Discussion Paper 1607*, London: Centre for Macroeconomics.

Bangham, G. and Leslie, J. (2020). *Rainy days*. London: Resolution Foundation. https://www.resolutionfoundation.org/app/uploads/2020/06/Rainy-Days.pdf

Bank of England. (2020). How has Covid affected household savings?. https://www.bankofengland.co.uk/bank-overground/2020/how-has-covid-affected-household-savings

Berry, C., Macfarlane, L. and Nanda, S. (2020). *Who wins and who pays? Rentier power and the Covid crisis.* London: IPPR. https://www.ippr.org/research/publications/who-wins-and-who-pays

Blakeley, G., Roberts, C., and Murphy, L. (2018). *A wealth of difference: Reforming the taxation of wealth*. London: IPPR. www.ippr.org/research/publications/a-wealth-of-difference

Blanchflower, D. and Oswald, A. (1998). What makes an entrepreneur?, *Journal of Labor Economics*, 16(1), pp. 26–60.

Bynner, J. and Paxton, W. (2001). *The asset-effect*. London: IPPR.

Christophers, B. (2019) *The new enclosure: the appropriation of public land in neoliberal Britain*. London: Verso.

Corlett, A. (2018). *Passing on: options for reforming inheritance taxation*. Resolution Foundation. https://www.resolutionfoundation.org/publications/passing-on-options-for-reforming-inheritance-taxation/

D'Arcy, C. and Gardiner, L. (2017). *The generation of wealth: asset accumulation across and within cohorts.* Resolution Foundation. http://www.resolutionfoundation.org/publications/the-generation-of-wealth-asset-accumulation-across-and-withincohorts/

Domeij, D. and Klein, P. (2002). Public pensions: to what extent do they account for Swedish wealth inequality?, *Review of Economic Dynamics*, 5(3), pp. 503–534.

Elwes, J. (2014). The mansion tax: Ed Miliband house of horrors'. Prospect. https://www.prospectmagazine.co.uk/politics/the-mansion-tax-ed-miliband-house-of-horrors

Fairer Share. (2021). Fairer Share gains national media coverage as the campaign reaches 100000 supporters, webpage. https://fairershare.org.uk/fairer-share-gains-national-media-coverage-as-the-campaign-reaches-100000-supporters/

Furman, J. and Orszag, P. (2015). A firm-level perspective on the role of rents in the rise in inequality. http://gabriel-zucman.eu/files/teaching/FurmanOrszag15.pdf

Glennerster, H. (2012). Why was a wealth tax for the UK abandoned? Lessons for the policy process and tackling wealth inequality, *Journal of Social Policy*, 41(2). http://eprints.lse.ac.uk/42582/

Goos, M. and Manning, A. (2007). Lousy and lovely jobs: the rising polarisation of work in Britain. *Review of Economics and Statistics*, 89(1), pp. 118–133. http://www.mitpress-journals.org/doi/abs/10.1162/rest.89.1.118?journalCode=rest

Green, J. and Pahontu, R. L. (2021). Mind the Gap: Why wealthy voters support Brexit. Available at SSRN: https://ssrn.com/abstract=3764889 or http://dx.doi.org/10.2139/ssrn.3764889

Haldane, A. (2015). Labour's share', Speech at the TUC, 12 November 2015. Bank of England. http://www.bankofengland.co.uk/publications/Pages/speeches/2015/864.aspx

Hills, J. and Glennerster, H. (2013). 'Public policy, wealth and assets: a complex and inconsistent story', in Hills et al., *Wealth in the UK: distribution, accumulation and policy.* 187. Oxford: Oxford University Press: University Press.

International Monetary Fund [IMF]. (2017). Drivers of declining labor share of income. https://blogs.imf.org/2017/04/12/drivers-of-declining-labor-share-of-income/

IPPR Commission on Economic Justice [IPPR]. (2018). *Prosperity and justice: a plan for the new economy.* Cambridge: Polity Press.

Khan, O. (2019). *Economic inequality and racial inequalities in the UK.* Friends Provident Foundation. https://www.friendsprovidentfoundation.org/library/resources/economic-inequality-and-racial-inequalities-in-the-uk/

Lawrence, M. and Mason, N. (2017) *Capital gains: broadening company ownership in the UK economy.* IPPR. https://www.ippr.org/publications/CEJ-capital-gains

Lawrence, M., Roberts, C. and King, L. (2017). *Managing automation: employment, inequality and ethics in the digital age.* IPPR. https://www.ippr.org/publications/managing-automation

Lawton, K. and Reed, H. (2013). *Property and wealth taxes in the UK: the context for reform.* https://www.ippr.org/files/images/media/files/publication/2013/03/wealth-taxescontext_Mar2013_10503.pdf

Marsden, J. (2015) *House prices in London – an economic analysis of London's housing market.* GLA Economics. https://www.london.gov.uk/sites/default/files/house-pricesin-london.pdf

McKnight, A. (2011). 'Estimates of the asset-effect: the search for a causal effect of assets on adult health and employment outcomes', *CASE Paper 149.* London: London School of Economics

Nanda, S. and Parkes, H. (2019) *Just tax: reforming the taxation of income from wealth,* IPPR. https://www.ippr.org/research/publications/just-tax

Office for Budget Responsibility [OBR] (2020). *Economic and fiscal outlook: November 2020*. http://cdn.obr.uk/CCS1020397650-001_OBR-November2020-EFO-v2-Web-accessible.pdf

Office of Tax Simplification. (2020) *OTS Capital Gains Tax Review: Simplifying by Design November*, https://www.gov.uk/government/publications/ots-capital-gains-tax-review-simplifying-by-design

ONS. (2018a). Estimating the impact of the self-employed in the labour share. https://www.ons.gov.uk/economy/economicoutputandproductivity/productivitymeasures/methodologies/estimatingtheimpactoftheselfemployedinthelaboursh are

ONS. (2018b). Analysis of real earnings and contributions to nominal earnings growth, Great Britain: September 2018. https://www.ons.gov.uk/employmentandlabourmarket/peopleinwork/earningsandworkinghours/articles/supplementaryanalysisofaverageweeklyearnings/september2018

ONS. (2019a). Total wealth: Wealth in Great Britain, dataset. https://www.ons.gov.uk/peoplepopulationandcommunity/personalandhouseholdfinances/incomeandwealth/datasets/totalwealthwealthingreatbritain

ONS.(2019b).Disposableincomeandexpenditureofhouseholdsbydecile,financialyearsending 2002 to 2018, dataset. https://www.ons.gov.uk/peoplepopulationandcommunity/personalandhouseholdfinances/incomeandwealth/adhocs/010109disposableincomeandexpenditureofhouseholdsbydecilefinancialyearsending2002to2018

ONS. (2020). Inheritance tax statistics – 2017–18. https://www.gov.uk/government/collections/inheritance-tax-statistics

Piketty, T. (2014). *Capital in the twenty-first century*. Cambridge MA: Harvard University Press.

Quilter-Pinner, H., Hochlaf, D., and McNeil, C. (2020). *The decades of disruption: new social risks and the future of the welfare state*. IPPR. https://www.ippr.org/research/publications/decades-of-disruption

Roberts, C. and Lawrence, M. (2018). *Our common wealth: A citizens' wealth fund for the UK*, IPPR. https://www.ippr.org/research/publications/our-common-wealth

Round, A., Nanda, S., and Rankin, L (2020). *Helping households in debt*, IPPR. https://www.ippr.org/research/publications/helping-households-in-debt

Rowlingson, K. (2012). Wealth inequality: key facts, Policy Commission on the Distribution of Wealth, University of Birmingham. https://www.birmingham.ac.uk/Documents/research/SocialSciences/Key-Facts-Background-Paper-BPCIV.pdf

Ryan-Collins, J., Macfarlane, L. and Lloyd, T. (2017). *Rethinking the economics of land and housing*. London: Zed Books.

Schmalz, M., Sraer, D., and Thesmar, D. (2017). Housing collateral and entrepreneurship, *The Journal of Finance*, 72(1), pp. 99–132.

Stirling, A. (2018). *Just about managing demand: reforming the UK's macroeconomic policy framework*. IPPR. https://www.ippr.org/research/publications/just-aboutmanaging-demand

Stirling, A. and King, L. (2017). *Financing investment: reforming finance markets for the long-term*. IPPR. https://www.ippr.org/publications/cej-financing-investment

Tax Justice UK. (2020). *Talking tax: how to win support for taxing wealth*. https://www.taxjustice.uk/uploads/1/0/0/3/100363766/talking_tax_-_how_to_win_support_for_taxing_wealth.pdf

World Inequality Database. (2020). Income and wealth inequality, United Kingdom, 1895–2019. https://wid.world/country/united-kingdom/

3 Social Mobility

Duncan Exley

Introduction

Social mobility, put simply, is experienced by individuals who occupy a higher or lower ranking—usually in financial and/or occupational terms—than their parents did at a similar age. Social mobility and the related concept of 'aspiration' have been major themes in political and media discourse for over four decades, with each successive Prime Minister making efforts to say how they will promote more upward mobility and thereby allow more of us to attain our aspirations.

This chapter will explore trends in the prevalence and type of social mobility since the middle-to-late 20th century: how social mobility levels affect the social, political, and economic functioning of the country as well as individuals' well-being; the mismatch between political and public understandings of and attitudes to social mobility; and the difference between policies favoured by policymakers and those that would make most impact.

Trends in social mobility

There are various ways of measuring social mobility. Taken together, they paint a picture of restricted or declining mobility:

Occupational measures

'Occupational mobility' refers to the process of individuals getting jobs in what are classified as higher-status (or lower-status) occupations than those their parents had at a similar age.

According to this measure, in the third quarter of the 20th century, the United Kingdom experienced high levels of upward mobility (Bukodi & Goldthorpe, 2018), including large numbers of individuals from working class backgrounds finding 'middle-class' jobs. In recent decades, however, things changed. People born since the early 1980s are the first group since comparable records began (in 1946) to have lower-status jobs than their parents had at the same age (Goldthorpe, 2016). In occupational terms, the United Kingdom is now, on aggregate, a downwardly mobile country.

The usefulness of occupational measures, though, may be declining. Goldthorpe describes the National Statistics Socio-Economic Classification ranking as 'quite

DOI: 10.4324/9781003104476-5

strongly associated with income level [...] income security, short-term income stability, and longer-term income prospects' (Goldthorpe, 2016), but this is decreasingly true. The (low) levels of income, security, stability, and prospects once associated with blue-collar work have now become common in white-collar occupations, eroding the 'old divisions between blue collar and white collar workers' (Taylor, Kamerāde & McKay, 2014).

Economic measures

Economic measures of mobility—movements in the position of individuals or households up or down the league table of incomes—also show reduced mobility in recent years. A landmark 2002 study using these measures showed that levels of economic mobility were lower for people born in 1970 than they were for those born in 1958. This, the study's authors concluded, 'flatly contradicts the common view that anyone can make it in modern Britain. Indeed, rather than weakening, the link between an individual's earnings and those of his or her parents has strengthened' (Blanden, Goodman, Gregg & Machin, 2002). Other data show that economic mobility in the United Kingdom is low compared to norm of other developed countries (OECD, 2018).

These economic measures also have their limitations. For example, the most widely cited studies measure income rather than wealth although the latter is increasingly important to individuals' chances of attaining their aspirations, especially in regard to home ownership.

Multidimensional measures

A ground-breaking study that measures class in terms of a combination of economic, social, and cultural capital was published in 2015. While lack of similar studies means it does not provide data that can be compared with other periods or other countries, it also sees social mobility in the United Kingdom as restricted, especially mobility into and out of the higher echelons: 'the small elite class is, in fact, much more exclusive than any of the other classes' (Savage, 2015). The observation that social mobility into the 'elite' is especially difficult is also found in an OECD report looking at *intra*generational—i.e. movements within an individual's lifetime—economic mobility. The OECD report classifies Britain as having relatively high numbers of people moving between low- and middle incomes but low numbers moving from high- to middle income and concomitantly low numbers entering the top tier (OECD, 2018).

Consequences

When social mobility is constrained, or when the populations is more likely to experience downward mobility than they are to 'go up in the world', it has adverse social and political consequences:

Alan Milburn, former Chair of the Social Mobility Commission, thinks there is a widely perceived failure of what he calls the 'post-war promise' of social mobility: that people who work hard and/or attain educational qualifications can expect to do better than their parents (Exley, 2019). Individuals born after 1980, despite having obtained a higher level of educational qualifications than any previous generation, find themselves rewarded not only with, on average, lower-status jobs than their parents had at the same age, but also a lower—and declining—chance of homeownership (MHCLG, 2020a). As a result of their constrained and insecure finances and housing situations, increasing numbers are also reluctantly delaying or cancelling plans to start a family (ONS, 2019, 2020). These phenomena pre-date Covid-19, war in Ukraine, and the subsequent economic problems.

This situation is likely to have consequences for mental health: psychological studies suggest—unsurprisingly—that individuals whose aspirations are frustrated are more likely to suffer depression (Greenaway, Frye & Cruwys, 2015). It is also likely to foster antagonism towards the 'establishment': international academic research suggests a link between frustrated—or downward—social mobility and the growth of anti-establishment political distrust and populism (e.g. Protzer, 2021; Daenekindt, van der Waal & de Koster, 2018), and in the United Kingdom, there appears to be a strong correlation between pro-Brexit voters and those whose 'socio-economic position was perceived to be declining and/or to be stagnant' (Antonucci, Horvath & Krouwel, 2017).

Constrained mobility also adversely affects the performance and effectiveness of our economy and institutions. Thirty-nine per cent of the 'elite' in politics, business, and the media are privately educated, compared to 7 per cent of the population (Sutton Trust, 2020). Analysis suggests that this phenomenon, and the reduction in the proportion of MPs from working-class backgrounds since the 1980s, has been accompanied by an increased tendency for MPs to support measures that 'contradict the interests of working-class voters' (O'Grady, 2019). Even if policymakers from middle-class backgrounds are motivated to address the challenges faced by working-class people, they will struggle to do so effectively because their lack of lived experience makes it harder to fully understand those challenges.

The UK economy's ability to 'bounce back better' from the pandemic will be enabled, said former Prime Minister Boris Johnson, by the 'ingenuity, dynamism [and] entrepreneurial spirit' (Houghton, 2020). But unfortunately, many would-be entrepreneurs from ordinary backgrounds are denied a chance to unleash their ingenuity and dynamism because 'successful entrepreneurs'… most commonly shared trait is not personality but access to financial capital, often through gifts and inheritance' (Roberts & Lawrence, 2017). An assessment carried out in 2010 estimated that 'weakening the link between background and achievement in the UK would contribute between £56 and £140 billion to the value of the economy each year by 2050' (Sutton Trust, 2010).

The ability of privilege to trump potential also applies to fields such as science: the Chief Executive of the British Science Association has acknowledged that there is a 'class barrier' to entry into scientific research (Gibney, 2016), which suggests that individuals from ordinary backgrounds with the potential to make extraordinary breakthroughs—in fields that might include the study of the next pandemic virus—are being kept out of the laboratory.

Political vs public discourses of social mobility and aspiration

Despite social mobility having been a major theme in the rhetoric of all recent Prime Ministers, and restricted or downward social mobility having relevance to some of the most important values, aspirations, and frustrations of the public, politicians have largely failed to engage the public with either narratives or policy programmes in this area. This is primarily due to there being two separate—political and public—discourses of social mobility.

The politics of social mobility

One of the defining ideas of Tony Blair's transformation of the Labour Party into 'New Labour' was the belief that Prime Minister Margaret Thatcher and her successor John Major had won elections in large part by positioning the Conservative Party, in contrast to Labour, as being on the side of aspirational voters (Heath, Jowell & Curtice, 2001). As Blair told the Labour conference in 1996: 'I can vividly recall the exact moment that I knew the last election was lost... I met a man polishing his Ford Sierra, self-employed electrician... his instincts were to get on in life, and he thought our instincts were to stop him' (Blair, 1996).

Since then, all our political leaders have had a lot to say about the interrelated concepts of social mobility and aspiration. Prime Minister Gordon Brown spoke of creating an 'age of aspiration'; David Cameron made social mobility the central theme of his first-party conference speech after winning a majority; Theresa May declared an intention to create 'the world's great meritocracy' (Exley, 2019), and Boris Johnson talked of 'levelling up' (Johnson, 2021). During the Conservative leadership contest in August 2022 to replace Boris Johnson as Prime Minister, both candidates agreed about the importance of social mobility. Rishi Sunak said 'I believe in hard work and aspiration and that's my story and if I'm prime minister then I'll be making the case for that with vigour' (Sunak, 2022) while Liz Truss spoke of building 'an aspiration nation' (Truss, 2022).

However, with exceptions such as Thatcher's Right to Buy policy, the political discourse of social mobility has remained conceptual and ideological rather than engaging with the tangible, specific aspirations and values of voters.

One side of this ideological debate on social mobility is exemplified in an article by Nick Clegg, who, shortly after becoming Deputy Prime Minister in 2010, wrote that 'social mobility is what characterises a fair society, rather than a particular level of income equality. Inequalities become injustices when they are fixed; passed on, generation to generation' (Clegg, 2010). Accordingly, the Child Poverty Commission was in 2012 renamed the Social Mobility and Child

Poverty Commission (Welfare Reform Act 2012) and, in 2016, became the Social Mobility Commission (Welfare Reform and Work Act 2016) Promoting social mobility was, thus, being pitched as a superior interpretation of fairness to reducing poverty and inequality.

The opposing side of the debate isn't so much a different conceptualisation as its mirror-image. It argues that reducing poverty and inequality is more important than promoting social mobility. This can be seen in the Labour Party's 2019 manifesto, which stated that 'the true measure of fairness is not social mobility but social justice [because] implicit in the notion of social mobility is the idea that poverty and inequality are acceptable provided some people can climb the social ladder' (Labour Party, 2019).

However, while politicians are writing speeches and articles about 'social mobility', polling shows that barely half (52 per cent) the public say they know what 'social mobility' means 'fairly well' or 'very well' (Social Mobility Commission, 2020).

Public preferences, perceptions, and experiences of social mobility and aspiration

Although the terminology of 'social mobility' has little appeal to voters, it does relate to some of the public's most strongly held values and some of their most salient aspirations and frustrations.

According to one opinion poll, the values which the British public—across all social classes—say are most important to them are 'family', 'fairness', and 'hard work' (Ainsley, 2018). These values were ranked significantly higher than 'equality'. When in 2011, the public were asked whether fairness was about 'getting what you deserve' or 'equality', the former beat the later by approximately two to one (O'Brien, 2011). Public opinion is not purely meritocratic, as most of us do think there is a 'socially acceptable' standard of living—significantly higher than that currently guaranteed by social security levels—below which we should not be left to fall (Padley & Stone, 2021). However, a 'fair reward for hard work' is a reasonable description of the view of the majority of the public.

But other polling suggests that the public thinks 'fair reward for hard work' does not reflect how the United Kingdom actually operates today. Asked which was the more important determinant of 'where you end up in society', more people chose 'who your parents were' than chose 'talent and hard work' by a margin of 11 percentage points (Social Mobility Commission, 2021).

This does not mean that the public will necessarily perceive the situation to be bad enough to constitute a problem. Some argue that the British public still 'think that opportunities are *equal enough* to count as a meritocracy' (Gaffney & Baumberg, 2014). However, constrained opportunity tends to acquire more salience when our own chances to attain our aspirations feel unfairly constrained. And a plurality of adults under 50 now feel that although they have become better educated than their parents, they are worse off in terms of housing, job security, and job satisfaction (Social Mobility Commission, 2021). As data quoted above suggest, these perceptions are reflected in the reality of declining opportunity to attain some of our most dearly held aspirations, including a home to call our own, a satisfactory job, and the economic security to start a family. These things matter to hugely to people and, as the studies on the links between constrained or downward social mobility and political distrust and populism suggest, that should matter to any politician.

Part of the reason why politicians have failed to engage with the public's strongly held values, frustrations, and aspirations around social mobility is that they have accepted the premise—exemplified in Nick Clegg's article and the 2019 Labour manifesto quoted above—that one has to choose between social mobility and social justice (with the latter focused on reducing poverty and inequality). As we have seen, the public do not see these as mutually exclusive, favouring both a minimum standard of living and, above that level, rewards proportionate to effort. Cross-country analyses also show a strong correlation between the low inequality and high social mobility (OECD, 2018), suggesting these are better seen as complementary rather than competing. Social mobility helps reduce inequality by—for example—giving a greater number of people with lived experience and relationships in the 'lower' classes the power, skills, and/or relationships to influence decision-making in favour of the members of those classes. Also, those whose priority is greater equality need not cede social mobility (as a discourse) to their opponents because the policies needed to promote greater mobility—some of which are outlined at the end of this chapter—also reduce inequality (Exley, 2019) and promoting such policies is more likely to be successful if it resonates with public preferences for both a decent minimum standard of living *and* 'fair reward for hard work'.

Drivers of social (im)mobility

Despite the huge amount of political discourse on social mobility, politician's actions typically have not addressed the most important factors that have restricted upward mobility.

Reviewing recent publications on social mobility for *Prospect* magazine in 2018, Tom Clark wrote, 'For all the methodological arguments between them, the new batch of books agree on one thing: fixating on education in isolation hasn't worked' (Clark, 2018).

As with any other large-scale social phenomenon, there are a complex and complicated range of factors involved. However, it is the interaction of limited 'room at the top' with the empowerment of wealth which is the key to understanding the United Kingdom's unusually poor levels of mobility.

Limited 'room at the top'

The upward occupational mobility that characterised the third-quarter of the 20th century was not the result of better education, but of a substantial increase in the availability of skilled and white-collar jobs (Bukodi & Goldthorpe, 2018). This had a direct effect of creating greater financial security for those workers and their families, which, in turn, meant higher tax receipts that helped fund a supportive social security system and improved public services, including a vast expansion of public sector housing. It was accompanied by substantial public investment both in physical infrastructure and, through the huge expansion of the public sector workforce and various industrial policies, high-quality jobs (Chick, 2002). Upward social mobility was, therefore, driven by deliberate public sector investment and was closely linked to the reduction in inequality seen in that period (Dorling, 2015).

Today, in contrast, high-quality jobs are in short supply. In the name of social mobility, we have educated more people to degree level than ever before, but almost a third of workers who have a degree don't have a job that requires one (Industrial Strategy Council, 2019). Education initiatives to boost social mobility have proliferated but, unlike the post-war decades, UK governments since the 1980s have favoured a laissez-faire approach to industrial policy, emphasising cost-incentives such as having the lowest corporation tax in the G7 (Conte, Miller & Pope, 2019). This has given a relative advantage to low-cost, low-skilled sectors (of the sort most heavily impacted by the Covid-19 pandemic) (Cominetti, Leslie & Smith, 2021) rather than the higher-paid, higher-skilled, higher-status jobs to which people are more likely to aspire.

The opportunity to attain another widely held aspiration, a 'home to call our own', is also constrained by the limited supply of housing. The number of new dwellings completed annually in England, which rose to a peak of approximately 350,000 in the late 1960s, fell to around half that level in the late 2010s. This was driven by a fall in local authority homebuilding from approximately 150,000 annual completions to virtually nothing by the early 1990s (MHCLG, 2020b), following Thatcher-era legislative restrictions on public sector housing investment (Fée, 2009). The effect of this has been (to borrow the Social Mobility Commission's wording) to strengthen the link between 'where you end up' and 'who your parents were': by the 1990s, 30-year olds whose parents had housing wealth were approximately twice as likely to be homeowners themselves, and, from the mid-2000s, almost three times as likely (Clarke & Wood, 2018).

The empowerment of wealth

The increasing importance of a wealthy family in determining the chances of attaining one's aspirations is not limited to housing. For example, entry to certain careers now often depends on having the means to fund living expenses during lengthy periods of unpaid work. For example, in journalism, portfolios of articles written without payment or during unpaid internships are now typically a prerequisite for being offered paid work, in contrast to the situation 'during the UK's first great wave of social mobility [when] journalists might have worked their way up through the local newspaper' (Milburn, 2009).

It is not the case that *levels* of wealth inequality are peculiarly high in the United Kingdom compared to those in other OECD countries—they are close to average, with the top 10 per cent of all British households owning approximately half of all household wealth (Balestra & Tonkin, 2018). However, policymakers have created a situation where family wealth has greater influence, relative to other factors, in determining individuals' chances of attaining their most widely held aspirations to own their own homes and gain entry to good jobs.

The United Kingdom has also adopted policies that have given wealthy families a greater advantage in *pursuing* opportunities. For example, the United Kingdom has one of the lowest rates of unemployment support among developed economies (OECD, 2021). This pushes those who lose work and lack a cushion of wealth to find immediately available jobs rather than take time to look for work—or undertake training—that unlock higher income and well-being in the longer term. The United Kingdom is also unusual in how little security it offers its rising number of private renters (Shelter, 2016), increasing the risk of 'poor health and negative educational, social or psychological outcomes' associated with enforced moves between homes (Children's Society, 2017). This means children in families unable to afford homeownership are more likely to be at a disadvantage in education and later career.

The prevalence of poverty, the low levels of support to mitigate it, and the under-resourcing of schools also means that wealth becomes a determinant of whether children have access to other resources associated with higher educational attainment. These include a good home-learning environment, good nutrition, an absence of stressors related to financial insecurity, and access to computers and the Internet. (Oddly, this is one aspect of the relationship between education and social mobility on which government has, in the last decade, not been fixated). Geraint Johnes, a specialist in the economics of education, has written that the United Kingdom is 'particularly striking' in the extent to which 'educational performance is very much driven by social factors' so that 'while tweaking educational policy may help or hinder at the margin, it is social policy that really has the power to secure large gains in educational attainment' (Johnes, 2018).

The experience of the pandemic has exacerbated these effects. An assessment carried out in autumn 2020—i.e. with approximately half a year of school closures still to come—estimated that Year 2 pupils from disadvantaged households were already seven months behind their peers in reading and mathematics (Rose et al., 2021). Earlier in the pandemic, an evidence assessment had concluded that 'school closures are likely to reverse progress made to narrow the gap [between attainment of disadvantaged children and that of their peers] in the last decade' (Education Endowment Foundation, 2020). This can be expected to be further exacerbated by the financial shocks of the current cost-of-living crisis.

An additional way in which wealth affects the degree of benefit children derive from their school years is through 'school choice' policy. This operates not just through the wealthy's ability to send their children to private schools whose pupils have higher odds of being admitted to 'top universities' than state-educated individuals with similar exam results (Montacute, 2018). It also applies to the way that school choice operates in the state school sector. Rich families can afford the higher cost of housing in the catchment area of 'high-performing' state schools (Department for Education, 2017). They also have far higher odds of being admitted into the remaining state grammar schools (Burgess, Crawford & Macmillan, 2018). School choice empowers wealth by giving the wealthy choices that the rest of us cannot afford.

Other areas of policy that have gradually strengthened the relative importance of coming from a wealthy family include the lower tax rates levied on income from wealth compared to income from employment: 'While the role of private wealth in the economy has more than doubled since the 1980s... taxes on it have not kept pace... And there are a range of tax advantages for the better off—many related to wealth tax exemptions' (Jung & Nanda, 2021).

What can be done?

At a time when social mobility is restricted, and in occupational terms mostly downward, politicians urgently need to find a way of presenting a narrative and programme around social mobility and aspiration that resonates with public values, aspirations, and frustrations. This cannot be achieved by talking about 'social mobility', but rather by talking about the things to which people aspire and are struggling to attain.

An effective policy programme to promote upward social mobility would cease to fixate on education alone. It must instead recognise that unless there are greater opportunities to fulfil our aspirations, there will be no increase in the numbers who attain those aspirations (and a greater incentive for wealthy families to use their advantage to hoard them). Such a policy programme might include:

- An industrial strategy that prioritises the creation of high-value jobs, and invests, using an 'entrepreneurial state' approach (Mazzucato, 2015), to anticipate and seize developing economic opportunities in, for example, sustainable technology.
- A recognition that if housing supply is to match the growth in demand, the public sector must be unleashed, preferably in partnership with private homebuilders to prevent segregation-by-income by creating developments with homes for private sale alongside those for social rent (Chetty, Hendren & Katz, 2016). It should also mean establishing a decent homes standard for private rented accommodation, requiring landlords to offer decent standards of health and safety, insulation and providing security for tenants, in recognition that housing has a large effect on children's educational performance and mental health.
- Creating a 'citizens' wealth fund' for individuals to invest in education, training, and other personal development opportunities (Roberts & Lawrence 2018).
- Investing in the resilience of the non-wealthy by restoring working-age social security to levels typical of our western European neighbours.
- Making more serious effort to promote diversity and inclusion in our politics, economy and society and the educational institutions that supply them with

personnel; including by adding socioeconomic background to the 'protected characteristics' listed in the Equalities Act 2010 so that the diverse majority of us are less underrepresented in the 'establishment'.
- Reducing the excessive power of wealth to buy advantage by rebalancing overall taxation to favour of income earned from work rather than assets.

Decision-makers and influencers still have the opportunity to change their discourse from one centred on abstract concepts and ideology to a narrative that engages with the more nuanced, pragmatic, and deeply held values, aspirations, and frustrations of the public. They also have the opportunity to engage with areas of policy that have already shown themselves to be effective, rather than pushing individuals to compete for a diminishing number of opportunities against an incumbent caste that can pay to load the dice in favour of their own families.

Unless these opportunities are taken, then the problem will worsen, as other countries continue with strategies that are likely to create, sustain, and attract high-quality future-focused industries, as our housing supply falls further behind supply, and as the power of wealthy families consolidates generation-on-generation, leading to an even more cynical, alienated population who see an establishment with unrelatable backgrounds and experiences who have failed to deliver a fair reward for hard work.

References

Ainsley, C. (2018) *The new working class*, Bristol: Policy Press.
Antonucci, L., Horvath, L. & Krouwel, A. (2017) 'Brexit was not the voice of the working class nor of the uneducated – it was of the squeezed middle', LSE *Politics and Policy* blog, 13 October.
Balestra, C. & Tonkin, R. (2018) *Inequalities in household wealth across OECD countries: Evidence from the OECD Wealth Distribution Database*, Paris: OECD.
Blair, Tony (1996) Leader's speech to Labour Party conference, Blackpool, 1 October. Accessed at http://www.britishpoliticalspeech.org/speech-archive.htm?speech=202.
Blanden, J., Goodman, A., Gregg, P. & Machin, S. (2002) *Changes in intergenerational mobility in Britain*, CEEDP (26), London: LSE.
Bukodi, E. & Goldthorpe, J.H. (2018) *Social mobility and education in Britain: Research, politics and policy*, Cambridge: Cambridge UP.
Burgess, S., Crawford, C. & Macmillan, L. (2018) Access to grammar schools by socioeconomic status, *Environment and Planning A*, 50(7), 1381–1385, October.
Chetty, R., Hendren, N. & Katz, L. (2016) The effects of exposure to better neighborhoods on children: New evidence from the moving to opportunity project, *American Economic Review*, 106(4), 855–902.
Chick, M. (2002) *Industrial policy in Britain 1945–1951*, Cambridge: Cambridge UP.
The Children's Society (2017) *Understanding childhoods: Growing up in hard times*, London: The Children's Society.
Clark, T. (2018) The social mobility trap, *Prospect*, Jan/Feb 2020.
Clarke, S. & Wood, J. (2018) *House of the rising son (or daughter): The impact of parental wealth on their children's homeownership*, London: Resolution Foundation.

Clegg, N. (2010) Inequality becomes injustice when it is passed on, generation to generation, *The Guardian*, 22 November.

Cominetti, N., Leslie, J. & Smith, J. (2021) *On firm ground? The impact of Covid-19 on firms and what policy makers should do in response*, London: Resolution Foundation.

Conte, M., Miller, H. & Pope, T. (2019) *How do other countries raise more in tax than the UK?*, London: Institute for Fiscal Studies.

Daenekindt, S., van der Waal, J. & de Koster, W. (2018) Social mobility and political distrust: Cults of gratitude and resentment?. *Acta Politica*, 53, 269–282.

Department for Education (2017) *House prices and schools: Do houses close to the best performing schools cost more?* London: Department for Education.

Dorling, D. (2015) *Inequality and the 1%*, London: Verso.

Education Endowment Foundation (2020) *Impact of school closures on the attainment gap: Rapid Evidence Assessment*, London: Education Endowment Foundation.

Exley, D. (2019) *The end of aspiration? Social mobility and our children's fading prospects*, Bristol: Policy Press.

Fée, D. (2009) Acknowledging the limits of Thatcherism : Housing policies during the Major years, *Observatoire de la société britannique*, 7 | 2009, 233–248.

Gaffney, D. & Baumberg, B. (2014) 'Perceptions of social mobility in Britain are characterised by a strange paradox', *LSE Politics and Policy* blog, London, 12 May.

Gibney, E. (2016) Is science only for the rich?, *Nature*, 537, 466–467, 22 September.

Goldthorpe, J.H. (2016) Social class mobility in modern Britain: Changing structure, constant process, *Journal of the British Academy*, 4, 89–111.

Greenaway, K., Frye, M. & Cruwys, T. (2015) When aspirations exceed expectations: Quixotic hope increases depression among students. *PLoS One*, 10(9), e0135477.

Heath, A. Jowell, R., & Curtice, J. (2001) *The rise of new labour: Party policies and voter choices*, Oxford: Oxford UP.

Houghton, T. (2020) Prime Minister Boris Johnson joins LinkedIn as he pledges to 'connect more directly' with businesses, *Business Live*, 2 September.

Industrial Strategy Council (2019) *UK skills mismatch in 2030*, London: Industrial Strategy Council.

Johnes, G. (2018) 'GCSE results: Why bright, poor students fail to achieve top grades', *The Conversation*, 23 August.

Johnson, B. (2021) *The Prime Minister's levelling up speech*: 15 July. Accessed at https://www.gov.uk/government/speeches/the-prime-ministers-levelling-up-speech-15-july-2021.

Jung, C. & Nanda, S. (2021) *Tax and recovery: Beyond the binary*, London: IPPR.

The Labour Party (2019) *It's time for real change: The Labour Party Manifesto 2019*, London: The Labour Party.

Mazzucato, M. (2015) *The entrepreneurial state: Debunking public vs. private sector myths*, New York: Public Affairs.

Milburn, A. (2009) *Unleashing aspiration: The final report of the Panel on Fair Access to the Professions*, London, Cabinet Office.

Ministry of Housing, Communities & Local Government (2020a) *English housing survey headline report, 2018–19*, London: Ministry of Housing, Communities & Local Government.

Ministry of Housing, Communities & Local Government (2020b) *House building; new build dwellings, England: September Quarter 2019*, London: Ministry of Housing, Communities & Local Government.

Montacute, R. (2018) *Access to Advantage: The influence of schools and place on admissions to top universities*, London: Sutton Trust.

O'Brien, N. (2011) *Just deserts? Attitudes to fairness, poverty and welfare reform*, London: Policy Exchange.

OECD (2018) *A broken social elevator? How to promote social mobility*, Paris: OECD.

OECD (2021) *Benefits in unemployment, share of previous income (indicator)*, Paris: OECD.

ONS (2019) *Conceptions in England and Wales: 2017*, London: ONS.

ONS (2020) *Conceptions in England and Wales: 2018*, London: ONS.

O'Grady, T. (2019) Careerists versus coalminers: Welfare reforms and the substantive representation of social groups in the British Labour Party. *Comparative Political Studies*, 52(4), 544–578.

Padley, M. & Stone, J. (2021) *Households below a Minimum Income Standard: 2008/09–2018/19*, York: JRF.

Protzer, E. (2021) 'Social mobility explains populism, not inequality or culture', CID Research Fellow and Graduate Student Working Paper Series 2021.118, Harvard University, Cambridge, MA, January.

Roberts, C. & Lawrence, M. (2017) *Wealth in the twenty-first century: Inequalities and drivers*, London: IPPR.

Roberts, C. & Lawrence, M. (2018) *Our common wealth: A citizens' wealth fund for the UK*, London: IPPR.

Rose, S., Twist, L., Lord, P., Rutt, S., Badr, K., Hope, C. & Styles, B. (2021) *Impact of school closures and subsequent support strategies on attainment and socio-emotional wellbeing in Key Stage 1: Interim Paper 1*, London: Education Endowment Foundation.

Savage, M. (2015) *Social class in the 21st century*, London: Penguin.

Shelter (2016) *Time for reform: How our neighbours with mature private renting markets guarantee stability for renters*. Accessed at https://assets.ctfassets.net/6sxvmndnpn0s/5dQOQ3 VrKnwulcrgUZRUYf/7948f25b6926e83805ba8fb3cf51667e/Time_for_reform_ FINAL.pdf

Social Mobility Commission (2020) *Social mobility barometer: Public attitudes to social mobility in the UK, 2019–20*, London: Social Mobility Commission.

Social Mobility Commission (2021) *Social Mobility Barometer: Public attitudes to social mobility in the UK, 2021*, London: Social Mobility Commission.

Sunak, R. (2022) *Today*, BBC Radio 4, 14 July.

Sutton Trust (2010) *The mobility manifesto. A report on cost-effective ways to achieve greater social mobility through education, based on work by the Boston Consulting Group*. London: Sutton Trust.

Sutton Trust (2020) *Elitist Britain 2019: The educational backgrounds of Britain's leading people*, London: Sutton Trust.

Taylor, R., Kamerāde, D. & McKay, S. (2014) *Reviewing the literature on pay and non-standard employment taking a cross sector perspective*, London: Third Sector Research Centre.

Truss, L. (2022) I will be unashamedly pro-business and show Global Britain is thriving and open to the world', *Sunday Telegraph*, 24 July.

4 Racial economic inequality

The visible tip of an inequality iceberg?

Kurt Barling

Introduction

When this edited collection was first conceived, after an exceptional conference, headlined by Nobel Laureate Professor Joseph Stiglitz, at Middlesex University in December 2019, the world was arguably a very different place. For very different reasons, two of the most dramatic events of 2020 have refreshed the debate on systemic racism in the UK. Both the death of George Floyd in the US and the global pandemic caused by Covid-19 have raised questions for social scientists about the lens through which systemic racism is investigated. These events demanded that I change the lens through which I approached this paper on economic inequality and race. They have highlighted rather complacent social attitudes towards enduring racial inequality in the media but also a recognition amongst younger activists that the problem hasn't gone away.

The shocking death of George Floyd at the hands of a police officer in Minneapolis, Minnesota, in May 2020 triggered a surge of outrage and global support for the Black Lives Matter movement (#BLM). While research linking poverty, inequality and systemic racism has been carried out for decades (Khan, 2020), #BLM has given rise to perhaps the most vigorous debate about systemic racism since the civil rights era of the 1960s. It has given rise to conversations and analyses that might not have happened without that tragedy and pushed the issue of racial inequality further up the political agenda. After four decades of anti-discrimination laws, the actual struggle to translate that into greater equality of economic outcomes has not always kept pace with optimistic public perceptions of how much positive racial progress has been made (Mirza, 2017).

Then there has been the enduring calamity of the global coronavirus pandemic. One of the issues that arose early on, both in the UK and the US, was an over-representation of black and ethnic minority people (BAME) in Covid-19 infection and death rates (ONS, 2020a; Runnymede, 2020; Race Disparities Unit, 2020b). There are several possibilities that might explain this trend. The first is a genetic pre-disposition that makes the BAME physiology more susceptible to the virus. The second is that infection rates are determined by socio-economic and environmental factors. Thirdly, that implicit or explicit racism in the healthcare system – despite NHS claims to fairness – means BAME patients are less likely to

DOI: 10.4324/9781003104476-6

receive support from public health professionals, less likely to go to hospital when ill, and less likely to have their symptoms taken seriously by doctors (Schifferes, 2020).

Early on, the scientific and medical communities discounted the more generalised genetic explanations, owing to the fact that there are few common genetic links between the diverse ethnicities comprising the BAME category. BAME is, after all, a statistical category, and not an ethnicity in and of itself. It bears no relation to kinship. Black (African, Afro-Caribbean or mixed); Asian (Indian, Pakistani, Caribbean, African); Asian (Chinese, Vietnamese) and other Minority Ethnic including Cypriots, Kurds, Syrians and other Middle Eastern nationalities do not form a homogenous group.

Moreover, the BAME category itself is increasingly contested by minorities themselves although it continues to be used by governments for statistical purposes. Indeed, the increasing disquiet over the BAME label is a consequence of a falsely implied homogenous characteristic that misrepresents the people it seeks to describe. The label itself may mask inequalities and be racist in its assumptions. It is worth considering that the labour market, income and wealth data we shall explore in this paper mask significant differentials within the BAME category which diminish its real value in reshaping discourse on remedies to racial inequality.

So, this leaves us with environmental factors or discrimination in medical treatment. Prima facie evidence suggests that it is, indeed, socio-economic factors driving the disproportionately high infection rates. So exactly what environmental factors have led to this outcome and why? And what about the higher death rate shown in ONS figures (ONS, 2020a, 2020c, 2020d and 2020e)? In the UK, the NHS promises emergency care to all at the point of delivery, and currently, there is little more than anecdotal evidence from patient surveys to suggest there is implicit bias in the quality of care given to BAME patients. Working backwards then, disparities in infection rates have likely arisen from differentials such as issues of housing, access to healthcare, and labour market roles (RDU, 2020a).

Britain's National Health Service is disproportionately staffed by BAME people, so, it may seem counter-intuitive to suggest that somehow there is inequality of access to NHS care which might have led to the disproportionate number of deaths recorded for Covid-19 amongst BAME groups. But that is an argument that goes to the heart of our need to be robust about how we identify and research racial inequality. The perceptions of black people of their NHS experiences are not overwhelmingly positive, with over 60 per cent saying they do not believe their health is as equally protected by the NHS when compared to white people (Schifferes, 2020). This does not sit well with the popular view of the essential fairness of the NHS and begs the question of whether deeper issues, such as racism, are at play in UK healthcare.

So here, we are looking through a very different lens at an age-old problem, a year into an epidemic, a year of #BLM protests, and now the election of Joe Biden as a US President who explicitly recognises the problem of systemic racism. In response, this paper looks at the socio-political challenge of racial inequality to see what insights might have come from these two dramatic and enduring debates of 2020. What do these insights offer us by way of deepening our understanding of the intersection of economic inequality and race? Is inequality appropriately mediated by journalists or are narratives of Britain's steady progress towards equality flawed? How might this help us re-evaluate policy approaches to tackling systemic racial economic inequality? Could we be seeing, through this coronavirus and #BLM long lens, focused on BAME inequality, the visual tip of the iceberg of an unjust society? First, I will focus on what we mean by racial economic inequality and how we have come to measure it. Then I will turn to how the idea is mediated in the press. Finally, I will look at the implications of this for the remedies we have chosen to tackle these inequalities, before concluding what the implications of all this are for actually identifying the nature and scale of the problem and tackling it in Britain.

What do we mean by racial economic inequality?

The relationship between the British state and its emerging ethnic minority communities and citizens was recast after the passing of the first Race Relations Act in 1965. Up until then, racial prejudice was thought of largely as something that reflected the behaviour of one individual to another or institutional prejudice against black and Asian people. There were, of course, many examples of this confrontational racism, ending in riots in Notting Hill in 1958 after persistent racial attacks by Teddy Boys on the new communities settling there. But, as numbers of immigrants from the Caribbean grew, it became clear that problems in housing, workplaces and racially motivated attacks on black people were rising and becoming more complex. Discrimination and the active monitoring of it became a theme of government. It gave rise to robust debates about the unequal status of black and Asian people in British society and the political just cause of proceeding towards equality. To some degree, this mirrored and borrowed from the US Civil Rights Movement, and research methods deployed there to study the issues have often been replicated or amended to study the issue of race and racism in the UK. This, in fact, has proven increasingly contentious (Mirza, 2017).

Subsequent Race Relations Acts in 1968 (to tackle discrimination in housing), 1976 (to tackle discrimination in employment) and 2000 (to impose on public institutions a duty of equal treatment to those it serves), all marked stages along a reform pipeline to equip ethnic minorities with the tools to challenge unequal treatment. At least that is the earnest hope underpinning legal statute. Ensuring that these laws are translated into best socio-economic practice present a different challenge. At the root of the reality of unequal status was the inability to improve employment prospects and, as a result, income. Economic inequality fuelled levels of need deprivation and crisis in housing, healthcare, criminal justice and other walks of life, where patterns of inequality were reported in the media and discovered by the increasing numbers of researchers focused on the problem of racial inequality (Khan, 2020; ONS, 2020b).

As levels of unemployment rose in the 1970s, it became clearer that prospects for black and Asian children of migrants were often worse than their white counterparts, and this shone a light on educational inequality. Debates in public discourse about *inequality of outcomes* became linked to a growing reflection on *inequality of opportunity*. These are the fundamentals of racial inequality rooted in historical circumstance. In the development of the modern British economy, British colonialism played a crucial role in the growth of manufacturing, for example, and the accumulation of wealth. These facts are undisputed. However, the question of whether these inequalities created by structural problems of systemic racism that persist today (Fanon, 1963; Foucault, 1979) has once again become contentious. What is clear is that inequality has not gone away. In fact, there is considerable evidence (Stiglitz, 2012; Piketty, 2014) that in a general sense, levels of inequality in society have worsened in recent decades.

Measuring racial economic inequalities

Measuring inequality is not an exact science, and more complex analysis is necessary to try and identify significant factors that might explain inequality at a more granular level. Employment statistics are critical. The types of jobs people have and the sums of money they earn is, however, a crucial indicator of variations of inequality between ethnic groups. The UK Labour Force Survey has provided important data since the 1980s illustrating significant ethnic inequalities in the labour market. While these inequalities persist, it is important to recognise that there are important variations across different ethnic minority groups. Employment rates have remained consistently worse for ethnic minorities and at least 10 per cent behind White British people in the latest available data from 2016 (Runnymede, 2020). Put another way, unemployment rates among ethnic minorities are much higher.

Whilst unemployment is clearly damaging in the short term, typically putting low-income families into the poverty bracket over longer periods, it can be corrosive along the trajectory of a working life (ESRC, 2019). There is evidence that even with a graduate education, ethnic minorities can find it disproportionately difficult to find work two and a half years after they have completed their degree course (Lessard-Phillips et al., 2014). On another measure of low-income differentiation, the National Minimum Wage, it is estimated that ethnic minorities are up to 6 times more likely to be paid below this rate in less regulated parts of the labour market (Peters, 2015). Figures also suggest that all BAME groups are more likely to be in the lowest paid work and, consequently, more likely to be living in poverty.

Unpacking the group BAME data is a complex but increasingly necessary part of getting to grips with targeting remedies to the right people (RDU, 2020b). On a broad measure of poverty, like the measure of the percentage of households below average income, there are some minority groups within the broader BAME classification, who undoubtedly experience racism in some shape or form, but they do not necessarily have the inequality profile that makes them a potential target for government relief.

In short, if you look for evidence of racial disparities, it is not difficult to find them. Ethnic minorities share characteristics in common with other groups who are disadvantaged in the economy. So, it is important to consider whether there are explanations other than racial discrimination which have a bearing on these disparity outcomes. In fact, the absolute numbers of disadvantaged people in those other groups are greater than the absolute numbers of minorities affected. So, the numbers may tell a partial story in inequality terms if not in racial terms. Social class remains a significant factor in determining opportunity of outcomes. Poverty, which is more closely aligned with social class, therefore, has a bearing on fundamental inequalities of income and wealth. These also statistically align with educational under-achievement, which, in turn, feeds into prospects in the labour market. Put simply, whether white or black, people with these shared characteristics are more likely to have a lower income, lower levels of savings wealth or other assets, and within this group, BAME are disproportionately over-represented.

It should be uncontroversial to expect that migration affects patterns of stable employment. Many non-professional migrants arriving in the UK cannot be reasonably expected to seamlessly slot into the labour market. However, one piece of research on the UK-born children of these migrants suggests that there is not always a natural trajectory towards progress and equality. UK-born ethnic minority men are more likely to be unemployed than their overseas fathers (Heath and Cheung, 2006) and downward class mobility means that many children of migrants find themselves at a disadvantage when trying to enter the labour market. This, of course, raises questions on causality and pushes the explanations further back down the pipeline of lived experience to educational outcomes and opportunities.

Ironically, Covid-19 has shone a bright light on this analytical conundrum. Race and class are observably aligned on the issue of Covid-19 rates of infection and death. Socio-economic factors should not mask the fact of the matter that people of colour are disproportionately in those jobs where you are most likely to be exposed to contagion risks. There is, therefore, a correlation between Covid-19, race and class. However, from the available evidence, it would not be true that Black and Asian people are more susceptible to Covid-19 infection genetically (i.e. no known causal link) nor that they are disproportionately affected independently of their socio-economic environment (i.e. it is the socio-economic factors which create the causal link). Following the data remains more important than following our hunches.

This picture painted of racial inequality is clearly not exhaustive. Finding these patterns of inequality is, sometimes, more art than science. They are not static and there is a danger of becoming too racially deterministic with research observations. But, the picture is representative of the difficulties that ethnic minorities face in education, the labour market and emerging out of the impoverished circumstances that migration often imposes on families from one generation to the next. Part of the challenge in facing these tests of inequality as a society is how we react to the problem in policy terms. This, in turn, relies on how seriously the problem is perceived by politicians, policymakers and the wider public. It is easier in #BLM times to gloss over the absence historically of race in public debate and fear of discussing it. George Floyd has sparked what appears to be a rigorous set of debates and concerted efforts to change the tone of the discourse on systemic racism. We might ask, from what quarters has this anger emerged?

Arguably, the dominant narrative across the media landscape is that society is becoming fairer and more merit based; overt racially discriminatory behaviour is less prevalent now, than in 1965 when the first Race Relations Act was passed. At face value, this may be true, but diving deep into the data, social scientists regularly identify consistent patterns of enduring inequality, some of which we have briefly looked at above. One thing that can be learned from US research is how the narratives on racial progress can often ignore the facts on the ground because of what people want to believe about broader society. The fact that many white people have historically not engaged with black people outside of the work environment makes experiential learning of black people's existential condition problematic and means perceptions rely on mediated interpretations of progress. Much more research is needed on how the UK media mediate stories of racial inequality, both social and economic.

Unpacking racism in the media

Let's try and unpack this point a little more. It was common in the early days of migration from New Commonwealth countries for the media to problematise those new communities. In other words, public discourse on the impact of these communities was done through a lens of the problems or conflicts that were raised. Housing, jobs and crime were a few of the areas that dominated news agendas. It was not common to see people of colour in the media space. But, it was common when you did see them, it was because of some social problem. Cultural studies scholars like Stuart Hall explored how these images created negative stereotypes of people of colour that reflected only part of a complex reality. If white people only experienced black people's lives through the media, Hall argued, it would be difficult for them to form an accurate portrait of the Black or Asian experience.

Psychologists believe that we form our views of the world around us when we are quite young and then resist challenges to those beliefs. These *cognitive biases* present a 'variety of ways of thinking (indeed a variety of routine ways of thinking) that constrain one's perceptions and interpretations of the world' (Stocking and LaMarca, 1989). These biases form stereotypes and can affect the way journalists interpret information. What the media produces is often viewed through the prism of personal bias and a predilection to seek out and only acknowledge views that fit with those that the journalist already has. The corollary of this is, as consumers of news, we often seek out what we know and are sceptical of alternative narratives that challenge that understanding. Some argue this *confirmation bias* affects the way we interpret the news (Christian, 2013). In short, this means that people are less willing to accept that society continues to be both unequal and unjust. The public, by way of the media, remains wilfully unaware of racial inequality, in general, and racial economic inequality, in particular, believing that historical patterns of discrimination have been overcome through recent legislative and cultural change. Race as myth, and racism as reality, creates cognitive dissonance (Kraus et al., 2019).

The dominant story-telling paradigm in news reporting is seeing stories through the prism of individual experience. The way stories are told from the anecdotal case study to a generalised problem fail to explore implicit or structural acts behind a particular event. They favour an understanding of social interactions as determined by individual behaviour and perpetuates the dominance of the values of individualism. So, whilst social science may be trying to deepen an understanding on 'systemic' or 'structural' factors in racial inequality, journalists using case-study stories guide the news consumer towards the idea of 'personal responsibility' for that inequality of circumstance. In short, 'who's to blame' stories focus on victims and fail to report on the structural, institutional or systemic constraints which would allow that person the agency to ameliorate their situation. Individual choices are conditioned by the values, behaviours and attitudes consistent with the social milieu. Put another way, individual agency to act depends on the world you actually live in. Writing in his seminal 1903 work, *Souls of Black Folk*, WEB Du Bois talked of double-consciousness, 'measuring of one's self by means of a nation that looked back in contempt'. This structural context, a kind of psychosocial construct, for mediation is an enduring structural impediment to racial progress, in as much as it reinforces existing biases rather than challenging them. Without journalistic context, reporting inequities across race will tend to reinforce existing assumptions and biases (Banaji and Greenwald, 1995).

Race and racism are problematic subject matter for the news media, not least because there have historically been so few BAME practitioners of the journalistic craft in the UK. This has meant that disrupting the narrative of positive racial progress and economic inequality would have relied on patterns of thinking that is not very widespread in broader society. When the Office for National Statistics released data on pay differentials across ethnic groups in October 2020 headlines heralded 'the end of the ethnicity pay gap' with some media reporting that in some categories, ethnic minorities (16- to 29-year olds) were earning more than their white peers (Doughty, 2020). This is the *positive progress* narrative. It is not necessarily untrue, but it masks the fact that ethnic minorities are still twice as likely to be unemployed (you need to be in work to earn more) or working in jobs where they have less legal protections in the workplace. A willingness to avoid the racial patterns of economic inequality remains part of the reason there are such powerful prevailing narratives on racial progress across British society.

The research into racial inequality is made more difficult to interpret because of the complexity of the demographic (as discussed above) that the BAME group is describing. This has given rise to a narrative that the focus on race is misleading and disruptive to good social relations. The government Equalities Minister, Kemi Badenoch, talked about banning critical race theory from schools because it is a segregationist ideology, feeds into this perception (House of Commons, 2020). It only heightens the controversy in the debate when the Minister is herself Black British. This kind of narrative does nothing to encourage exploration of genuine racial inequality or its causes. In essence, it encourages a narrative that it doesn't really exist. Munira Mirza, who is now Chief of Staff to Prime Minister Johnson put it another way: *'By appeasing the anti-racism lobby and affirming its culture of grievance, public institutions and business leaders are not making Britain a fairer place. In fact, they are harming the very people they aspire to help'* (Mirza, 2017).

This is contested ground and the #BLM Movement in the UK has revived public discourse on this very issue. The idea that singular success stories can mitigate the effects of racism is an easy argument to make, but a difficult one to sustain just looking at the government's own Race Disparity Unit data. Black visible success is not fiction, but it does have the potential to make racial economic inequality less visible, and the data suggest that it remains a chimera.

What's to be done about racial economic inequality?

The important thing to recognise is laws, even good laws, do not necessarily change behaviour. Discrimination has consistently been recognised as leading to poorer outcomes in the labour market. Discrimination in housing and education lead to significant disadvantage and this sets access barriers to employment. It's also clear from the research evidence (Khan, 2020) that the more characteristics ethnic minorities share with other disadvantaged groups, the more likely they will be amongst those who struggle to lift themselves out of poverty. An increasingly contentious debate in the UK is about whether race is the key determinant driving these inequities.

Robust government enforcement (primarily through the Equalities & Human Rights Commission or EHRC) and employer and service provider compliance with regulations and the law would help tackle individual cases of unequal treatment. The EHRC has been mired in controversy since former Chief David Isaac complained that political interference is affecting its regulatory role (Isaac, 2021). Over the past decade, access to the law has become more expensive and, therefore, more difficult for people to seek legal remedy to a complaint of discrimination, making individual challenges to structural impediments far harder to overcome. When the EHRC was created in 2006, it was charged with the promotion and enforcement of equality and non-discrimination laws across the board. But, it has been increasingly criticised for shying away from identifying issues of systemic racism (Runnymede, 2020). In the field of journalism, it is clear that whilst the problem of racism is recognised and reported on, within it there are serious complaints that it has not sufficiently challenged the consequences of that recognition in its own recruitment and progression processes (Henry and Ryder, 2021). Professional progression depends on the trust of your peers and that appears to have been a commodity in short supply in many professional walks of life when it comes to people of colour. It is also something that it is difficult to legislate for. Leadership on negotiating our differences and deconstructing the mythical codes of race in employment should be tackled at the cultural level of business ethics. Law sets a framework; the workplace needs to broker the change.

In 2017, Prime Minister Theresa May set up an administrative branch of the government, the Race Disparity Unit (RDU), to look at government data to identify racial disparities across society. Its job is to serve the Cabinet Office, which coordinates government business across the great offices of State. This explicitly recognised that in some areas of the economy and society disparities exist between ethnic groups in the UK. The bigger question it wanted to understand was what causes these, how significant these disparities are and what can be done about it? This was a big shift of emphasis at government level. However, since Boris Johnson became Prime Minister in 2019, there has been a subtle change in its objectives. It now is acting as the Secretariat for the Commission on Race and Ethnic Disparities established in July 2020. It remains unclear if the data it will continue to collect will be used to influence policy decisions or just adorn government statements on racial disparity. A degree of scepticism has emerged as the number of those people appointed by the government to the Commission has spoken against the idea of systemic racism. Remember that while from a scientific standpoint, race is a myth, *racism* from a data standpoint remains a reality.

The Coronavirus crisis has been widely recognised to have had a disproportionate impact on ethnic minority groups (PHE, 2020). Data suggested Black people were up to two times more likely to die than white people from the disease. The PHE report, which interpreted the data, suggested a range of socio-economic and geographical factors contributed to the higher infection and mortality rates for ethnic minorities. These include occupational exposure, as care staff in nursing homes and medical staff in hospitals, population density in the localities they live in, household composition and pre-existing health conditions (RDU, 2020a). Whilst more research is needed to clarify why this is the case, it is an example of outcomes of systemic inequality not being visible until a crisis forces the specific questions on structural racial injustice to be asked. Despite the early data findings that BAME groups are more susceptible to worse outcomes, the UK government's advisers have concluded that ethnicity is a 'proxy' for the highest risk factors associated with deprivation and that it requires a universal approach to deprivation to tackle the problem effectively.

It raises the important question of whether universal approaches are an effective remedy. There is a general presumption that universal policies will equally benefit everyone targeted by the policy. There is also evidence that some universal solutions, or those that avoid identifying race as a factor, can end up overlooking inequalities. One of the more significant challenges would be to devise targeted remedies which can benefit disadvantaged groups with the same characteristics as a particular ethnic minority group. The RDU in one of its early studies discovered significant disparities between Pakistani and Bangladeshi and White British women in the West and East Midlands areas. The Department for Work and Pensions were encouraged to devise a package of measures to target all women in those hot spot areas looking for work which potentially also benefited those ethnic minorities affected (RDU, 2017). The same RDU audit on disparities noted that ethnic minority children were being suspended and expelled from schools at significantly higher rates. This triggered a review by the Department of Education to explore the reasons for the disparity.

Tackling discriminatory practices in the workplace is arguably an important place to improve an unbiased operation of the labour market. Here, the effects of income inequality can be addressed by ensuring recruitment, development and progression processes are fair and transparent. The Race Equality Charter in the UK Higher Education sector is an example of workplace interventions to improve the equality of outcomes and opportunities for BAME staff and students. This is just one of several such initiatives, but inevitably they rely on goodwill, good leadership and only effect those in regular employment. They also take time to bed in and deliver results. Cultural shift takes time.

When it comes to wealth accumulation, BAME people have significantly lower levels of saving and assets than White British people. Wealth is tracked by the ONS Wealth and Assets Survey (ONS, 2019). The trends suggest a pattern of wealth inequality that accentuates income differentials. White British households hold the most wealth, followed by Indian households. Pakistani households have under half of the wealth of White British households with Black Caribbean having much lower levels of accumulation, and Black African and Bangladeshi even less. The Runnymede Trust (Khan, 2020) characterised this wealth inequality by showing the proportions of the proverbial pound in your pocket each group has accumulated. If White British have a full £1, Indian households have 90–95p, Pakistani households have roughly 50p, Black Caribbean households have around 20p and Black Africans and Bangladeshis have around 10p. The cumulative effects of the labour market and recent migration are key factors, but so too are the fact that pensions and inherited homes account for much accumulated wealth. Redistribution of wealth will take time.

Other points of progress also take time. For example, well-qualified immigrants tend to catch up with British-born people in the labour market, but it can take over a decade. Measuring change needs to take advantage of advances in the real-time analysis of data. AI-generated research outcomes could offer more effective ways of understanding the scale of the problem and more accurately monitor a rapidly moving target. What the statistics tell us about Britain five years ago may not reflect reality on the ground today. We could introduce more dynamic economic modelling which uses AI algorithms to give more of a real-time picture of the patterns of employment and, therefore, the shifting patterns of inequality. If ethnic minorities genuinely began to share a more equitable status with their white peers, the debate would simply shift to the persistent challenge faced by the large numbers of people still struggling with economic disadvantage. Economic inequality is increasing, so the solutions in a society that wants more just and equitable outcomes lie in economic system change or policies with redistributive objectives. In the meantime, social science should not ignore the impact of race on patterns of inequality because doing so is likely to perpetuate some of the mistaken ideas about racial progress. Race is a myth, racism isn't. Treating economic inequality as a colour-blind issue over-simplifies the complex demographic landscape which politicians perhaps misguidedly use to fashion economic policies (Brown-Iannuzi et al., 2017).

Sometimes though structural or systemic inequalities for ethnic minorities arise out of hidden systemic failure only revealed after someone joins up the dots of many individual cases. The Windrush Scandal only came to light because of the government's decision to implement a 'hostile environment' strategy to make life difficult for migrants. It progressively revealed that thousands of West Indian migrants who had quite legally been in the UK for decades were being deprived of a right to stay in the country, or work, or claim benefits because of paperwork irregularities (Gentleman, 2019). A catalogue of deportations, sackings, impoverishment without access to state benefits and refused healthcare were all symptoms of systemic discrimination based on ethnicity. All the victims were ethnic minorities originally from the Caribbean. It highlights how systemic racial inequality can play out without state intervention or, indeed, unintentionally with it. Despite an acknowledgement by government that serious errors were made and instituting a compensation scheme, that state effort has still failed to deliver correction to ethnic minorities. There can be little argument that the discrimination and remedy fall far short of equality (Gentleman, 2020).

Conclusions

Race has, over several centuries, been instrumental in the exercise of power and has become embedded in structures and institutional behaviour. We have slowly striven to dismantle these discriminatory barriers in Britain. The history of race has made us sometimes lazy, searching for explanations of discrimination in the wrong places. The reality is that discounting race as a factor in disadvantage does not help resolve the problem any more quickly. More interdisciplinary research is needed to deconstruct the complex layers of relations affecting racial economic and social inequality, its causes and impacts.

Britain is not as riven with the deeply embedded racial cleavages as the United States, which provides much of the social science evidence on racial inequality. In UK law since 1965, discrimination has been recognised as a problem that has no place in a just and fair society. But the raw data suggest that persistent racial economic inequality persists. There are divergences between ethnic groups and often these reflect class, educational attainment and levels of enduring poverty.

Racial economic inequality is also a way of shining a light on structural components of how race is perceived in society and how people experience racism in education, the workplace and health outcomes. It helps us understand how prejudice extends from individuals to the institutions that serve them and back again. Racial economic inequality sits at the tip of a very large economic inequality iceberg and finding the means to tackling it has potential consequences for all those beset by the same characteristics of inequality.

It remains very difficult to blame the media in the UK for over-emphasising positive narratives of racial progress. Everyone likes a good news story. Unfortunately, there remains a paucity of serious research on the link between media portrayal of inequality and the potentially inaccurate public perceptions of progress. However, given there are few means of sharing information on enduring discrimination, beyond experiencing it within the community we live in, it seems reasonable to assume that non-ethnic minority media consumers who, for example, see very positive images of individual BAME progress would draw the conclusion that this is a positive reflection of broader societal change. Nevertheless, failing to change the way we mediate the stories of those who live in circumstances, which have structural causes at their root, will not help counterbalance dominant narratives of positive racial progress. We will continue to believe we live in a country that is becoming more equal and that the arc of history bends towards justice, as President Obama put it. That might be the hope, but this cannot be achieved without creating policies which move us towards more just outcomes.

Economic inequality remains a defining political challenge of our time. The more unequal we become, the more challenges there will be in preserving a system which claims to be fair, but to many citizens, it is perceived as grossly unfair. There is a very real danger that by failing to recognise the gravity and enduring nature of racial inequalities that we will not tackle the sources of the problem and instead preserve those very injustices.

References

Banaji, M. R. and Greenwald, A. G. (1995). 'Implicit stereotyping in false fame judgments'. *Journal of Personality and Social Psychology*, 68, pp. 181–198.

Brown-Iannuzzi, J. L., Dotsch, R., Cooley, E., and Payne, B. K. (2017). 'The relationship between mental representations of welfare recipients and attitudes toward welfare'. *Psychological Science*, 28, pp. 92–103.

Christian, S. (2013) 'Cognitive biases and errors as cause and journalistic best practices as effect'. *Journal of Mass Media Ethics*, 28(3), pp. 160–174.

Doughty, S. (2020), 'End of the ethnic pay gap: Young employees from Ethnic minorities now earn MORE than white British workers', *Daily Mail*, 13th October, accessed at https://www.dailymail.co.uk/news/article-8833247/Young-white-workers-earn-money-hour-ethnicity-age.html

Du Bois, W.E.B (1903, republished 2004) *The Souls of Black Folk*, Abington: Routledge.

DWP (March 2020) *Households below average income*, accessed at, https://www.gov.uk/government/collections/households-below-average-income-hbai--2

Economic and Social Research Council (2019) *Unemployment scarring*. Accessed at https://esrc.ukri.org/about-us/50-years-of-esrc/50-achievements/unemployment-scarring/

Fanon, F. (1963). *The Wretched of the Earth* (Vol. 36). New York: Grove Press.

Foucault, M. (1979). *Discipline and Punish* (A. Sheridan, Trans.). New York: Vintage.

Gentleman, A. (2019). *The Windrush Betrayal: Exposing the Hostile Environment*. London: Guardian Faber.

Gentleman, A. (2020). *The Guardian*, 'Black official quits 'racist' Windrush compensation scheme,' 18 November, accessed at https://www.theguardian.com/uk-news/2020/nov/18/black-official-quit-allegedly-racist-windrush-compensation-scheme

Heath, A. and Cheung, S-Y. (2006). *Ethnic Penalties in the Labour Market: Employers and Discrimination*. London: HM Government, DWP Research Report 341.

Henry, L. and Ryder, M. (2021). *Access All Areas: The Diversity Manifesto for TV and Beyond*. London: Faber.

House of Commons. (2020). *Speech by UK Equalities Minister Kemi Badenoch, Black History Debate*, 20th October, London: Hansard.

Isaac, D. (2021), 'EHRC Undermined by Pressure to Support No. 10 Agenda says ex-chief', *The Guardian*, 18 January, accessed at https://www.theguardian.com/society/2021/jan/18/ehrc-undermined-pressure-support-no-10-agenda-david-isaac

Khan, O. (2020). *The Colour of Money Report: How Racial Inequalities Obstruct a Fair and Resilient Economy*. London: Runneymede Trust.

Kraus, M., Onyeador, I., Daumeyer, N., Rucker, J., and Richeson, J. (2019). 'The misperception of racial economic inequality'. *Perspectives on Psychological* Science 2019, 14(6), pp. 899–921.

Lessard-Phillips, L., Swain, D., Pampaka, M. and Nwabuzo, O. (2014). *When Education Isn't Enough*. London: Runnymede Trust.

Mirza, M. (2017). 'Theresa May's Phony Race War is Dangerous and Divisive' *The Spectator*. 13th September. Accessed at https://www.spectator.co.uk/article/theresa-may-s-phoney-race-war-is-dangerous-and-divisive

ONS. (2019). *Wealth & assets survey*, accessed at https://www.ons.gov.uk/peoplepopulationandcommunity/personalandhouseholdfinances/debt/methodologies/wealthandassetssurveyqmi

ONS. (2020a). *Coronavirus (COVID-19) related deaths by ethnic group, England and Wales: 2 March 2020 to 10 April 2020*, accessed at https://www.ons.gov.uk/peoplepopulationandcommunity/birthsdeathsandmarriages/deaths/articles/coronavirusrelateddeathsbyethnicgroupenglandandwales/2march2020to10april2020

ONS. (2020b). *Labour market status by ethnic group*, table A09, accessed at https://www.ons.gov.uk/employmentandlabourmarket/peopleinwork/employmentandemployeetypes/datasets/labourmarketstatusbyethnicgroupa09

ONS. (2020c). *Rates of deaths involving the coronavirus (COVID-19) by comorbidity and ethnic group, England* accessed at https://www.ons.gov.uk/peoplepopulationandcommunity/birthsdeathsandmarriages/deaths/datasets/ratesofdeathsinvolvingthecoronaviruscovid19bycomorbidityandethnicgroupengland

ONS. (2020d). *Model estimates of deaths involving the coronavirus (COVID-19) by ethnic group for people in care homes, England*, accessed at https://www.ons.gov.uk/peoplepopulationandcommunity/birthsdeathsandmarriages/deaths/datasets/modelestimatesofdeathsinvolvingthecoronaviruscovid19byethnicgroupforpeopleincarehomesengland

ONS. (2020e). *Model estimates of deaths involving the coronavirus (COVID-19) by ethnic group for people in private households, England*, accessed at https://www.ons.gov.uk/peoplepopulationandcommunity/birthsdeathsandmarriages/deaths/datasets/modelestimatesofdeathsinvolvingthecoronaviruscovid19byethnicgroupforpeopleinprivatehouseholdsengland

Peters, S. (2015). 'Ethnic inequalities and the minimum wage', *Race Matters*, March 18. Accessed at https://www.runnymedetrust.org/blog/ethnic-inequalities-and-the-minimum-wage

Piketty, T. (2014). *Capital in the Twenty First Century*. Cambridge, MA: Harvard University Press.

Public Health England. (2020). *COVID-19: understanding the impact on BAME communities*, June 16, accessed at https://www.gov.uk/government/publications/covid-19-understanding-the-impact-on-bame-communities

RDU (Race Disparities Unit) (2017). *Race disparity audit,* accessed at https://assets.publishing.service.gov.uk/government/uploads/system/uploads/attachment_data/file/686071/Revised_RDA_report_March_2018.pdf

RDU. (2020a). Author interview with Marcus Bell, Director of the Race Disparities Unit.

RDU (2020b) https://www.gov.uk/government/publications/ethnicity-data-how-similar-or-different-are-aggregated-ethnic-groups/ethnicity-data-how-similar-or-different-are-aggregated-ethnic-groups

Runnymede Trust (2020), Haque, Z, Becares, I, and Treloar, N, 'Over-exposed and Under-protected: The Devastating Effect of Covid-19 on Black and Minority Communities in Britain', accessed at https://assets.website-files.com/61488f992b58e687f1108c7c/61c31c9d268b932bd064524c_Runnymede%20Covid19%20Survey%20report%20v3.pdf

Schifferes, S (2020), 'Coronavirus inequalities in health care may explain worse outcomes for BAME people', *The Conversation,* 11 November, accessed at https://theconversation.com/coronavirus-inequalities-in-healthcare-may-explain-worse-outcomes-for-bame-people-149314

Stiglitz, J.E. (2012). *The Price of Inequality.* London: Penguin.

Stocking, S. H. and LaMarca, N. (1989). 'How journalists describe their stories: Hypotheses and assumptions in newsmaking'. *Journalism Quarterly,* 67, pp. 295–301.

5 Homeownership

The key to wealth inequality?

Pirmin Fessler and Martin Schürz

In this chapter, we put forward the argument that the way the media approach the representation of wealth is misguided, as they mask important and relevant social distinctions. The question of whether the rich are getting richer, and, if so, by how much, is a frequent and recurring theme in media coverage. Media narratives often focus on specific groups in society, billionaires, the middle class, or the asset poor, measured by their net wealth. But this perspective on wealth inequality neglects the changes in quality that come with greater wealth, as well as the social relations these changes are grounded in, therefore ignoring important issues such as power and social class.

We put forward a class-based approach, which is grounded in the functions of wealth, and we provide empirical evidence that inequality between classes is more prevalent than differences between countries.

Experts typically assess changes in overall wealth inequality with measures such as the Gini coefficient (which measures how unequally wealth is distributed across the whole population) or alternatively the ratio of the top 10 per cent to the bottom 90 per cent of wealth holders. Academic economic literature is also rather narrow. It examines wealth concentration and the evolution of top shares of wealth over time (Kopczuk and Saez, 2004; Piketty, 2014). It has no explicit reference to power or production relations. At first glance, it seems to be purely data driven. It also seems to be agnostic to the social context and conditions. However, differences in quantities imply qualitative differences regarding the functions of wealth. And the meaning of differences in wealth levels depends on the context in a given society at a given point in time.

A purely numerical one-dimensional measure of wealth masks the implicit distinction between the different functions that wealth can have for people in different wealth percentiles. Without narratives about power relations between social classes, such analyses are not particularly meaningful. The alternative is to make the power relations explicit in the statistical analysis. This creates a more transparent analysis of wealth inequality and it allows a deeper public debate on what constitutes an adequate degree of wealth inequality in society.

Our approach distinguishes between wealth as a means of capitalist production, wealth as a substitute for welfare state measures, and wealth as a source of non-cash income. We apply this approach to wealth inequality based on

DOI: 10.4324/9781003104476-7

household data for continental Europe, the UK, and the US and illustrate the conceptual advantages in focusing on different functions of wealth, such as precaution, use, and power. Legitimation of wealth inequality needs to be understood in relation to the distinctive functions of wealth.

We use data from the Survey of Consumer Finances (SCF) for the United States, the Household Finance and Consumption Survey (HFCS) for continental Europe, and the Wealth and Asset Survey (WAS) for the UK to apply such an approach and illustrate its advantages.

Functions of wealth

Currently, researchers define household net wealth as the monetary value of all assets minus its liabilities (OECD, 2013). While Fessler and Schürz (2018) give a comprehensive discussion of the definitions of private and public wealth, Davies and Shorrocks (2000) summarise some major stylised facts of the literature:

- In developed countries, net wealth is very concentrated and distributed much more unequally than income.
- The bottom 50 per cent in the wealth distribution of households holds only a tiny fraction of aggregate wealth.
- Non-financial assets outweigh financial assets and consist mainly of households' main residences.
- The distribution of financial assets is substantially more unequal across households than the distribution of non-financial assets.

In the OECD's definition, wealth must be transferable. It, therefore, excludes all forms of public pension entitlements as well as company 'defined benefit schemes' which are not transferable. We follow the literature and the OECD's recommendation and stick to the definition of marketable wealth as our main variable of interest.

The favoured focus on the top share of the richest 1 per cent (Piketty, 2011, 2014; Alvaredo et al., 2013) implicitly assumes that the rich are different from the rest of society. But this claim cannot be substantiated directly with the data as this approach uses percentiles of the net wealth distribution and not socio-economic variables or different functions of wealth. While this approach is limited by the restrictive nature of most administrative datasets, there is now widely available survey data to which we can draw on to show a different pattern.

Furthermore, in cross-country comparisons of percentile shares, it remains unclear what the underlying households in the different countries have in common. Households around the 90th percentile might mostly hold business wealth in one country, while in other countries, home ownership might be the dominant pattern around this percentile. The bottom half in one country might consist mostly of homeowners having non-cash income from imputed rents, while in another country, it might be mostly renters depending almost only on their labour income.

70 *Pirmin Fessler and Martin Schürz*

Since a specific perspective on the data must be taken, the chosen perspective influences what we see – and what we do not see. That is why it is a necessary precondition to reveal and describe the chosen perspective to understand empirical findings.

Figure 5.1 shows a schematic illustration of a potential structure of functions of wealth across the wealth distribution. At the very bottom of the distribution, associated with low amounts of usually very liquid wealth holdings, the main function of wealth is **provision**. Households save for all kinds of precautionary reasons, for example, the need to replace a broken washing machine or repair their car, but also for the unexpected loss of income through periods of unemployment or illness. How much households need to save for a rainy day heavily depends on welfare state policies. With increasing net wealth levels, **use** becomes more prevalent, particularly in the form of home ownership. And with even higher wealth, the function of **income generation** becomes more important. This might include households that own their own businesses and/or real estate, which they rent out to earn capital income. At the top of the distribution is this specific form of wealth (ownership of the means of production) that becomes a source of considerable power in society.

We use these three functions of wealth, namely, provision, use, and income generation, as a base for a relational approach. Of course, there are important further functions of wealth, such as status and transfer, e.g. in the form of bequests to future generations. Even though with rising wealth levels, use is added

Functions of Wealth

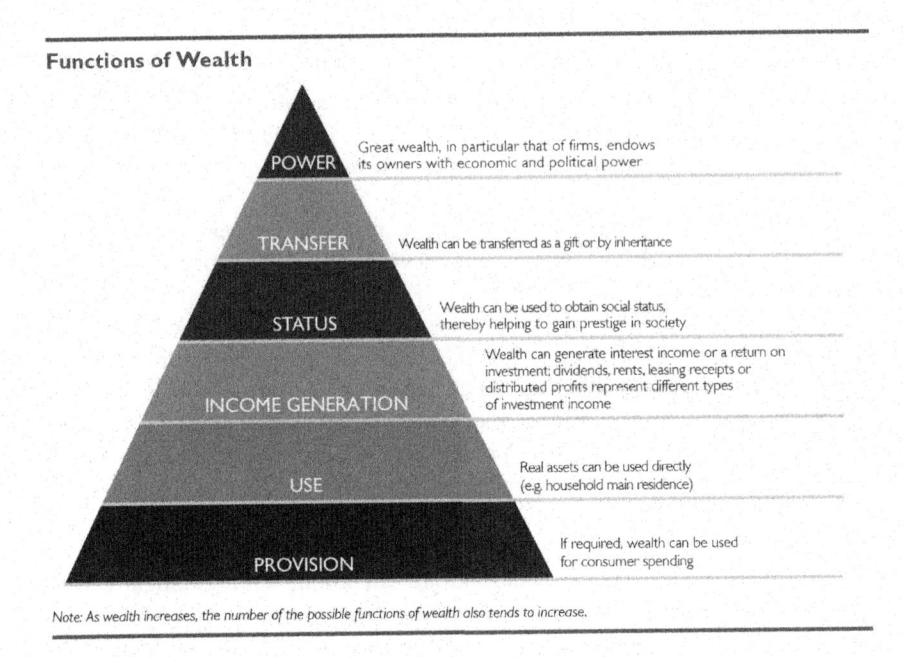

POWER	Great wealth, in particular that of firms, endows its owners with economic and political power
TRANSFER	Wealth can be transferred as a gift or by inheritance
STATUS	Wealth can be used to obtain social status, thereby helping to gain prestige in society
INCOME GENERATION	Wealth can generate interest income or a return on investment; dividends, rents, leasing receipts or distributed profits represent different types of investment income
USE	Real assets can be used directly (e.g. household main residence)
PROVISION	If required, wealth can be used for consumer spending

Note: As wealth increases, the number of the possible functions of wealth also tends to increase.

Figure 5.1 Functions of Wealth. Illustration authors' own.

to provision, and further up the wealth ladder income generation to use and provision, not all functions of wealth are additive, and the relationship between them is complex. Some are substitutes, some are complimentary, and others, such as provision and use, just overlap. Aside from the idea that higher net wealth implies more possible functions of wealth for wealth holders, the precise actual functions of wealth in a specific context at a specific point in time must be studied empirically. Many of them are difficult or even impossible to measure. But a focus on different functions of wealth has conceptual advantages.

Renters, owners, and capitalists

The distribution of wealth shapes society in a manner that it determines to a large degree inequality in income and consumption as well as different forms of human and social capital (Bourdieu, 2002) and, therefore, power relations, production relations, and class locations. As Hugrée et al. (2020) argue, power relations cannot be reduced to the actions of a few billionaires. Much rather, they are constructed in different areas of social life (Hugrée et al., 2020).

The classical Marxian notion implies an antagonism of those who have capital (capitalists) and those who do not (workers). But, the rise of the middle class in the 20th century meant that people could accumulate a considerable amount of assets not directly related to means of production (Sparkes and Wood, 2020).

Our class-based approach is grounded in the functions of wealth. These functions are linked to both the forms of wealth and the relations between the social classes:

1 Renters are those who do not own their home. They need to pay a rent to capitalists (or the state) to live in their houses or apartments. Their only main income source is labour income. Renters have mostly precautionary wealth.
2 Owner–occupiers (additionally) use their wealth by living in their own house or apartment. In most cases, this house or apartment is also their single most valuable asset. They do not pay a rent to live in their houses or apartments. Living in their own home generates a rent, the imputed rent, which is a form of non-cash capital income.
3 Capitalists (additionally) either rent out additional real estate to the renters or own a business and make a profit selling goods or services to renters and owner–occupiers or other capitalists (or businesses), and/or by using renters and owner–occupiers as their workforce.

Renters must sell their labour to pay for their home and rent from capitalists or the state. Owner–occupiers get an imputed rent. However, they still earn income by selling their labour. Capitalists employ both renters and owners and receive the lion's share of their income from wealth and self-employment. All classes show within-class income inequality as well as within-class wealth inequality.

One of the most obvious is the differences between small business owners and landlords and owners of large multinational companies or vast holdings of real estate. While within-class heterogeneity is considerable, note that in all countries, between-class inequality explains a much larger share of overall wealth inequality than within-class inequality.

Furthermore, the patterns of class prevalence across the wealth distribution are rather robust to changes in definitions. Also, note that we do distinguish between direct business owners and people holding traded stocks or bonds, which, in itself, does not qualify them as capitalists in our definition (Fessler and Schürz, 2020). Besides direct social relationships among social classes, such as landlord and renter, employer and employee, or producer and consumer, the functions of wealth refer to different forms of assets. This also creates antagonistic interests. This class antagonism has implications for class consciousness and issues of identity. Note, however, that while our approach allows us to compare different classes across countries in a more meaningful way than other inequality measures, there are still many institutional differences between countries which influence class formation and wealth positions differently in different countries (Fessler and Schürz, 2018).

While coverage issues and underreporting are especially problematic for survey-based top-share estimates, such as the share of the 0.1 per cent or 1 per cent of the top-wealth holders in total wealth, our approach is more robust to these measurement problems. Nevertheless, it is likely to have led to a very small underreporting of the share of capitalists in the population, and a bigger underestimation of their wealth and income – so our estimates are conservative, and inequality could be even higher than we have found.

Hierarchical pattern in the wealth distribution

For centuries, homeownership was a main foundation of political visions and projects. Quite often, it is framed and misunderstood as synonymous with wealth. As early as 1872, Engels wrote that *'the worker who owns a little house to the value of a thousand talers is certainly no longer a proletarian, but one must be Dr. Sax to call him a capitalist'* (Engels, 1872).

Social classes and wealth

In Europe, the share of renters ranges from about 15 per cent in Slovakia to about 56 per cent in Germany; it is about 36 per cent in the US. The share of owner–occupiers ranges from roughly 30 per cent in Germany to about 73 per cent in Slovakia and lies at about 48 per cent in the US. The share of capitalists is lowest in the Netherlands, with about 3 per cent, and largest in Ireland, where more than 23 per cent of the household population fall into that category. In the US, about 15 per cent of households are capitalists (Figure 5.2).

Generally, the variety across countries is rather large. However, in all countries, apart from Germany and Austria, homeowners are the largest class.

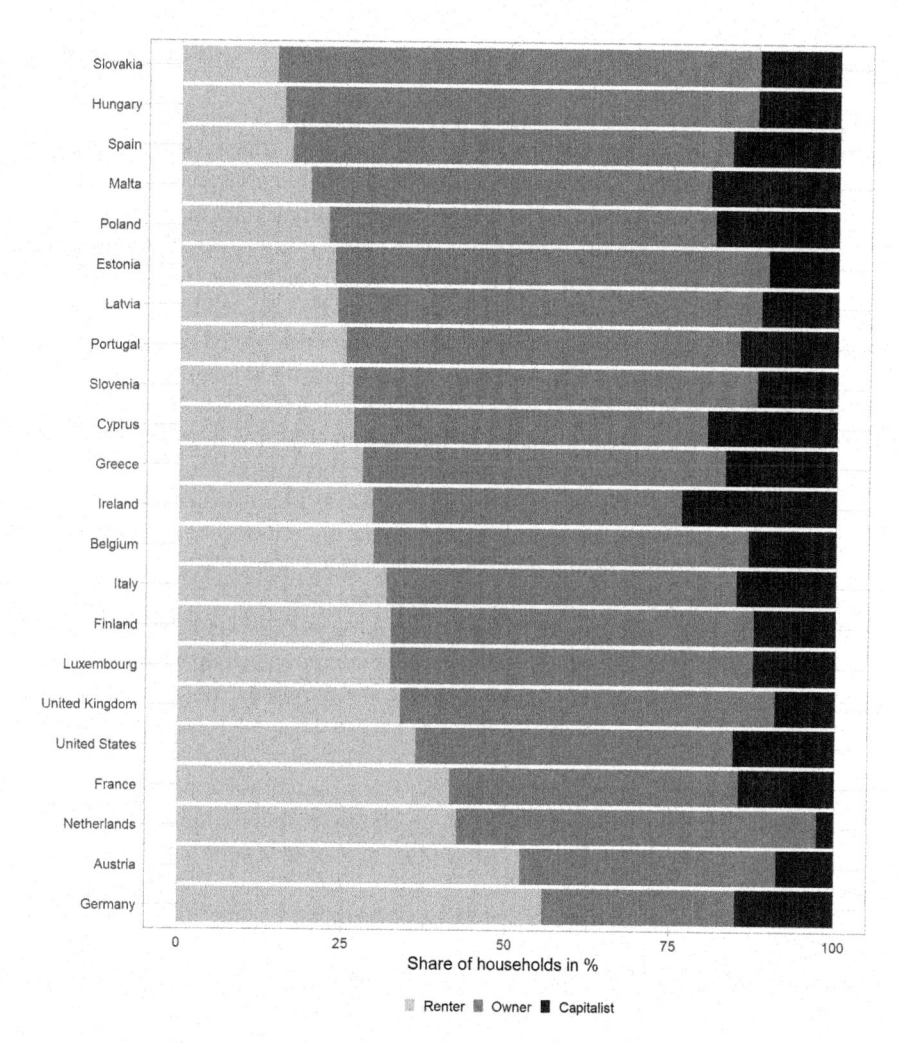

Figure 5.2 Renters, owners, and capitalists in the US, the UK and continental European countries.

Source: SCF 2016 for the US; WAS 2014–16 for the UK; HFCS 2014 for continental Europe.

Homeowners in the middle of the wealth distribution

Homeowners are in the middle of the wealth distribution; renters are found in the lower half of the wealth distribution and capitalists dominate the very top. In the UK, owners are the dominant class, in the sense that they are most prevalent, from the 25th percentile up to the very top, while in Germany, renters are the dominant class up to the 75th percentile. And while capitalists dominate the top of the income distribution in the US, Germany, and France, they do not in the UK.

In some ways, the UK is a special case. It has by far the largest owner–occupier class, which is likely related to its rather low level of wealth inequality by international comparisons.

However, the exact patterns differ across countries and depend on differences in institutional settings. For example, there are significant differences in the availability of home loans for mortgages. There are many more homeowners at the bottom of the wealth distribution in the US, partly because they are more easily able to obtain mortgages without large deposits or a low loan-to-value ratios. Some of those households end up having negative net wealth, which shows up in a rather high share of owner–occupiers at the very bottom of the US wealth distribution.

Because of the different wealth components of different social classes, similar policies will have divergent effects in different countries. For example, while the former tax deduction of interest payments for a mortgage might have increased the net income for a large proportion of UK households, it will not have such a big effect on the income distribution in Germany, where many more are renters. Inequality measures will be affected in different ways. This translates into different interests vis-à-vis policies and influences the formation of coalitions supporting certain policies. Beckmann et al. (2020) show that homeownership is usually positively associated with voting for centre-right parties.

While in the US, capitalists are dominant at the top of the wealth distribution, the UK is the only country where owners are the dominant group right up to the very top. In France, owner–occupiers become the dominant group around the 40th wealth percentile; in Germany, homeowners make up most households only between the 55th and 88th percentiles. Owner–occupiers are much less dominant in Germany than in the UK or the US. The strong prevalence of capitalists at the top in Germany reflects the fact that widespread shareholding is less common in Germany and that the structure of that economy is dominated by family businesses (Fessler and Schürz, 2020).

Especially in the lower parts of the wealth distribution, state pension systems, public health provisions, public education, unemployment insurance, and other forms of public welfare are substitutes for the precautionary function of private wealth (Alessie et al., 2013; Feldstein, 1974; Fessler and Schürz, 2018; Jappelli, 1995). All these elements, the tax system, rental subsidies, tenancy laws, and social housing influence the threshold at which renters turn into owners. And inheritance, property, and other capital taxes, as well as labour market conditions, and the environment for small enterprises, will be relevant for the concentration of business wealth and, therefore, the prevalence of capitalists across the distribution. Historical events such as wars or land reforms, but also the collapse of the Eastern bloc and different paths of transition towards market economies for those countries, shaped the patterns of the wealth distribution. For example, most households in eastern Germany became renters of their homes formerly owned by the state, while most Slovak households became homeowners. These political decisions made in the transition period are the main reason why Germany has the largest share of renters and Slovakia has the lowest share of renters among all observed countries.

Wealth and income shares

Capitalists' shares in total wealth are markedly larger than their shares in total income, while renters' shares in income are larger than their shares in wealth. For homeowners, the pattern is less clear although there is a bigger variation in the share of wealth than the share of income across the sample as a whole. While owners in some countries have lower wealth shares than income shares, their wealth shares are considerably higher than their income shares in others. The Netherlands, the UK and Slovakia stand out with particularly high levels of wealth shares held by homeowners (see Table 5.1).

Figure 5.3 relates the share in gross income as well as the share in net wealth to the respective population shares of renters, owners, and capitalists. This ratio is close to one in all countries and for both income and wealth. A ratio of one means that the households in that class are close to the overall average. In other words, the share of a given class in income and wealth is very close to its share in the population.

In all countries, capitalists have a disproportionately high share in income and wealth, whereas renters have in all countries a disproportionately low share of income and wealth. As the wealth distribution is more unequal than the income distribution, wealth ratios generally show higher variation than income ratios. For income, the highest and lowest ratios are to be found in the US: they are

Table 5.1 Class shares in percentage of total income and wealth

	Gross income			Net wealth		
	Renter	Owner	Capitalist	Renter	Owner	Capitalist
Austria	41.9	43.7	14.4	10.8	47.6	41.7
Belgium	19.9	60.5	19.6	9.8	58.4	31.8
Cyprus	17.9	52.5	29.6	7.6	36.8	55.5
Germany	41.2	33.2	25.6	13.5	30.6	55.9
Estonia	15.5	62.8	21.7	7.9	56.8	35.3
Spain	12.4	63.4	24.2	4.4	54.8	40.8
Finland	19.6	59.5	20.8	3.4	63.6	33.1
France	29.4	47.2	23.5	8.6	47.4	44.0
Greece	23.9	53.3	22.8	7.3	58.7	34.0
Hungary	12.6	65.7	21.7	3.3	59.0	37.7
Ireland	20.0	46.1	33.8	4.3	36.2	59.5
Italy	21.0	51.4	27.6	4.2	58.5	37.3
Luxembourg	22.3	55.1	22.6	6.8	50.0	43.1
Latvia	18.0	57.4	24.6	11.3	49.7	38.9
Malta	13.7	60.7	25.6	2.9	51.0	46.1
The Netherlands	30.9	65.1	4.0	9.1	82.5	8.3
Poland	16.3	57.2	26.5	2.7	49.9	47.3
Portugal	16.5	58.2	25.3	7.1	50.4	42.5
Slovenia	20.9	60.4	18.6	10.3	53.8	35.9
Slovakia	11.0	67.3	21.7	1.9	72.0	26.1
The United States	17.1	44.5	38.3	4.7	35.1	60.2
The United Kingdom	21.7	61.0	17.3	5.9	72.0	22.1

Source: SCF 2016 for the US; WAS 2014–16 for the UK; HFCS 2014 for continental Europe.

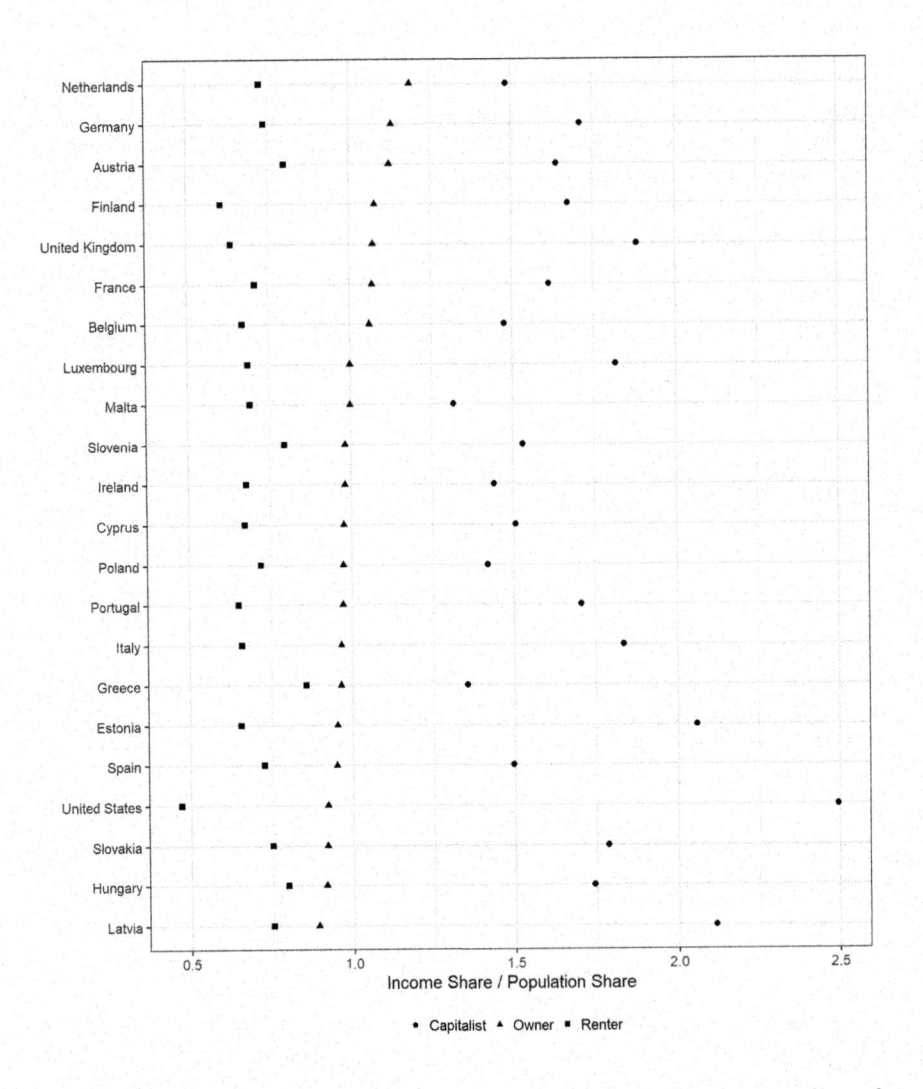

Figure 5.3 Shares of income in relation to the population share of renters, owners, and capitalists for all countries.

Source: SCF 2016 for the US; WAS 2014–16 for the UK; HFCS 2014 for continental Europe.

smallest for renters there (0.47, i.e. on average about half of the overall mean) and highest for capitalists there (2.5). For wealth, they are smallest for renters in Finland (0.1) and largest for capitalists in Austria (4.7).

The fact that homeowners' shares in income and wealth are so close to their population share means that to a large degree overall inequality in both income and wealth is driven by differences between renters and capitalists.

The capital-to-income ratio is used by Piketty (2017) as a measure of capital accumulation. This ratio shows the importance of inherited wealth versus wealth created each year. We show how this relation varies for different social classes.

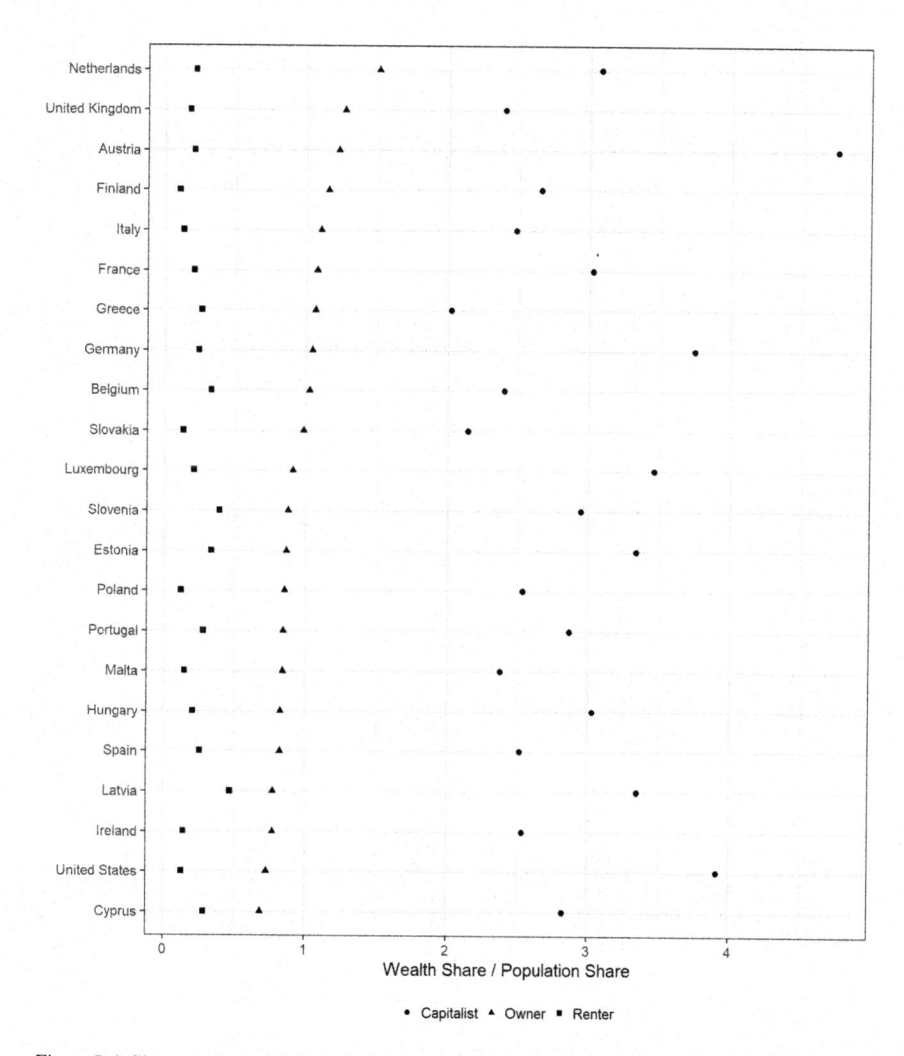

Figure 5.4 Shares of wealth in relation to the population share of renters, owners, and capitalists for all countries.

Figure 5.4 shows class-specific wealth-to-income ratios. The owners' ratios are about the size of the overall ratio for the whole population, while the renters have substantially lower wealth-to-income ratios in all countries. Capitalists, on the other hand, have substantially higher ratios. Their large ratios reflect the higher probability of inheritances in this class as well as the larger amounts of wealth they inherit. Again, the UK is together an outlier. Owner–occupiers have the largest share of net wealth which is mostly due to their large number (see Table 5.1 and Figure 5.3), but their wealth-to-income ratio is almost as high as that of capitalists in the UK.

Differences in income and wealth in capitalism are legitimised by the meritocratic principle that success is due to hard work. This has to be questioned

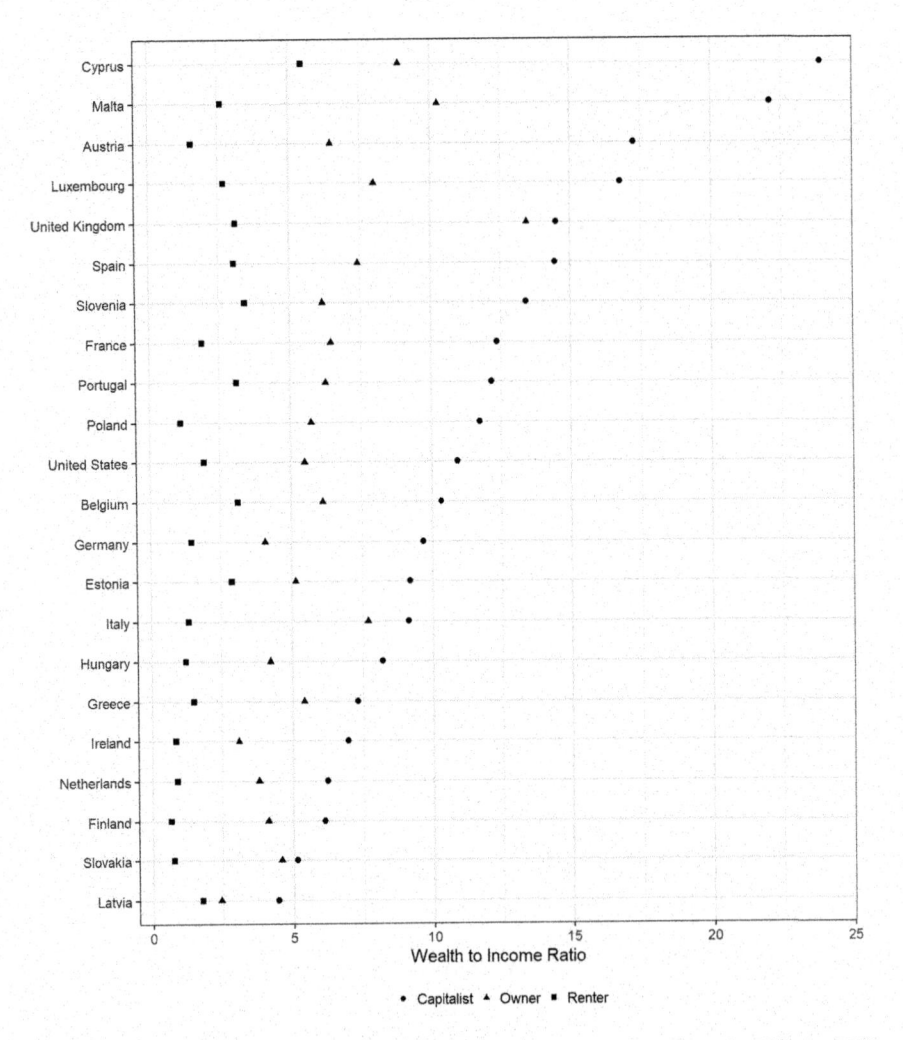

Figure 5.5 Wealth-to-income ratios for renters, owners and capitalists in the US, the UK and continental European countries.

Source: All statistics are calculated considering multiple imputations and survey population weights.

empirically by pointing to the role of wealth transfers across generations (see Piketty, 2020). Differences between classes are by far larger than differences between countries for which wealth-to-income ratios are usually reported.

One can decompose the overall inequality of income and wealth as measured by the Gini coefficient into a part due to inequality within and between classes, and an overlap of both. In all countries, the between-class inequality explains much more of the overall inequality in the case of wealth (more than half in most countries) than in the case of income (less than half in all countries). Classes relate to specific wealth components and, consequently, have different forms of income: Certain policies targeting specific wealth or income components will likely more clearly align with the wealth distribution than with the income distribution. For example, taxing income from renting out real estate will concern capitalists who are concentrated at the top of the wealth distribution, while if we look at the income distribution, they are more widespread over the whole distribution. There are forms of income which are relevant in certain countries – especially the US – and for certain groups of the population such as top managers. Today, the role of top incomes is especially difficult to assess because of the role that stock buy-backs play in raising executive compensations (Lazonick and Hopkins, 2016).

Taxing imputed rent would increase the tax burden mostly for owners in the middle of the wealth distribution, but it would be broadly neutral regarding the overall income distribution. Common interests of a social class are related to the degree of homogeneity within class as well as the distance to another class. Within-class inequality differs a lot among classes. But regarding income, within-class inequality is very similar across all classes. And regarding wealth, homeowners are rather homogenous. Owners show the lowest within-class inequality of wealth. Their single most important wealth item is their home. Their status as homeowners is an important part of their identity and daily life. Therefore, homeowners are easier to target, and it is easier to mobilise them politically.

The renters show the highest within-class inequality. This heterogeneity has implications for class identity. It means their status as renters might be less important for their identity than the real estate asset is for homeowners. Renters will find it harder to understand themselves as a social class as their wealth levels differ a lot. And when it comes to certain policies, the diverging interests might be largest within this class (Fessler and Schürz, 2020).

Conclusion

The wealth distribution is typically analysed by observing percentiles, and top shares of wealth. The media concentrate on recent development of top shares. And too often, the media add rather arbitrary narratives to this data on top shares.

However, to understand wealth inequality in society, we must distinguish functions of wealth connected to social classes. Only by understanding how wealth functions will provide a picture of the social implications of wealth inequality. We are able to gain additional insight by classifying households based on the functions of their wealth holdings. Employing data for Europe and the US, we show that our relational approach aligns well with the wealth distribution. In every country we consider, renters are primarily located in the bottom, owners in the middle, and capitalists at the top of the income and wealth distributions. What considerably varies across countries, however, are the two switching points in the wealth distribution, going upward, where the majority tips from renters to owners and, at an even higher wealth level, from owners to capitalists.

All in all, we see different forms of wealth to be dominant for different social classes: financial wealth (savings) for renters at the bottom, real estate wealth for owners in the middle, and business and real estate wealth for capitalists at the top of the wealth distribution. These distinctions in the forms of wealth corresponds with different absolute levels and different functions of wealth. To exercise power in society, an owned main residence is not sufficient. But in order to hide these differences of functions, the ideology of homeownership is a crucial element of the approach of an ownership society. It focuses on one function only: use.

Owners have average levels of income and wealth. Most inequality is explainable by differences between renters and capitalists. Differences between classes are by far larger than differences between countries. Regarding wealth, renters show the highest within-class inequality in all countries, which might hinder the formation of common interests and coalitions.

The main advantage of a class-based approach is that, otherwise, implicitly assumed links to power are made explicit. Furthermore, such an approach can be directly linked to questions of justification of wealth inequality (see also Schürz 2019). Thus, it contributes to an urgent and up to now largely missing rational debate on questions of justice.

References

Alessie, R., Angelini, V. and Santen, P. (2013). Pension wealth and Household Savings in Europe: Evidence from SHARELIFE, *European Economic Review*, 2013, 63, pp. 308–328.

Alvaredo, F., Atkinson, A. B., Piketty, T., and Saez, E. (2013). The Top 1 Percent in International and Historical Perspective, *Journal of Economic Perspectives*, Summer, 27(3), p. 20.

Beckmann, P. Fulda, B., Kohl, S. (2020). Housing and Voting in Germany. *MPIfG Discussion Paper*, 20(6).

Bourdieu, P. (2002). The Forms of Capital. *Readings in Economic Sociology*, London: Blackwell Publishers.

Davies, J. B. and Shorrocks, A. F. (2000). The Distribution of Wealth. In: A.B. Atkinson and F. Bourguignon, eds., *Handbook of Income Distribution*, Amsterdam: Elsevier, pp. 605–675.

Engels, F. (1872). *The Housing Question*. New York: Pathfinder Press (reprinted 1995).

Feldstein, M. (1974). Social Security, Induced Retirement, and Aggregate Capital Accumulation, *Journal of Political Economy*, 82(905), p. 926.

Competition in an Age of Hunger Games: Donald Trump and the 2018 Presidential Election, *Institute for New Economic Thinking Working Paper Series*, 2018, pp. 66.

Fessler, P. and Schürz, M. (2018). Private Wealth across European Countries: The Role of Income, Inheritance and the Welfare State, *Journal of Human Development and Capabilities*, 19(521), p. 549.

Fessler, P. and Schürz, M. (2020). Structuring the Analysis of Wealth Inequality Using the Functions of Wealth: A Class-Based Approach. In: R. Chetty, J. N. Friedman, J. C. Gornick, B. Johnson, and A. Kennickell, eds. *Measuring and Understanding the Distribution and Intra/Inter-Generational Mobility of Income and Wealth*. Chicago: University of Chicago Press, https://www.nber.org/chapters/c14446

Hugrée, C., Penissat, E., and Spire, A. (2020). *Social Class in Europe. New Inequalities in the Old World*. London: Verso.

Jappelli, T. (1995). Does Social Security Reduce the Accumulation of Private Wealth? Evidence from Italian Survey Data. *Ricerche Economiche*, 49(1), p. 31.

Kopczuk, W. and Saez, W. (2004). Top Wealth Shares in the United States, 1916–2000: Evidence from Estate Tax Returns, *National Tax Journal*, June Cita, 57(2), pp. 445–487.

Lazonick, W. and Hopkins, M. (2016). If CEO Pay Was Measured Properly, It Would Look Even More Outrageous, https://www.ineteconomics.org/perspectives/blog/-ifceo-pay-was-measured-properly-it-would-look-even-more-outrageous

OECD (2013). *OECD Guidelines for Micro Statistics on Household Wealth*. Paris: OECD Publishing, https://doi.org/10.1787/9789264194878-en

https://www.ons.gov.uk/peoplepopulationandcommunity/personalandhouseholdfinances/incomeandwealth/datasets/totalwealthwealthingreatbritain

Piketty, T. (2011). On the Long-Run Evolution of Inheritance: France 1820 2050. *The Quarterly Journal of Economics*, 126(3), pp. 1071–1131.

Piketty, T. (2014). *Capital in the Twenty First Century*. Cambridge, MA, Harvard University Press.

Piketty, T. (2017). Toward a Reconciliation between Economics and the Social Sciences, In: J. Heather Boushey, B. DeLong, and M. Steinbaum, eds., *After Piketty – The Agenda for Economics and Inequality*. Cambridge, MA: Harvard University Press.

Piketty, T. (2020). *Capital and Ideology*. Cambridge, MA: Harvard University Press.

Schürz, M. (2019). *Überreichtum*. Campus Verlag. Frankfurt am Main/New York.

Sparkes, M. and Wood, J.G.D. (2020). The Political Economy of Household Debt & The Keynesian Policy Paradigm. *New Political Economy*, https://doi.org/10.1080/13563467.2020.1782364

II
Framing poverty and inequality

6 Poverty and the media

Poverty myths and exclusion in the information society

Peter Golding

When the *Sun* newspaper covered its front page with a disconcerting headline revealing a 'Space Alien Found Claiming Benefits in Cardiff' (4/11/10), it seemed like merely the kind of grotesque if entertaining 'story' the popular paper specialised in. But it was, too, an ingenious conflation of the xenophobia and 'scroungerphobia' that had become constants of popular discourse throughout the second half of the 20th century. This chapter charts the long history and dispiriting continuity of such refrains. It then argues that lower-income groups not only are rendered culpable and marginal by such rhetoric and imagery but are also, by denial of access to the resources increasingly necessary for full, informed, and active citizenship, obstructed from the means to enter the alluring world of civic participation, that is to say, they are rendered relatively powerless. Condemned for their poverty, in a consistent and effective frame of blaming the victim, the poor are further punished by their partial exclusion from the capacity to engage with political and social process.

Peter Townsend's now classic definition reminds us of the multi-dimensionality of poverty. As he wrote, people

> can be said to be in poverty when they lack the resources to obtain the types of diet, participate in the activities and have the living conditions and amenities which are customary, or at least widely encouraged or approved, in the societies to which they belong.
>
> (1979, p. 31)

Since Townsend wrote that, our notions of what constitutes the amenities and necessities of daily life have changed, not least with the evolving technologies of communication which have become permanent, often essential elements of the mundane activities which comprise consumerism and everyday social and political activity. But the other side of Townsend's definition is important too, in that what is 'widely encouraged and approved' has come to embrace the ownership and routine use of a range of communications resources and devices.

This chapter explores the double jeopardy this entails, examining both the variety of ways in which the media have insistently delivered hostile and ideologically loaded imagery of poverty and welfare but also how income inequality

DOI: 10.4324/9781003104476-9

has profound implications for the curtailment of citizenship among lower-income groups. To the recurrent castigation of the poor has been added an ever-increasing obstacle to their social and political participation in the society from which they are significantly excluded.

The deep historical roots of late 20th century 'scroungerphobia'

Hostility to and deep scepticism about the probity and morals of the poor have been central motifs in the history of British social policy. From attempts in the middle ages to distinguish 'God's poor' from the Devil's, the core of welfare policy has been the urge to discriminate the culpably deprived (vagrants, single parents, 'fallen women', the idle, and feckless), from those entitled to both sympathy and actual support (the very elderly and genuinely very sick and disabled) – in other words to separate the deserving and undeserving poor. The Elizabethan Poor Law of 1601 set out clear demarcation between the support appropriate for the 'impotent poor', and employment or correction for those wilfully idle and for the able-bodied.

The focus on control of vagrancy (more latterly homelessness and having 'no fixed abode') has endured in a perennial conflation of regulation of the poor with actual assistance, much complicated by its conditionality. The most significant manifestation of this dimension of welfare and poverty policy is found in the principle of 'less eligibility', ensuring that the poor 'shall not be made really or apparently so eligible as the situation of the independent labourer of the lowest class', as it was defined by the 1834 Poor Law Act (Checkland and Checkland, 1974, p. 335). The fundamental desire to judge and contain the poor, while ensuring their lot was palpably and demonstrably worse than that of the plainly more worthy and virtuous labourer, has become a constant dimension of the moralistic underpinning of more recent legislation, and of the undertone of righteous indignation and social separation inherent in its ideological foundation. It surfaces, for example, in the simplistic formula of 'workers' and 'shirkers' of recent political rhetoric.

That long history and enduring backdrop of perceptions and policy lay behind a study of broadcast and print media, both national and local, undertaken in the late 1970s (Golding and Middleton, 1982). Examining both media portrayals of poverty and welfare, and public attitudes to them, the study uncovered a depth and range of 'scroungerphobia' of depressing magnitude. Social security, the administrative rubric for the broad array of transfer payments and welfare support then available, was the major topic of roughly a third of all news stories about any aspect of social policy in the national media analysed. Both categories were a major feature of news, however, and social security was more likely to make news when it overlapped with more enticing categories like crime, sex, or even political conflict.

The most dramatic illustration of this was the finding that over a fifth of all lead news stories about this area of social policy reported the legal proceedings arising from cases of alleged abuse of social security. When social security made it into the headlines, it was very likely to be as a result of accusations of illicit action by the unemployed. Indeed, it was this latter category of the poor who dominated the population of all those in poverty made visible by news. By contrast, the low paid were relatively obscured in the demography of the media world, a territory formed from news values rather than social values. The crime focus becomes even more prominent in the evidence that roughly one in eight of all news stories examined in the research, which was about any aspect of social services, welfare, or social security, dealt with the trial, prosecution or conviction for fraud, claimants, and over a third of such stories appeared as front-page news. At the other end of the scale, the limited take-up of means-tested benefits was mentioned in fewer than four per cent of all such stories.

This snapshot of a period of virulent-mediated malevolence against the poor can, of course, be dismissed as a capture of something ephemeral or atypical. Content analysis of the media has a perennial problem of sampling and representativeness – is the study indicative or representative of its time only, of the decade, of all years since some arbitrary year zero? However, innumerable studies conducted at other times, or reviewing a range of studies undertaken at different times, have all reached similar conclusions (*inter alia* see Devereux, 1998; De Benedictus et al., 2017; Morrison, 2018; Redden, 2014). The deep moral presumptions and attitudes embedded in the distinction between 'God's Poor and the Devil's' are, in varying vocabularies and iconographies, perennial features of poverty policy and perceptions.

Any lingering hope that such popular virulence was an unusual spasm in the history of popular culture has been sadly demolished by the continuation of similar material in more recent times. Indeed, that very continuity rather confirms the view that indignation about and contempt for the poor are endemic and perennial, rather than unusual or only periodic, even if their intensity and substance are historically variable. In the torrent of disdain and opprobrium that has continued to pour from the press, four streams predominate: that welfare benefits bestow an exceptional and unusually luxurious lifestyle; that fraud in obtaining such largesse is commonplace; increasingly that the invalidity or disability that are the intended condition for some benefits are easily and readily feigned; and that there are far too many foreigners among the many improper beneficiaries of 'our' exploited generosity in the welfare system.

The excessive generosity of our easily duped benefits system and the consequent opulence enjoyed by its undeserving and exploitative recipients have continued to receive regular proclamation. The *Daily Star* (5/4/15) covered its front page with news of a 'Benefits Scrounger Mum's £10m Vegas Trip'. In 2017, it followed this with another prominent story aggrieved at news that a 'Benefits Cheat Queen Swindled Nearly £250k to Fund Luxury Holidays to US and Designer Bags' (12/2/17), and later, in the summer with news of the 'Benefits Cheat Mum of 4 caught snorkelling in the Maldives' (31/7/17). In the *Daily Express*, front-page revelations of the 'Benefits Cheats in Paradise' matched the paper's regular news about similar outrages, including the reassuring news of the jailing of the 'Benefits Cheat Who Lived on a Tropical Isle' (19/8/11) and the equally comforting story of the uncovering of a '£30k Benefits Fraud by Cruise Dad' (9/2/11).

The Sun reinforced its sense of who its readers are with the revelation that 'You Pay £52,000 Benefits for Superhouse Family of 12' (9/10/13).

Objection to the enviable lifestyles obtained by benefits recipients is, thus, readily coupled with anger about their being financed fraudulently. The lengths people will go to are implied by a *Daily Express* story (18/10/17) which opened with the alarming news that 'A benefit fraudster who scammed £60,000 in state handouts has walked free from court after claiming she was "barely literate" and could not understand the form she was signing'. Endless stories of renewed 'crackdowns' to locate and penalise the perennial and criminal underclass reinforce the sense of 'us' and 'them' built into this refrain. It is a problem whose sheer scale is frequently highlighted. In the *Daily Express'* (2/9/11), a front page revealed the stunning discovery of '4M Scrounging Families in Britain'; among many similar announcements of the obviously essential periodic suppression required for this population was a *Daily Mail* front page confirmation of a 'New Welfare Crackdown on Workshy' (27/1/15). Ever creative, *The Sun* invented spoof awards, 'the welfies', to give prominence to 'Brits with Talent for Playing the Benefits System' (15/1/15). Its readers were entertained with revelations about 'the nation's doss idols' and 'awarded' them with prizes for being 'graspers who find a way to claim as much welfare as possible'. These included an 'amnesia award', a 'put a knot in it award', the 'excess pounds award' for the 'slobbo with no jobbo', a 'miracle cure award', and so on; an ingenious compilation of a compelling array of prejudices and myths to fuel its humour.

Perhaps, more conspicuous in recent years has been the migration of the sick and disabled across the border increasingly into the territory of the underserving. As I note below, attitudes to the disabled have become more sceptical and harder, and again, the link between their support and fraud is pervasive. It appears that '75% of Incapacity Claimants Are Fit to Work' (*Daily Mail*, 23/4/13), and if this front-page story spelled it out insufficiently, a lengthier headline subsequently in the *Mail Online* explained that 'Almost a Million People Who Could Work Have Been on Benefits for 3 of the Last 4 Years Despite the Government's Employment Drive' (20/4/16).

Equally virulent and persistent in more recent media coverage of welfare has been the insistent xenophobia that many have detected as, among other things, a constituent part of the driver behind the 'Brexit' referendum result. The *Daily Star* assured its readers in a front-page spread (13/7/10) that the paper had been instrumental in securing a just result, proclaiming that '£2M Asylum Seeker Gets Booted Out Thanks to the *Daily Star*'. After all, it was incontrovertible fact, *Daily Mail* front page readers were informed, that 'Foreign Families Rake in Benefits' (24/10/12), including, explained a later *Sun* front page, 'Pole Chancers', whose exploitation of an 'EU Welfare farce', was aided by their unscrupulous use of a handy 'Migrants' Guide to Raking In UK Benefits (26/12/16).

The arrival of television 'poverty porn'

The continuity evident in this sustained and perpetual demonology has been extended by one unlovely and important innovation in recent years, the arrival on television of a genre rapidly dubbed 'poverty porn'. The epithet is deeply misleading and inappropriate, in compounding the stigmatisation of low-income families and individuals by the association of their lot and lifestyle with pornography. Indeed, in its first incarnation, as a term of distrust for the kind of exposure of 'third world' poverty designed to encourage charitable giving, it also attracted much criticism from campaigners uneasy at the negative images of passivity such material encouraged. But the mix of cheap production, voyeurism, and easily confected righteous indignation proved irresistible for a number of successful 'reality television' series. These series exploited an insatiable appetite for a moralising contempt for the poor with exploitation of carefully compiled vignettes of their apparently alarming and indefensible behaviour and attitudes (De Benedictus et al., 2017). The potent assembly of all this with a ready supply of unpaid or low paid and readily biddable stars fostered innumerable programmes and series, including *Benefits Street* (2014), *Britain's Benefit Tenants* (Ch 4, 2015), *On Benefits and Proud* (Ch 5 2013), *We All Pay Your Benefits* (BBC, 2013), and regular prominence on chat shows like *Jeremy Kyle* or *Tricia*.

Such programmes have been hugely successful. The first series of *Benefits Street* gave Channel 4 the highest viewing figures it had obtained for many years. Reaction was intense – the regulatory body O*fcom* received hundreds of complaints, while the people featured found themselves the recipients of death threats on Twitter. Love Productions, who made the series, increased its value that year by 25 per cent. In 2014, Sky/News International took a 70 per cent stake in the production company. It was that series that prompted a parliamentary election candidate to wonder (on their Facebook page) whether the kind of people displayed on the programme should be 'put down' (Murphy and Perkins, 2019). Series of this kind proved popular internationally too. Keo Films, who made *Skint* (2013), franchised the format to Australia as *Struggle Street*, which ran on SBS in Australia in 2015, 2017, and 2019.

Central to such material were the deployment and amplification of familiar myths. They frequently featured large families (in fact, the overwhelming majority, about 90 per cent, of couples with 3 or more children have at least one adult in work) and reinforced the views that such people do not seek to work given the generosity of easily obtained benefits and that fraudulently obtained benefits were rife. In fact, official data on fraud show that, while the net government loss due to benefit fraud and error in 2018–9 was, after recoveries, £3.0 billion, or 1.6 per cent of benefit expenditure, 1.1 per cent of total benefit expenditure (or £2.0 billion) was *underpaid* due to fraud and error (DWP, 2019).

Series like these had, and continue to have, widespread appeal and durability, given the large appetite of cable TV channels for repeat and relatively inexpensive series. *Can't Pay, We'll Take It Away*, a Channel 5 series featuring the exciting life and times of bailiffs, or High Court Enforcement Officers, dealing with defaulters, ran for five series from 2014 to 2018. One memorable episode shows an eviction officer telling a tenant 'say what you like, just give it some wellie, it makes good television', highlighting a deep and enduring truth about the appeal of such entertainment for producers. Among many objections that the programme received, it found itself the subject of litigation after complaints about privacy invasion arising from the use of body cameras. Programmes like this are telling reinforcers of a panoply of welfare stereotypes and mythologies (see, for example De Benedictis et al. 2017). In a study of audience responses to *Benefits Street*, it was shown that viewers use the programmes not only for entertainment but in reinforcing negative perceptions of benefit recipients and of the benefits system more generally (Paterson et al., 2016).

A permanent mood of moral disdain

Against such a backdrop of enduring scepticism about, and moral disdain for, so many categories of the poor, and of explicit antipathy to the systems that support them or seem so easily and outrageously exploited, the movement of public attitudes has been predictably limited, remaining largely negative about welfare and benefits generally. This is examined in closer detail elsewhere in this volume (see especially chapters in Part 3). However, it is important to recognise the reinforcing and continuing impact of the kind of media coverage described here. The *British Social Attitudes* studies produced annually by the National Centre for Social Research indicate that negative perceptions of welfare recipients are a more or less stable element in British public opinion (National Centre, 2020; see also Taylor-Gooby and Taylor, 2015). Indeed, despite some current and possibly temporary 'softening' of attitudes, recent decades have shown much evidence of a continuing hardening of attitudes towards both the benefits system and claimants. The British Social Attitudes studies, for example, show a fall in the proportion of those who think more should be spent on benefits from 61 per cent in 1989 to 27 per cent in 2009. The enormities and unprecedented privations resulting from the Covid-19 pandemic seemed to have resulted in some shift in such attitudes, though at the time of writing with no certainty about either the significance or durability of such shifts (National Centre for Social Research, 2020).

Since the turn of the century, shifts in government policy and the severe economic crisis provided a backdrop of growing turmoil that affected the formation of attitudes. Following the cataclysm of the 2008–9 financial collapse and ensuing recession, a period of severe austerity was imposed by the incoming coalition government, and the 2012 Welfare Reform Act introduced enormous changes, mainly in the form of restrictions and cuts, to the welfare and benefits systems. Despite the severity of the impact of these changes on the living standards and welfare of the country's poorest families, negative media portrayals continued to have a major influence. As Clery and Dangerfield note, while media coverage tended still to limit the visibility and impacts of poverty per se, examination of public attitudes to it revealed 'stark differences between readers of tabloid and broadsheet newspapers, many of which [writing in 2019] have only emerged over the past decade' (Clery and Dangerfield, 2019, p. 20).

Central to these attitudes is an apparent distaste for the dependency which receipt of benefits is believed to instil into recipients. In the 2016 British Social Attitudes study, for example, 61 per cent were reported as thinking that a working-age couple without children who are struggling to make ends meet should look after themselves rather than look to the government for help. The suspicion that 'generosity' harms its recipients by encouraging their dependence, and their failure to even seek any form of independence, has been a constant refrain in both media stories about benefits and in public belief systems.

Equally persistent has been the distinction described earlier between the deserving and undeserving poor, with the latter most often represented by the unemployed. The 2016 BSA survey found that 45 per cent of respondents wanted to see less spending on benefits for the unemployed, though the equivalent figure for retired beneficiaries was 7 per cent (Clery, 2016). Between 1998 and 2011, the proportion of people agreeing that 'ensuring people have enough to live on if they become unemployed' fell from 85 per cent to 59 per cent (op. cit.), and a regularly asked question similarly shows the persistence of the view that 'around here, most unemployed people could find a job if they wanted one'. Such views were given much prominence in 2010 in the widely reported view of the then Conservative Chancellor, George Osborne, in launching major cuts in benefits that 'People who think it is a lifestyle to sit on out-of-work benefits ... that lifestyle choice is going to come to an end. The money will not be there for that lifestyle choice'. He went on, 'The welfare system is broken. We have to accept that the welfare bill has got completely out of control and that there are five million people living on permanent out-of-work benefits' (Wintour, 2010). At the 2012 Conservative Party annual conference, he added, 'Where is the fairness for the shift-worker, leaving home in the dark hours of the early morning, who looks up at the closed blinds of their next-door neighbour sleeping off a life on benefits?' By 2019, such views appeared partially to have relented, and the 2020 BSA report suggests a sharp fall in the numbers regarding unemployment benefits as unduly generous, though the proportion thinking them as too high and discouraging work remained above a third (National Centre for Social Research, 2020). Attitudes are complex and varied, though the general ungenerous tenor of underlying view remains and, indeed, are recurrently reinforced by popular imagery (see the chapter by Clery in this volume for more detailed discussion).

That claimants are prone to fraud also remains a constant in popular belief, not altogether surprisingly given the prominence of that aspect of the benefits system in media coverage. Attitudes have been persistently tougher on benefits fraud than on tax evasion, with BSA surveys finding a consistently higher proportion of people (typically about two-thirds) regarding it as wrong not to declare casual work to the benefits office, while rather fewer regard it as wrong similarly to withhold information from HMRC. Such beliefs have fuelled encouragement to people to provide incriminating reports of wrong-doing where they think they have detected it, even though few such reports are ever confirmed. An Ipsos-Mori survey in 2013 found that the public believed 24 per cent of benefits were fraudulently claimed, some 34 times the figures indicated by government statistics. Between 2010 and 2015, the Department for Work and Pensions received more than 1.6 million reports from the public about people believed to be fraudulently claiming; it closed over a million such reports after finding insufficient or no evidence of fraud in the majority of them (Cowburn, 2016).

One shift in recent years has been in the demography of those denoted undeserving, especially a significant increase in hostility to and scepticism about the disabled and long-term sick. One study noted an increase in anti-disability rhetoric between 2004 and 2011 in the media, especially in aligning the disabled with 'scroungerphobia' and the like. In that period, the authors found a big increase in benefit fraud as a theme in articles about the disabled (Briant et al., 2013). Typical of this is a story in the *Mail online* (4/8/17) 'exposing' that a 'Fraudster who claimed £38,000 in disability benefits claiming he is a "frail old man and 70 per cent disabled" is pictured running the London Marathon Twice'. A study sponsored by a disability charity looked especially at the impact of negative media imagery on people with disabilities. They found that disabled people increasingly felt the press to be discriminating and contributing to disability hate crimes and abuse. Over three-quarters (77 per cent) of respondents cited negative press articles about disabled people; only a third (35 per cent) named a positive story; 94 per cent suggested press portrayal of disability equality issues was 'unfair'; 76 per cent said the volume of negativity was 'significantly increasing'; and 91 per cent said there was a link between negative press portrayal of disabled people and rising hostility/hate crime (Disability Rights UK, 2012; see also Cooke et al., 2000).

The invisibility of an alternative

Not altogether surprisingly, against this background of persistent mythology and sceptical attitudes, the benefit system has become ever more conditional and restrictive. From 2013 onward, a benefit cap has ensured that claimants cannot receive more than average household income. By 2019, 250,000 households had been capped, including 210,000 who had their housing benefit capped, and in May 2020, 150,000 households were having their benefits capped. At the same time, the severity and implementation of benefits sanctions have been increasing. Between May 2010 and December 2014, 3.5 million Job Seekers' Allowance claimants were the subject of sanctions, over half a million more than in the previous decade. More than 900,000 of these were claimants who reported a disability. By 2020, the average duration of sanctions for Universal Credit was a month.

The core concern here is with the visibility and dissemination of imagery. Wealth and the world of the rich are rarely evident in the media except occasionally in the form of the exceptional and extravagant excesses of the superrich. The jet-setting and opulent life styles familiar from the grope-and-greed television of yesteryear, like *Dallas*, onward, readily present as exceptional, levels of privilege that are rapidly growing in all societies even as the scale of inequality has increased. Yet most people perceive themselves as 'middling', and in the absence of any alternative, generally underestimate the extent of inequalities (Irwin, 2018). The sheer exoticism of extreme wealth easily masks the less commonly evident routine privileges of the merely well-to-do. One reason for this is that the news media are better able to convey event rather than process. This is not the place to rehearse the complex theorisation that such analysis entails (see *inter alia*, Golding and Elliott, 1979; Iyengar, 1991), but it raises immediately the difficulty of providing cultural resource for understanding the processes that produce inequality and poverty, rather than the relative ease with which the misbehaviour and apparent misdeeds of the downtrodden may be narrated in 'stories'.

Alternative and, indeed, quite contrary, imagery and analysis of poverty and welfare exist in the public domain of course. To suggest there is undiluted 'scroungerphobia' or only masking of the dire, realities of poverty and benefit levels would be to suggest an unlikely uniformity and completeness to ideology. Feature films like Ken Loach's *I Daniel*, front-page stories like an anti-royal piece headlined 'The Queen and Charles Cash in on Benefits' *(Daily Mirror* 24/2/2014*),* or numerous investigative documentaries uncovering the sheer scale of relentless impoverishment resulting from meagre and punitively administered benefits are testimony to the power and possibility of varying the tenor of coverage of this area of social policy. In the 1970s and 1980s, and, indeed, more recently, there have always been occasional worthy TV documentaries and newspaper articles making plain the sheer extent and persistence of widespread poverty. The London Weekend Television series *'Breadline Britain'* was based on extensive surveys and repeated after its original 1983 broadcast in 1991 and 2013 (see the chapter by Mack in this volume). But, they are the exceptions that prove the rule, and such tendencies are unlikely to change as a result of well-intentioned initiatives such as a recent guide aimed at journalists (Joseph Rowntree Foundation, 2020).

Information inequality

It is, therefore, imperative that it is possible for people to acquire information and background to inform understanding of social process and policy from a variety of sources. The capacity to seek and obtain such information is, sometimes, described as having enormously blossomed with the expansion of 'social media' – indeed, by 2018 virtually half the population was using 'social media' as their main source of news, and expenditure on them exceeded that on books, magazines, and newspapers (Ofcom, 2020). But not only is there ever-diminishing trust in the veracity of the material such media distribute, but crucially, alternative sources of publicly available civic information are reducing in scope, scale, and availability. Two examples illustrate this point (for elaboration, see Golding, 2017).

Firstly, almost 800 libraries closed between 2010 and 2018, the period that the Coalition government implemented austerity (CIPFA, 2019). The closure of almost a fifth of the UK's libraries over the last 10 years comes against a backdrop of a 29.6 per cent decline in national spending on the service, which topped £1bn in 2009/10 but dropped to under £750m in 2018/9. At the same time, the number of paid librarians has also plunged. In 2009/2010, there were 24,000 salaried staff working in libraries; in 2019, there were 15,300. In recurrent surveys, it has been shown to what extent public libraries are preferred sources for citizenship information (see, e.g. Marcella and Baxter, 2000).

Secondly, the BBC has been subject to recurrent cuts in staffing and income and arrives in the 2020s unsure even of its future existence (Mair and Bradshaw,

2020). A government white paper, in 2016, argued for the BBC as a source of distinctive output—in other words, output unattractive or unprofitable for commercial providers—in direct contrast to evidence from elsewhere in Europe, showing that where public service broadcasters competed with commercial providers across the full range of services, the public received the highest quality of service from both (e.g. Ibarra, Nowak, and Kuhn, 2015). The finances of the BBC were savaged by a new requirement that it meet the cost (previously met by public expenditure) of providing free licenses to people over 75, partly in 2018–19 and fully from 2020-21, a reduction of £650 million in the corporation's income. BBC news services have been a regular victim of pressures on its income. After the license fee was frozen in 2010, the corporation announced it would seek £800 million in efficiency savings. Roughly 2,000 job cuts were announced in 2011 on top of the 7,000 lost in the previous seven years. In 2014, came a move to cut 415 jobs in the news department, and in early 2016, the corporation announced it would seek to save £550 million in news services by 2021–22. Further cuts in news staffing have followed regularly, and in 2020, the Corporation announced plans to cut a further 70 posts in its news division, an announcement coming hard on the heels of plans to cut 450 jobs in regional programmes. The results of these cuts argued the National Union of Journalists would be hugely damaging to the BBC's 'ability to represent all parts of the country and produce high-quality local news and investigative journalism' (Waterson, 2020).

It becomes even more essential, therefore, that people have the capacity and resources to seek information from as wide a range of sources as possible. Yet, it is here that the double whammy faced by the poor cuts deepest. When the information necessary for active citizenship is only available at a price and is becoming ever scarcer and more difficult to obtain, then poverty enforces the disempowerment of those with limited means to either communicate or seek information. The extent of this 'citizen detriment' resulting from information poverty is illustrated in Tables 6.1 and 6.2.

Table 6.1 shows the ownership of communication goods among differing income groups, and it highlights the substantial and enduring gradient in ownership of such goods from lower-income groups up to the better off. Table 6.2 shows that information goods and services have acquired a distribution pattern

Table 6.1 Percentage of households owning selected communication goods, UK 2019

	Income group		All Households
	Top 10%	Lowest 10%	
Home computer	100	63	89
Internet connection	99	69	91
Phone	90	70	83
Mobile	99	88	96

Source: Calculated from Office for National Statistics (2020). Table A46.

Table 6.2 Household expenditure on communications, UK 2018/19

	(£/week)		As % of all expenditure		£/wk all
	Poorest 10th	Richest 10th	Poorest 10th	Richest 10th	
Telephone and so on	5.5	12.9	2.35	1.08	10
Internet	0.5	1.3	0.21	0.11	0.8
TV (cable, licences, and so on)	2.9	7	1.24	0.58	4.5
Newspapers, magazines, and so on	1.3	2.8	0.58	0.19	2
TOTALS	£ 10.20	£ 24.00			
Total Household exp/week	£234.00	£1,196.60			£585.60

Source: Calculated from Office for National Statistics (2020) Table A6.

paralleling that of essentials such as food, clothing, and housing generally. While lower-income groups spend a higher proportion of their disposable income on such goods, in absolute terms, they spend very much less than higher-income groups. In other words, inequality of incomes and spending power determine citizen detriment, the inherent inability of the poorest to seek, obtain, and possess the necessities for informed citizenship. The poor, whatever their changing demographic composition, are not only condemned and blamed for their financial deprivation but also, at the same time, find themselves excluded from many of the opportunities to participate actively in society and, indeed, to have access to a range of sources of information and means of action open to the better off. It is in that sense that poverty invites double jeopardy – the obloquy of popular disdain, distrust, or condemnation illustrated by the media and public attitudes described earlier, and the inability to either challenge such demonology or obtain an alternative range of informed opinion or analysis in an increasingly online world shaped by price and marketability.

References

Briant, E., Watson, N. and Philo, G. (2013). *Reporting Disability in the Age of Austerity*, *Disability & Society*, 28(6), pp. 874–889.
Chartered Institute of Public Finance and Accountancy (CIPFA). (2019). *Decade of Austerity Sees 30% Drop in Library Spending*, 6 December, London CIPFA. Available at: https://www.cipfa.org/about-cipfa/press-office/latest-press-releases/decade-of-austerity-sees-30-drop-in-library-spending (Accessed 30 October, 2020).
Checkland, S. G., and Checkland, E. O. A. (eds.). (1974). *Poor Law Report, 1834*. Harmondsworth: Penguin Books.
Clery, E. (2016). Welfare: Support for Government Welfare Reform. In Swales, K. (ed.) *British Social Attitudes 33*. National Centre for Social Research. London: NCSR. Available at: https://www.bsa.natcen.ac.uk/latest-report/british-social-attitudes-33/welfare.aspx (Accessed 29 October, 2020).

Clery, E., and Dangerfield, P. (2019). Poverty and Inequality: Have Attitudes Evolved in Line with Official Trends or Political and Media Discourse?. In J. Curtice, E. Clery, J. Perry, M. Phillips, and N. Rahim (eds.) *British Social Attitudes 36*, London: NCSR.

Cooke, C., Daone, L. and Morris, G. (2000). *Stop Press: How the Press Portrays Disabled People*. London. [Online]. Available at: https://www.disabilityrightsuk.org/sites/default/files/pdf/disabilitypresscoverage.pdf (Accessed July 15, 2018)

Cowburn, A. (2016). Public Tips on Benefit 'Frauds' Are Mostly False', *Observer*, 27 February, 2016. [Online] Available at: https://www.theguardian.com/society/2016/feb/27/false-benefit-fraud-allegations.

De Benedictis, S., Allen, K. and Jensen, T. (2017). Portraying Poverty: The Economics and Ethics of Factual Welfare Television, *Cultural Sociology*, 11(3), pp. 337–358.

Devereux, E. (1998). *Devils and Angels: Television, Ideology and the Coverage of Poverty*. Luton: University of Luton Press.

Disability Rights UK. (2012). *Press Portrayal of Disabled People: A Rise in Hostility Fuelled by Austerity?* London. [Online]. Available at: https://www.disabilityrightsuk.org/about-us/press-office/press-and-media-2012/press-portrayal-disabled-people-rise-hostility-fuelled

DWP [Department for Work and Pensions] (2019) *Fraud and error in the benefit system: financial year 2018 to 2019 estimates*. London. [Online]. Available at: https://www.gov.uk/government/statistics/fraud-and-error-in-the-benefit-system-financial-year-2018-to-2019-estimates (Accessed: 26 October, 2020).

Golding, P. (2017). Citizen Detriment: Communications, Inequality, and Social Order, *International Journal of Communication*, 11 [Online]. Available at: http://ijoc.org/index.php/ijoc (Accessed 28 September, 2017).

Golding, P., and Elliott, P. (1979). *Making the News*. London: Longman.

Golding, P., and Middleton, S. (1982). *Images of welfare: press and public attitudes to poverty*. Oxford: Martin Robertson.

Ibarra, K. A., Nowak, E., and Kuhn, R. (eds.). (2015). *Public Service Media in Europe: A Comparative Approach*. London: Routledge.

Irwin, S. (2018). Lay Perceptions of Inequality and Social Structure, *Sociology*, 52(2), pp. 211–227.

Iyengar, S. (1991). *Is Anyone Responsible? How Television Frames Political Issues*. Chicago, IL: University of Chicago Press.

Joseph Rowntree Foundation. (2020). *Reporting Poverty: A Guide for Media Professionals*. Available at: https://www.jrf.org.uk/report/reporting-poverty-guide-media-professionals (Accessed: 19 October, 2020).

Mair, J., and Bradshaw, T. (eds.). (2020). *Is the BBC Still in Peril?* Goring: Bite-Sized Books.

Marcella, R., and Baxter, G. (2000). Information need, information seeking behaviour and participation, with special reference to needs related to citizenship: Results of a national survey, *Journal of Documentation*, 56(2), pp. 136–160.

Morrison, J. (2018). *Scroungers: Moral Panics and Media Myths*. London: Zed Books.

Murphy, S., and Perkins, L. (2019). Tory candidate wrote people on Benefits Street should be 'put down, *the Guardian*, 3 November, 2019. [Online] Available at: https://www.theguardian.com/politics/2019/nov/03/tory-candidate-francesca-obrien-wrote-people-benefits-street-should-be-put-down.

National Centre for Social Research. (2020). *British Social Attitudes 36*. National Centre for Social Research. Available at: https://www.bsa.natcen.ac.uk/latest-report/british-social-attitudes-36/poverty-and-inequality.aspx (Accessed October 25, 2020).

Ofcom. (2020). *Online Nation: 2020 Summary Report*. London. [Online]. Available at: https://www.ofcom.org.uk/__data/assets/pdf_file/0028/196408/online-nation-2020-summary.pdf

Office for National Statistics. (2020). *Family Spending in the UK: April 2018 to March 2019*. London. [Online]. Available at: https://www.ons.gov.uk/peoplepopulationandcommunity/personalandhouseholdfinances/expenditure/bulletins/familyspendingintheuk/april2018tomarch2019#family-spending-data (Accessed: 29 September, 2020).

Paterson, L. L., Coffey-Glover, L., and Peplow, D. (2016). Negotiating Stance within Discourses of Class: Reactions to Benefits Street, *Discourse & Society*, 27(2), pp. 195–214.

Redden, J. (2014). *The Mediation of Poverty: The News, New Media, and Politics*. Boulder, CO.: Rowman and Littlefield.

Taylor-Gooby, P., and Taylor, E. (2015). Benefits and welfare: Long-term trends or short-term reactions? In: J. Curtice and R. Ormston (eds.) *British Social Attitudes, 32*. London: National Centre for Social Research, pp. 74–101.

Townsend, P. (1979). *Poverty in the United Kingdom*. Harmondsworth: Penguin Books.

Waterson, J. (2020). One in Six Jobs To Go as BBC Cuts 450 Staff from Regional Programmes, *The Guardian*, 2 July, 2020. [Online] Available at: https://www.theguardian.com/media/2020/jul/02/local-tv-stars-to-go-as-bbc-cuts-450-staff-from-regional-programmes

Wintour, P. (2010). George Osborne to Cut £4bn More from Benefits, *The Guardian*, 9 September, 2010.

7 The rhetoric of recessions

How British Newspapers Talk About the Poor When Unemployment Rises 1896–2000*

Daniel McArthur and Aaron Reeves

Introduction

The global financial crisis of 2008 seemed to coincide with a rise in stigmatising rhetoric about people in poverty and welfare recipients across a range of print and television media outlets (Harkins and Lugo-Ocando, 2016; Tyler, 2008, 2013). This language legitimised welfare retrenchment by 'othering' (Lister, 2015) people in poverty and representing them as part of an outgroup who were lazy, immoral and living fraudulently at the expense of hard-working taxpayers (Jensen, 2014). Anti-welfare narratives permeated public discourse over this period and, in some cases, even had a demonstrable impact on attitudes towards welfare recipients (Reeves and De Vries, 2016).

This latest crisis is one recent example of how parts of the media stigmatise the poor during periods of rising unemployment. A number of studies have argued that media rhetoric about the poor responds to macroeconomic conditions, becoming more stigmatising when times are hard (Golding and Middleton, 1982; Macnicol, 1987). However, the existing quantitative evidence linking economic crises and newspaper rhetoric about the poor remains limited. Existing work relies on time-consuming hand-coding (Gilens, 1996; Misra et al., 2003), which limits the ability of researchers to examine long-term trends in the language newspapers use to describe the poor. We know of no quantitative studies that investigate whether the prevalence of stigmatising language about the poor is affected by underlying economic conditions. Case studies have generated crucial insights into how the print media frame poverty during economic downturns and periods of high unemployment, but they have done so by examining precisely those periods in which stigmatising rhetoric increased. This logic of case selection may inadvertently overlook periods when, for example, unemployment rises, but there is no change in stigmatising rhetoric (Deacon, 1976).

We address this gap in research on the link between economic crises and newspaper rhetoric about poverty by drawing on a unique dataset measuring how often five right-wing and centrist British newspapers and periodicals use stigmatising language about people in poverty throughout the 20th century (1896–2000). We find that stigmatising rhetoric about the poor becomes more common when

---

* This chapter is adapted from 'The Rhetoric of Recessions: How British Newspapers Talk about the Poor When Unemployment Rises, 1896–2000', published in *Sociology* (53,6), April 2019.

DOI: 10.4324/9781003104476-10

unemployment increases, but this association weakens when unemployment rates are especially high (>10 per cent), such as during the 1930s and the 1980s.

Outside these exceptional periods, we conclude that British centrist and right-wing newspapers deploy deeply embedded Malthusian anxieties about the behaviour of the poor when unemployment is rising. In doing so, they draw on a powerful set of ideas to explain an economic phenomenon that by itself might threaten the hegemony of individualistic interpretations of unemployment and poverty. Adopting an historical perspective reveals how deeply embedded ideas, such as Malthusian explanations for poverty, are deployed when they resonate with the structural context. Media stigmatisation of the poor following the global financial crisis was consistent with how our sample of newspapers responded to changing economic conditions across the 20th century.

Recycling Malthus: media responses to high unemployment in historical context

While the media reaction to the global financial crisis in the UK intensified anti-welfare rhetoric (Jensen, 2014; Jensen and Tyler, 2015), such concerns about the numbers and morality of the poor and the unemployed are not new and can be traced back over many centuries (Day, 2001; Welshman, 2007). Thomas Malthus' Essay on the Principle of Population (2008), first published in 1798, has had an enormous influence on how poverty is understood in British society (Golding and Middleton, 1982; Harkins and Lugo-Ocando, 2016; Macnicol, 1998).

Malthus argued that providing welfare is counterproductive because it breaks the natural check that starvation places on the numbers of the poor. In his view, the poor would not work if they are not required to do so to survive, and so providing them with food would erode their work ethic. Furthermore, their inability to exercise sexual restraint means that their numbers would inexorably increase, leading to collective immiseration and eventual societal collapse. When people refuse to work, unemployment rises, and so rising unemployment becomes a symptom of the moral decay that will make societies unsustainable unless action is taken to reduce welfare uptake and disincentivise welfare dependency. To this end, Malthus argued that welfare receipt should be stigmatised: 'hard as it may appear in individual instances, dependent poverty ought to be held disgraceful' (Malthus, 2008: III.VI.5).

Malthusian ideas have had a profound influence on public and policy discourse over the last 200 years, shaping the Poor Law debates of the 1830s (Malthus, 2008; Polanyi, 2002), the welfare reforms of the 1980s and 1990s (Somers and Block, 2005) and austerity policies following the Great Recession (Harkins and Lugo-Ocando, 2016; Jensen and Tyler, 2015).

Malthus' influence can be clearly seen in media responses to unemployment. Public debates about poverty during the 1890s and early 1900s – an economically turbulent period when unemployment fluctuated wildly – were dominated by concerns about the spread of a 'degenerate nature' among the worst off in society, the 'social residuum' or 'unemployables' (Welshman, 2007: 2, 21; see also Day, 2001). In 1894, only a year after the peak of a recession, Geoffrey Drage (1894: 142)

(Secretary to the Labour Commission) argued that unemployment was mostly attributable to 'faults of character – habits of intemperance, idleness, or dishonesty'.

When the Great Depression hit, parts of the press blamed 'dole' abusers for the country's economic difficulties rather than speculators or financiers (Deacon, 1976; Golding and Middleton, 1982). In August 1931, the Daily Telegraph called on the government to 'not be moved by the threatening invective of those who … [cry] "Hands off our dole"'. The government cut unemployment benefit by 10 per cent.

Between 1973 and 1976, a moral panic about welfare fraud coincided with a doubling of unemployment rates from 1.9 per cent to 3.9 per cent. On 15 July 1976, the Daily Express' front page read 'Get the scroungers!' This war on benefits cheats was widespread enough that around 30 per cent of all social policy-related news stories in 1976 were concerned with welfare abuse. Such stigmatising rhetoric punctured the thin 'veneer of an apparent "welfare consensus"' that had existed since the Second World War (Golding and Middleton, 1982) and legitimised major cuts to public spending.

Ideational embeddedness and the media

These historical episodes make it clear that the print media have repeatedly played a crucial role in framing recessions in Malthusian terms, raising the question about why journalists recurrently deploy this language amid rising unemployment. Part of the explanation seems to be that Malthusian ideas have been 'ideationally embedded' in the culture of Anglophone countries: they have become central features of the narratives and explanatory systems that social actors use to explain the world, often without realising their source (Somers and Block, 2005: 264). The success of Malthusian explanations of poverty is rooted in the capacity of this theory to make itself true by changing the features of the world that appear salient to people, including journalists (Bourdieu, 1998: 95). For example, living in a society where Malthusian explanations are central to how people understand poverty means people can now see the perverse effects of welfare almost everywhere they look. Despite the fact that there are vanishingly few people who actually refuse to work, the dominance of the Malthusian narrative makes it possible for people to believe that such behaviour is commonplace (Macdonald et al., 2014). By 'making themselves true', Malthusian ideas have become a form of common sense, accepted across society. So deeply embedded are these narratives in the Anglophone world that even those in poverty often deploy such images and tropes (Shildrick and MacDonald, 2013).

From this perspective, journalists are not the sole creators of stigmatising rhetoric, they are simply one set of actors who are 'engaged in the production and maintenance of meaning' and who are part of a discourse that renders some kinds of occurrences more meaningful than others (Benford and Snow, 2000). Like politicians and the general public, journalists deploy Malthusian ideas because they are engaged in a process of reproducing and recirculating widely accepted ways of understanding the social world (Couldry and Hepp, 2016). Journalists also possess a high degree of power to shape public opinion and government policy through the way they deploy these discourses in framing the issues of day.

Therefore, it is worth considering how journalists' relationship to their readers, and the economic context, may make them more or less likely to draw on Malthusian explanations for poverty.

Why newspapers use Malthusian ideas in recessions

Whatever their goal or agenda, journalists need to effectively communicate with their readers. To do so, journalists draw on evocative and recognisable tropes, metaphors or images. As described above, Malthusian ideas provide a rich and compelling set of narratives journalists can use to frame their explanations of social phenomena (Gamson and Lasch, 1983; McKendrick et al., 2008). Malthusian ideas will not be ever-present in media discourse, rather, journalists are more likely to deploy them when they resonate most strongly with readers' experiences and the broader context (Benford and Snow, 2000; Gamson, 1992). Rising unemployment is a set of circumstances that Malthusian ideas explain well by providing a simple theory, whereby an increasing population in poverty is a natural result of the immorality of the poor (Somers and Block, 2005). As a result, when unemployment rates go up, stigmatising rhetoric in the print media should increase because this is when Malthusian ideas are at their most relevant as a way of making sense of changing economic conditions. By contrast, when unemployment declines, and the Malthusian explanation of poverty becomes less relevant to the circumstances, stigmatising rhetoric should decline as well.

This 'Malthusian' theory has never been tested quantitatively. Thus, it is also possible that when unemployment is rising it becomes harder to maintain that 'faults of character' (Drage, 1894) are the cause of joblessness, and as a result, structural explanations of poverty may resonate more strongly with economic context and newspaper readers' experiences (Benford and Snow, 2000; Van Oorschot, 2006). From this perspective, when unemployment rates go up, stigmatising rhetoric in the media will decline, reflecting the increased resonance of structural explanations of poverty.

The central question of this article is, thus, whether newspapers use stigmatising rhetoric about people in poverty more frequently when unemployment rates go up or when they decline. Our analysis addresses this question by drawing on a novel dataset covering the entire 20th century, allowing us to connect macroeconomic conditions with how newspapers talk about people living in poverty.

Measuring Stigmatising Rhetoric in Newspapers

We construct a unique dataset measuring the frequency of stigmatising language about people in poverty over the 20th century. The Gale NewsVault database contains archives of five British newspapers from their inception to the present day: the Mail (daily and Sunday editions); the Telegraph (daily and Sunday editions); the Times (daily and Sunday editions); the Financial Times and the Economist. While there is some diversity among these papers in their political alignment and readership demographics, they are all predominantly centrist or right-wing in orientation and are read by a largely middleclass audience (see Appendix for further information). Unfortunately, the Gale NewsVault database does not contain any left-wing newspapers. As a result, we are unable to say whether left-wing newspapers are more likely to use stigmatising language when unemployment increases.

We restrict our sample to 1896–2000 when all five newspapers are available. To calculate the frequency of stigmatising language about people living in poverty, we utilise Gale NewsVault's search function. This returns the frequency of articles containing specific terms by year.

Word choice

Stigmatising language about the poor frames people in poverty as members of an outgroup and associates poverty with negative stereotypes asserting immoral behaviour. The specific language used to describe the poor has changed substantially over time; words used frequently in one period, such as 'unemployables' or the 'residuum' in the late 19th century, later drop out of common usage. Political entrepreneurs create new terms, such as the 'underclass' in the 1980s, to express a set of ideas that remains fairly static (Gamson and Lasch, 1983; Welshman, 2007). We select words following earlier research on how poverty is presented in the media (Day, 2001; Golding and Middleton, 1982; Tyler, 2013; Welshman, 2007), choosing a large number of words (28) on the assumption that historical idiosyncrasies in usage should average out. Our set of words includes terms which are used to describe people in poverty in a stigmatising or demeaning manner such as 'scrounger', 'skiver' or 'underclass' (Golding and Middleton, 1982) and terms that denote negative attributes that are commonly asserted to be associated with poverty such as 'lazy', 'feckless' or 'unemployable' (Welshman, 2007). When such terms are used, they invoke negative stereotypes linking poverty with deviant and immoral behaviour, thus presenting poverty as shameful and othering the poor (Lister, 2015).

Our focus is on measuring the prevalence of stigmatising and othering rhetoric about the poor. We are not trying to measure the net 'mood' (balance of positive vs negative coverage) of print media discourse about the poor (Rose and Baumgartner, 2013) because apparently positive words about poverty can be used with a stigmatising intent (consider the negative connotations of the word 'benefits' in contemporary political discourse), and the framing of articles can provoke stigmatising reactions in their readers even if the words they use are generally neutral (see Gilens, 1996 for evidence of how ostensibly neutral images change perceptions of welfare recipients).

We use the frequency (the absolute number of uses) of each word rather than a measure of popularity (the proportion of articles published in a year in which a given word appears), in both descriptive statistics and the regression models. This is because the total number of articles fluctuates substantially from year to year (including a drop at the start of the Second World War because of

Table 7.1 Descriptive statistics for words measuring stigmatising rhetoric about the poor

Word	Average per year	Min	Max	Sparkline
Peasant*	948.30	467	2413	
Tramp*	659.21	195	1216	
Beggar*	332.31	46	1313	
Peon*	305.90	46	587	
Pauper*	175.58	10	844	
Dependency	103.70	14	511	
Idler*	85.61	22	202	
Lower class	72.03	8	181	
Delinquent	62.16	7	272	
Loafer*	56.02	4	201	
Delinquency	55.58	2	242	
Indigent	50.02	2	241	
Vagrant	40.94	4	138	
Feckless	39.27	0	216	
Indolent	30.60	5	85	
Unemployable	24.62	0	80	
Vagrancy	23.47	0	93	
Underclass	22.19	0	225	
Deserving poor	22.00	0	153	
Shirker*	19.19	1	230	
Scrounger*	16.80	0	130	
Residuum	10.72	0	52	
Skiver*	9.71	0	67	
Dependent on benefits	7.86	0	45	
Criminal class	7.30	0	19	
Workshy	6.64	0	39	
Dangerous class	5.20	0	15	
Riff raff	1.66	0	20	

Notes: Data from Gale NewsVault. Words ordered by descending average frequency. Sparklines are intended to give a sense of relative frequency of word across time (1896–2000) and should be read with respect to minimum and maximum for each word.

paper rationing) and so artificially shifts the relative popularity far more than the absolute frequency.

Table 7.1 provides descriptive statistics for our set of words. We include sparklines to show differences in how often these words are used over the period.

Some words are used fairly consistently, such as 'tramp'. Others are popular only in the early 20th century, such as 'deserving poor', while others gain in popularity such as 'underclass', which was unused prior to the late 20th century.

Newspaper rhetoric and unemployment over the 20th century

Unemployment rates are a major driver of hardship for which measures are available covering the entire 20th century (unlike measures of poverty, which are not regularly available until the mid-1960s). Furthermore, the morality and behaviour of the unemployed are central to how poverty has historically been discussed in the British print media, as the case studies cited above indicate. Therefore, we focus on the relationship between unemployment rates and stigmatising rhetoric to understand how newspaper rhetoric about the poor depends on levels of poverty and hardship.

In Figure 7.1, we plot the average frequency of stigmatising rhetoric against unemployment rates across the 20th century, taken from the Bank of England's 'Three Centuries of Macroeconomic Data' series (Thomas and Dimsdale, 2016). Across much of the 20th century, these two lines seem to move together, suggesting that as unemployment rises so does stigmatising rhetoric (r = 0.705), providing some evidence in support of the 'Malthusian' hypothesis.

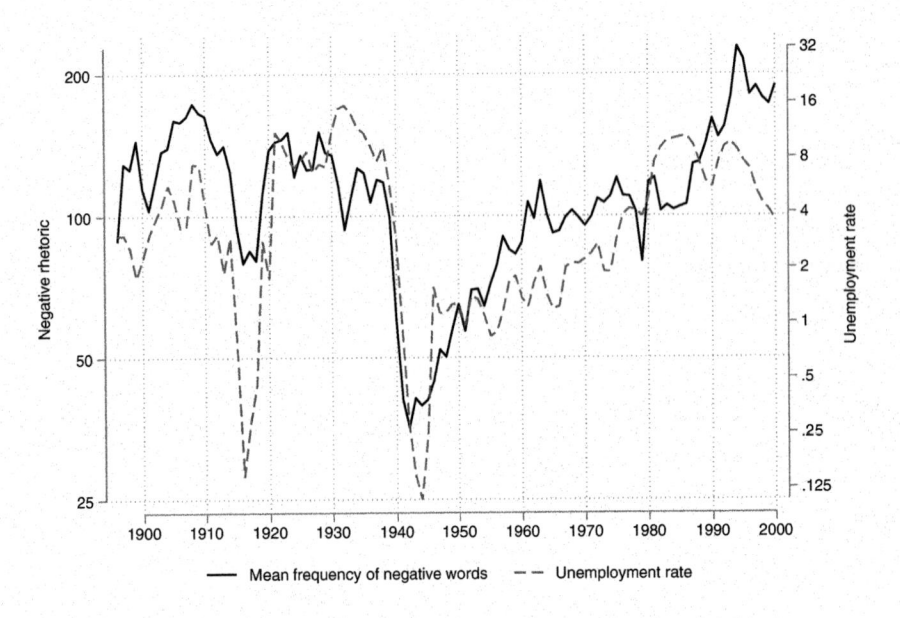

Figure 7.1 Unemployment rates and stigmatising rhetoric about the poor in Britain, 1896–2000.
Note: Both vertical axes are on a logarithmic scale.

Looking more closely, there are periods when this relationship does not hold. For example, at the beginning of the 1930s, there is a sharp rise in unemployment that coincides with a reduction in the amount of stigmatising rhetoric. Then, as unemployment rates gradually fall through the middle of the 1930s, stigmatising rhetoric rises again. Similarly, during the 1980s, we see this relationship becomes less clear. As unemployment rates rose between 1979 and 1980, there was a sharp increase in stigmatising rhetoric, but as unemployment continued to increase throughout the middle of the 1980s, stigmatising rhetoric seemed to decline, before rising steadily as unemployment fell.

Are Changes in Unemployment Associated with Changes in Stigmatising Rhetoric?

We further investigate the association between unemployment rates and stigmatising rhetoric using regression models. As our theory suggests, stigmatising rhetoric should respond to changes in unemployment because journalists and editors are probably more responsive to short-term changes in the economy (e.g. 2 per cent rise in unemployment) than long-term structural conditions (e.g. low unemployment over the last 10 years). We estimate whether annual changes in unemployment are associated with annual changes in stigmatising rhetoric. This 'first difference' approach reduces the risk of identifying a spurious relationship, especially if long-run trends in our key variables are correlated with other macroeconomic or political variables. We, therefore, model the response of the print media to changes in economic conditions rather than the underlying levels, taking into account the total number of articles published in any given year.

This analysis provides evidence for the 'Malthusian' hypothesis. Rising unemployment is positively correlated with rising stigmatising rhetoric even after accounting for the number of articles published in that year (Table 7.2). Other variables may potentially explain this relationship: in Figure 7.1, unemployment and stigmatising rhetoric both dramatically decline during the First World War and the Second World War, and so we include government spending on defence (per cent of GDP) in our models (Mitchell, 2007), but this does not substantively alter our main finding. Political factors, such as the party in power, may shape media rhetoric during times of rising unemployment through their 'agenda-setting' capacity (Tyler, 2013). However, we see no clear change in our results once we control for the political party composition of government.

The health of public finances is another possible confounder: during the Great Recession, conservative media often blamed welfare recipients for high levels of public sector debt. Therefore, we add measures of public debt, tax revenue and non-defence public spending, all as a proportion of GDP, to our models (Thomas and Dimsdale, 2016). The coefficient on unemployment remains positive and statistically significant although there is some evidence that increased non-defence public spending is associated with increased stigmatising rhetoric. Taken together, the stability of our regression results offers further evidence in favour of the 'Malthusian' hypothesis that stigmatising rhetoric becomes more common when unemployment rises.

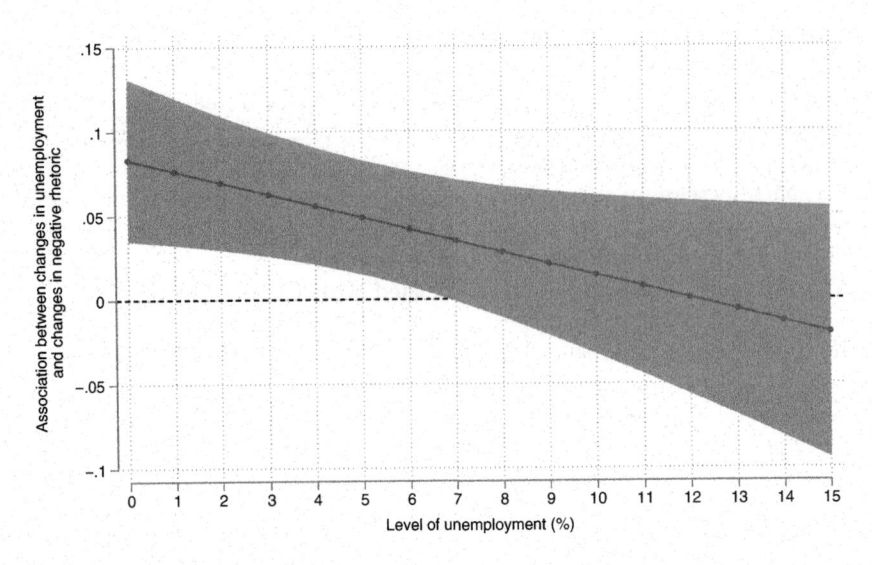

Figure 7.2 Increases in unemployment and stigmatising rhetoric.

Why Does the Relationship between Unemployment and Stigmatising Rhetoric Weaken in the 1930s and 1980s?

Figure 7.2 showed that the association between unemployment and negative rhetoric breaks down in periods of especially high unemployment rates, potentially suggesting some non-linearity in the association between unemployment and stigmatising rhetoric.

Stigmatising rhetoric may not increase with rising unemployment if the starting level of unemployment is already very high. To test this, we re-estimate the relationship between unemployment and stigma from Table 7.2 adding an interaction between the change in the unemployment rate and the level of unemployment. Figure 7.2 plots the estimated effect of a 1 per cent increase in unemployment on changes in negative rhetoric, at a variety of different starting levels of unemployment. A 1 per cent increase in unemployment is associated with a greater increase in stigmatising rhetoric when the initial level of unemployment is low. At higher rates of unemployment, the effect of an increase in unemployment on stigmatising rhetoric gets smaller. At levels of unemployment above 7 per cent, the association between change in unemployment and stigmatising rhetoric is not significantly different from 0. In fact, at very high levels of unemployment, an additional increase in unemployment – for example, from 13 per cent to 14 per cent – may even reduce the amount of stigmatising rhetoric (although the confidence intervals cover 0). This is the situation we see in the early 1930s when the use of stigmatising rhetoric falls once unemployment rates became exceptionally high increase in unemployment given the pre-existing level of unemployment. While an unemployment rate of 0 is strictly outside of our sample, there are years when unemployment rates are very low (~0.1 per cent).

Table 7.2 Association between unemployment rate and stigmatising rhetoric adjusting for covariates, 1896–2000

Annual change in the average frequency of stigmatising words

	(1)	(2)	(3)	(4)
Increase in the unemployment rate (log)	0.058**	0.042*	0.044**	0.033*
	(0.019)	(0.017)	(0.016)	(0.016)
Increase in the number of published articles (log)	0.77***	0.68***	0.82***	0.77***
	(0.13)	(0.14)	(0.11)	(0.13)
Defence spending (%GDP)		−0.0047***		−0.0027
		(0.00099)		(0.0020)
Conservative party (ref)				
Labour		−0.023		−0.025
		(0.020)		(0.021)
Coalition		−0.014		−0.022
		(0.022)		(0.029)
Whig/Liberal		−0.041		−0.046
		(0.027)		(0.027)
Increase in public debt (%GDP)			−0.000057	0.00063
			(0.00062)	(0.00093)
Increase in tax revenues (%GDP)			−0.0035	−0.0012
			(0.0050)	(0.0058)
Increase in non-defence government spending (%GDP)			0.012***	0.0073
			(0.0030)	(0.0054)
Constant	−0.0069	0.0062	−0.0083	0.0076
	(0.0085)	(0.014)	(0.0080)	(0.015)
Observations	105	105	100	100

Notes: Standard errors in parentheses. *p < .05, **p < .01, ***p < .001. All models estimated using Newey-West standard errors which are adjusted for heteroscedasticity and serial correlation up to the second lag. Descriptive statistics for control variables in Web Appendix 2. https://journals.sagepub.com/doi/full/10.1177/0038038519838752

Is Rising Unemployment Associated with Changes in Words Unrelated to Poverty?

It is possible that the association between unemployment and stigmatising rhetoric could be spurious and driven by some unobserved factor that affects the words newspapers use unrelated to changes in unemployment rates. To test our hypothesis, we explore this possibility to see whether our measure of unemployment is correlated with a set of placebo words that we would not theoretically expect to be associated with changes in unemployment. Using the same data and method described above, we construct a sample of 12 commonly used words in four categories: historical figures (Shakespeare, Mozart); past-times (football, cricket, opera, theatre); countries (France, Germany, the USA) and rooms of the house (bedroom, bathroom, kitchen). We hypothesise that changes in the

Table 7.3 Association between unemployment rate and placebo words adjusting for covariates, 1896–2000

Annual change in the average frequency of placebo words	(1)	(2)	(3)	(4)
Increase in the unemployment rate (log)	0.025 (0.017)	0.020 (0.014)	0.013 (0.013)	0.0031 (0.011)
Increase in the number of published articles (log)	0.71*** (0.13)	0.67*** (0.13)	0.81*** (0.10)	0.75*** (0.11)
Defence spending (%GDP)		−0.0018 (0.0012)		−0.0027 (0.0018)
Conservative party (ref)				
Labour		−0.020 (0.013)		−0.022 (0.013)
Coalition		−0.013 (0.017)		−0.022 (0.019)
Whig/Liberal		−0.0088 (0.016)		−0.016 (0.017)
Increase in public debt (%GDP)			0.00028 (0.00042)	0.00096 (0.00061)
Increase in tax revenues (%GDP)			−0.0016 (0.0027)	0.00076 (0.0029)
Increase in non-defence government spending (%GDP)			0.0012 (0.0020)	−0.0028 (0.0030)
Constant	0.0030 (0.0065)	0.012 (0.0090)	0.0032 (0.0057)	0.016 (0.0083)
Observations	105	105	100	100

Notes: Standard errors in parentheses. *p < .05, **p < .01, ***p < .001. All models estimated using Newey-West standard errors which are adjusted for serial correlation up to the second lag and heteroscedasticity.

logged frequency of these 'placebo' words should not be associated with changes in logged unemployment rates. If they were, this would raise serious doubts about our argument. Table 7.3 replicates the findings from Table 7.2 with logged mean frequency of placebo words as the dependent variable. In each example, the relationship is positive but statistically insignificant. Moreover, the size of the association is far smaller. For example, in the fully adjusted models (model 4 in Tables 7.2 and 7.3), the coefficient for stigmatising rhetoric ($\beta_{stigmatising}$ = 0.033) is 10 times larger than the coefficient for the placebo words ($\beta_{placebo}$ = 0.0031). These models increase our confidence that the relationship between unemployment and stigmatising rhetoric is not spurious.

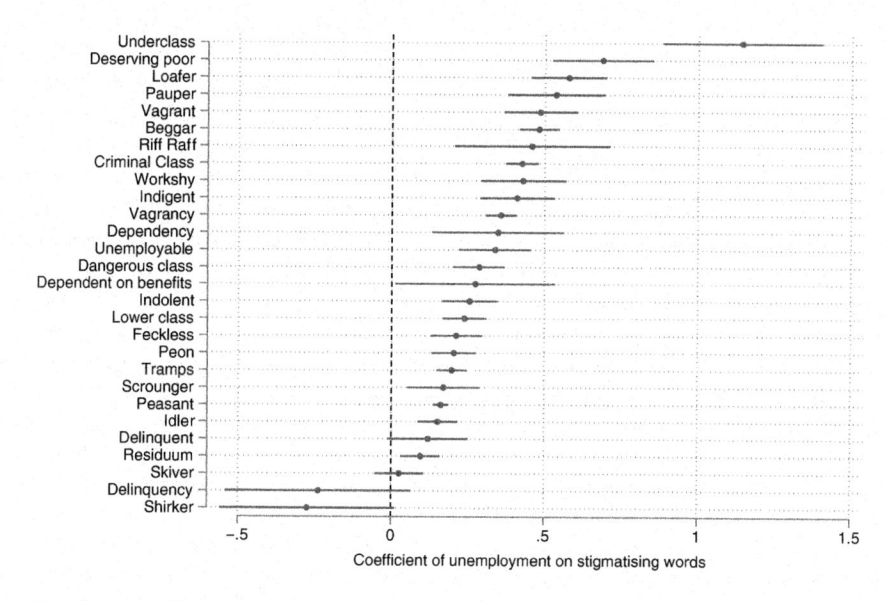

Figure 7.3 Association between unemployment and the frequency of stigmatising words or phrases, 1896–2000.

Are our results robust to measurement error?

Measuring stigmatising rhetoric about the poor by counting the number of times particular words or phrases is used will necessarily entail measurement error. In this section, we explore whether and how measurement error may bias our results.

We first investigate whether a few specific words are driving our results by estimating regression models where the frequency of each individual word is treated as a separate response variable. Figure 7.3 presents the association between logged unemployment rates and each of the 28 words we use to measure stigmatising rhetoric. Of the 32 words analysed, 30 (94 per cent) have positive associations with unemployment – meaning they are used more often in years when unemployment is higher. Moreover, the confidence intervals around the coefficient for logged unemployment do not include zero for 28 of the 32 words (88 per cent). The vast majority of the stigmatising words in our sample are used with higher frequencies in years with higher levels of unemployment, providing evidence their usage is driven by a common underlying process.

Frequency of word use is an imperfect measure of stigmatising rhetoric because all of the words used in this analysis are polysemic even if they are primarily recognisable as words associated with poverty. Ambiguity of meaning creates some uncertainty in our results: perhaps, the correlations we observe are driven by uses of words that are unrelated to poverty. To address this concern, we conduct a content analysis of newspaper articles in years where our regression model fits well (i.e. typical cases) and years where our model fits poorly (i.e. deviant cases). Typical case analysis is primarily confirmatory – exploring whether the words and phrases used in our measure of stigmatising rhetoric are, in fact, being deployed in a poverty-related context. Deviant case analysis, however, is particularly good at discovering measurement error or omitted variables (Seawright, 2016).

We identify two typical (1901 and 1991) and two deviant (1934 and 1980) cases using the absolute value of the residuals from Table 7.2 and we selected words for further analysis based on whether they were rising in that year or were unusually elevated in that period. We also chose a variety of words to ensure our results are not driven by idiosyncrasies of any particular term. In each year, we read the first 100 randomly selected articles or, if there were fewer than 100 articles, we read every article. The second author then coded each usage of each word according to whether the word was used in reference to the poor (if it was not, it was classed as 'irrelevant') and if the word was used in reference to the poor, we then determined whether the word was used in a stigmatising, sympathetic or neutral way. The first author also coded half of these cases to check intercoder reliability. We provide some illustrative examples of this coding in Table 7.4.

Table 7.4 Examples of newspaper word usage by relevance and sentiment

Stigmatising/negative	Sympathetic/positive	Neutral	Irrelevant
'A family of paupers, extending to three generations, has cost the ratepayers of the Paddington Union a sum of £3,000' (Hereditary pauperism, Daily Mail, 21 November 1901) 'Gangs of drunken beggars ... aggressive vagrants' (Menace of the beggars who strike fear in heart of London, Daily Mail, 17 June 1991)	'A pathetic letter, which throws a flood of light on the terrible monotony of life in a workhouse' (A day in a pauper's life, Daily Mail, 29 October 1901) 'An underclass is formed by a physical concentration of social problems' (The underclass is no illusion, Financial Times, 22 April 1991)	'Mr How is highly educated, and spends most of his time travelling about the country, mixing with tramps and other outcasts' (A pauper millionaire, Daily Mail, 9 October 1901) 'His chosen descent into the underworld of the workless and vagrant' (Making it seem virtuous to eat bacon, Daily Telegraph, 19 October 1991)	'The man found dead under a hedge ... and since buried in a pauper's grave, was John Howard Bullheid' (Solicitor's strange death, Daily Telegraph, 9 October 1901) 'Jimmy finds a vagrant who has moved in' (TV listing for Casualty, 8 November 1991)

The typical case analysis confirms our main findings, but it also highlights some of the challenges with this approach to measuring stigmatising rhetoric. Both 'pauper' and 'underclass' were almost always used in relation to issues of poverty, but this was not always true of 'loafer' and 'vagrant', where around 40 per cent of mentions were not directly related to poverty. Importantly, of the uses of 'loafer' and 'vagrant' that pertain to poverty, the majority are negative (40 per cent–50 per cent, compared to 0 per cent –18 per cent that are sympathetic). This suggests that increases in stigmatising words are a good measure of increasing stigmatising rhetoric and do not simply capture increasing discussion of poverty, in general, at times of high unemployment.

The deviant case analysis brings out a different but equally important perspective. In those years where our model fits poorly, there are a higher number (30 per cent–70 per cent of all uses) of 'irrelevant' uses of tramp (e.g. 'tramp shipping'), beggar (e.g. 'The Beggar's Opera') and workshy (e.g. the name of a race-horse). These cases fit our model poorly because the words are not being used to describe the poor at all, confirming the presence of measurement error in our dependent variable (Seawright, 2016).

Our content analysis of typical and deviant cases provides additional evidence supporting the 'Malthusian' hypothesis that stigmatising rhetoric increases when unemployment rises. Counting word frequencies is not a perfect strategy for measuring negative rhetoric. It clearly captures both signal (uses of the words in relation to poverty) and noise. The noise that we measure, however, seems more likely to be random (uses of the words unrelated to poverty) rather than biasing our results.

Discussion

This analysis draws on a dataset measuring how often five centrist and right-wing newspapers used stigmatising language about people in poverty across the 20th century. Case studies of media rhetoric have often argued that the poor are stigmatised more by the media during recessions because the media frame unemployment through a Malthusian lens (Harkins and Lugo-Ocando, 2016). Consistent with this argument, we find that when unemployment increases so too does the frequency of stigmatising rhetoric about the poor. This association is not explained by other political, economic or fiscal variables. Our content analysis of articles suggests that the words we selected are used in a predominantly stigmatising or negative way in years where unemployment is increasing.

Stigma and attitudes towards people on benefits

One possible consequence of the recurrent stigmatisation of the poor is its effect on public attitudes towards people in poverty and welfare recipients. Media

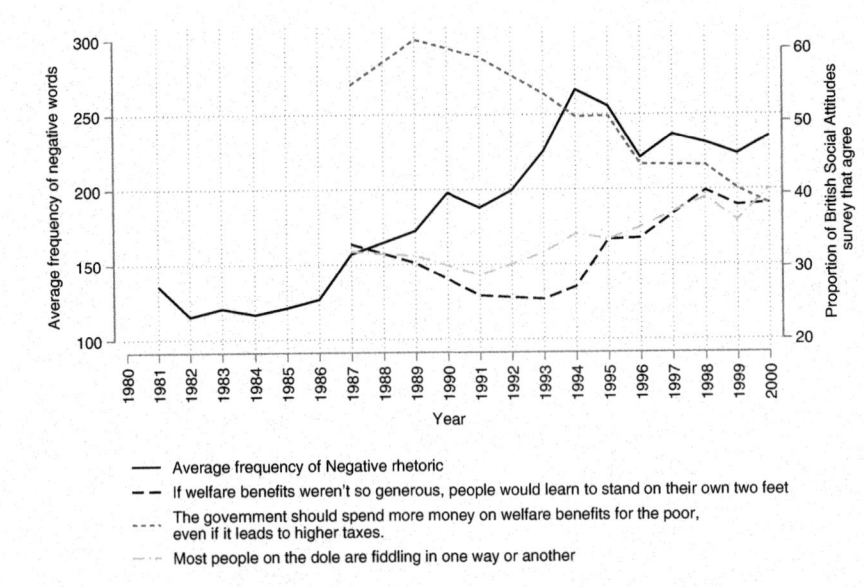

Figure 7.4 Trends in the frequency of stigmatising rhetoric and welfare attitudes in the UK.

Note: Public opinion data from the British Social Attitudes Survey 1987–2000.

framings have a great deal of power to 'construct' and 'normalise' certain ways of viewing poverty (Gamson et al., 1992). Unfortunately, data on public opinion towards welfare is too sparse before the 1980s to systematically investigate whether shifts in media rhetoric influenced attitudes (Hudson et al., 2016). Looking just at attitudinal shifts towards welfare recipients since the start of the British Social Attitudes Survey (covering 1987–2000), we find increasing stigmatising rhetoric about welfare recipients in the media during the late 1980s and 1990s appears to have preceded increasingly negative social attitudes (Figure 7.4). This trend is consistent with a wide body of empirical evidence documenting the effect of the media on attitudes (King et al., 2017) and political outcomes, like voting (Reeves et al., 2016).

Causality, mechanisms and media production

The temporal reach of our analysis allows us to avoid relying on case studies of specific periods when media stigmatisation of the poor was highly salient. Our modelling attempts to address both long-term confounding through first differencing and short-term confounding through our control variables – a strategy which is reinforced by our placebo analyses. However, we are still cautious about a causal interpretation of our results, in part, because of the usual difficulties involved in causal inference from observational data but also because the account we provide does not fully specify or test the mechanisms involved in producing articles about people in poverty. The content and tone of newspaper articles are determined by a complex set of interactions among journalists, editors, newspaper proprietors and the perceived or actual response of readers; these are processes that our results do not address (Gamson et al., 1992; Golding and Middleton, 1982; Herman and Chomsky, 1994).

An additional reason for caution is that our theory does not fully account for those periods when the relationship between unemployment and stigmatising rhetoric weakens. When unemployment is already very high (e.g. the 1930s and 1980s), then further increases in joblessness do not necessarily lead to more stigmatising language. One possible explanation is that structural understandings of poverty may become more plausible in periods when unemployment is exceptionally high and it becomes difficult to blame the moral failings of the unemployed. It is also possible the economic situation of journalists might affect the content of their articles. If journalists become at particular risk of losing their jobs during extremely deep recessions, they might become more sympathetic towards the poor.

Given these caveats, we argue future research should trace how processes of media production affect the way people in poverty are presented. This work could deploy detailed discourse analysis or archival research to unpick how actors such as proprietors or editors shape journalistic decisions about how to cover stories about poverty and how they respond to changing economic conditions (Baker, 2007).

History, context and ideational embeddedness

One insight we gain from our historical approach is the degree to which Malthusian explanations of poverty have become 'ideationally embedded' in British politics and culture (Somers and Block, 2005). The very fact that we observe a relatively stable association between rising unemployment and the frequency of stigmatising rhetoric is indicative of how particular ideational regimes are redeployed to 'construct, ... explain, and normalise market processes', particularly in moments of 'crisis' when the logic of Malthusianism might be dislodged by some other 'more compelling public narrative' (Somers and Block, 2005: 264, 271). For example, the experience of personal or family unemployment may lead individuals to support greater redistribution if they are not countered by a narrative that blames the crisis on the immoral behaviour of the poor. The ideational embeddedness of Malthusian ideas may help us explain why people living in poverty deploy stigmatising language themselves: their interpretation of the social world is framed by, and draws on, the same set of narratives, symbols and discourses.

Our article has broader theoretical relevance beyond poverty stigma because it provides an account of the conditions under which deeply embedded cultural understandings are differentially activated when they resonate with the structural context. This theoretical apparatus, when combined with our long historical focus, might prove useful for understanding the resurgence of anti-immigrant sentiment and nationalism in the press, and how these trends may reflect longer processes connected with imperialism, decolonisation and mass immigration to the UK (Bonikowski, 2017).

Limitations

Error in our measure of stigmatising rhetoric is a limitation of our analysis. There will be occasions when we count the usage of a word as 'stigmatising' even though it is being used in another context; this issue is exacerbated by the way that the language used to talk about poverty changes over time. However, our content analysis suggested that measurement error predominantly occurred in years where model fit was poor, implying that error in our measure of stigmatising language likely undermines our ability to observe a relationship between economic conditions and stigmatising rhetoric. Another concern is the generalisability of our results, which are limited because the archive used in our analysis only provides access to a set of centrist and right-wing publications. We cannot draw any conclusions about how left-wing papers respond to rising unemployment. We are also unable to address the extent to which journalists are responding to the attitudes of their readers. While we cannot rule out this possibility entirely, it is unlikely during the first three-quarters of the 20th century because newspapers did not have access to regular and consistent polling data on the attitudes of their readers towards welfare recipients (Hudson et al., 2016). This may change in the future as such data have now become far more readily available.

Conclusion

The rise in stigmatising media rhetoric about the poor following the Great Recession was consistent with a pattern we observe across the 20th century: as unemployment increases, so does newspaper stigmatisation of the poor. Although our data end during the earliest years of New Labour, there is little reason to expect that much has changed since then. The Blair government presented itself as no soft touch on welfare, a trend that was only amplified by the Conservative-led coalition.

The Cameron government attacked 'scroungers' and 'skivers', language that was also picked up by newspapers (Jensen and Tyler, 2015). The phenomenon of 'poverty porn' too is symptomatic of the ideational embeddedness of Malthusian ideas, revealing how producers, viewers and, to some extent, subjects of these 'documentaries' draw on and reproduce these narratives (Jensen, 2014). These ideas are deeply rooted in the British cultural imagination and so such language will return in the future, likely in a different form, but with the same purpose of 'holding dependent poverty disgraceful' (Malthus, 2008: III.VI.5). Though the specific words used might vary, the rhetoric of recessions among centre-right British newspapers is unlikely to change in the near future.

Appendix: Replication materials

The data and code to replicate the analysis is available here: https://github.com/asreeves/ rhetoric-recessions.

References

Baker CE (2007) *Media Concentration and Democracy: Why Ownership Matters*. Cambridge: Cambridge University Press.

Benford RD and Snow DA (2000) Framing processes and social movements: An overview and assessment. *Annual Review of Sociology* 26: 611–639.

Bonikowski B (2017) Ethno-nationalist populism and the mobilization of collective resentment. *British Journal of Sociology* 68(S1): 181–213.

Bourdieu P (1998) *Acts of Resistance: Against the New Myths of Our Time*. Cambridge: Polity.

Couldry N and Hepp A (2016) *The Mediated Construction of Reality*. Cambridge: Polity Press.

Day G (2001) *Class*. London: Routledge.

Deacon A (1976) *In Search of the Scrounger: The Administration of Unemployment Insurance in Britain, 1920–1931*. London: Bell for the Social Administration Research Trust.

Drage G (1894) *The Unemployed*. London: Macmillan.

Gamson WA (1992) *Talking Politics*. Cambridge: Cambridge University Press.

Gamson WA and Lasch KE (1983) The political culture of social welfare policy. In: Spiro SE and Yuchtman-Yaar E (eds) *Evaluating the Welfare State: Social and Political Perspectives*. London: Academic Press, 397–415.

Gamson WA, Croteau D, Hoynes W, et al. (1992) Media images and the social construction of reality. *Annual Review of Sociology* 18: 373–393.

Gilens M (1996) Race and poverty in America: Public misperceptions and the American news media. *The Public Opinion Quarterly* 60(4): 515–541.

Golding P and Middleton S (1982) *Images of Welfare: Press and Public Attitudes to Poverty*. Oxford: M Robertson.

Harkins S and Lugo-Ocando J (2016) How Malthusian ideology crept into the newsroom: British tabloids and the coverage of the 'underclass'. *Critical Discourse Studies* 13(1): 78–93.

Herman ES and Chomsky N (1994) *Manufacturing Consent: The Political Economy of the Mass Media*. London: Vintage.

Hudson J, Lunt N, Hamilton C, et al. (2016) Nostalgia narratives? Pejorative attitudes to welfare in historical perspective: Survey evidence from Beveridge to the British Social Attitudes Survey. *Journal of Poverty and Social Justice* 24(3): 227–243.

Jensen T (2014) Welfare commonsense, poverty porn and doxosophy. *Sociological Research Online* 19(3): 3.

Jensen T and Tyler I (2015) 'Benefits broods': The cultural and political crafting of anti-welfare commonsense. *Critical Social Policy* 35(4): 470–491.

King G, Schneer B and White A (2017) How the news media activate public expression and influence national agendas. *Science* 358(6364): 776–780.

Lister R (2015) 'To count for nothing': Poverty beyond the statistics. *Journal of the British Academy* 3: 139–165.

Macdonald R, Shildrick T and Furlong A (2014) In search of 'intergenerational cultures of worklessness': Hunting the Yeti and shooting zombies. *Critical Social Policy* 34(2): 199–220.

McKendrick JH, Sinclair S, Irwin A, et al. (2008) *The Media, Poverty and Public Opinion in the UK*. New York: Joseph Rowntree Foundation.

Macnicol J (1987) In pursuit of the underclass. *Journal of Social Policy* 16(3): 293–318.

Macnicol J (1998) Perspectives on the idea of an 'underclass'. In: Edwards J and Revauger J-P (eds) *Discourses on Inequality in France and Britain*. Aldershot: Ashgate, 161–174.

Malthus T (2008) *An Essay on the Principle of Population*. Ed. Gilbert G. Oxford: Oxford University Press.

Misra J, Moller S and Karides M (2003) Envisioning dependency: Changing media depictions of welfare in the 20th century. *Social Problems* 50(4): 482–504.

Mitchell B (2007) *International Historical Statistics 1750–2005: Europe*. Basingstoke: Palgrave Macmillan.

Polanyi K (2002) *The Great Transformation: The Political and Economic Origins of Our Time*. Boston, MA: Beacon Press.

Reeves A and De Vries R (2016) Does media coverage influence public attitudes towards welfare recipients? The impact of the 2011 English riots. *British Journal of Sociology* 67(2): 281–306.

Reeves A, McKee M and Stuckler D (2016) 'It's The Sun Wot Won It': Evidence of media influence on political attitudes and voting from a UK quasi-natural experiment. *Social Science Research* 56: 44–57.

Rose M and Baumgartner FR (2013) Framing the poor: Media coverage and U.S. poverty policy, 1960–2008. *Policy Studies Journal* 41(1): 22–53.

Seawright J (2016) The case for selecting cases that are deviant or extreme on the independent variable. *Sociological Methods and Research* 45(3): 493–525.

Shildrick T and MacDonald R (2013) Poverty talk: How people experiencing poverty deny their poverty and why they blame 'the poor'. *The Sociological Review* 61(2): 285–303.

Somers MR and Block F (2005) From poverty to perversity: Ideas, markets, and institutions over 200 years of welfare debate. *American Sociological Review* 70(2): 260–287.

Thomas R and Dimsdale N (2016) Three centuries of data – version 3.0. Bank of England. Available at: http://www.bankofengland.co.uk/research/Pages/onebank/threecenturies.aspx.

Tyler I (2008) 'Chav mum chav scum'. *Feminist Media Studies* 8(1): 17–34.

Tyler I (2013) *Revolting Subjects: Social Abjection and Resistance in Neoliberal Britain*. London: Zed Books.

Van Oorschot W (2006) Making the difference in social Europe: Deservingness perceptions among citizens of European welfare states. *Journal of European Social Policy* 16(1): 23–42.

Welshman J (2007) *Underclass: A History of the Excluded, 1880–2000*. London: Continuum International Publishing.

8 Factual television in the UK

The rich, the poor and inequality

Joanna Mack

One of the functions of factual television is to provide information on the nature of society and the tools by which to understand it. Yet, one of the most fundamental changes of the last 40 years – the sharp rise in inequality – has rarely been examined in any depth. There has been the occasional one-off documentary on the impact of inequality on health or social mobility, but there has been no major series. While factual television in Britain has covered the two opposite ends of the inequality spectrum, the poor and the rich, it has not been a part of a debate on inequality but presented as independent phenomena.

In this chapter, I will be looking at how factual television has framed debate about inequality over the last 40 years by examining the output of documentaries, educational programmes, current affairs and newer forms of informational programming with a more entertainment-orientated focus and by drawing on my own experience in making programmes for broadcast television. Using the documentary *Breadline Britain* as a case study, I trace political and economic developments and commercial imperatives of the past four decades to highlight why factual television today is so peculiarly prone to de-contextualisation.

Highlighting injustice

Television documentaries have been a strength of British television and have a distinguished record of highlighting the injustice of poverty. Channel 4's *Growing Up Poor: Britain's Breadline Kids*, transmitted in December 2019, is a recent and powerful example. The film focused on three children living in poverty and their daily struggles. It did what television can do really well: tell people's stories, give people a voice – in this case, the children themselves – and provide a sympathetic understanding of the consequences of poverty for viewers who have not experienced it first hand.

While *Growing Up Poor* contained some facts and figures, there was, however, no explicit analysis and the focus was instead on individual stories. Poverty was, therefore, seen primarily through the lens of those featured in this film, and it could be seen as the result of divorce, domestic violence and bereavement, compounded by failures in the benefit system.

DOI: 10.4324/9781003104476-11

The genre can, and does, point to underlying structural causes of poverty through its use of context. In *A Northern Soul* (transmitted on BBC2 in November 2018), the director Sean McAllister returns to his hometown, Hull, where he encounters Steve, a struggling warehouse worker with a dream to take hip-hop music to disadvantaged kids through his Beats Bus. McAllister set out to tell the story of people who fall prey to a system over which they have no control, showing how debt, low pay and insecure work restrict opportunities (Morris, 2018). By allowing the main protagonist to tell his story in depth, and with dignity and respect, the programme achieves this aim, and powerfully so. Poverty is seen as the result of structural, not individual, failure.

There is a tension, however, in documentary-style television between being compelling and accessible, on the one hand, and providing analysis and explanation, on the other hand. Not surprisingly, *A Northern Soul* does not incorporate an analysis of the economic and social changes that have resulted in a country where low pay and insecure work are endemic; nor *Growing Up Poor* of how political choices have resulted in a social security system which is less protective of the most vulnerable. It would slow down the narrative and the films would not work so well on the emotional level that television operates on so successfully.

In addition, today's programme-makers often shy away from the politics of poverty. In June 2019, the Sheffield International Documentary Festival ran a session on "Poverty in the UK: how to tell stories that inspire change". The session kicked off with Abigail Scott Paul of the Joseph Rowntree Foundation arguing that "presentations of poverty that use politicised language really turn off those audiences that are not warm to the issue … it evokes this really dangerous reaction in the Daily Mail", a sentiment echoed by Daniel Horan, head of factual programming at Channel 4, who stated that his concern when commissioning programmes was how "to get the Daily Mail or the Sun reader or the Telegraph" (Sheffield Doc/Fest, 2019). While there was a recognition of the need to provide background context, the recommendation of the panel was clear: avoid politicising poverty.

But when the makers of television programmes routinely self-censor political explanations, and if the background context provided remains at a superficial level, viewers risk seeing poverty as a kind of "orphaned" phenomenon. They are left with no clear political understanding of the causes of poverty and why it has risen in recent years, nor of the kinds of change needed to tackle poverty. This problem is not specific to television. Across all media, poverty is rarely explored in any depth, with little critique of the role of the present economic system in its creation (McKendrick et al., 2008; Redden, 2011; Chauhan and Foster, 2014).

But is there something about television that makes it particularly prone to this sort of de-contextualisation?

This concern can be traced back to 1975 when John Birt and Peter Jay, two senior figures at ITV's London Weekend Television (LWT), one of the regional companies that constituted what was then the ITV franchise, described television as having a "bias against understanding" (Public Interest Investigations, 2010). In a series of articles in *The Times* they argued, among other things, that features, being determined by the "film-making imperative" of narrative storytelling, failed to present the bigger picture (Birt, 1975). They wanted factual television to be driven by "a mission to explain".

From 1979 to 1988, I worked at LWT in their factual programming department, and in 1982, I was asked to make a series of four one-hour programmes for ITV's educational output, part of the public service remit placed on ITV at that time.

Breadline Britain, a case study: part 1

In the general election of 1979, Margaret Thatcher and the Conservative Party had won power with their radical agenda to roll back the state and promote market forces, shattering the post-war consensus on the welfare state. By the early 1980s, the UK was in the depth of recession, and unemployment was reaching record levels with more than a million having been unemployed for over a year. We decided, therefore, that the focus of the series should be on "poverty".

When this was proposed, there were concerns that the subject of poverty would be "too political" for an educational programme (Browne and Coueslant, 1984). In Margaret Thatcher's view, shared by her party, "people who are living in need are fully and properly provided for" (Hansard, 1983b). Such a series was essentially questioning this. Standing by their decision, the senior executives argued that it was valid "to place the question of living standards firmly on the public agenda in a way that asked viewers to think about the kind of society they lived in and wanted to live in" (Browne and Coueslant, 1984).

Television, at this time, had a strong commitment to this public service ethos, on ITV as well as the BBC. The ITV companies prided themselves on being fiercely independent (Fitzwalter, 2008) and had an impressive track record of hard-hitting current affairs series taking on powerful interests, such as Granada Television's *World in Action* or Thames Television's *This Week*. The previous year, the BBC had transmitted a four-part series on the politics of poverty presented by Professor David Donnison (BBC Scotland, 1982). In the television environment of that time, while LWT was conscious of potential political controversy, this was never going to be a constraint.

In making the series, we, as programme makers, felt it critical that we did not impose our value judgements to define poverty and, in line with the culture of factual programming at LWT, we also wanted to ensure our work was based on current academic thinking. We decided to conduct a large-scale, face-to-face survey to find out which of a wide range of items people thought were "necessities" for living in the Britain, items which no-one should have to be without – and who could or could not afford these items. A deprivation index was calculated based on the numbers who could not afford items classed by a majority as necessities. Those in poverty were defined as those whose "enforced lack of socially-perceived necessities" had a pervasive impact on their lives; they were falling below the minimum standards set by society (Mack and Lansley, 1985).

This approach developed Peter Townsend's (1979) measure of poverty using an index based on relative deprivation by taking account of criticisms put forward by David Piachaud (1981) on the importance of choice in any measure of poverty, and by Amartya Sen (1983) on the need to take account of people's views to define deprivation. For a television audience, it had the additional advantage that it would chime with their understanding of unacceptable hardship, of what you need to live in society and, therefore, of poverty.

Breadline Britain was broadcast in 1983 on the network's prestigious noon-on-Sunday slot. At its heart were the survey's central findings that the public saw the necessities of life in relative – as opposed to absolute – terms and that 14 per cent of households (around 7½ million adults and children) were falling below the minimum standards as set by society as a whole. Through the lives of seven households, chosen on the basis that they reflected the survey's findings on the groups most vulnerable to poverty, it aimed to combine personal stories (the "film-making imperative") with analysis (the mission to explain). It explored, for example, the foundation and working of the welfare state, the deterioration in public housing, educational and health inequalities and the rapid de-industrialisation of Britain at that time (LWT, 1983).

Audience figures were good and feedback from viewers was positive (Browne and Coueslant, 1984). But, the real reach of the *Breadline Britain* series was not on its broadcast but through the extensive educational back-up given to it, provided because the series was part of ITV's statutory requirement to include "educational" programming. A free 20-page booklet (Mack and Lansley, 1983) summarising the results was sent out, on request: around 10,000 were distributed to individuals and organisations, including politicians, trade unions, church groups, charities, tenants' associations and so on. ITV support staff from each of the regions across the ITV network produced detailed study packs for their area and organised events. These included discussions in a wide range of centres – such as pre-school playgroups, unemployment centres, homeless hostels and adult education groups – and public meetings. There was an exhibition at Birmingham central library and much else (Browne and Coueslant, 1984). The programmes, which were cleared of copyright restrictions for educational use, were widely recorded for use in schools and colleges. There was collaboration with the Independent Local Radio Network (the radio equivalent of ITV), resulting in phone-in discussions at a local level.

This helped the series have a longer-term impact than the fleeting moment of a broadcast transmission. It helped move the political debate as to where the poverty line should be drawn. Back in 1983, the Conservative government dismissed its findings on the basis that this was just a relative measure and included as necessities items that, in the words of the Minister for Social Security, Rhodes Boyson, "50 years ago, or even 25 years ago, people merely aspired to" (Hansard, 1983a). But the public accepted that minimum standards should reflect contemporary not past styles of living, so while the core of items seen to be necessities related to basic needs – such as "a damp-free home", "heating to warm living areas of the home", or "two meals a day for adults" and "three meals a day for children" – most people also saw a range of contemporary items – such as a "refrigerator" or "washing machine" – as items that adults living in Britain should be able to afford (Mack and Lansley, 1985). As lifestyles change, new goods become critical for coping. And people also saw poverty as being about more than just subsistence: most people regarded a variety of social items – such as "celebrations on special occasions" or a "hobby or leisure activity" – as necessities. People accepted that everyone should have access to a certain quality of life. This held true across all social groups, including by political affiliation. In subsequent years, politicians of all parties, including the Conservative Party, have come to accept that poverty is relative to time and place (Mack, 2018).

Breadline Britain achieved its aim of providing a level of analysis to help viewers understand the changes taking place and encourage debate about it. But it was a product of its time. The ITV companies were cash rich, enabling a large resource commitment in its making. ITV also had strong public service requirements placed upon it. This was why, in a commercial environment, a series of that length and depth was made. It was also why the series had such an extensive educational follow-up.

But, by the 1990s, television was rapidly changing.

The marketisation of British television

Margaret Thatcher, throughout her premiership, wanted to deregulate British broadcasting and bring in new competitive forces, to break up the duopoly of the BBC (1 and 2) and ITV (made up of regional franchises). The first shake-up came with the launch of Channel 4 in 1982, a new public service channel funded by advertising and with all output to be supplied by a new sector of independent producers (Catterall, 1998) (Seaton, 1991). Overseen by the Independent Broadcasting Authority (IBA), the regulator at the time, its remit was to cater for "tastes and interest not generally catered for".

In the mid-1980s Thatcher tried – and failed – to shift the BBC's funding from the licence fee to advertising. By the late 1980s, she had turned her attention to ITV, announcing at a Downing Street summit in 1987 that ITV was "the last bastion of restrictive practices" (Bonner and Aston, 1998). Soon, government relations with the ITV companies hit a new low, after the production of a series of hard-hitting investigative programmes, most particularly Thames Television's *Death on the Rock* (broadcast in 1988, it exposed evidence that three unarmed members of the IRA had been shot dead by the SAS in Gibraltar). The government became determined to overhaul the system.

In 1990, the resulting Broadcasting Act was passed. This abolished the IBA and replaced it with two light-touch regulators, the Independent Television Commission (ITC) and the Radio Authority. It changed the system for the franchises for each ITV region. The existing system, where franchises were awarded to applicants on the basis of evidence of quality programming and strong financial controls, was replaced by blind, highest-bidder auctions to determine the winner (Bonner and Aston, 1998). This bidding system (in which Thames Television lost its licence) created a new generation of more commercially driven, more lightly regulated, franchise holders who, under the Act, were then allowed to merge – eventually leading to the dismantling of the ITV regional network of companies and the formation of ITV plc in 2005 (Brown, 2009).

In a move to bring market mechanisms into the BBC, the Act required the BBC to commission 25 per cent of its output from the new independent production sector that had developed after the launch of Channel 4, thereby creating an internal market where BBC production units bid against external companies. And finally, the Act also allowed for the creation of a new terrestrial channel, which, in 1997, was launched as Channel 5.

In the meantime, in 1989, Rupert Murdoch's News International Group launched Sky Television, which heralded the start of paid-for television. The new Sky service was initially unlicensed in the UK and to get round this transmitted from a base in Luxembourg via satellites – all unchallenged by the government (King, 1998).

British television had started its transition from being based on ideas of supporting an educated and democratic society to one based on "choice" and "consumer sovereignty" (Berry, 2019b).

Breadline Britain, a case study: parts 2 and 3

By 1990, I was running my own independent production company and, against the background of a sharp rise in inequality during the 1980s, I pitched a second series of *Breadline Britain* to LWT. By then, it was already a different television environment. Money was tighter, longer programmes were being edged out, serious programmes more marginalised in the scheduling. Nonetheless, LWT commissioned six half-hours, for a late-night slot on the ITV network. As was the case in 1983, the series would be based on a large-scale, face-to-face survey to find a consensually agreed minimum standard of living. This time the survey required additional outside funding, which we raised from the Joseph Rowntree Foundation (JRF).

Breadline Britain in the 1990s (LWT, 1991) was broadcast in the spring of 1991. It revealed a sharp increase in poverty: up from 14 per cent to 21 per cent of households. Apart from a booklet summarising the findings (Frayman, 1991), there was no educational backup. There was no longer a requirement for this and my concern, as an independent producer, was the next commission.

By the late-1990s, the impact of the 1990 Act was becoming clear and measurable. Despite the rhetoric of greater choice, in practice, the variety of types of programming was becoming more restricted: in particular, there had been "a decline in the volume of programmes relevant to making informed decision about political, social and economic issues" (Leys, 2001, p. 161). Investigative programmes, which require a deeper financial commitment, were less likely to be made, and in 1998, Granada's *World in Action* was axed. Independent producers had become more cautious, many were financially insecure. The sector was no longer a source of diversity but of a downward pressure on production costs through their employment practices, which was arguably Thatcher's aim all along (Bennett, 2015).

In 1999, the JRF funded a third survey of poverty in Britain based on the methodology developed in *Breadline Britain*, but by then, there was little chance of getting a series or programme based on its findings, even though the survey costs had been paid for. It was not "saleable" enough to pitch.

By the start of the millennium, digital television was taking off. Up until then, broadcasters had transmitted to viewers through analogue signals; moving to digital brought with it a vastly increased channel capacity. The number of channels, which had already expanded from 5 at the start of cable and satellite television in 1989 to 50 when digital television was launched in 1998, had reached over 200 by the mid-2000s (BARB, 2021). This segmented audiences, increased competition for viewers, decreased the revenue of existing commercial public broadcast channels, and opened the sector to global markets (Starks, 2007) (Cave, 2006). While regulation on public service broadcasters (the BBC channels, ITV, Channel 4, and Channel 5) to produce programming that has "educative value" and promotes "civic understanding" and "well-informed debate" remained (Communications Act, 2003), its enforcement was largely through self-regulation with a new regulator, Ofcom, acting as a backstop (Smith, 2006). The result was a further "serious loss of quality public service and original production" (Hardy, 2012).

The public broadcasting channels, faced with a declining audience share, looked to meet their public service obligations through new formats. Serious factual programming was going out of fashion: in was factual television as entertainment (Brunsdon et al., 2001).

Glamorising wealth

By the early 2000s, the top 1 per cent had doubled their income share from 6.9 per cent when Margaret Thatcher took power in 1979 to around 13 per cent (WID, 2019) (Atkinson, 2015). Letting the rich get richer had been the aim, said to be a driver of growth which would ultimately benefit the poor through a "trickle down" of wealth. This neo-liberal agenda, as it became known, was largely adopted by the Labour Party after Tony Blair took over the leadership in 1994; the party was, in the words of their chief strategist, Peter Mandelson, "intensely relaxed about people getting filthy rich as long as they pay their taxes" (Parker, 2009). In this new era, shows which glamorised wealth – whether it be the gaining of it or the spending of it – flourished.

From the mid-2000s, the idea of the entrepreneur moved onto mainstream British television. In January 2005, the BBC launched *Dragon's Den* (BBC2, 2005–present), swiftly followed in February by *The Apprentice* (BBC2 2005–6, BBC1, 2007–present), formats imported from Japan and the United States, respectively. Both series are based on the notion that anyone who works hard enough or has a good enough idea can get rich.

In *Dragon's Den*, a series of contestants ask a panel of multi-millionaires to invest in their idea for a product. It promotes the view that entrepreneurship is all about the pitch, about an individual idea rather than a collective effort – with the unspoken implication that it is to the individual that the rewards should flow. In *The*

Apprentice, presented by Lord Alan Sugar, contestants compete, in the original series, for a six-figure job in one of Sugar's firms and, in later series, an investment. Its essence is summarised when Sugar declaims: "I don't care what you do, clean cars, clean windows, whatever. Just get out there and make me some money".

By the late 1990s, a particular ideological view of business that saw it in terms of individual entrepreneurship had become mainstream. It was one in which, as Anthony Sampson argues, "the capitalist was reinterpreted as a heroic lifeforce, a bringer of growth and innovation and riches to others as well as himself" (Sampson, 1998, p. 169). Since winning the 1997 election, the new-look Labour party had promoted the "enterprise-orientated culture" and, in these commissions, the BBC was explicitly reflecting these aims (Kelly and Boyle, 2011); the programmes were seen as "exemplars of contemporary public service content" (Boyle and Kelly, 2012, p. 14).

As to the spending of wealth, the rich were projected as either philanthropists or just to be envied. In 2006, Channel 4 first aired *The Secret Millionaire,* which went on to run for ten series. The format of the show is that a millionaire goes incognito into impoverished communities and agrees to give away a slice of their money (a small percentage) to an individual or project that takes their fancy. Channel 4 described it as an example of "new formats and approaches being applied to important social issues, such as poverty" (Lygo, 2007). While the programme does bear witness to the divides in society (McKendrick et al., 2008), this "do-gooder" type of television essentially promotes the idea of a post-welfare state where individual generosity can solve problems (Ouellette, 2010). The show might make the millionaire feel better and might even help the chosen person or project, but the idea that the rich handing out a little bit of money is going to have anything but the most superficial impact on impoverished communities is simply absurd.

Then, there were, and are, the "lifestyle" shows. In 2011, E4 launched *Made in Chelsea* chronicling the lives of affluent, young people, living in West London. The participants admit to living off their wealthy parents and the show is little more than a parade of expensive fashion, beautiful locations, glamour, and vacuity. Ten years later, the show is still running strong.

Such shows have become a staple of broadcast television since the 2000s. They proved popular; like drama, they delivered characters, a story, and an ending. They were relatively cheap to produce, a matter of importance given the increasing financial constraints of the multi-channel era. They could be (and were) endlessly repeated. And, they were successful global formats (Boyle and Kelly, 2012). But, their cumulative effect was to feed into the idea that wealth is simply to be admired, to be aspired to. Such shows reflected, and re-enforced, the underlying values of a free market culture – the importance of individualism, the identification of self through consumption and the right to accumulate wealth (Philo and Millar, 2000). As such, they are cheerleaders for inequality.

During this period, there were very few programmes on poverty at all. Looking at all of the output of BBC's flagship current affairs series, *Panorama,* from the start of the millennium to the financial crash (BBC Panorama, 2000–8), there was one programme, in 2001, on debt. Searching the BBC archives for this period using the terms "poverty in Britain", apart from short items on regional news, chat shows and political discussion programmes, there is little: an episode on rural poverty in Wales in a series on BBC1 in 2000 called *The Real World*; a five-part series on homelessness on BBC1, *Britain's streets of poverty*, in 2004; and *Evicted*, a documentary on homelessness broadcast in 2006, also on BBC1. The only mention of poverty in Channel 4's annual reviews for this period relates to *The Secret Millionaire*. That is about it. This absence of programming is somewhat surprising, given that, in 1999, Tony Blair had announced ambitious plans to halve child poverty in a decade and, by the mid-2000s, it was already clear that, while progress was being made, more would need to be done to hit the target (Brewer et al., 2002) (Harker, 2006). Poverty existed in what the JRF described as a "media shadow", whereby systematic and cultural biases in the media led to little meaningful light ever being shone on it (McKendrick, et al., 2008, pp. 37–8).

It was equally rare for factual television to examine extreme levels of wealth. There was a *Panorama* in 2004 "Winner takes it all" (BBC Panorama, 7/11/2004) on the pros and cons of run-away wealth and a BBC's *Money Programme* "Superstar, super-rich" in 2007 on global franchising (BBC Money Programme, 2007). The pickings are thin.

It wasn't until 2015, in Jacques Peretti's BBC2 two-part series *The super-rich and us* (Peretti, 2015), that the policies that have brought the arrival of astronomical wealth were actually challenged. By then, there were high-profile books – from Wilkinson and Pickett (2009), Danny Dorling (2010), Joseph Stiglitz (2012) and many more – examining the detrimental impact of extreme levels of inequality and wealth on society and the economy. Factual television remained dominated by gloss about the glamour of wealth.

Austerity unchallenged

On September 14, 2007, Northern Rock, one of the UK's biggest mortgage lenders, failed. A year later, Lehman Brothers went bankrupt and the world went into financial meltdown. In the initial phases of the financial crisis, the media laid much of the blame on "greedy" bankers operating without control (Berry, 2019a). The idea of an "undeserving rich" whose actions damaged, rather than contributed to, British society gained currency (Taylor-Gooby, 2013). For a time, it seemed that the current economic system might be reappraised.

Indeed, there were series that examined the role the lack of regulation of the financial sector played in the crash, important issues that needed to be addressed (BBC2, 2009a) (BBC2, 2009b). But, the structural flaws in Britain's economic system with its dependency on the financial system were unexamined. There were no factual series tackling how widening inequality might have contributed to the failure: of how the growth of the previous decades had resulted in the very rich getting far richer with none of the promised "trickle down"; of how this linked into the stagnation in wages that lay behind the spiralling of personal debts and how these debts were, in an environment of weak regulation, exploited by the banks for their own enrichment and in such a risky way that it eventually set off the crash (Stiglitz, 2018).

To some extent, this reflected the lack of a wider political debate among the main established political parties (Schifferes and Knowles, 2014). But, factual television, unlike television news, has the space to step back from the immediate politics of a situation to provide a deeper understanding. It failed to do so.

The door was open for an opportunist re-writing of history. The Conservatives successfully turned public perception of the crisis from one of a failure of the banking system into one of a failure of government to keep government spending under control (Lewis, 2018). There had, indeed, been a rise in the government deficit; it was the result the subsequent recession not of earlier government overspending (Berry, 2018). This reframing of events was not true (Wren-Lewis, 2018a; Wren-Lewis, 2018b), but it was politically successful. Following the 2010 election, the Conservatives and Liberal Democrats formed the Coalition government and set about an agenda to cut government spending. That Coalition politicians pushed the line that state spending was excessive is, perhaps, not surprising. Their aim was a permanent shrinking of the size of the state and austerity provided the excuse (Tooze, 2018, p. 350).

Looking at factual programmes through this period, the need for action to bring down the national debt does not get questioned but "explained", typically by using household analogies for government spending, such as "maxing out" on the credit card – analogies which any introductory economic textbook will tell you don't apply (Wren-Lewis, 2018b; Krugman, 2012). The failure of broadcasters (which are held to higher standards than the press) to challenge this highly partisan version of events is shocking, a lapse of its public service obligations (Lewis, 2018). When, on rare occasions, academic economists were interviewed explaining why cutting the deficit would be counter-productive, it was presented as an opinion to be balanced by another opinion.

Simon Wren-Lewis has made the observation, in *The Lies we are told*, that "broadcast media impartiality was becoming a bias against knowledge" (Wren-Lewis, 2018a, p. 3). This goes to the heart of questions about the interpretation of "balance". Broadcasting regulation places a statutory duty for "due impartiality" in news reporting and over a series of factual programmes taken as a whole. This is extremely important and has, to a large extent, protected British television from the more outrageous biases and propaganda seen in American television, on, for example, Fox News. But what is seen as balance and impartiality is open to different interpretations.

If this is seen to be met by simply having one person on one side of an argument and another with a diametrically opposed view, irrespective of the accuracy and factual basis of their respective positions, then this is problematic. It runs directly counter to requirements for factual accuracy and can mislead viewers. The dangers of "false balance" are clearly seen in the BBC's coverage of climate change. Even when the fact of man-made climate warming had become uncontested among an overwhelming majority of scientists, BBC factual programming on the subject would give climate change sceptics (generally with no specialist knowledge) an equal platform with climate scientists. In 2018, the BBC admitted that it had got this wrong: "you don't need a denier to balance the debate", it, belatedly, told staff (Carrington, 2018).

The problem in the austerity debate was less a question of balance than a lack of balance: the anti-austerity position was seldom heard and, when it was, it was dismissed. The idea that Britain was overspending, that it needed to balance its budget and that there needed therefore to be cuts was taken-for-granted as the account of what had happened and what was needed. Many academic economists were arguing for the reverse: that higher levels of government spending were needed to secure employment, a productive economy and a return to growth (Nutti, 2013). But nothing of this debate got reflected in factual programming. Austerity was causing impoverishment, but the basis on which it was built remained unchallenged.

There was a "politicisation" of the truth so deep that it wasn't even seen as politicisation, a "cognitive capture" by the dominant political ideology (Stiglitz, 2014). For broadcast television, TINA (Margaret Thatcher's "there is no alternative") was alive and well. The ways these two interpretations of impartiality played out for global warming and austerity are perhaps unsurprising given the dominance of neo-liberal economics over the last 40 years. In both cases, the positions adopted by broadcasters reflect the interests of those benefiting from the current economic system. In that sense, there is no conflict of principle.

Benefit-bashing

With austerity unchallenged, the Coalition government immediately set out plans to cut £20 billion from working-age benefits (Browne and William, 2015). British television turned its attention to claimants with a plethora of programming reflecting the government's agenda that benefits were too generous, that living on them was a "lifestyle choice", an agenda that had already been taken up full-heartedly by the right-wing tabloid press (Taylor-Gooby, 2012) (Morrison, 2019) (Baumberg, et al., 2012).

In 2011, the BBC broadcast *The Future of Welfare*, presented by Radio 4's lead presenter on the *Today* programme, John Humphrys. Promoting the series in the *Daily Mail*, Humphrys talked of: "the predictable effect of a dependency culture that has grown steadily over the past years …. A sense that not only is it possible to get something for nothing but that we have a right to do so" (Humphrys, 2011). Following a complaint by the Child Poverty Action Group, the BBC trustees ruled that the series depended on anecdotal evidence, lacked sufficient statistical information, and that there was a "failure of accuracy" and a "breach of impartiality" (BBC Trust, 2013). The ruling was welcome, but the anti-benefit narrative continued. In 2013, the BBC transmitted *Nick and Margaret: We All Pay Your Benefits*, pitting "taxpayers" against "claimants". Critics at the time described it as playing into "the 'striver versus scrounger' conflict that this government has so successfully worked into the popular consciousness" (Porter, 2013).

In 2014, Channel 4 broadcast the first series of *Benefits Street*, a fly-on-the-wall documentary following residents of one of Britain's most benefit-dependent streets. Such documentaries could, in principle, tell stories about the participants which retained their dignity. This series was not one of them. It was edited to provoke a response and it did (Price, 2014). It was dogged by controversy, labelled by many as "poverty porn" (Jensen, 2014; Patrick, 2017) and alienated the participants. Any subtleties in its portrait of the participants were ignored by the biases of the tabloid press and its audience. It fed into the benefit-bashing rhetoric that was flourishing. It was recommissioned.

In 2015, Channel 5 transmitted a constant stream of voyeuristic programmes promoting the idea of a something-for-nothing dependency culture with titles such as *The Great Big Benefits Wedding: LIVE!* and *Benefits Brits by the Sea*. These programmes, like *Benefits Street*, fed back into the *Daily Mail*, *Express* and *Sun* and then onwards into social media where the initial framing of benefit claimants as cheats and scroungers became ramped up into hatred (Morrison, 2019).

Breadline Britain, a case study: part 4

In 2012, I approached ITV offering the results of a new research project, *Poverty and Social Exclusion in the UK*, investigating poverty using the method pioneered in the first *Breadline Britain* series back in 1983. It was a major, multi-university collaboration (of which I was a part) and was undertaking the largest-ever survey of living standards in the United Kingdom (PSE UK, 2012). In the aftermath of the financial crisis and with austerity beginning to bite, ITV were keen and proposed a special edition of their flagship current affairs programme, *Tonight*. It wasn't the level of commitment of the past, but a prime-time slot, nevertheless, suggested that poverty was coming back on the agenda. Indeed, in 2011, BBC1 had transmitted a powerful documentary on children in poverty, *Poor Kids* and, in early 2013, Channel 4's *Dispatches* tackled the failing disability benefits system.

In March 2013, the *Tonight* programme, *Breadline Britain*, set out the key findings (ITV, 2013): the proportion of households falling below society's minimum standards had doubled since 1983, up from 14 per cent to nearly 30 per cent (Gordon et al., 2013). During this thirty-year period, in some respects, living standards had risen, virtually everyone now had the kind of consumer items (such as a washing machine) that, thirty years back, Rhodes Boyson and the Conservative Party had scoffed at as not being essential for living in Britain. But what is needed to take part in society had also changed; for example, in 2012, "a computer and internet" – not even around for the consumer of 1983 – was seen by most people as essential for school-aged children. Those on lower incomes had not kept pace with these changing requirements, resulting in a sharp rise in relative poverty since 1983. But, the 2012 survey also found that there had been a rise in absolute deprivation compared to 1999, with higher percentages unable to afford many of the most basic of necessities: more people couldn't afford to heat their homes, or eat properly, and more children were living impoverished and restricted lives, missing out on educational and social opportunities (Mack, 2018) (Lansley and Mack, 2015).

The programme attracted an audience of 3.4 million and clearly resonated with ITV's viewers; the accompanying twitter feed was packed with sympathetic comments. Unlike the benefit-bashing programmes of this time, this programme sought to understand the structural reason why people fell into poverty – highlighting low-paid and insecure work, long-term unemployment, declining housing standards and the inadequacy of the benefit system. This framing was reflected in the viewer response.

As austerity began to bite more deeply, other such programmes followed: in May 2013, BBC1 transmitted, as part of its ongoing partnership with the Open University, a four-part series *Living with Poverty*, an exploration of contemporary poverty in different areas of England (Open Learn, 2013); *Channel 4 News* ran a series of extended feature items on aspects such as homelessness (Long, 2014) and foodbanks (Lees, 2016). But, these programmes remained outliers – and, although they exposed the consequences, none challenged the need for austerity.

A renewed focus on poverty

On winning the 2015 election, the Conservatives announced a further £12 billion in benefit cuts, hitting, as before, the poorest the hardest (Elming and Hood, 2016). The government also started to rollout out its flagship policy of replacing a range of benefits with universal credit and reduce, yet further, government funding for local authorities (National Audit Office, 2018). The warning signs that this combination was pulling families deeper and deeper into poverty were there right from the start: foodbank use was soaring (The Trussell Trust, 2017), life expectancy for the poorest declining and health inequalities widening (Marshall et al., 2019). The ability of the state to provide protection was being dismantled – and with devastating consequences (Cooper and Whyte, 2017). When, in 2018, the UN Special Rapporteur on extreme poverty, Philip Alston, visited the UK, his verdict was damning: "the bottom line is that much of the glue that has held British society together since the Second World War has been deliberately removed and replaced with a harsh and uncaring ethos" (Alston, 2018, 2019). The opposition Labour Party, on the election of Jeremy Corbyn as leader in 2015, became far more outspokenly critical. There was beginning to be a groundswell against austerity.

And television responded. In 2019/20, *Channel 4 News* ran its own special, in-depth, series called *Breadline Britain* (Channel 4 news team, 2019). There were hard-hitting documentaries on poverty (discussed earlier) and, following the 2016 vote to leave the European Union, programmes exploring whether parts of the UK had been "left behind" in documentaries such as BBC2's *The Mighty Redcar*. But, as discussed earlier, these programmes de-politicised poverty.

The way television combines raising concern about poverty while de-politicising its solutions is illustrated by two shows that have been on air, annually, since the 1980s: *Children in Need* and *Comic Relief/Sports Relief*. These mega-fundraising telethons bring to the audience heart-rending stories of, for *Children in Need*, disadvantaged kids and, for *Comic Relief/Sports Relief*, people in poverty in the UK and worldwide. They raise substantial sums for charitable causes and, in many ways, illustrate television at its best, encouraging people to give their time and money to help others. But they airbrush the causes of need and of poverty. Why one of the richest nations on earth requires such events to meet children's needs is not asked (Ryan, 2018). Nor, more specifically, why child benefit has lost a quarter of its value over the last ten years (CPAG, 2021).

But, nevertheless, these telethons, like the documentaries, do highlight the injustice of poverty and that these programmes were all made for the public service broadcast channels, with their remit to operate for "public benefit rather than purely commercial purposes" (Ofcom, 2015), is significant. There was little elsewhere. Only a small percentage of the output of the commercial subscription broadcast channels is even factual television (Ofcom, 2020). The new subscription video-on-demand channels, such as Amazon Prime or Netflix, which are growing rapidly, do produce high-budget, high-quality documentaries, but these are designed to appeal to consumers across the world (Ofcom, 2020). Apart from the occasional buying-in of documentaries such as *The Divide*, a crowd-funded film based on Wilkinson and Pickett's book *The Spirit Level*, there is little interest in inequality or poverty, and even less if the focus is on the UK.

The challenge of the future

Since the start of 2020, Covid-19 has raged across the world. The UK has (as of early 2021) seen both one of the highest mortality rates and one of the most severe economic impacts in the world, impacts which have fallen heavily on low-paid workers, deprived communities and black and ethnic minorities (Brewer and Patrick, 2021; Government Actuarial Department, 2020; Johnston, 2021).

Could there be this time, unlike the financial crisis of 2007/8, a reappraisal of the social and economic system that has created such deep inequalities? Will factual television take up this challenge?

Over the last forty years, the mainstream broadcast channels, faced with greater competition and lighter regulations, changed: they produced less serious and more entertainment-orientated programming. This interacted with a changing political climate that became increasingly dominated by the neo-liberal consensus, resulting in a long period in which rising inequality went unchallenged. If the public and political consensus shifts to seeing a need to tackle inequality, then factual television has an opportunity be at the heart of this debate. It could, once again, ask what kind of society do we want to live in?

But then, the government, regarding the broadcast media as unsupportive, is eyeing up changes to its current structure and regulation to allow more right-wing partisan channels and less regulation. This does not bode well. Which of these alternatives wins depends, as ever, on political choices and on public pressure and engagement.

References

Alston, P. (2018). *Statement on Visit to the United Kingdom by United Nations Special Rapporteur on Extreme Poverty and Human Rights*. Geneva: United Nations.

Alston, P. (2019). *Report of the UN Special Rapporteur on Extreme Poverty and Human Rights in the UK*. Geneva: United Nations.

Atkinson, A. B. (2015). *Inequality*. Cambridge, MA: Harvard University Press.

BARB, 2021. *TV Since 1981*. [Online] Available at: https://www.barb.co.uk/resources/tv-facts/tv-since-1981/2004/reported/ [Accessed 8 March 2021].

Baumberg, B., Bell, K. and Gaffney, D. (2012). *Benefits Stigma in Britain*. London: Turn2Us.

BBC Money Programme. (2007). *How the Super-Rich Just Get Richer*. [Online] Available at: http://news.bbc.co.uk/1/hi/business/7118991.stm [Accessed 9 February 2021].

BBC Panorama. (2000–8). *Archive 2000–2008*. [Online] Available at: http://news.bbc.co.uk/1/hi/programmes/panorama/archive/2000/default.stm [Accessed 9 February 2021].

BBC Panorama. (2004). *Winner Takes It All - Transcript*. November 7. [Online] Available at: http://news.bbc.co.uk/nol/shared/spl/hi/programmes/panorama/transcripts/winnertakesall.txt [Accessed 10 February 2021].

BBC Scotland. (1982). *Hard Times: The Poltics of Poverty Programme 1*. [Online] Available at: https://www.youtube.com/watch?v=yXi0Dl_VggE [Accessed 19 February 2021].

BBC Trust. (2013). *Editorial Standards Findings*. [Online] Available at: http://downloads.bbc.co.uk/bbctrust/assets/files/pdf/appeals/esc_bulletins/2013/may_jun.pdf

BBC2. (2009a). *The City Uncovered*. [Online] Available at: https://www.bbc.co.uk/programmes/b00gtljy [Accessed 31 January 2021].

BBC2. (2009b). *The Love of Money*. [Online] Available at: https://www.bbc.co.uk/programmes/b00mq36b [Accessed 31 January 2009].

Bennett, J. (2015). From independence to independent, from public service to profit. In: J. Bennett and N. Strange, eds. *Media Independence*. Abingdon: Routledge, pp. 71–94.

Berry, M. (2018). Austerity, the media and the UK public. In: L. Basu, S. Schifferes and S. Knowles, eds. *The Media and Austerity*. London: Routledge, pp. 43–62.

Berry, M. (2019a). *The Media, the Public and the Great Financial Crisis*. Cham: Palgrave Macmillan.

Berry, M. (2019b). Neoliberalism and the media. In: J. Curran and D. Hesmondhaigh, eds. *Media and Society, sixth edition*. London: Bloomsbury Academic, pp. 57–82.

Birt, J. (1975). Broadcasting's journalistic bias is not a matter of politics but of presentation. *The Times*, 28 February, p. 14.

Bonner, P. and Aston, L. (1998). *Independent Television in Britain: Volume 5, ITV and IBA 1981–92*. London: Palgrave Macmillan.

Boyle, R. and Kelly, L. (2012). *The Television Entrepreneurs*. Farnham: Ashgate.

Brewer, M., Clark, T. and Goodman, A. (2002). *The Government's child poverty target: How much progress has been made*. London: Institute for Fiscal Studies.

Brewer, M. and Patrick, R. (2021). *Pandemic Pressures*. London: Resolution Foundation.

Brown, M. (2009). How ITV got where it is today. *The Guardian*, 4 March.

Browne, D. and Coueslant, P. (1984). *A Report on the National Backup Inititiative to the LWT Series "Breadline Britain"*. London: IBA.

Browne, J. and William, E. (2015). *The effect of the coalition's tax and benefit changes on household incomes*. London: Institute for Fiscal Studies.

Brunsdon, C., Johnson, C., Moseley, R., and Wheatley, H. (2001). Factual entertainment on British television. *European Journal of Cultural Studies*, 4(1), pp. 29–62.

Carrington, D. (2018). BBC admits 'we get climate change coverage wrong too often'. *The Guardian*, 7 September.

Catterall, P. (1998). The origins of Channel 4. *Contemporary British History*, 12(4), pp. 79–115.

Cave, M. (2006). The development of digital television in the UK. In: M. Cave and K. Nakamora, eds. *Digital Braodcasting*. Cheltenham: Edward Elgar, pp. 105–118.

Channel 4 news team. (2019). *Breadline Britain*. [Online] Available at: https://www.channel4.com/news/breadline-britain-2

Chauhan, A., and Foster, J. (2014). Representations of poverty in British newspapers: a case of 'othering' the threat?. *Journal of Community and Applied Social Psychology*, 24(5), pp.390–405.

Communications Act. (2003). *Act of Parliament*. London: HMG.

Cooper, V. and Whyte, D. (2017). Introduction. In: *The Violence of Austerity*. London: Pluto Press, pp. 1–31.

CPAG, 2021. *2021 Budget Representation*. London: Child Poverty Action Group.

Dorling, D. (2010). *Injustice - Why Social Inequality Still Persists*. Bristol: Policy Press.

Elming, W., and Hood, A. (2016). *Distributional Analysis*. London: Institute for Fiscal Studies.

Fitzwalter, R. (2008). *The Dream That Died: The Rise and Fall of ITV*. Leicester: Matador.

Frayman, H. (1991). *Breadline Britain in the 1990s*. London: LWT.

Gordon, D. et al. (2013). *The Impoverishment of the UK: PSE-UK First Report*. [Online] Available at: http://www.poverty.ac.uk/sites/default/files/attachments/The_Impoverishment_of_the_UK_PSE_UK_first_results_summary_report_March_28.pdf [Accessed 8 February 2021].

Government Actuarial Department. (2020). *Mortality insights*. [Online] Available at: https://www.gov.uk/government/publications/mortality-insights-from-gad-december-2020/mortality-insights-from-gad-december-2020 [Accessed 26 January 2021].

Hansard, 1983a. *Report on Proceedings in House of Commons 28 June 1983*. London: House of Commons.

Hansard, 1983b. *Report on the Proceedings in the House of Commons 20 December 1983*. London: House of Commons.

Hardy, J. (2012). UK television policy and regulation, 2000–10. *Journal of British Cinema and Television*, 9(4), pp. 521–547.

Harker, L. (2006). *Delivering on Child Poverty: What Would It Take?*. London: Department of Work and Pensions.

Humphrys, J. (2011). Our shameless society: How our welfare system has created an age of entitlement. *Daily Mail*, 24 October.

ITV. (2013). *Breadline Britain*. [Online] Available at: https://www.itv.com/news/2013-03-28/breadline-britain

Jensen, T. (2014). Welfare common sense, poverty porn and and doxosophy. *Sociological Research online*, 19(3), pp. 277–283.

Johnston, A. (2021). *Lessons Learnt - The Economic and Health Impacts of Covid-19*. London: Women's Budget Group.

Kelly, L. and Boyle, R. (2011). Business on television. *Television and New Media*, 12(3), pp. 228–247.

King, A. (1998). Thatcherism and the emergence of Sky Television. *Media, Culture and Society*, 20, pp. 277–293.

Krugman, P. (2012). The austerity agenda. *The New York Times*, 31 May.

Lansley, S. and Mack, J. (2015). *Breadline Britain – The Rise of Mass Poverty*. London: Oneworld.

Lees, J. (2016). *Food Banks: On the Front Line with Britain's Poorest*. [Online] Available at: https://www.channel4.com/news/trussell-trust-figures-foodbanks-one-million-people-blog

Lewis, J. (2018). Foreward. In: L. Basu, S. Schifferes and S. Knowles, eds. *The Media and Austerity*. London: Routledge, pp. viii-xi.

Leys, C. (2001). *Market-Driven Politics*. London: Verso.

Long, J. (2014). *Rubbish Tips and Mice: One Mum's Story of the Private Rental Sector*. [Online] Available at: https://www.channel4.com/news/by/jackie-long/blogs/housing-landlords-shelter1045

LWT. (1983). *Breadline Britain 1983 Transcripts*. [Online] Available at: https://www.poverty.ac.uk/living-poverty/breadline-britain-1983-2013 [Accessed 8 February 2021].

LWT. (1991). *Breadline Britain in the 1990s Transcripts*. [Online] Available at: https://www.poverty.ac.uk/living-poverty/breadline-britain-1983-2013. [Accessed 8 February 2021].

Lygo, K. (2007). *Channel 4 Annual Review of 2006*. London: Channel 4.

Mack, J. (2018). Fifty years of poverty in the UK. In: *Poverty and Social Exclusion in the UK: Volume 2 – The Dimensions of Disadvantage*. Bristol: Policy Press, pp. 27–55.

Mack, J. and Lansley, S. (1983). *Breadline Britain – The Findings of the Television Series*. London: London Weekend Television.

Mack, J. and Lansley, S. (1985). *Poor Britain*. London: George, Allen and Unwin.

Marshall, L., Finch, D., Cairncross, L., and Bibby, J. (2019). *Mortality and life expectancy trends in the UK: stalling progress*. London: The Health Foundation.

McKendrick, J., Sinclair, S., and Irwin, A. (2008). *The media, poverty and public opinion in the UK* New York: Joseph Rowntree Foundation.

Morris, B. (2018). *Why A Northern Soul Challenges Tv's War on the Poor*. [Online] Available at: https://www2.bfi.org.uk/news-opinion/news-bfi/interviews/northern-soul-sean-mcallister [Accessed 28 January 2021].

Morrison, J. (2019). *Scoungers: Moral Panics and Media Myths*. London: Zed.

National Audit Office. (2018). *Financial Sustainability of Local Authorities 2018*. London: House of Commons.

Nutti, M. (2013). *Austerity Can Kill You*. [Online] Available at: https://dmarionuti.blogspot.com/2013/07/austerity-can-kill-you.html [Accessed 19 February 2021].

Ofcom. (2015). *Public Service Broadcasting in the Internet Age*. London: Ofcom.

Ofcom. (2020). *Small Screen: Big Debate – A Five Year Review of Public Service Broadcasting*, London: Ofcom.

Open Learn. (2013). *OU on the BBC: Living with Poverty*. [Online] Available at: https://www.open.edu/openlearn/whats-on/tv/ou-on-the-bbc-living-poverty [Accessed 23 February 2021].

Ouellette, L. (2010). Reality television gives back: on the civic functions of reality entertainment. *Journal of Popular Film and Television*, 38, pp. 66–71.

Parker, G. (2009). A fiscal focus. *Financial Times*, 7 December.

Patrick, R. (2017). *Inaccurate, Exploitative, and Very Popular: The Problem with 'Poverty Porn'*. [Online] Available at: https://blogs.lse.ac.uk/politicsandpolicy/for-whose-benefit/

Peretti, J. (2015). *The Super-Rich and Us*. [Online] Available at: https://watchdocumentaries.com/the-super-rich-and-us/ [Accessed 8 February 2021].

Philo, G. and Millar, D. (2000). Cultural compliance and critical media studies. *Media, Culture and Society*, 22, pp. 831–839.

Piachaud, D. (1981). Peter Townsend and the holy grail. *New Society*, Issue 10 September.
Porter, A. (2013). Nick and Margaret: we all pay your benefits (and judge you while we do so). *Huffpost*, 26 July.
Price, G. (2014). Decoding benefits street: how Britain was divided by a television show. *The Guardian*, 22 February.
PSE UK. (2012). *PSE Research*. [Online] Available at: https://www.poverty.ac.uk/pse-research [Accessed 9 February 2021].
Public Interest Investigations. (2010). *Mission to Explain*. [Online] Available at: https://powerbase.info/index.php/Mission_to_explain#cite_note-5 [Accessed 28 January 2021].
Redden, J. (2011). Poverty in the news. *Information, Communications & Society*, 14(6), pp. 820–849.
Ryan, F. (2018). Children in need is wonderful, but we shouldn't need Pudsey to feed our children. *Guardian*, 13 November.
Sampson, A. (1998). *Company Man*. London: Harper Collins.
Schifferes, S. and Knowles, S. (2014). The "first crisis of globalization". In: S. Schifferes and R. Roberts, eds. *The Media and Financial Crises*. London: Routledge, pp. 42–58.
Seaton, J. (1991). How the audience is made. In: J. Curran and J. Seaton, eds. *Power without Responsibility: The Press and Broadcasting in Britain*. London: Routledge, pp. 212–233.
Sen, A. (1983). Poor relatively speaking. *Oxford Economic Papers*, 35(2), pp. 153–169.
Sheffield Doc/Fest. (2019). *Poverty in the UK: How to Tell Stories That Inspire Change*. [Online] Available at: https://www.youtube.com/watch?v=lpoLpP-pwsc [Accessed 28 January 2021].
Smith, P. (2006). The politics of UK television policy: the making of Ofcom. *Media, culture and society*, 26(6), pp. 929–938.
Starks, M. (2007). *Switching to Digital Television*. Bristol: Intellect Books.
Stiglitz, J. (2012). *The Price of Inequality*. New York: W. W. Norton & Company.
Stiglitz, J. (2014). Media: an information theoretic approach. In: S. Shifferes and R. Roberts, eds. *The Media and the financial crisis*. London: Routledge, pp. 140–152.
Stiglitz, J. (2018). *Ten Years Later*. New York: Roosevelt Institute.
Taylor-Gooby, P. (2012). *A Left Trilemma: Progressive Politics in the Age of Austerity*. London: Policy Network.
Taylor-Gooby, P. (2013). *The Double Crisis of the Welfare State and What We Can Do About It*. Basingstoke: Palgrave Macmillan.
The Trussell Trust. (2017). *Early Warning: Univeral Credit and Foodbanks*. London: Trussell Trust.
Tooze, A. (2018). *Crashed*. London: Allen Lane.
Townsend, P. (1979). *Poverty in the United Kingdom*. London: Penguin.
WID. (2019). *The World Inequality Database*. [Online] Available at: https://wid.world/country/united-kingdom/ [Accessed 25 January 2021].
Wilkinson, R. and pickett, K. (2009). *The Spirit Level – Why More Equal Societies Almost Always Do Better*. London: Allen Lane.
Wren-Lewis, S. (2018a). *The Lies We Are Told*. Bristol: Bristol University Press.
Wren-Lewis, S. (2018b). Why the media ignores economic experts. In: L. Basu, S. Schifferes and S. Knowles, eds. *The Media and Austerity*. London: Routledge, pp. 170–182.

9 The Attention Cycle of Income Inequality in the UK and US Print Media, 1990–2015

Martin W. Bauer, Patrick McGovern and Sandra Obradovic

Introduction

Why are people not angrier about rising levels of economic inequality? By the late 2000s, income inequality had risen noticeably within 17 of the 22 OECD countries, with major increases in the UK and the US (OECD, 2015). Yet, public attitudes to inequality have remained remarkably steady. Though the public generally accepts that income differences are too large, the proportion holding this view has not increased over time in either the UK or the US (Mijs, 2019). We examine elsewhere this absence of a 'Tawney moment', by which we mean 'the unambiguous public shaming of inequality as a social evil that calls for urgent action' (McGovern et al., 2020). With this term we are calling upon Richard H Tawney (1880-1962; LSE Economic Historian), who did exactly so with his 1931 seminal book 'Equality'.

How might we explain this paradox of stable social attitudes in the face of unprecedented increases in income inequality? So far, three explanations have been offered: political ideology, meritocracy, and ignorance. In terms of ideology, the argument is that the political centre of gravity moved firmly to a Neo-Liberal/Neo-Conservative right in the 1980s giving rise to Thatcherism in the UK and to Reaganism in the US (see Brooks and Manza, 2014 for a review). The second argument is that rising inequality is explained by the dominant public belief that, in our society, anybody's economic success has been achieved entirely on individual merit; anybody not achieving has only him or herself to blame (Sandel, 2020). Indeed, Mijs (2019 – his paper is republished in this volume) finds that the more unequal a society, the more likely its citizens rationalise success in these meritocratic terms otherwise known as 'The American Dream'. We must then assume that the UK is buying into this dream.

The third explanation is simply that a lack of wide-spread awareness of economic inequality, and of rising levels of income inequality inhibits public reaction. In other words, the public is unlikely to get angry about an issue when it barely knows of its existence. A sense of grievance is a requirement for social mobilisation. As one of the important sources of information about the economy is the mass media, an analysis of news reporting of inequality will help us understand the relationship between rising income inequality and unchanging public attitudes. Of course, the news sources that people consult have changed over time with broadcasting radio and television and, most recently, new Internet media all challenging the dominance of printed news. Even so, we note that many of those who consult their preferred social media sites for news still follow up with national newspapers to confirm major stories of mainstream news, either in print or online (Mitchell, 2018).

To date, the only substantial empirical study of news of economic inequality has been undertaken by the American sociologist Leslie McCall (2013) who investigated this very idea that Americans permitted growing inequality largely because they did not know about it. To test what she calls the ignorance perspective, McCall searched for articles that mentioned income inequality within mainstream US periodicals over a 30-year period (1980–2010). Significantly, she finds that coverage in *Newsweek*, *Time* and *US News & World Report* was not much greater in 2010 than it had been in 1980. However, she noted that coverage rose and fell in waves, peaking in the early 1980s and after mid-1990s. From this, McCall concludes, somewhat cautiously, that Americans did know about rising inequality, or at least those aspects that were easy to understand such as the growing gap between the pay of CEOs and that of an average employee.

Having established that income inequality was not a complete media blind spot, McCall then examined whether the surges in coverage were influenced by changes in economic conditions. She found that the rise in coverage in the early 1980s corresponded with a rise in income inequality, but the subsequent peaks and valleys in coverage did not mirror the shifts of inequality across the 1990s. Nor did the fluctuations in media coverage correlate with the business cycle as lack of interest in this topic was evident in periods when the economy was growing as well as in decline.

Following McCall, we examine how traditional print news media might play a role in understanding the puzzling quiescence of public opinion. Taking her lead, we test whether the mass media contribute to the ignorance hypothesis by choosing not to cover the topic. This need not be the result of a conspiratorial plot by right-wing media to keep the subject off their pages, but rather it may arise from a professional logic of chasing news value and journalists struggling to turn what is a relatively complex, abstract economic concept into attention-grabbing headlines (Hansen, 2016).

In any case, the social constructionist perspective on social problems reminds us that there are numerous economic and social conditions that have a negative impact on people's well-being, but only some are selected for presentation to the public (Hilgartner and Bosk, 1988). As it is not at all inevitable that a harmful societal trend will develop into a major public issue, the reporting during a 'claims making' stage is an essential first step on that journey (Best, 2008, pp. 18–19). By increasing topic salience, the media migrate an issue from the margins to mainstream public attention, thus rendering a problem less ambiguous, legitimate and part of routine editorial activity and public conversations, and spectacular events or scandals will help in that transition (Strodthoff et al., 1985).

Drawing on systematically compiled news data from the UK and the US between 1990 and 2015, we collected close to 60,000 articles to examine the extent to which the mass media took income inequality out of academic and policy circles and made it an issue of wider public attention. To do so, we first examine media salience over time. We then benchmark the level of attention to inequality against other issue cycles which have become recognised 'social problems' such as genetically modified (GM) crops and food and the Gulf War. We then compare similarities and differences in news coverage across the Atlantic. Finally, we consider explanations for the trends in coverage and relate these to the economic and political context before considering the influence of mounting academic research on the topic.

A corpus of news media coverage of income inequality

Drawing on a 25-year timeframe, from 1990 to 2015, we examine media discourse on income inequality over time to understand better the agenda-setting process in the public sphere. Media issue attention measures are one part of an agenda-setting approach to social problems, which assesses the flow of salience from mass media to public perception and ultimately into government action (McCombs and Shaw, 1972; McCombs 2004). Mass mediation inevitably reflects both real-world events, as in 'dog bites postman', and the news media operational logic, i.e. news values favouring 'postman bites dog'. News operations are coping with limited and shrinking editorial space, a 'herd mentality' among journalists chasing the same story in fear of being left out (FOBO), and uneven access to pundits and sources. Journalists rely on timely and regularly updated data streams on an issue. Equally, large-scale events, such as wars, political upheaval, epidemics, or pandemic health scares, can suddenly dominate the news flow (Luhmann, 2000). On any news topic, two aspects are key for public resonance: issue salience and framing. In this chapter, we focus on issue salience, while we focus on the framing of income inequality elsewhere (McGovern et al., 2020).

Given our focus on continuous long-term trends, we opted for legacy print news outlets rather than the more recent social media which came on stream massively only after 2000 and the Internet bubble. Our corpus of media outlets includes four daily newspapers (see Table 9.1).

The data were collected using the online databases *LexisNexis* and *Factiva*. For each newspaper, we initially explored the potential corpus size by searching for the term 'income inequality'. A codebook was developed with primary and secondary keywords, which guided the selection of articles. Primary keywords included 'income inequality' and potential synonyms (such as 'economic inequality' and 'pay inequality'), while the secondary keywords included words for closely related concepts (i.e. 'pay differentials' and 'wealth distribution').

Any count of 'salience' depends on the issue definition. Different sets of keywords spread the semantic net more widely on the 'issue'. Comparing across different criteria allows us to gauge keyword sensitivity of any count and to reach more robust conclusions. We use here two corpora, the full and the small corpus.

Table 9.1 Research corpus of print media, 1990–2015

News outlet	Print run 2013 (per 1000 pop)	Source	Items[Full corpus]	Number of words [1000s]
Financial Times (UK) Business	275,000 (4.35)	Nexis Lexis	14,976	9,995
Guardian (UK) Liberal	204,000 (3.23)	Nexis Lexis	20,752	17,832
New York Times (US) Liberal	1,865,000 (5.89)	Nexis Lexis	14,172	14,883
Wall Street Journal (US) Business	2,378,000 (7.52)	Factiva	7,321	6,679
UK + US pooled			57,221	49,389

Source: The print-run numbers are taken from the Audit Bureau of Circulations (UK) and the Alliance for Audited Media (US) for 2013. The general trend in print news circulations is downward for all outlets, in the UK and also the US by 2020 to about 50 per cent of 2000, which is only, in part, compensated by an increasing online presence of the same titles. In 2013, the UK population was 63.2 million and the US was 316.4 million.

Note: The print-run numbers are taken from the Audit Bureau of Circulations (UK) and the Alliance for Audited Media (US) for 2013. The general trend in print news circulations is downward for all outlets, in the UK and also the US by 2020 to about 50 per cent of 2000, which is only, in part, compensated by an increasing online presence of the same titles. In 2013, the UK population was 63.2 million and the US was 316.4 million.

For trend analyses, we rely on the restricted small corpus, and figures are indexed to peak year 2015 = 100. For reporting salience of 'inequality' in comparison with other social issues, we consult our full corpus. And for reporting 'topic salience', i.e. the ratio of specific 'income inequality' in the context of 'wider inequality terms', we consider the figures of the small corpus divided by figures of the full corpus (the overall topic salience of 'income inequality' is 10.3 per cent, which means we estimate that overall about 1 in every 10 articles on 'economic inequality' is specifically on 'income inequality'). Salience figures over time are further weighted against the entire newshole (i.e. running estimates of all news items per year and newspaper), and we report time-series indexed to the peak years (2014/15 =100).

1. *Full corpus (N=57211):* The full corpus includes all items retrieved using all 19 keywords. This corpus represents the wider semantic field of 'economic inequality'.
2. *Small corpus (N=5909):* The small corpus includes all articles with the specific keyword 'income inequality' only and comprises the more homogeneous set of topical items.

Results: the attention cycle of income inequality

Our analysis enables us to make three observations on changing media attention to income inequality. First, media salience rises significantly but unsteadily, and this contrasts with the steady increase in 'income inequality' and the academic attention to it between 1990 and 2015; second, the peak levels of media attention to 'income inequality' can be benchmarked on other large news stories on an issue cycle; third, the UK and US broadly move in parallel though slightly out of step over the years. We take these three observations in turn.

1   *The rise of income inequality, the steady academic attention to it, and the unsteady rise of media salience*

Our first observation combines UK and US inequality news to see if the coverage in our dataset is consistent with a 'hype-cycle' model (Van Lente et al., 2013). Figure 9.1 shows a stylised 'hype cycle' of public discourse around an emerging social issue. A hype cycle has an important agenda-setting effect; it moves an issue from a small group of key specialist actors working in an 'echo chamber' to the attention of mainstream mass media, effectively 'sounding the alarm' and drawing public attention to the issue. This creates a heightened issue awareness, which, in turn, creates a sense of urgency for political action (McCombs and Shaw, 1972; McCombs 2004). During the alarm phase, the general media exceed the trend of specialist outlets before falling back only to later exceed them again.

In Figure 9.1, we also report the trend in number of articles within the Social Sciences Citation Index that carried 'income inequality' in the title. We did this to see if there was a parallel movement in topic interest across academic and media circles. Over the observation period, we found that academic publications on 'inequality' increased exponentially ($Y = 3.1278\ e^{0.1346X}$; $R^2 = 0.92$).

Taking a three-year moving average across all newspapers, we can identify a bi-model cycle on inequality news: an initial wave started in the early

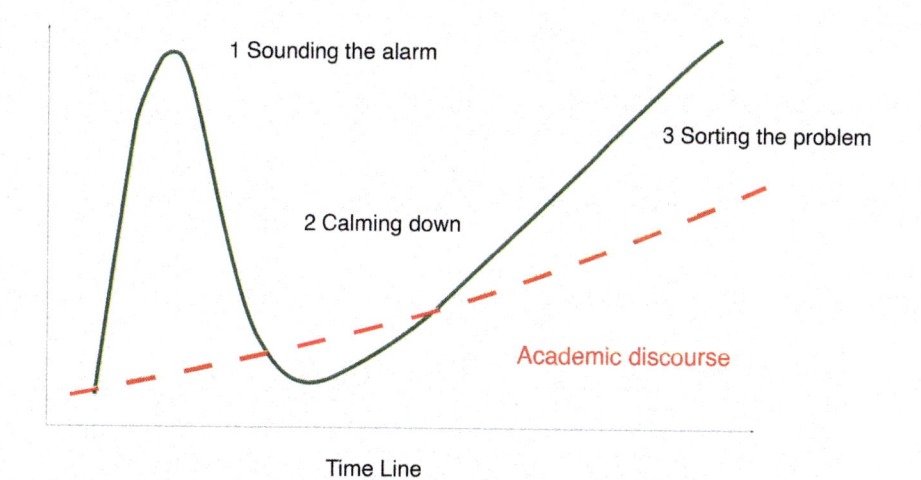

Figure 9.1a Public discourse in relation to academic publications, with the three phases of 'sounding the alarm', 'calming down', and 'sorting the problem'.

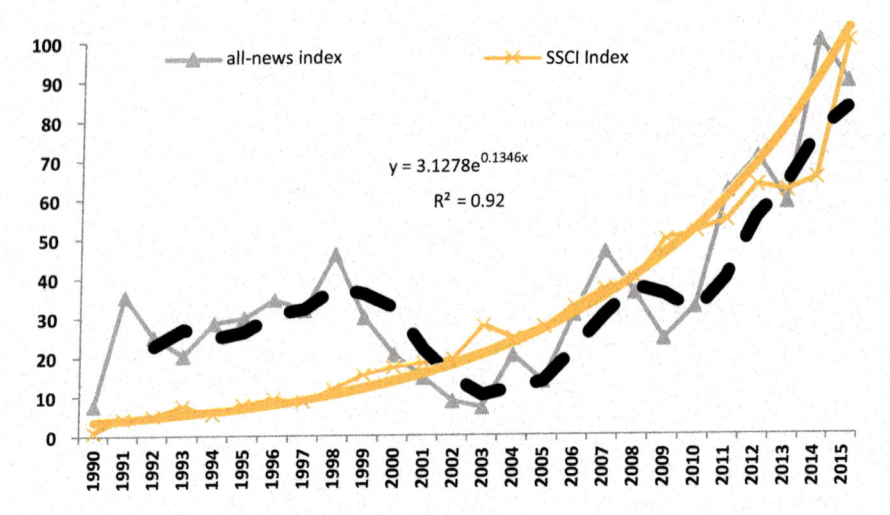

Figure 9.1b The growth of scholarly economic literature on 'income inequality' and combined UK and US salience of 'income inequality' relative to newshole.

1990s and peaked in 1997/98 before declining into the mid-2000s when a second wave emerges. This second wave took off 2005/6, stalled between 2008 and 2009 at the level of the previous surge, and then rose vigorously into the 2010s. Until 2000, media coverage of inequality is far above the trend in specialist academic literature, indicating the alarm phase; however, after 2000, the media coverage falls below the specialist trend and stays there over the rest of the period.

Overall, we conclude that inequality news between 1990 and 2015 in the UK and US is increasing and consistent with a bi-model hype cycle; however, it never reached its third phase of generating news coverage above and beyond the academic trend. Our observations end in 2015 on a peak, so we, therefore, cannot say whether this recent surge had reached its final peak or continues to date; this is a matter for further research to clarify. It is likely that the pandemic of 2020/21 created another surge in public attention to income inequality.

We have shown above that 'inequality' has clearly gained in salience in all newspapers. What was in the 1990s at most an occasional news item on a monthly cycle, is by 2015 clearly a regular news item on a weekly if not shorter news routine. These findings contrast with those of McCall (2013) in that we show a significant increase in the coverage of income inequality over the period (1990–2015). However, we can confirm, in convergent validity, the surge in inequality news in the later 1990s reported by McCall; most of the later surge that we identify occurs in the five years after her study ends (2010–15). What is also striking is that these waves of inequality news appear at broadly the same rhythm in both the UK and the US [see below].

2   *Benchmarking inequality news: how strong a salience compared to other issues?*

A second observation arises from comparing the peak of inequality news with other issue attention cycles over the same period. We ask ourselves, is the peak of 2015, which we recognise in the coverage of inequality, a massive peak or not? We find that in 2014/15, *The Guardian* carries about 2000 (92), the *FT* 950 (172), the *NYT* 1450 (526), and *WSJ* 650 (149) news items on 'inequality' (in brackets figures from the small corpus).

The most studied long-term issue cycle is probably that of the 'environment' (Djerf-Pierre 2013). Environmental attention saw at least four waves moving from water and air pollution (1950s) to over-population (late 1960s), to oil spills (1970s), to large-scale disasters such as the Chernobyl nuclear accident and Bhopal or Seveso type chemical disasters (1980s), and then via the ozone hole and global warming to present-day climate change debates (Bauer, 2015; Mazur and Lee, 1993; Tennant, 2012). This episodic pattern is consistent with Downs' (1972) model of an 'issue-attention cycle'. Lowe and Goyder (1983, p. 32) show that attention rose during periods of economic expansion and relative prosperity and responded to dramatic events (e.g. the drought of the summer of 1988). Critically, they emphasise the importance of the wider socio-economic situation that gives resonance to a topic when it emerges in the media. Similar attention cycles can be found on 'globalisation' (Fiss and Hirsch, 2005) and on emergent technologies such as 'biotechnology' (Bauer et al. 2002), 'nanotechnology' (Gaskell et al., 2005), and AI (Btesh and Bauer, 2019).

Considering the episodic nature of issue attention, our question must be: when attention about inequality reaches its peak, how high is this peak? Here, we compare inequality with other social problems. For instance, as shown in Table 9.2, evidence from the UK shows that climate change news might have peaked in 2009 with 4,217 items in the London *Times* (Tennant, 2012). Biotechnology reached its news peak in 1999 during the 'great food debate' with 1,666 items in the London *Times* (Bauer, 2015, p. 188), the coverage of 'the internet' peaked in 2000 with 7,329 items (average across three newspapers) (Bauer, 2015, p. 137).

Considering these UK comparators, 'inequality' falls far short of surges in news coverage of topics (see Table 9.2) such as the Internet, climate change, the Gulf War of 1990, or the credit crunch of 2008. It is, in fact, more in line maybe with GM food in the late 1990s if we consider the wider semantic field of the term [our full corpus]. Using the stricter net of a 'single keyword' [small corpus], 'inequality' only amounts to one-tenth of the 'Great Food Debate' of the late 1990s.

3   *Cross-Atlantic comparisons: business news versus general news*

Those familiar with the political scene in the UK and the US might be surprised by the broadly similar patterns of media reporting over time. After all, the UK has a trade union-funded Labour party while the US is the only advanced capitalist economy without a party representing the labour movement. Surely, the UK newspapers write for a more left-wing readership that distinguishes between 'socialism' and 'liberalism'?

142　Martin W. Bauer et al.

Table 9.2 Compares peak levels of media salience for different issues since 1990; the basis of comparison is the number of items in a single news source [citation sources, see text]. Bottom figures compare topic salience in four news sources overall, a ratio of 'income inequality [single keyword]'/'inequality' [19 keywords]

Topic	Single-source baseline	Peak year	Number of new items
'Biotechnology'	London TIMES	1999	1,666
'inequality'	**Full corpus**	**2015**	**Max. 2,000**
'Gulf War'	Guardian	1990	4,185
'Climate change'	London Times	2009	4,217
'Credit Crunch'	Guardian	2008	5,320
'The Internet'	Average GUA, Times, Telegraph	2000	7,329
News source	**Full corpus (%)**	**Small corpus (%)**	***Topic salience***
Guardian QUA [UK]	20,752 (36.3)	622 (10.5)	3%
Financial Times FT [UK]	14,976 (26.2)	1,537 (26.0)	10%
NY Times NYT [US]	14,172 (24.8)	2,946 (49.9)	21%
Wall Street Journal WSJ [US]	7,318 (12.8)	804 (13.6)	11%
Total	57,221 (100)	5,909 (100)	10.3%

Overall salience and topic salience

Might we, therefore, expect that the UK newspapers would, on average, give more attention to income inequality even if this rose and fell in a similar pattern to US papers? And, indeed, as shown in Table 9.2 above, 63 per cent of our 'inequality corpus' arises in British newspaper, and 38 per cent in US newspaper of similar orientation. Also, and as might be expected, the topic was much more in evidence in the liberal-left papers (71 per cent; *NYT* and *GUA*) than in the business press with (29 per cent; *FT*, *WSJ*).

The situation is, however, slightly different if we consider the topic salience of the term 'income inequality'. Here, the situation is exactly reversed as US papers carry 63 per cent of the coverage, while the UK shows 38 per cent of the material. This suggests, that in the US, the inequality discourse is dominated by 'income inequality' while this is less the case in the UK where the reporting beyond the term includes other forms of economic inequality (see Table 9.2).

This transatlantic reversal is also evident when we consider the trends over time. Figure 9.2 shows that topic salience of 'income inequality' remains between 5 per cent and 10 per cent of inequality news in the UK and the US; it then picks up (mainly in business news) to a new level of 15 per cent – 25 per cent, except in the *NYT*, where 'income inequality' becomes the prototypical inequality news with 45 per cent topicality by 2015.

Overall, we can state that 'income inequality' was more topical in US papers than in UK papers. The peak year of 2015, the *NY Times* carried 600 (47 per cent) topical items in a total 1,388 inequality news as compared to only 92 (14 per cent)

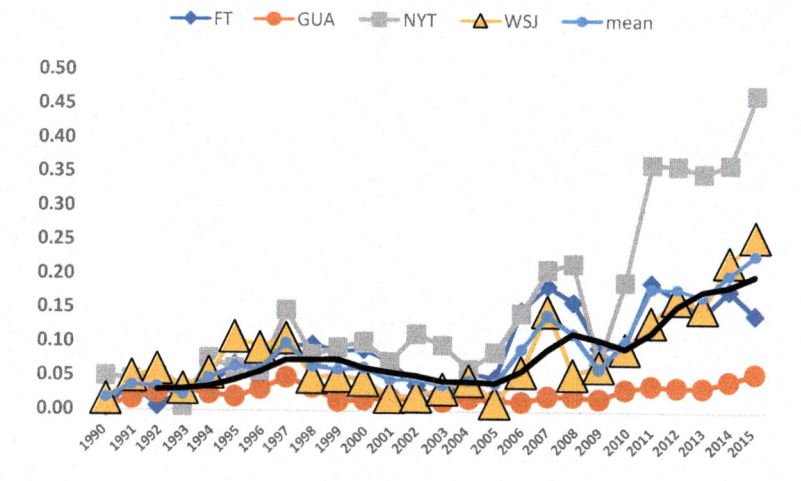

Figure 9.2 Topic salience of 'income inequality' as percentage of all inequality items in any one year and for all newspapers.

of 1,639 items in the *Guardian*. This is considerably less, even if we also consider that, in our estimates, the newshole of the *Guardian* is about three-quarters of the *NY Times*.

Comparing UK and US news surges

However, when considering the trend surges over time, the US mostly lags the UK as shown in Figure 9.3. The UK led on the issue in the early 1990s, only to lose momentum towards the end of the 1990s to the US media. The second rise in salience pre-credit crunch of 2008 occurs in parallel for the UK and the US, maybe with a short UK lead in 2004. The post-2009 massive increase in attention to inequality was spearheaded by the UK, which the US trend then followed.

There is only the short period 1996/97 when the US exceeds the UK relative coverage of 'income inequality'; the *WSJ* was pushing the issue and the *NYT* was following suit. This falls into the year of Clinton's re-election for a second term in office. In the UK, the salience responds to this US surge in the first year of the Blair/Brown Government of 1998, after which the issue salience declined. In 1998, Peter Mandelson, speaking as an architect of New Labour to US computer executives, had famously declared "*We are intensely relaxed about people getting filthy rich as long as they pay their taxes.*" Overall, we observe four surges of inequality news in the UK (1991, 1998, 2006/07, and after 2010) and three such surges in the US (1996/97, 2006/7, and after 2011).

Business vs general news outlets

Both in the US and the UK, the business news outlets, i.e. the *FT* and *WSJ*, were leading the surges in the discussion of income inequality. As shown in Figure 9.4

144 Martin W. Bauer et al.

'Inequality' news salience indexed at 100

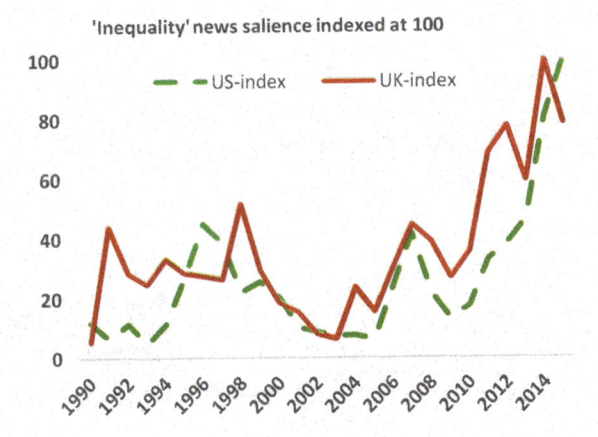

Figure 9.3 The surge of inequality news in the US and in the UK, indexed to the peak year.

'Inequality' news salience indexed at 100

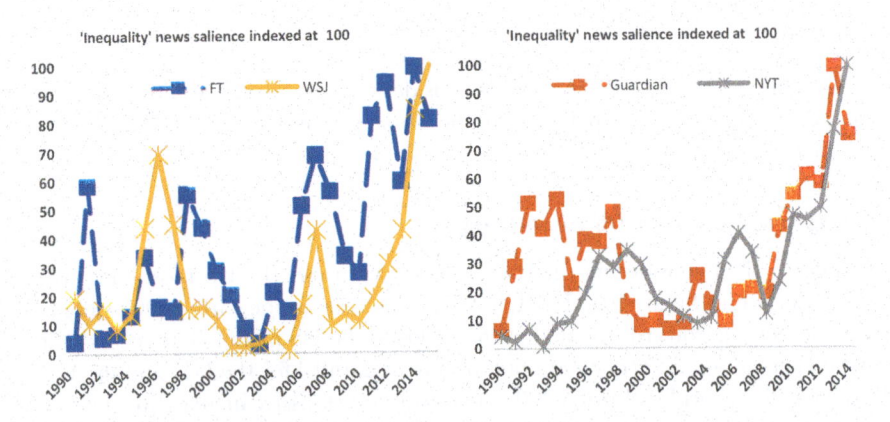

Figure 9.4 The surge of income inequality news in the US and the US, comparing business news outlets (WSJ, FT, on the left) with general news outlets (NYT, GUA, on the right) indexed to peak year.

over the period, the *FT* has seen four surges into the public debate over income inequality (1991, 1998, 2006–8, and 2011–12). The *WSJ* surges three times, namely, in 1995–97, 2007, and 2014–15. The running commentary in the general news in the *GUA* and in the *NYT* was following their lead after 1991 and 1996, respectively, and they all ran in parallel between 2006 and 2008 and again after 2010.

Explaining the changing media attention to inequality

We examine four explanations for these observations on the cycles, rhythms, and peaks in news coverage of economic inequality over the period 1990-2015: a mirror of shifting reality, business cycles, political cycles, and the news value of academic studies.

A shifting reality mirrored

How might we explain this surge in media interest over this period? For a topic like income inequality, it is always tempting to claim that it is driven by economic factors. An obvious proposition here would be that the increased news value is simply a direct response to rising levels of inequality in society. As inequality grows, so also does media attention and public interest. To investigate this possibility, we compiled data for the Gini coefficient for both the UK and the US between 1990 and 2015. We found that the Gini increased noticeably for the US across this period (41.8–45.4) but remained at roughly the same level in the UK (33.9–34.7). Even if the long-term media coverage had corresponded to the rise in the US Gini coefficient, this still raises the question of why there were fluctuations in the coverage of income inequality in *New York Times* and in The *Wall Street Journal*. To put it another way, rising inequality cannot explain rising media attention because inequality rose only in one of the two countries during this period while the media index rises regularly or stalls. This is consistent with a social construction model of social issues; reality is not a news value in-itself (Hansen, 2016; Hilgartner and Bosk 1988). News coverage depends on the regular feed of new data on inequality and academics and pundits readily available to comment on it. There is no evidence of routine institutional updates on such data that could rival how the IPCC informs the public about climate change.

Business cycle

Given that the economies of the UK and the US, along with that of many other countries, entered a major recession in 2008, we should consider the possibility that income inequality gives way to other matters when the economy takes a downturn. To address this, we undertook a simple correlation of the frequency of media coverage in each year with changes in the Annual Real Gross Domestic Product for the UK and the US. Here, the correlation was zero. Similarly, when we did the same correlation for the UK, the result was also close to zero (0.02). In short, the cyclical fortunes of the economy have little or no relation with the salience of inequality within the print media.

Political cycle

Another possible explanation is that rising interest in the issue is related to the political cycle. For instance, left of centre parties might be more likely to raise the issue of income inequality in the public discourse while in government. One can speculate whether the three phases we described earlier have anything to do with the electoral cycle. For much of the 1990s, the UK was still emerging from Thatcherism and a critical assessment of her legacy in terms of increased inequality was setting in; a similar discussion sets in with the Clinton Presidency after 1992. In the UK, the arrival of the Blair government in 1997 seems to calm the discourse of inequality. During the second phase from 2003 to 2008, Blair's New Labour are still in power in the UK and Bush Jr is President of the US; we think this phase was very much distracted by other matters, not least 9/11 and its aftermath in Iraq and Afghanistan. Phase three coincides in the US with the Obama administration and in the UK with the Tory-Liberal coalition of Cameron and Clegg.

To measure the impact of the political cycle, we conducted correlations that compared annual frequencies in articles with whether the Labour party was in government in the UK or the Democrats in the Presidency in the US. The results suggest some support for the US (bi-serial correlation r=0.38) but not for the UK (r = -0.64). Regarding the US case, it is worth mentioning that President Obama delivered an influential speech, in 2013, in which he described rising income inequality as the 'defining challenge of our time' [a Tawney Moment?] and went on to proclaim that tackling it was one of the cornerstones of his second administration (*The Times*, 2013). Blair's New Labour government was much more reluctant to engage directly with issues of income inequality and redistribution. Instead, it focused on 'social exclusion' and established a Social Exclusion Unit some months after taking office in 1997.

Though Blair's government never formally defined the concept, it gradually became clear through subsequent government discussions that it was a shorthand term for multiple forms of deprivation. In any case, the failure to directly address income inequality was noted. In a letter to the *Financial Times*, some 54 social policy and sociology professors welcomed the new unit but asked the government to reconsider its strategy for a more equal society. By ignoring the need for income redistribution, 'the government was trying to tackle social exclusion with one hand tied behind its back' (Lister and Moore, 1997). A subsequent assessment of the performance of the New Labour governments found that average income did increase across the period (1996–7 to 2006–7) but so also did income inequality as the income of the top ten per cent grew rapidly (Hills et al., 2009, pp. 342–3).

But, as McCall has also observed, perhaps the most striking development in this period was the Occupy Wall Street protests that began in New York's financial district in 2011. As the movement rallied round the slogan 'we are the 99 per cent', it placed a harsh light on the economic inequality between the wealthiest 1 per cent and the rest of the population. A noticeable spike in press attention followed in both countries.

News value of academic studies

Obama's 2013 speech drew on a range of statistical evidence about rising inequality. Ultimately, public understanding of this abstract phenomenon is dependent on the rendering of facts by experts. Here, we highlighted the exponential rise in academic interest, especially among economists. When we examined the number of papers on 'income inequality' in the Social Sciences Citation Index, we found a clear year-on-year accelerating increase between 1990 and 2015 (see Figure 9.1 above).

Certainly, some of the increase in media coverage may simply be picking up on this growing number of academic studies, especially when they are undertaken by major research bodies that cultivate media relations and prepare press releases. However, the news is picking up this growth not directly, but consistent with a hype cycle as demonstrated above. Perhaps newspaper editors showed that stories on economic inequality resonated with the public and that this, in turn, fuelled a demand for evidence produced by social scientists. Journalists are most likely taking their cues for news from politics, and then seeking out the academics to comment on it, which, in turn, creates reputation and relevance for academic research under an impact audit.

In sum, having considered the reality of inequality, the business and political cycles, and academic attention of increasing income inequality, there is no one explanation for fluctuating trends in coverage that can be traced directly to changes in the economic and political environment (see also McCall, 2013, pp. 87–88). A major catalyst of inequality news coverage moving from fringe to mainstream might have been the short-lived Occupy Wall Street movement, generally considered to have started in October 2011; this coincides with a massive surge in media attention to inequality both in the US and in the UK. Even then, this effect was unlikely to fuel the remarkable surge up to 2015. Nonetheless, the fact that there is now a well-established pipeline of research means that 'inequality' has the potential to become a routine news item on the state of the economy, much like the reporting of growth, unemployment, or productivity figures. However, it might need a catalyst event to really put it there.

Conclusions

We conclude that, with regard to media salience, in contrast to previous analysis (McCall, 2013), income inequality increased greatly in salience between 1990 and 2015, particularly after the credit crunch of 2008/09. If the public did not get angry about rising inequality over the past three decades, then we can hardly say it was because of ignorance or a media blind spot. That said, inequality does not reach the critical mass that other news event cycles have reached over the same period. It compares at best with the 'great food debate' over genetically modified crops of the late 1990s in Europe in terms of volume, but it falls far short of events such as climate change, the credit crunch of 2008, or the Gulf War of 1990.

Furthermore, our evidence indicates that the issue-attention cycle of inequality resembles that of a hype cycle, often observed in supply driven emergent technology developments. As it grows within the technical-academic literature, it unwinds a bi-modal surge of news in three phases: an initial alarm is followed by a calmer phase, after which the surge resumes into a different stage. Overall, the issue-attention cycle of inequality looks more like a social-scientific hype-cycle than the fully politicised issue-attention cycle that emerged over climate change.

While overall the coverage of inequality and income inequality has increased significantly since 1990, in particular, since the crisis of 2008, we conclude that as of 2015, inequality has *not yet* reached the critical mass that is necessary to define an urgent social problem in society, what we would call the 'Tawney Moment'. In this respect, income inequality resembles a Brahminic issue resonating among an academic elite, but it has so far (nota bene to 2015) been unable to generate larger resonance with the wider public. It might well be that the Covid-19 pandemic of 2020/21 leaves a legacy of shared experience that brings income inequality finally into the focus of public attention and into the centre of policymaking.

References

Bauer, M W. (2015). *Atoms, bytes and genes: Public resistance and techno-scientific responses*, London: Routledge.

Bauer, M W., Gaskell, G., and Durant, J. (2002). *Biotechnology: The making of a global controversy*, Cambridge: Cambridge University Press.

Best, J. (2008). *Social problems*, New York: W. W. Norton.

Brooks, C. and Manza, J. (2014). Prisoners of the American dream? Americans' attitudes toward taxes and inequality in a new gilded age, Unpublished. Available at: http://as.nyu.edu/docs/IO/3858/PrisonersoftheAmericanDream.pdf.

Btesh, V. and Bauer, M W. (2019). From expert systems to deep learning: A study of hype cycles and representations of artificial intelligence in the French public sphere, 1980–2018, [manuscript based on LSE MSc Thesis 2018].

Djerf-Pierre, M. (2013). Green metacycles of attention: Reassessing the attention cycles of environmental news reporting 1961–2010, *Public Understanding of Science*, 22 (4), pp. 495–512.

Downs, A. (1972). Up and down with ecology: The issue-attention cycle, *The Public Interest*, 28, pp. 38–50.

Fiss, P C. and Hirsch, P M. (2005). The discourse of globalization: Framing and sense-making of an emerging concept, *American Sociological Review*, 70 (1), pp. 29–52.

Gaskell, G. et al. (2005). Imagining nanotechnology: cultural support for technological innovation in Europe and the United States, *Public Understanding of Science*, 14 (1), pp. 81–90.

Hansen, A. (2016). The changing uses of accuracy in science communication, *Public Understanding of Science*, 25 (7), 760–74.

Hilgartner, S. and Bosk, C L. (1988). The rise and fall of social problems: a public arenas model, *American Journal of Sociology*, 94 (1), pp. 53–78.

Hills, J., Sefton, T., and Stewart, K. (2009). *Towards a more equal society? Poverty, inequality and policy since 1997*. Bristol: Policy Press.

Lister, R. and Moore, R. (1997). Government must reconsider its strategy for more equal society, *Financial Times*, sec. Letters p. 20.

Lowe, Philip and Jane Goyder. 1983. *Environmental groups in politics*. London: George Allen & Unwin.

Luhmann, N. (2000). *The reality of the mass media*, Stanford CA, Stanford University Press.

Mazur, Allan and Jinling Lee. 1993. Sounding the global alarm: environmental issues in the US national news, *Social Studies of Science*, 23(4), pp. 681–720.

McCall, L. (2013). *The undeserving rich: American beliefs about inequality, opportunity, and redistribution*, Cambridge: Cambridge University Press.

McCombs, M E. (2004). *Setting the agenda – The mass media and public opinion*, Cambridge: Polity Press.

McCombs, M E. and Shaw, D L. (1972). The agenda-setting function of mass media, *Public Opinion Quarterly*, 36 (2), pp. 176–87.

McGovern, P., Bauer, M W., and Obradovic, S. (2020). Income inequality and the absence of a Tawney moment in the mass media, Working paper (53). International Inequalities Institute, London School of Economics and Political Science, London, UK. http://eprints.lse.ac.uk/107535/.

Mijs, J B. (2019). The paradox of inequality: Income inequality and belief in meritocracy go hand in hand, *Socio-Economic Review*, 19(1), pp.7–35.

Mitchell, A. (2018). *Americans still prefer watching to reading the news–and mostly still through television*, Washington, DC: Pew Research Center.

OECD. (2015). *In it together: Why less inequality benefits all*. Paris: OECD publishing.

Sandel, M. (2020). *The tyranny of merit: What's become of the common good*, London: Allen Lane.

Strodthoff, G G., Hawkins, R P., and Schoenfeld, A C. (1985). Media roles in a social movement: A model of ideology diffusion, *Journal of Communication*, 35 (2), 134–153.

Tennant, C. (2012). *On the threshold: A social psychological study of different standpoints in the climate change debate*, London School of Economics and Political Science.

Times, New York. (2013). The president on inequality, *New York Times*, 5 December, 2013, sec. A.

Van Lente, H., Spitters, C., and Peine, A. (2013). Comparing technological hype cycles: Towards a theory, *Technological Forecasting and Social Change*, 80(8), pp. 1615–1628.

10 Comparative trends in the portrayal of poverty and inequality

Jairo Lugo-Ocando and Brendon Lawson

If one wanted to describe the way the news media report poverty in society, one would need to start by acknowledging that overall, and with few exceptions, most segments of the news media fall far from fulfilling its normative aspirations of being a Watchdog that speaks truth to power. Rather – in the majority of cases – it is a docile lapdog that occasionally barks when allowed (Lugo-Ocando, 2014). Indeed, the mainstream news media as a collective of individuals working together as an interpretative community and, journalism as a political institution in liberal democracy, have lagged behind over the years in relieving the plight of people living in poverty both on a national as well as an international level (Harkins and Lugo-Ocando, 2016b; Lugo-Ocando, 2014).

However, while this very broad generalisation holds a great deal of truth in it, it is nevertheless inaccurate in the wider context of the media landscape. It is also, to a degree, misleading as there are numerous examples in which journalists all over the world are truly committed to highlight the suffering of people, the struggles they go through and denounce openly the injustices they face. Therefore, the problem is not necessarily the commitment of journalists to report poverty, injustice and human suffering but rather the aesthetics and manner in which they do so. Therefore, we should not question, for a moment, the very real commitment that many news reporters individually and collective have in relation to exposing injustices around poverty.

Having said that, we cannot claim the same about the mainstream news media outlets they work for. This is because they are mostly commercial enterprises with their own political economy and therefore their own organisational ideologies and sets of practices. In these cases, structure is characterised by a mode of production that reproduces existing discourses of power rather than challenging them. Consequently, it is important to study past and current trends in reporting poverty in order to understand the nature of this coverage and why organisational culture tends to prevail upon professional autonomy when it comes to this issue.

This chapter examines the current and past trends in relation to how journalists, and the news media in more general terms, provide news coverage of poverty and social exclusion. In so doing, it explores the ways the mainstream news media report poverty and inequality while looking at comparative trends and issues.

DOI: 10.4324/9781003104476-13

The section studies not only how this coverage is shaped by history, individual ideologies and organisational cultures, but also how the news coverage tends to be driven by ideology, structure and agency. The evidence presented here suggests that far from being a "watchdog" to power, mainstream journalism – as a political institution – tends instead to reflect the prevailing worldviews of the elites while reinforcing existing discursive regimes of power.

Indeed, the chapter examines the historical context in which news on inequality and poverty developed over the years, while dissecting how this news coverage affects both the public imagination and political approaches to the problem. It employs a comparative and international perspective, pointing out continuities and changes in the global news reporting of inequality, and highlighting trends and differences between national and international news organisations when they report these issues.

At the centre of this analysis are the issues of professional autonomy and objectivity; two of the core notions in news reporting deontology. It is argued here that while most journalists feel comfortable in reporting poverty as an objective manifestation of social exclusion, it is not so much the case when it comes to inequality, which is perceived to be a more ideologically-driven and contested issue. This, in turn, has come to define past and current trends of news coverage of poverty.

Methodology and approaches

To do this analysis we examined a corpus of news items that included 613 articles from 2019 produced by a variety of news media outlets that included newspapers both in the Global North as well as in the Global South. These Western news outlets included broadcasters' websites such as BBC and CNN as well as the digital version of newspapers such as the Guardian in the UK, the New York Times and the Australian. From the South we incorporated Al Jazeera (Aldroubi) as a broadcaster and the online content from the newspapers the Cape Times (South Africa) and the Indian Times. At no point are we are claiming that this is a representative sample nor that it is possible to generalise conclusions drawn from the analysis of the data. However, we do find the data consistent in helping us illustrate the central arguments of this chapter.

For this research project, we compiled two corpora. The first corpus focused on articles produced during 2019 by the eight news outlets described above that referred to the nodes of poverty and inequality. This corpus was primarily used to assess the relationship between poverty and inequality in international reporting. A second corpus focused on articles referring to poverty and inequality only from *The Guardian Online* from 2002, 2009 and 2019. This historical corpus was used to provide a longitudinal analysis of the relationship between these two nodes in press coverage. The reason as to why we issued the Guardian is because it is considered left-wing media in relation to how the mainstream media tend to portray both poverty and inequality.

To create the main corpus, we selected eight digital news outlets from across the world: The Guardian (UK), Indian Times (India), New York Times (US),

The Australian (Australia), BBC News Online (UK), The Cape Times (South Africa), CNN (US) and Al Jazeera (Qatar). We focused on alternative months from 2019 (January, March, May, July, September, November) and examined a one-week sample from the third Monday of the month to (and including) the following Sunday. Within these parameters we conducted two searches using Google News. The first set of words focused on the node of "poverty" and the second set of words focused on the node of "inequality".

The second query was necessarily more complex than the first as it used ambiguous words. To just examine socio-economic inequality, we adopted the "AROUND (10)" function which only retrieves content where the second set of words appear within ten words of the first set of words. Once all the results had been retrieved for both searches, we excluded certain types of content. We excluded words if they were proper nouns (e.g. Southern Poverty Law Centre) and if the words were part of a URL to another article or not part of the headline and body of the article. We also focused on the specific genre of *news articles*. This excluded opinion pieces, letters to the editor, obituaries, sports pieces, culture articles (and other non-news article genres). This resulted in a corpus of 613 articles.

To create the second corpus, we followed the same rules as described above but only focused on content from *The Guardian* over three years: 2002 (n = 27), 2009 (n = 46) and 2019 (n = 197). In total, there are 270 articles in this corpus. It should be noted that the articles from 2019 (n = 197) also form part of the main corpus. To code each article in the corpora, we relied on a codebook with ten variables. We recorded the basic details of the article: the Year (V1) and Month (V2), the News Outlet (V3), Author Gender (V4) and whether News Agency content was used (V5). This was followed by the geographical focus of the article, recording whether it was a domestic or international story (V6).

To code the text of the article itself, we used the Pearl Extension in Google Chrome to detect the use of certain words. Variable 7 determined whether the "poverty" node was used, determined using the following words: poverty, impoverishment, impoverished, poor, destitution, scarcity, developing, pay, deprivation, slum and the poor. Variable 8 determined whether the "inequality" node was used, determined using the following words: inequality, poorer, disparity, exclusion, marginalised, marginalisation, disadvantage, disadvantaged, difference, gap, discrimination, discriminatory, disproportionate, disproportionately, privilege, privileged, segregation, backward, divide. Variable 9 determined whether the "gender" node was referred to in the article, determined by the presence of the following words: gender, female, male, women, men, girls, boys. For V7–V9, the specific words used were set in context to determine if they were coded as a node of their respective concepts. For example, if the word for V8 referred to water "scarcity" without reference to socio-economic inequality then it was not coded as a node of socio-economic inequality.

The final variable was concerned with the most used source in each article. This involved three stages. First, looking within the article for an identified source. This includes all direct quotations (even if the person saying it is not identified) or reference to someone stating, saying or announcing something but not including vague references to "people", "report", "activists" without a clear attachment to an organisation (this attachment can come later in the report, e.g. first a "report" is mentioned and then the provenance of that report is discussed). Second, categorising each named source as one of the following categories: government/state, third sector/civil society, experts/scholars, private sector, general public, other or N/A (no source). If one source is referred to multiple times, it was coded only once. The exception to this rule was when the same organisation was referred to in multiple ways: e.g. "a representative from Oxfam says..." and "a report from Oxfam shows". In this case, they were coded as two sources. Third, coding the article for the category with the most number of sources. If there are two sources with the most references, we coded the one that appears in the article first. If the person represents two types of sources (e.g. a private chef who also campaigns for better government policy on food) categorise depending on what capacity that person is operating within – are they advertising their restaurant or referring to their campaigning?

The results of this content analysis were analysed using SPSS Version 23. We conducted simple frequencies and more complex tests for association and correlation. The analysis of the historical corpus was also set in relation to other studies that have looked at longitudinal coverage of news reporting on poverty.

Finally, we have incorporated views and opinions from journalists working in these media outlets. We did so by carrying out a series of semi-structured interviews. Following the ethical recommendation from our university, and in order to allow reporters, editors and producers to speak free and critical about their own practices and that of their organisations, we have anonymised the data. We have referred to the organisation they work with, however, as this provides important markers in the analysis. All the data was all compiled between January and August 2020.

Poverty versus inequality

Looking at other studies available, we can highlight several features. First, overall poverty as a news beat receives scarce attention by the media both in terms of airtime and display space allocated to the issue. Indeed, according to previous research on the topic, news coverage of poverty accounts for between 5 per cent and 7 per cent of the overall news content, on average depending of which media outlet (Carey, 2017; Kitzberger and Pérez, 2009). A second aspect is that most of the reporting about the issue tends to centre on the manifestations rather than upon the cause of poverty, something that has been already noticed in previous works (Harkins and Lugo-Ocando, 2017; Lugo-Ocando, 2014). Third, that inequality seldom appears to be used as an explanatory element in analysing poverty. Forth but not least, mentions of inequality in the news on poverty tends to peak in times of financial crisis and for a short period after that. Then, there seems to be a regression to the mean.

The first feature is not surprising and has been over the years highlighted by a series of studies (Clawson and Trice, 2000; Kim, Carvalho and Davis, 2010;

Redden, 2011). Nevertheless, from a deontological point of view it continues to be baffling given that journalism as a political institution makes the normative claim that stands for the vulnerable and the voiceless. Hence, given the little attention provides to what is perhaps the most central issue in society, aside from the environment, one has to ask: what does the news media stand up for?

One possible answer, according to one of the interviewees is that,

> *Overall the news media these days is struggling to catch up with social media platform in terms of the audiences they reach and the advertisement they attract comparatively to the effort and resources they deploy. So, poverty does not add up in this equation, sadly I would say (...). Poverty is only news when is exacerbated or is related to particular events such as the death of George Floyd in the hands of the police. Other than that, it is less and less present in our screens. It only appears in the news agenda when it gets worst or it triggers violence.*[1]

The next two trends, highlights that not only poverty is often left unexplained in the news but that inequality is almost never used as an explanatory feature for it. Moreover, as our own data suggests, inequality is left out of the discursive regimes that define the narratives about poverty. Consequently, poverty is then – to more or less degree – explained by agency rather than structure. Therefore, poverty is often attributed to people's (wrong) choices or to the state intervention in the face of welfare. This focus elides structural circumstances that define those choices, policies and ultimately the lives of those individuals (Harkins and Lugo-Ocando, 2017).

The last trend, in which mention of inequality tends to peak in crisis, is rather distinctive in the sense that seems to follow a different rational. Why does the news media report more inequality in times of economic crisis and turmoil? After all, poverty is always present although they tend to go up in times of crisis. The logic would dictate that if journalists do not embrace inequality as an explanatory feature of poverty in normal times, they should not do that either in times of economic crisis. Why then does it seem to be that inequality is more of an issue in the aftermath of the great crises?

Looking at the set of data, one can see that there is a difference between news coverage of poverty and that of inequality. In all the media outlets from our sample, inequality lags behind poverty. Where this difference is most noticeable is the gap among broadcasters. Interestingly, there is almost no difference between media outlets from the West or from the Global South in regard to this (Figure 10.1).

This is a very interesting finding indeed. Of 514 articles from our sample that included a reference to "poverty" in the 2019 corpus, only 137 items included a reference to inequality (26.7 per cent). Whereas there were 236 articles that referred to "inequality" in which 137 articles referring to poverty (58.1 per cent). From this it is possible to argue that most news articles referring to poverty do not use inequality as an explanatory framework. However, this feature – which is predominant across the sample – does vary significantly depending of the news outlet.

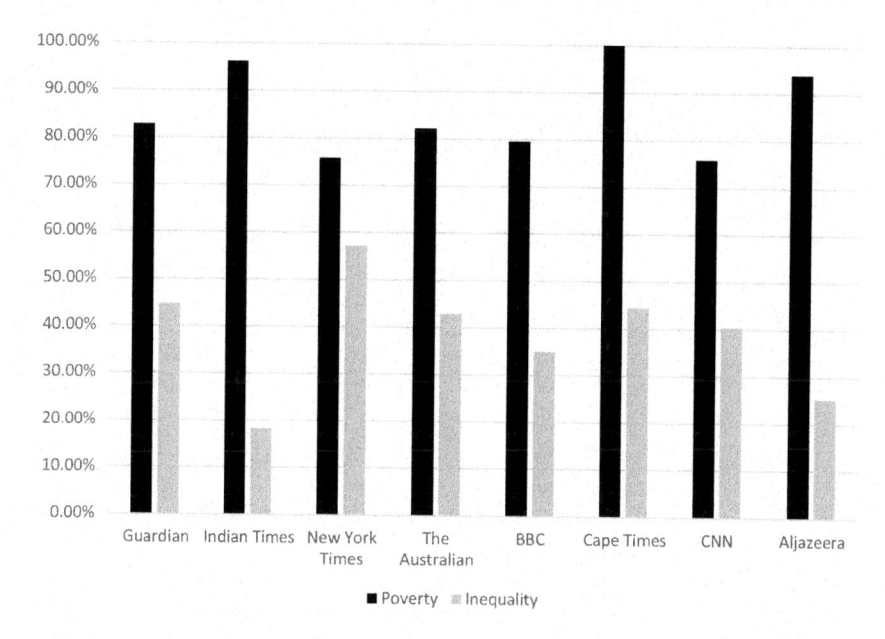

Figure 10.1 Nodes present in article by news outlet.
Source of data: 613 articles collected using Google news 2019.

In this sense, from the overall selection of news stories that had both nodes during that period of time, poverty accounted for far more content than inequality in general terms. Poverty was found in fact in 83.8 per cent of articles, whereas the inequality was found in only 38.5 per cent of articles. Again, this data indicates that journalists are more prone to report poverty than inequality in their stories. This is underpinned by the data that shows that there were only 16.2 per cent of articles where *only* "inequality" was referred to (with no reference to poverty), compared to 61.5 per cent where *only* "poverty" was identified (with no reference to inequality).

More interesting, in only 22.3 per cent of articles do the nodes for "poverty" and "inequality" appear together. In other words, inequality is rarely associated with poverty. This reiterates our thesis that inequality is not perceived, considered or embraced as a possible explanation for poverty. Based on the semi-structured interviews with journalists, it is possible to argue that reporters avoid including inequality because it implies that they have taken a position on poverty. As one of the interviewees, who is a producer in a mayor international broadcaster pointed out

> In most of our coverage poverty and inequality appear to be interchangeable. At least that is the way I see it in my own mind. But to be fair, inequality rarely appears at all in our daily coverage. Now, I do agree with the fact that poverty is an objective matter despite some disparities in the way is measured. That is not the case, I am afraid, of inequality, which seems to be far more politicised. Particularly in the current polarized environment here in the US.[2]

Table 10.1 Frequency and percentage of news stories that feature poverty

		Frequency	Percent	Valid percent	Cumulative percent
Valid	Guardian	197	32.1	32.1	32.1
	Indian Times	77	12.6	12.6	44.7
	New York Times	70	11.4	11.4	56.1
	The Australian	28	4.6	4.6	60.7
	BBC	103	16.8	16.8	77.5
	Cape Times	9	1.5	1.5	79.0
	CNN	62	10.1	10.1	89.1
	Aljazeera	67	10.9	10.9	100.0
	Total	613	100.0	100.0	

Source of data: 613 articles collected using Google news 2019 (January, March, May, July, September, November).

The data also highlights which news outlets provide the greatest coverage of poverty. In terms of the number of stories, the Guardian in the UK produced and published over a third of all news stories on poverty in the entire sample during that period (Table 10.1).

One has to question why The Guardian produced the largest proportion, by far, of articles? It does not seem that political leaning is an explanation given the low number of articles produced by other left-wing outlets. When we consider that BBC News Online produced the second highest number of articles, we are pointed in the direction of ownership structures. Both news outlets are not owned by private shareholders. If we analyse this in relation to the widely accepted thesis around how the political economy of the media and media ownership has defined organisational and professional ideologies in the newsroom, then it is possible to speculate to a degree that there might be some sort of relationship between both factors.

However, other alternative – and perhaps more grounded – explanation in the case of the Guardian and the BBC is the fact that 2019 was an election year in the UK. In particular, the main opposition party had as its leader Jeremy Corbyn who had particularly explicit redistribution agenda that often brought back narratives around inequality and socialism. Consequently, both the Guardian which was sympathetic towards Corbyn and the BBC, which is bounded by the norm of impartiality set in its charter, were perhaps more influenced by Labour's political agenda and had to reflect that in its own pages. Nevertheless, the data is insufficient to corroborate either of these possible explanations and further studies about the relationship between coverage of poverty and media ownership is required.

Having said that, what is clear is that news coverage on poverty is scarce and at times patchy. In very few occasions there are sustained campaign on poverty or continuity in the coverage as happens with other news beats. As one of our interviewee pinpoints,

> One of the key problems is that we rarely do follow-ups on our own stories on poverty. We broadcast them when they happen and that is that. We rarely go back to see what happen

Comparative trends 157

to the people of the first story nor we go month later to see if things have improved or change. We just do not have the resources nor is it commercially sustainable.[3]

This pattern of reporting can also be linked to the relationship between the source and the journalist. The news sources used by journalists is a fundamental element not only in defining both the basis of the storyline and the framing of any news item but also in conferring credibility to the reporter's claims of being objective and impartial (Manning, 2000; Tuchman, 1972). What we know from most studies around journalists and sources, particularly in relation to the coverage of poverty, is that they overwhelmingly access official sources (Harkins and Lugo-Ocando, 2016a; Lewis, Williams, and Franklin, 2008).

This is corroborated, once more, in our own data for this section. The most cited source was what we call "state apparatus", which accounts for all sources within government, related official institutions. In our sample, these sources were the most used source in just over half the articles (50.7 per cent). This was followed by Third Sector and Civil Society, that encompass NGOs, the UN system, professional organisations, unions etc. This type of source was the most used source in just under a quarter of all articles (23.8 per cent). The least used source was the private sector, being used the most in only 4.4 per cent of articles in the corpus. In five cases there was no source cited (Table 10.2).

Despite this being an expected finding, it is important to notice that previous studies from around the world in the past document an even higher dependency upon government (official) sources. One of the reasons as to why the percentage of Third Sector and Civil Society voices has grown over the years is perhaps due to the increasing investment that these organisations have made over the years in their PR and communication departments. Indeed, many studies have now come to un underline how NGOs, charities and others have now become far more influential in defining the news agenda and the nature of the news coverage (Scott, Bunce, and Wright, 2017; Wright, 2018).

One interesting trend that we found was that that media outlets are increasingly producing their own content on poverty. In doing so, they are becoming less dependent upon news agencies. Of all the articles in the corpus, only 9.6 per

Table 10.2 Most cited source by news outlet

		Frequency	Percent	Valid percent	Cumulative percent
Valid	Government (official)	311	50.7	50.7	50.7
	Third sector/civil society	146	23.8	23.8	74.6
	Experts/scholars	57	9.3	9.3	83.8
	Private sector	27	4.4	4.4	88.3
	General public	67	10.9	10.9	99.2
	No source	5	.8	.8	100.0
	Total	613	100.0	100.0	

Source of data: 613 articles collected using Google news 2019 (January, March, May, July, September, November).

cent used news agency content. However, this was not distributed evenly among all the outlets. Of the 59 articles that used press agency content in our corpus, Al Jazeera produced 37 of them (62.7 per cent). Whereas *The Australian* and *BBC* did not use any press agency content. This fact, in times of a massive reduction of resources in the newsroom, can be read as good news. It suggests that the media outlets have greater authorial control over what is being published.

It is also important to mention that the split between domestic news coverage (n=308) and international news coverage (n = 305) was even across the overall sample. This did vary from news outlet to news outlet: Al Jazeera's content was entirely international (n = 67) whereas most of the articles from Indian Times were domestic (93.5 per cent). Overall the data suggests that media outlets in our sample are producing themselves the stories on poverty that they disseminate. This has implications for action and intervention given that by changing cultures in the newsrooms one could improve also coverage of poverty.

Historical corpus

In addition to the broad picture we have analysed above it is also important to place these findings within historical trends. For example, as we said before, inequality as a theme tends to appear more in the aftermath of crisis. According to some interviewees this has been due to the fact that the crunch is often felt also at home. As one of the interviewees put it,

> *I can't speak for the others nor for those who covered the 1929 crash. But I can talk for myself and how I felt in 2008, particularly after [the collapse of] Lehman [Brothers]. We saw and felt how many lost their jobs while watching the bankers get away with murder. I mean, you know... one starts to wonder. But to be fair it wasn't us it was suddenly Obama taking about inequality. Books came out on the topic such as Piketty's one and before that The Spirit Level. Then everyone was talking about inequality.*[4]

Accordingly, the increased mentions of inequality in the coverage of poverty could be attributed to a matter of change in the wider political discourse that is reflected in news media coverage. Furthermore, it could be driven by the personal experiences of journalists who come to directly identify with those worst affected by the crisis. This was the same point made by John Rawls in A Theory of Justice (2009 [1971]) many years ago. Indeed, as some studies have already suggested, there is a strong element of utilitarian logics in the process of defining empathy among journalists (Lugo-Ocando and Andrade, 2019). We believe this empathetic element is key in underpinning the term inequality when reporters articulate news on poverty.

Nevertheless, not all newspapers and broadcasters are the same. Some outlets such as the Guardian have intrinsically and historically embraced inequality as an explanatory element when covering poverty; far more than any other media outlet. Because of this, we chose it as a particular case study to examining some of our ideas.

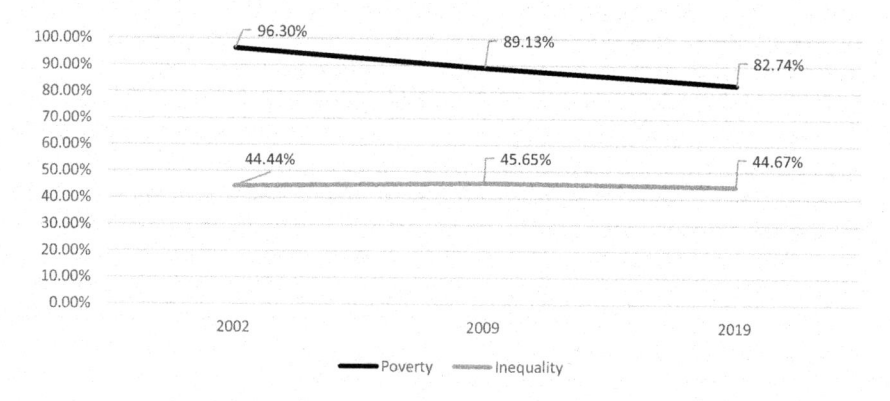

[Chart: Percentage of nodes (Poverty and Inequality) in The Guardian across 2002, 2009, 2019.
Poverty: 96.30% (2002), 89.13% (2009), 82.74% (2019).
Inequality: 44.44% (2002), 45.65% (2009), 44.67% (2019).]

Figure 10.2 Percentage of nodes present in The Guardian over three years: 2002 (n = 27), 2009 (n = 46) and 2019 (n = 197).
Source of data: Google news.

In the case of the London-based broadsheet, the historical variance has been minimal and atypical, even after the 2008 crash as shown in the chart below (Figure 10.2).

This means that not only the Guardian provides more coverage than the other media outlets but also that the percentages in relation to the mentions of inequality as an explanation for poverty has remain similar over the years but went slightly up after the crash of 2008; this despite the fact that the overall node on poverty decreased over the same years.

Another important trend historically was the fact that the most cited source in all news articles in the Guardian were government (official) sources. In 2002, 40.7 per cent of articles used this source the most, increasing to 50 per cent by 2009 and 50.3 per cent by 2019. Similarly, the use of "experts/scholars" also increased from 0 per cent in 2002 to 9.1 per cent in 2019. This stands in opposition to the use of the general public as a source, which decreased. In 2002, there were around a quarter of articles (25.9 per cent) where the "general public" were the most cited source. This decreased to 17.4 per cent in 2009 and reduced further to 9.6 per cent in 2019. This suggest that ordinary people are making it less into the news, which further narrows the range of voices on poverty in journalist's reporting about poverty (Sainath, 2017 [1996]).

Conclusion

Overall, data suggests that inequality is scarcely used as an explanation of poverty and that is seen by journalists as a more ideological and subjective matter than poverty, which is perceived rather as a more objective news item. It is also clear that professional ideologies, organisational cultures, the political economy of the news outlets and media ownership all come together to define the ways news on poverty is covered. Hence, we can explain these general trends partially as the result of the influence of normative values, such as objectivity, and partially due to the political economy of the news media.

Having said that, there is a great deal of leverage placed upon agency as suggested by the interviews. Empathy, for example, can go a long way in convincing journalists, editors and producers not only to increase the space and airtime they give to poverty but also to include more structural explanations to the phenomenon (i.e. inequality). Nevertheless, as we have also indicated here, inequality will remain a contested notion in the news coverage given the strong association that many reporters make between that notion and explicit ideological and subjective discourses. This is bad news for those of us who actually think that in order to address poverty in society one needs to actually engage with wealth redistribution and a degree of state intervention in the form of welfare.

Notes

1 Interview with broadcast producer No. 1 on August 3, 2020.
2 Interview with journalist No 4 on July 14, 2020.
3 Interview with broadcast producer No. 2, 2020.
4 Interview with broadcast news editor No. 1, 2020.

References

Aldroubi, M. (2017). Bahrain says Qatar's media is making diplomatic crisis worse. Retrieved from https://www.thenational.ae/world/gcc/bahrain-says-qatar-s-media-is-making-diplomatic-crisis-worse-1.620047

Carey, M. C. (2017). *The news untold: Community journalism and the failure to confront poverty in Appalachia.* Morgantown: West Virginia University Press.

Clawson, R. A., and Trice, R. (2000). Poverty as we know it: Media portrayals of the poor. *The Public Opinion Quarterly, 64*(1), pp. 53–64.

Harkins, S., and Lugo-Ocando, J. (2016a). All people are equal, but some people are more equal than others. In J. Servaes and T. Oyedemi (Eds.), *The Praxis of Social Inequality in Media: A Global Perspective* (pp. 3–20). Lanham, Maryland: Rowman & Littlefield.

Harkins, S., and Lugo-Ocando, J. (2016b). How Malthusian ideology crept into the newsroom: British tabloids and the coverage of the 'underclass'. *Critical Discourse Studies, 13*(1), pp. 78–93.

Harkins, S., and Lugo-Ocando, J. (2017). *Poor news: Media discourses of poverty in times of austerity.* London: Rowman & Littlefield International.

Kim, S.-H., Carvalho, J. P., and Davis, A. C. (2010). Talking about poverty: News framing of who is responsible for causing and fixing the problem. *Journalism & Mass Communication Quarterly, 87*(3–4), pp. 563–581.

Kitzberger, P., and Pérez, G. J. (2009). *Los pobres en papel. Las narrativas de la pobreza en la prensa latinoamericana.* Buenos Aires: Fundación Konrad Adenauer.

Lewis, J., Williams, A., and Franklin, B. (2008). A compromised fourth estate? UK news journalism, public relations and news sources. *Journalism studies, 9*(1), pp. 1–20.

Lugo-Ocando, J. (2014). *Blaming the victim: How global journalism fails those in poverty.* London: Pluto Press.

Lugo-Ocando, J., and Andrade, G. (2019). Selling the lottery to earn salvation: Journalism practice, risk and humanitarian communication. In M. Lawrence and R. Tavernor (Eds.), *Global humanitarianism and media culture* (pp. 187–204). Manchester: Manchester University Press.

Manning, P. (2000). *News and news sources: A critical introduction.* London: Sage.

Rawls, J. (2009 [1971]). *A Theory of Justice.* Cambridge, MA: Harvard University Press.

Redden, J. (2011). Poverty in the news: A framing analysis of coverage in Canada and the UK. *Information, Communication & Society, 14*(6), pp. 820–849.

Sainath, P. (2017 [1996]). *Everybody loves a good drought: Stories from India's poorest.* London: Penguin Books.

Scott, M., Bunce, M., and Wright, K. (2017). Donor power and the news: The influence of foundation funding on international public service journalism. *The International Journal of Press/Politics, 22*(2), pp. 163–184.

Tuchman, G. (1972). Objectivity as strategic ritual: An examination of newsmen's notions of objectivity. *American Journal of sociology, 77*(4), pp. 660–679.

Wright, K. (2018). *Who"s reporting Africa now?: Non-governmental organizations, journalists and multimedia.* Oxford: Peter Lang.

III
Public opinion, inequality, and the media

11 Public attitudes to poverty and inequality

Elizabeth Clery

Introduction

Recent analysis has highlighted a recent and emerging disconnect between trends in levels of poverty and inequality in Britain and the public's perceptions of and attitudes towards them (Clery and Dangerfield, 2019). Levels of poverty and inequality, as measured by official statistics, have remained relatively stable, at the population level at least, since the time of the 2008 financial crisis. However, the public is now more likely to perceive and anticipate high levels of poverty in Britain and is less accepting of and more sympathetic towards those experiencing these phenomena. It has been argued elsewhere that this divergence has been driven by an increasing, and more sympathetic, focus by politicians and the media on poverty and inequality. This trend has been particularly pronounced among Labour Party politicians in their expressed opposition to the austerity and welfare reform that followed the 2008 financial crisis, subsequently being reflected in the media. It has included a tendency for these concepts to be discussed in a holistic way, incorporating elements such as homelessness and food bank use, to which the public is sympathetic, rather than focussing on the long-term income trends measured by official statistics (Clery and Dangerfield, 2019). In this chapter, we consider the specific role played by the media in contributing to these changes in public attitudes, considering how recent changes in views about and perceptions of poverty and inequality may have been influenced by levels and types of media consumption specifically.

Poverty and inequality: a divergence in trends and attitudes

Analysis of time series data collected by the cross-sectional British Social Attitudes survey and by the UK element of the European Social Survey shows that the public's attitudes to poverty and inequality have changed in a number of ways in the past decade or so (all of the data below are taken from the British Social Attitudes survey, unless stated otherwise). Starting with the often-debated matter of what constitutes "poverty", we see that the public is now slightly more inclined to adopt a more inclusive definition of poverty than has traditionally

DOI: 10.4324/9781003104476-15

been the case. Around nine in ten people have consistently adhered to the view that someone would be in poverty if "they had not got enough to eat and live without getting into debt". The proportions agreeing that this would be the case for someone who "had enough to eat and live, but not enough to buy other things they needed" or someone who "had not got enough to eat and live without getting into debt" rose by six percentage points between 2006 and 2018. Fifty-five per cent and 28 per cent of the public, respectively, now support these definitions.

However, public perceptions of the recent, current, and future prevalence of poverty in Britain have changed far more markedly. While 52 per cent thought that there was "quite a lot" of poverty in Britain in 2006, by 2018, this proportion had risen to 65 per cent. More markedly still, 62 per cent of people in 2018 indicated that poverty had increased in the past ten years, almost double the proportion who stated this 12 years before. Similarly, 61 per cent of people in 2018 anticipated that poverty would increase further in the next ten years, compared with 44 per cent who anticipated such a change in 2006.

While the proportion of the public perceiving high and rising levels of poverty in Britain has, therefore, increased, at the same time, support for the premise that poverty and inequality are acceptable or inevitable appears to be in decline. In 2018, 78 per cent of people expressed the view that the gap between those on high and low incomes was too large, a proportion that has remained remarkably stable (and the majority view) across the lifetime of the British Social Attitudes survey. A decline in public acceptance of income inequality was observed in data collected in the UK as part of the European Social Survey. It shows that 53 per cent of people in 2016 thought that "large differences in people's incomes are acceptable to properly reward differences in talents and efforts", a decline from 64 per cent in 2008. Similarly, support for the view that, "for society to be fair, differences in people's living standards should be small" experienced an increase over the same period (although less marked), rising from 50 per cent to 55 per cent. In summary, the public appears to view large differences in people's incomes or living standards, which might be seen as representing, or consequences of, inequality, as less desirable or acceptable than it did in the past.

When we consider these attitudinal shifts against a backdrop of trends in poverty and inequality levels, as measured by official statistics, there is clear evidence of an emerging disconnect. Approaches to the measurement of poverty and inequality remain contested (Full Fact, 2019), with a number of alternative approaches under discussion, leading to the formation of the Social Metrics Commission in 2018, to develop an additional measure of poverty that "better reflects the nature and experiences of poverty that different families in the UK have, and can be used to build a consensus around poverty measurement and action in the UK" (Social Metrics Commission, 2019). It should be emphasised that current official measures exclude certain elements, which many people are likely to regard as indicators of poverty and inequality, such as homelessness, food bank use, and short-term hardship experienced as a result of changing benefit circumstances.

Accepting that poverty and inequality measurement remains an area of contention, it is, nevertheless, the case that none of the most frequently cited measures of these phenomena indicate a marked shift in poverty or inequality levels, at the population level at least, over the past decade or so – although there is a substantial literature, discussed elsewhere in this volume, documenting a rise in inequality, in particular, over a longer time period. The latest data from the government's "Households below average income" statistical series indicate that, in 2018–19, the level of relative poverty stood at 17 per cent before housing costs (BHC) and 22 per cent after housing costs (AHC), compared with 18 per cent and 22 per cent, respectively, in 2006–7. The comparable levels of absolute poverty in 2018–19 were 15 per cent BHC and 20 per cent AHC, compared with 18 per cent and 22 per cent in 2006–7. In terms of inequality, the Gini co-efficient figures for 2018–19 were 35 per cent BHC and 39 per cent AHC, continuing a largely flat trend since its reduction in 2010–11 (Department for Work and Pensions, 2020).

However, such comparative stability in levels of poverty and inequality, as officially measured, is at odds with public views and perceptions of these issues. As depicted in Figure 11.1, looking back across the entire period over which data on absolute poverty levels has been collected by the government, we see that objective measures and public perceptions of the prevalence of poverty appeared to move largely in tandem up until the time of the financial crisis. Specifically, as levels of absolute poverty declined, so did the proportion of the public perceiving there to be "quite a lot" of poverty in Britain or viewing this as having increased over the past decade. However, from that point onwards, while the official measures of poverty remained relatively stable, the proportions perceiving there to be

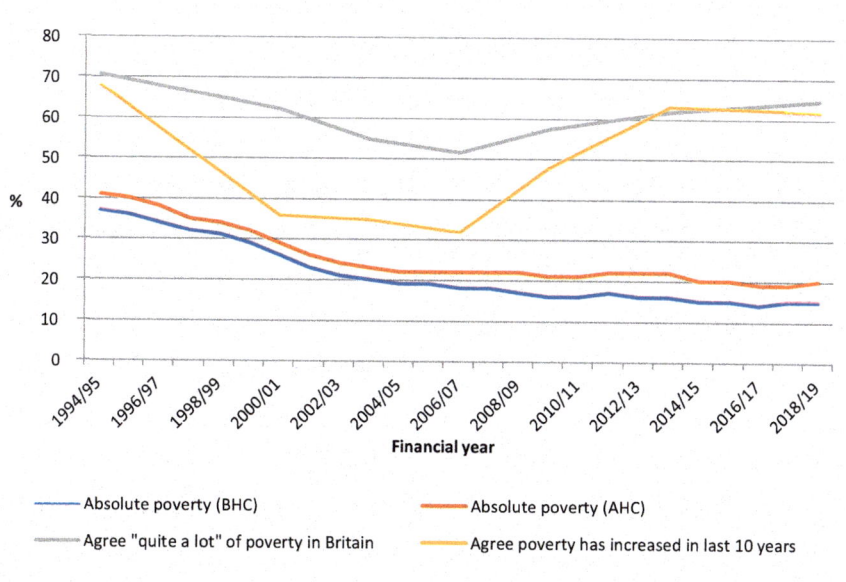

Figure 11.1 View that there is "quite a lot" of poverty, by HBAI absolute poverty measures, 1994/95–2018/19.

Source: Households below average income 1994/95–2018/19. (Department for Work and Pensions, 2020) and British Social Attitudes survey, 1994–2018.

"quite a lot" of poverty in Britain and for this to have risen in the past decade (where we would logically have expected to see a time lag) increased markedly. A comparison of public perceptions of the prevalence of poverty with measures of relative poverty tells a similar story.

This divergence might lead us to suspect that public perceptions of poverty and inequality are not simply mediated by the trends encapsulated in official measures of it (or that the role of such trends is in decline). Such a conclusion is lent weight by the fact that, among those sections of society where poverty rates have changed most markedly over the past decade – namely, pensioners (for whom they have declined) and those in households with children (for whom they have increased), there is little evidence that perceptions of current poverty levels have responded to these changes by becoming less and more pessimistic, respectively (Clery and Dangerfield, 2019). Specifically, while pensioners have always been less likely to perceive or to be concerned by poverty than the population at large (Clery et al., 2013), despite historically low levels of pensioner poverty, there is little evidence of further divergence in views.

In this volume, Obolenskaya and Hills consider a similar disconnect between the relative stability in levels of inequality in Britain over the past 25 years and the heightened levels of public concern about it. They conclude that this may be explained by the persistence of a high level of inequality, stagnation in average income growth, austerity fatigue, the increased salience of group inequalities, and the knock-on effects on social mobility. In the remainder of this chapter, we consider an alternative (although potentially related) explanation – that attitudes to poverty and inequality are increasingly being influenced by political and media presentation and discussion of these issues. We focus on the role of the media specifically, while recognising that it cannot be isolated from the broader context of political and social discussion and debate in which it operates.

Changes in media coverage of poverty and inequality

We begin by considering how media coverage of poverty and inequality has changed over the past decade. If the media have contributed to changing public attitudes towards poverty and inequality, we would anticipate its coverage of this issue to have moved in an equivalent direction to that discussed in relation to public attitudes above, that is, to have become more pessimistic (in terms of current and future levels of poverty and inequality) and more sympathetic towards those experiencing these phenomena. However, coupled with a change in tone, an increase in the extent to which the media cover these issues could also have contributed to a shift in public attitudes – by a process of raising public awareness – although this could arguably have influenced public attitudes in either direction, not just the more pessimistic and sympathetic shift observed in practice. We, therefore, first consider in what ways media coverage of poverty and inequality may have changed over the past decade, before attempting to determine whether and how these changes influenced public attitudes.

While recent trends in media coverage of poverty and inequality have received a certain amount of attention from researchers, this has tended to focus on the content and tone of coverage, rather than establishing how it has changed quantitatively over time. Nevertheless, there is some evidence to suggest that the media are now covering issues relating to poverty and inequality in more detail than they did previously. A review of media coverage of poverty conducted in 2007 typified this, at the time, as "a marginal issue in mainstream media" (McKendrick et al., 2008). From subsequent content analysis, we can tentatively conclude that this situation may have changed. A comparison of news coverage between two randomly chosen one-month periods in 2001 and 2011 found the number of articles covering poverty in four mainstream newspapers to have risen from 112 to 162 (Chauhan and Foster, 2014). Meanwhile, an analysis of coverage of benefit recipients identified two peaks, in the late 1990s and in 2010-11 – the latest point at which data were collected (Baumberg et al, 2012). Alternatively, an analysis of newspaper coverage of food banks found no newspaper articles before 2008 across nine national UK titles, with few before 2012, after which the number increased dramatically (Wells and Caraher, 2014).

In another chapter in this volume, Bauer et al. have demonstrated that the coverage of economic inequality in both the UK and US print media increased between 1990 and 2015, with most of the surge occurring between 2010 and 2015. Meanwhile, in terms of non-print media, a new genre of television programmes termed "poverty porn" emerged in the early 2010s, including "We pay your benefits", "Benefits Britain" and "Benefits Street" (Jensen, 2014). This is documented in the chapter by Mack in this volume, which describes a rise in "benefit bashing" television coverage from 2010 but also identifies the "beginning of a counter narrative" – with the number of programmes focussing on poverty beginning to rise.

We can, therefore, tentatively conclude that media coverage of poverty and inequality has increased in Britain over the past decade. But has this coverage mirrored trends in public attitudes by becoming more pessimistic about levels of poverty and inequality and more sympathetic towards these causes? While we find little evidence of such shifts in tone across the media as a whole, there has been a historic tendency, demonstrated by content analysis, for poverty and related issues to be covered more frequently and sympathetically in both the broadsheet and left-wing media (Sippit and Tranchese, 2015). This trend is supported by a 2008 study, which calculated the average number of articles covering poverty across a one-week period as 8.8 in Sunday broadsheet newspapers and 4.6 in daily broadsheet newspapers (the equivalent figures for "daily red tops" and "Sunday red tops" were below 2 and below 1, respectively) (McKendrick et al., 2008). Furthermore, the aforementioned analysis of articles on food banks in nine publications found 79 per cent of these articles to be concentrated in three publications that were either left-leaning and/or broadsheets (Wells and Caraher, 2014).

If these changes in media coverage have contributed to recent trends in public attitudes to poverty and inequality, which have become more pessimistic and less sympathetic, we would logically expect these shifts to have been most marked among those sections of society most exposed to recent changes in media coverage. We might, therefore, hypothesise that the views of individuals with the greatest levels of media engagement and consumption in general, and of the broadsheet media specifically, should logically have become markedly more sympathetic and pessimistic, compared with other sections of society, if the media are to have played such an influential role. To test this theory, we next examine how the attitudes to poverty and inequality of those with different levels and preferences in terms of media engagement have shifted over the past decade.

What are the links between media consumption and changes in attitudes to poverty and inequality?

Individual engagement with the media has been measured by social surveys in a variety of ways. While time series surveys, such as the British Social Attitudes survey, have sought to measure such behaviour consistently (to facilitate time series analysis), it has also been necessary to develop new measures in light of shifts in behaviour in this area – most notably a long-term decline in traditional newspaper readership and a concurrent rise in online media consumption (Curtice and Mair, 2008). Whilst the British Social Attitudes survey has asked respondents, since its inception, whether they "normally read any daily morning newspaper at least three times a week", since 2010, respondents have also been asked how often they "watch all or part of a news programme on television" or "look online at a news or newspaper website". To obtain a measure of media consumption, we added together the number of types of media which respondents said they viewed, "at least several times a week". While 14 per cent did not view any type of media with this regularity, the majority viewed one (39 per cent) or two (38 per cent) types of media with this frequency, while fewer than one in ten (8 per cent) did this in relation to all types of media asked about.

We have hypothesised that an increasing media focus on poverty and inequality may have prompted the shifts in public attitudes discussed earlier. However, on none of the measures of attitudes to poverty and inequality considered do we find substantial differences between those who engage with different numbers of media regularly, or between groups defined by levels of media consumption over time. This suggests that if media consumption has contributed to the growing pessimism about and sympathy in public attitudes towards poverty in inequality, this is not simply a function of the quantity of coverage that individuals are receiving.

When we consider the type[1], rather than level, of media consumption, however, stark differences emerge between the attitudes of those who engage with broadsheet and tabloid media specifically[2] – with the former tending to express more pessimistic and sympathetic views than the latter. While 55 per cent of readers of tabloid newspapers in 2018 thought that there was "quite a lot" of poverty in Britain, this view was expressed by 68 per cent of readers of broadsheet titles. Similarly, this view was endorsed by 64 per cent of those who read a tabloid newspaper website and 76 per cent of those who read a broadsheet newspaper website (these proportions are likely to be higher than those found in relation to traditional newspaper readership, as both mode of newspaper readership and attitudes to poverty are known to be associated with age, with younger age groups being more likely to be pessimistic about the amount of poverty in Britain, and to read newspapers online). Similar differences are evident in views about past and future poverty levels, with readers of broadsheet newspapers being more likely to think poverty had increased and is set to increase further. Mirroring the trends in relation to current poverty levels reported above, we found that 51 per cent of readers of tabloid newspapers thought that levels of poverty in Britain would increase over the next ten years, compared with 58 per cent of readers of broadsheet newspapers (the equivalent proportions for readers of online news websites, where these could be defined as tabloid or broadsheet, were 63 per cent and 74 per cent, respectively). Finally, we found similar differences in relation to the acceptability of poverty and inequality, with 74 per cent of readers of tabloid newspapers thinking the income gap is too large, compared with 88 per cent of readers of broadsheet newspapers.[3]

More crucially, however, we found that many of the differences in views noted above have only emerged over the past decade – and there is some evidence to suggest that this is the result of shifts in the views of readers of broadsheet media specifically. Figure 11.2 shows how the perceptions of the amount of poverty in Britain of readers of tabloid and broadsheet newspapers, and news websites, have changed since the period before the financial crisis. It shows that support for the view that there is "quite a lot" of poverty in Britain increased by 19 percentage

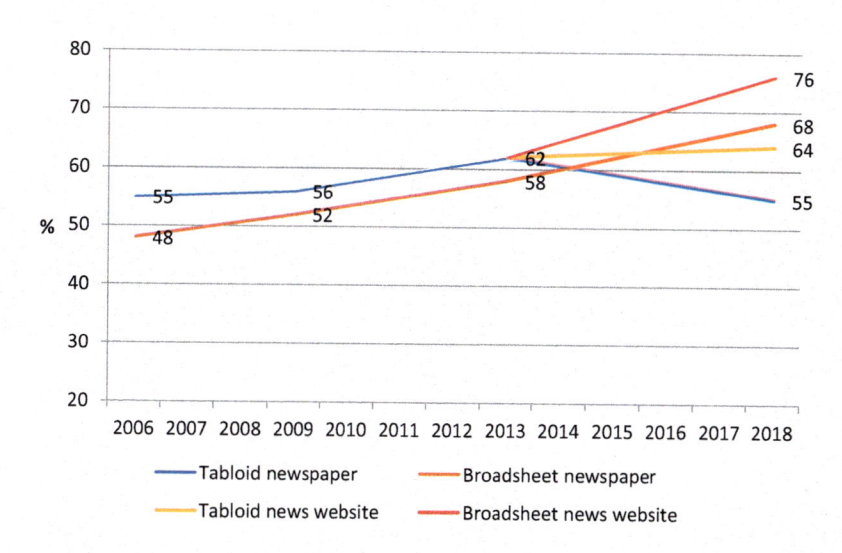

Figure 11.2 Proportions agreeing there is "quite a lot" of poverty in Britain, by type of media consumed, 2006–18.
Source: British Social Attitudes survey, 2006–18.

points among readers of broadsheet newspapers between 2006 and 2018, while remaining unchanged, despite some fluctuations, among readers of tabloid newspapers. Similarly, while the British Social Attitudes survey has only collected details of online news website readership for a shorter time period, we see that, between 2013 and 2018, the proportions of broadsheet and tabloid news website readers, who thought there was "quite a lot" of poverty in Britain, increased by 15 percentage points and just two percentage points, respectively.

We find similar patterns of change in relation to other perceptions relating to the prevalence of poverty in Britain. While the proportion of readers of tabloid newspapers who thought that poverty would increase over the next decade rose by three percentage points between 2006 and 2018 (now standing at 51 per cent, as noted previously), this view rose by 24 percentage points among readers of broadsheet newspapers and now stands at 58 per cent. Among those who read news websites, the perception that poverty would increase over the next decade rose by just three percentage points (to 63 per cent) among readers of tabloid news websites, compared with a rise of 19 percentage points (to 74 per cent) among readers of broadsheet news websites. Similarly, the view that the income gap is "too large" declined by four percentage points (to 74 per cent) among readers of tabloid newspapers between 2006 and 2018, while increasing by ten percentage points (to 88 per cent) among readers of broadsheet newspapers over the same time period.

Clearly then, there is substantial evidence to suggest that the changes in attitudes to poverty and inequality that have occurred over the past decade have been driven by very marked changes in the views of readers of broadsheet media. Pessimistic assessments of the prevalence of poverty in Britain, and the view that it is not acceptable, have increased markedly among consumers of broadsheet media, while the views of tabloid readers have, in most instances, remained relatively unchanged. This trend suggests that changes in the coverage of poverty and inequality in the broadsheet media (albeit an increase in coverage, more sympathetic coverage or a greater focus on issues such as homelessness, food bank use – or some of the aspects of inequality covered in the chapter by Hills) may bear some responsibility for the shift in attitudes to these issues, seen at a societal level.

However, it must be borne in mind that the media do not operate in a vacuum. Choices regarding media consumption are known to be associated with a range of demographic characteristics – which may themselves be driving changing attitudes to poverty and inequality. Historically, readers of broadsheet media tend to be better-educated than readers of tabloids; this remained the case in 2018, where 49 per cent of readers of broadsheet newspapers had a degree, compared with 10 per cent of readers of tabloid titles (there is also a well-documented relationship between political party affiliation and newspaper readership although this does not neatly operate along tabloid-broadsheet lines). Recent analysis has shown that shifts in attitudes to poverty and inequality have occurred disproportionately among supporters of particular political parties and in groups with certain levels of education. Specifically, these have primarily occurred among

Labour Party supporters and among those who are more highly educated, with society consequently becoming more divided, by political party allegiance and level of education, in its views on these issues (Clery and Dangerfield, 2019). The increasing concern among Labour Party supporters about poverty and inequality has been attributed to the fact that, in its opposition to austerity and welfare reform, the Party has frequently cited a rise in these phenomena; for instance, its 2017 manifesto stated, "After seven years of rising poverty and inequality, Labour will rebuild and transform our social security system" (The Labour Party, 2017). Inevitably, such pronouncements will have been quoted and analysed by the media, and the broadsheet media, in particular – highlighting the interconnectedness of political and media discourse.

Furthermore, none of the identities that have shown to be correlated with changing attitudes to poverty (namely, media consumption, political party allegiance, and level of education) are static. In addition to choosing to acquire more educational qualifications, an individual might change their political party allegiance or newspaper readership to more accurately reflect their emerging views about poverty and inequality. In other words, the composition of the groups of broadsheet and tabloid readers about whom we have drawn comparisons across a period of a decade or so may have been rather different at various points in time (this is particularly likely to be the case due to the migration of readers from traditional newspapers to online news websites, many of which cannot be classified on this basis).

Setting these limitations aside, however, when regression analyses were undertaken to identify the characteristics that independently predicted the view that there is "quite a lot" of poverty in Britain, it was found that the type of newspaper read was independently associated with views on this matter at both time points examined, along with a range of characteristics including political party affiliation, age, and level of education (Clery and Dangerfield, 2018). Clearly then, the media do appear to have an ongoing role in shaping public attitudes to poverty and inequality although this needs to be understood within a complex web of interacting identifies and factors.

Conclusion

Public attitudes to media and inequality in Britain have shifted over the past decade or so in a direction that diverges from official statistics; the public is more pessimistic about the prevalence of poverty now than it was in the period before the financial crisis, and less accepting of this as an inherent aspect of society. Our analysis suggests that changes in media coverage of these issues may be partly responsible for this shift. The views of readers of broadsheet media (both traditional and online) have shifted markedly in the directions described above, while the views of readers of tabloid media have remained relatively static. However, it must be acknowledged that changes in the readership of both types of media, as well as changes in their actual content, may have played a role – along with other characteristics of readers of both types of media, such as political party affiliation and level of education, which have also been shown to be linked to changing attitudes in this area.

Looking forward, it has been predicted that poverty levels in Britain are set to rise as a result of the Covid-19 crisis (Parkes and McNeil, 2020). Although trends in poverty, as objectively measured, have played little part in driving shifts in attitudes over the past decade, it remains to be seen whether this will continue to be the case going forward. The continued influence of the media (and the broadsheet media, in particular) in changing attitudes to poverty may be influenced by their specific coverage of poverty engendered by the Crisis, and the extent to which this is distinct or uniform across different types of media. Analysis of future waves of survey data including the British Social Attitudes survey and the European Social Survey will be vital to understand if and how the links between media coverage of poverty and inequality and public attitudes to these issues are changing.

Notes

1 On the British Social Attitudes survey, respondents who read a daily morning newspaper at least three times a week are asked to identify which newspaper this is, enabling their classification as tabloid or broadsheet readers. Since a measure of online newspaper readership was introduced on the survey in 2010, a similar follow-up question has been asked, enabling a comparable classification (although many readers view websites not associated with particular newspapers, with the BBC News website being the most popular).
2 Our analysis focuses on the differences between readers of broadsheet and tabloid media, rather than left-leaning and right-leaning newspapers. This is because all newspaper titles can be assigned to the former classification. In addition, we have analysed the relationship between political party affiliation and attitudes to poverty and inequality separately (and this factor is highly correlated with choices regarding political leanings of newspapers).
3 More detailed analysis in relation to the acceptability of poverty and inequality was not possible, as the European Social Survey has not measured media engagement in a consistent way over time.

References

Baumberg, B., Bell, K. and Gaffney, D. (2012). *Benefits Stigma in Britain*. London: Turn2Us. Available at: https://wwwturn2us-2938.cdn.hybridcloudspan.com/T2UWebsite/media/Documents/BenefitsStigma-in-Britain.pdf [Accessed May 2019].

Chauhan, A. and Foster, J. (2014). Representation of poverty in British newspapers: a case of 'othering' the threat? *Journal of Community and Applied Social Psychology*, [online] Volume 24(5), pp. 390–405. Available at: https://onlinelibrary.wiley.com/doi/abs/10.1002/casp.2179 [Accessed May 2019].

Clery, E. and Dangerfield, P. (2019). Poverty and inequality: have attitudes evolved in line with official trends or political and media discourse? In: J Curtice, E Clery, J Perry, M Phillips and N Rahim, ed. *British Social Attitudes: The 36th Report*. London: The National Centre for Social Research.

Clery, E., Lee, L. and Kunz, S. (2013). *Public Attitudes to Poverty and Welfare, 1983–2011: Analysis Using British Social Attitudes Data.* London: The National Centre for Social Research, available at: http://www.natcen.ac.uk/media/137637/poverty-and-welfare.pdf

Curtice, J. and Mair, A. (2008). Where have all the readers gone?: popular newspapers and Britain's political health. In: Park, A., Curtice, J., Thomson, K., Phillips, M., Johnson, M. and Clery, E., ed. *British Social Attitudes: The 24th Report.* London: Sage.

Department for Work and Pensions. (2020). *Households Below Average Income: An Analysis of the UK Income Distribution: 1994/95–2018/19.* London: Department for Work and Pensions. Available at: https://assets.publishing.service.gov.uk/government/uploads/system/uploads/attachment_data/file/875261/households-below-average-income-1994-1995-2018-2019.pdf [Accessed September 2020].

Full Fact. (2019). Poverty in the UK: a guide to the facts and figures. Available at https://fullfact.org/economy/poverty-uk-guide-facts-and-figures/ [Accessed May 2019].

Jensen, T. (2014). Welfare common-sense, poverty porn and doxosophy. *Sociological Research Online*, [online] 19(3), p. 3. Available at: http://www.socresonline.org.uk/19/3/3.html [Accessed May 2019].

Labour Party. (2017). *For the Many Not the Few: The Labour Party Manifesto 2017.* London: The Labour Party, available at: https://labour.org.uk/wp-content/uploads/2017/10/labour-manifesto-2017.pdf

McKendrick, J., Sinclair, S., Irwin, A., O'Donnell, H., Scott, G. and Dobbie, L. (2008). *The Media, Poverty and Public Opinion in the UK.* York: Joseph Rowntree Foundation. Available at: https://www.jrf.org.uk/report/media-poverty-and-public-opinion-uk [Accessed May 2019].

Parkes, H. and McNeil, C. (2020). Estimating poverty impacts of coronavirus: microsimulation estimates. Available at https://www.ippr.org/files/2020-06/estimating-poverty-impacts-of-coronavirus.pdf [Accessed September 2020].

Sippit, A. and Tranchese, A. (2015). *How Did the Media and Politicians in the UK Discuss Poverty in 2015?* York: Joseph Rowntree Foundation. Available at: https://www.jrf.org.uk/report/howdid-media-and-politicians-uk-discuss-poverty-2015 [Accessed May 2019].

Social Metrics Commission website, accessed April 2019: http://socialmetricscommission.org.uk/

Wells, R. and Caraher, M. (2014). UK print media coverage of the food bank phenomenon: From food welfare to food charity? *British Food Journal*, [online] 116(9), pP. 1426–1445. Available at: http://openaccess.city.ac.uk/8666/1/Wells%20print%20media.pdf [Accessed May 2019].

12 Debating inequality
The case of Piketty's capital in the 21st century

Andrea Grisold and Hendrik Theine

In the past couple of years, the issues of economic and social inequality have re-entered the stage of political attention and debate in many countries, after decades of benign neglect. This chapter is based on the research findings of an international and transdisciplinary project on the media coverage of economic inequality (Grisold and Preston, 2020). In this empirical research, the media treatment of Thomas Piketty's book serves as a paramount example of the mediation of economic inequality,[1] and one which sheds light on the neglected topic of media coverage on economic inequality. As a major transnational and cross-disciplinary study, it analysed the highly controversial discourse on inequality topics that were raised by Piketty's best-selling book in selected print media in four European countries: the UK, Ireland, Germany and Austria.

In this chapter, we problematise that the information news media provide about economic inequality and the respective remedies they suggest. The paper is structured in the following way: After a short introduction on the methods and data used, we present the major findings of our empirical work, showing that the media coverage of economic inequality favours a justification of neoliberalism through an overemphasis on meritocracy, deals with the economic consequences of inequality, but hardly with the interconnectedness of the political and economic spheres. With a general scepticism regarding redistribution policies, they are discussed to a lesser extent than rising inequality. We conclude by embedding those findings in the broader terms of inequality studies.

Introduction: inequality and the "media event" of Piketty's book

Critical media scholars have highlighted a construction of reality of inequality that is centrally shaped by mass media (Gandy, 2007; Schifferes and Roberts, 2015). Economic discussions concerning questions of economic inequality predominantly focus on its quantitative evaluation (Antonelli and Rehbein, 2018; Galbraith, 2012). The topic of how these research findings are mediated to the public is barely addressed although it is of particular relevance to how non-experts

DOI: 10.4324/9781003104476-16

are informed and how their notions of economic inequality are framed; indeed, the acceptance of redistribution policies correlates with the concept of inequality people have in mind (see, for empirical evidence, Gimpelson and Treisman, 2018).

The unexpected popularity of Thomas Piketty's book "Capital in the twenty-first Century" (C21) in 2014/2015 was a clear – and media-effective – sign of this increased interest in the topic of economic inequality. It reached the top of the bestseller lists and was described as a "media sensation", Piketty himself as a "rockstar economist". Piketty's key thesis stated that inequality is destined to worsen and that the post-war Keynesian period of progress, in terms of a flattening inequality curve, was, in fact, just a small deviation from the norm. What Piketty termed "patrimonial capitalism" (2014, p. 173) is a formation that is characterised by continual increases in economic inequality, which will continue unless drastic action is taken.

Piketty's approach intentionally includes an historical focus and methods to improve understanding around the mechanisms and implications of economic inequality. The book represents both a summary and a popularisation of more than 20 years of research by Piketty and his colleagues (Atkinson et al., 2011; Piketty, 2011; Piketty and Saez, 2014; Piketty and Zucman, 2014). Piketty shows that economic inequality within developed countries follows a U-shape relationship in the twentieth century up to now: first, inequality fell, but since the 1980s income and wealth inequality gained momentum with the "conservative revolution" (Piketty, 2014, p. 333). His figures show that today, the lower half of the population has about 5 per cent of the overall wealth at its disposal, whereas 95 per cent of wealth is in the hands of the upper half. Piketty's insights included suggestions for policy to tackle the widening inequality gap, such as a new wealth tax policy (see below for further details) (Piketty, 2014). The academic as well as the public discussion varied tremendously in their assessments of Piketty's scientific achievements[2]: notable scholars argued it is "one of the watershed books in economic thinking" (Milanovic, 2014, p. 519) and described it as "a revolution in our understanding of long-term trends in inequality" (Krugman, 2014).

Nonetheless, Piketty's was also criticised by a broad array of economists. Several major mainstream economists rejected and challenged the whole of Piketty's analytical framework by critically examining his interpretation of the laws of capitalism and the (meanwhile notorious) formula of $r > g$. Many used the standard mainstream argument that increasing capital stocks will, over time, result in decreasing returns on capital, and hence, inequality will not rise substantially (Rognlie, 2014; Summers, 2014). Others argued that inequality would almost exclusively originate from housing as the most important single component of capital income (Homburg, 2014; Jones, 2015). Acemoglu and Robinson (2015, 4) criticise that Piketty does not allow political factors to have "a systematic role" in his analysis, while heterodox economists faulted his theoretical foundations as flawed and, hence, not useful (Kapeller, 2014).

The empirical study

This chapter asks the following questions: What are the main positions on economic inequality depicted in media coverage in Europe? How does media coverage portray and judge potential redistribution policies?

To address these questions, we refer to our research findings of an international and transdisciplinary project that covers two different language regions (the English and German language discourse) as well as a good mix of "big" and "small" polities in the European Union setting. In each country, two dailies that are classified as quality newspapers and one major general interest weekly paper (see Table 12.1) were analysed in the period between March 2014 and March 2015. This coincided with the publication of the English translation of C21 in April 2014 and the German translation in the following October.[3]

The final corpus consisted of 329 articles (76 from Germany, 75 from Austria, 118 from UK and 60 from Ireland). All articles were read and manually coded with the qualitative data analysis software MaxQDA, following a detailed coding scheme. Methodologically, we applied critical discourse analysis, as it investigates the linguistic elements of discourse in their wider social and political contexts (Huckin, 2002; Jäger, 2015; Van Dijk, 2004).

There are significant similarities and differences in the political and economic systems of the respective countries being analysed, and they are instructive for the analysis of our data set. The UK had, before Thatcher and pre-1980s, strong Keynesian politics. Post 1980s, Thatcher's leadership made the UK a forefront of neoliberalism, with privatisation and individualisation becoming two important policy targets. Ireland, on the other hand, switched from a conservative, catholic agrarian society to one dominated by the service sector in the late 20th century, according to neoliberal principles as well. Germany established a Social Market Economy in the 1950s, while Austria had a strong social partnership and a Keynesian tradition, the latter especially associated with the charismatic chancellor Bruno Kreisky in the 1970s and early 1980s. These German-speaking countries have been interventionist in many of their policies (be it industrial policy or housing or social security), and more so than their English-speaking counterparts. Ireland, with its strong (and EU permitted) *Standortpolitik*, has specifically attracted several US multinationals to move their headquarters there,

Table 12.1 List of selected news outlets

	Daily newspapers	Weekly newspapers
Germany	Frankfurter Allgemeine Zeitung Süddeutsche Zeitung	Spiegel
Austria	Der Standard Die Presse	Profil
The United Kingdom	The Guardian The Financial Times	The Sunday Times
Ireland	The Irish Times	Sunday Independent

and so, it can be argued that they too have been interventionist in their economic policy approaches.

There is some comparative academic work, which has analysed different models of capitalist economies, and which distinguishes between liberal market economies (UK and Ireland) and coordinated market economies (Germany and Austria) (Hall and Soskice, 2001). Esping-Andersen (first published in 1990) identified different welfare state regimes, where the UK and Ireland are classified as "Liberal Regimes" with rather minimal and often privately oriented welfare schemes, while Germany and Austria are part of the "Conservative Regimes", typically shaped by traditional family values and social security benefits based on employment.

Other comparative research focuses on the interdependencies between the media and their respective political systems, with a focus on the different roles attributed to media in politics (Hallin and Mancini, 2004). Of the three major models of media systems, Ireland and the UK are considered part of the "Liberal Model" (this is market dominated, except public broadcasting well developed in Britain and Ireland, as is its medium newspaper circulation, and a strong professionalisation in journalism). Germany and Austria are, by comparison, part of the "Democratic Corporatist Model" (this refers to high newspaper circulation, press subsidies and protection for press freedom, and institutionalised self-regulation of journalism). As a general trend, Hallin and Mancini (2004) also observe a transformation process of convergence and homogenisation between the models.

A key characteristic of the traditional newspaper industry is that it has been under enormous pressure from certain large and powerful, external commercial competition in recent years. Turnover, advertising income and circulation have been shrinking, even if the patterns of ownership of newspapers have remained relatively stable over the years. More precisely, for the four countries of our study, individuals and especially family clans represent the predominant form of ownership; exemptions are three of the newspapers (*Frankfurter Allgemeine Zeitung (FAZ)*, *The Guardian* and *The Irish Times*) established under private non-profit foundations, albeit from very different ideological backgrounds (Bureau van Dijk, 2017; Ferschli et al., 2019).

The discourse on economic inequality in the press – key findings

Let us first look at the general stance towards inequality in our corpus. Table 12.2 contains the number of newspaper articles grouped according to their attitude within the period of analysis. In total, we found 178 articles with an explicit stance on economic inequality. Although the remaining 151 articles in our sample do report about Thomas Piketty, C21 and the great inequality debate, they do not explicitly take any position on economic inequality. Such articles, for instance, report only the key figures and statistics given in the book.

Of the 178 articles that have a clear stance, over half of them, 108, consider economic inequality to be a problem, while 51 portray inequality as not being a problem and another 19 remain neutral. There was no significant time difference for the stance towards inequality, except for many articles appearing in May and October 2014, corresponding with the publication dates of the English and German version of Piketty's book.

Table 12.2 also sheds light on the differences in the reception to Piketty's work, and economic inequality more generally, across the four countries. In the English-speaking countries, the number of articles which portray inequality as problematic is higher compared to the ones that do not. While there are several articles of the latter kind in Germany and the United Kingdom, the Irish coverage, by comparison, seems to be overtly pro-Piketty (see line "Ineq prob" and "ineq no prob" of Table 12.2). Austria marks a striking difference, as the majority of the articles do not assess inequality as a problem.

Table 12.2 Number of newspaper articles with a stance towards economic inequality

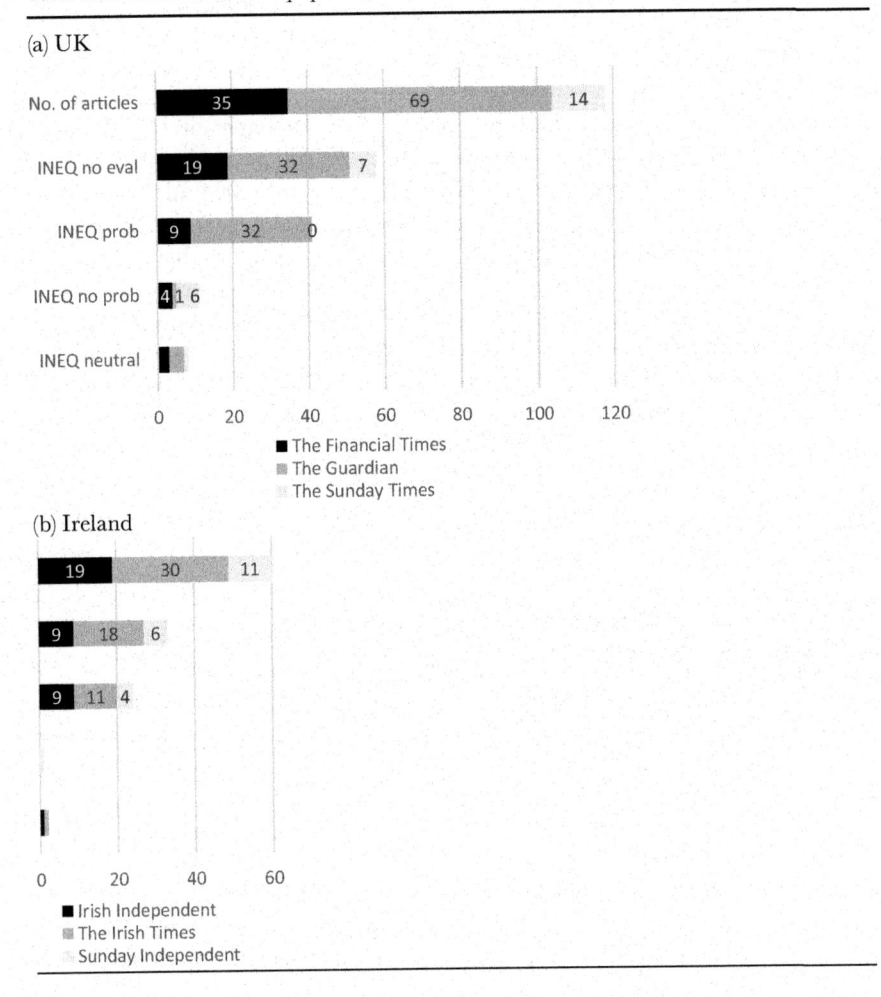

(a) UK

Category	The Financial Times	The Guardian	The Sunday Times
No. of articles	35	69	14
INEQ no eval	19	32	7
INEQ prob	9	32	0
INEQ no prob	4	1	6
INEQ neutral			

(b) Ireland

Category	Irish Independent	The Irish Times	Sunday Independent
	19	30	11
	9	18	6
	9	11	4

Table 12.2 continued

(c) Germany

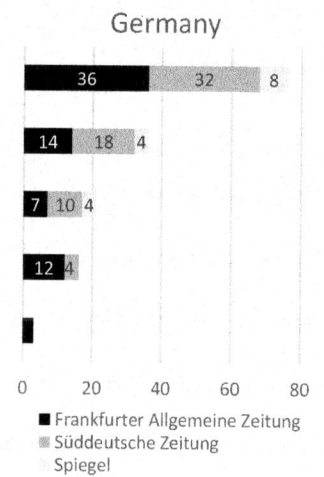

Germany

	FAZ	SZ	Spiegel
	36	32	8
	14	18	4
	7	10	4
	12	4	
	1		

- Frankfurter Allgemeine Zeitung
- Süddeutsche Zeitung
- Spiegel

(d) Austria

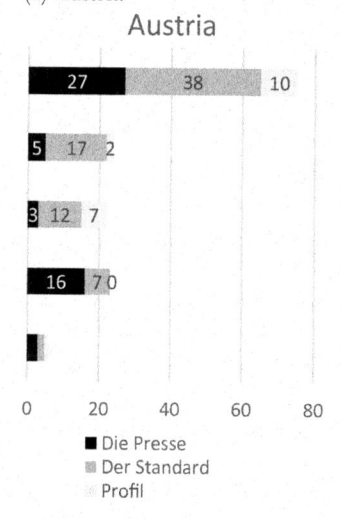

Austria

	Die Presse	Der Standard	Profil
	27	38	10
	5	17	2
	3	12	7
	16	7	0
	1		

- Die Presse
- Der Standard
- Profil

To further analyse Table 12.2, the publications that tend to share a more critical perspective, and view economic inequality as a problem, are mostly centre-left/ social-liberal newspapers (*The Guardian, Irish Times, Süddeutsche Zeitung* and *Der Standard*) – this holds true for all of the four countries in question. By contrast, the total number of articles that assess inequality as unproblematic is comparably higher (line "ineq no prob" of Table 12.2) in centre-right/market-liberal newspapers (*Frankfurter Allgemeine Zeitung, Die Presse, Financial Times* and *Sunday Times*). Within the weekly or Sunday papers in our sample, only the Murdoch-owned

Sunday Times is highly critical of Piketty's problematisation of inequality. Again, Ireland seems to represent a specific case as the *Irish Independent*, a rather conservative outlet, does not contain articles uncritical to economic inequality.

Concerning authorship, almost 80 per cent of the articles were written by staff or freelance journalists, while the remaining 20 per cent are opinion pieces or regular columns, most of them written by economists. And, it is rather stunning that 80 per cent of the authors are male.

In addition to assessing the effects of quantitative analysis sketched above, on the general attitudes towards inequality, a major focus of our empirical work is concerned with the qualitative findings, applying a critical discourse analysis. Derived out of this qualitative analysis of the corpus, the following specific framings of economic inequality can be grouped in the following categories: *reference to common conventions of society, economic consequences, political consequences and social consequences.*

Common conventions of society – meritocracy

Regarding the first category, it came quite as a surprise that the category *reference to common conventions of society* turned out to be the most frequently discussed in articles on the good or bad of economic inequalities. In this category, the societal conventions and *Leitbilder* meritocracy, social justice and social mobility are referred to.

Meritocracy, in its essence, refers to the idea that effort and talent should be the primary indicator for higher income and wealth, closely connected to success in the social hierarchy. It is crucial to note that, in almost all articles, individual effort is equated to "hard work"[4], rewarded through markets and attributed to individual efforts. Thus, neither questions of group efforts, which might not be assigned to individuals exclusively, nor unpaid work are considered relevant – except one article only out of the entire sample.

Within the body of articles that highlight problems of rising inequality, it is widely acknowledged that individual efforts and the appropriate remuneration in terms of wealth, income and – sometimes – societal status diverge. The significant tendency identified is that, instead of effort and talent, it is inheritance and birth that determine social status. Individual wealth based on inheritance is sharply criticised, for example, in the *Süddeutsche Zeitung*: "birth is a lottery, not a merit"[5] (Schulz, 2014).

In line with the normative principle of a presumed meritocracy, the problem of growing inequality is interpreted under the paradigm of whether meritocracy leads to unequal opportunities. The existence of economic inequality is considered legitimate if "justice" is guaranteed through equality of opportunities. Accordingly, the highly uneven distribution of inheritances is identified as the main obstacle: "You inherit not only wealth but also opportunity", thus resulting in "unearned privileges"; even the "best educated have no chance if they start without wealth" (Monbiot, 2014, p. 29).

Not very surprisingly, in those articles which portray inequality as not problematic, the reference to common societal conventions and, again, meritocracy turns out to be a central argument for the sheer necessity of economic inequality. If inequality is an outcome of merit due to equal opportunities and, thus, equality of chances, then – in contrast to its threatening potential – it is something that should be celebrated. In general, if inequality is a market outcome, there is nothing much we can, or should, do about it. On the contrary, it can serve as an incentive to "take risks" and – as a consequence – be rewarded with "economic success".

The market as default: economic aspects

Topics of *economic aspects and consequences* of inequality, the second most common category in quantitative terms, are likewise taken up by articles which conceive of inequality as a problem and those displaying the reverse argumentation. In both types, this category is salient, as it holds approximately a third of the overall number of coded segments. Articles of this category are often concerned with the consequences of (rising) inequality for economic growth, while the respective arguments are usually dichotomous or in polar opposition to each other.

On the one hand, there is a line of argument that increasing inequality will negatively affect the economy, and, in particular, its growth rates. Redistribution measures to relieve inequality consequently turn out to be a productive way to restore positive and high growth rates as well as a stable economy. On the other hand, other arguments make use of the reverse causality, namely, that high inequality does not harm growth but is instead an important prerequisite to ensure high growth rates. Here, the rationale goes that inequality and the concentration of capital are indispensable for growth, as it provides a solid base for investment and rewards incentives. Those argumentative strategies often stress the importance of capital and wealth for private investment and risk-taking. Wealth is portrayed as "highly productive" capital, tied up in small- and medium-sized businesses and is, thus, essential for the well-being and functionality of the whole of society. The latter arguments are particularly strong in UK articles.

In addition to the dispute over the mechanisms between growth and inequality, there is another relevant, recurring economic topic, namely, that inequality poses a problem for *employment conditions*. UK articles, in particular, frequently assess rising inequality as immersed with impacts on employment conditions because workers are increasingly being forced to accept lower working standards as well as lower wages due to increased competition. This debate is almost non-existent in German articles, even though the empirical evidence for deteriorating working conditions is to be found in those countries as well (e.g. a growing low-paid sector especially in Germany).

There is one peculiar economic rationalisation that is found in articles from all four countries in question – the claims that inequality produces growth, that the poor are actually dependent on the rich and that the rich "create value for other people". Semantically positive descriptions of agents are being introduced, such as wealthy entrepreneurs "transferring wealth", "taking risks" and "creating jobs". The underlying – and very explicit – rationale being that if politicians were to follow Piketty's call to "slap huge taxes on the rich, [...] they will find that it comes back and bites them" (Smith, 2014, p. 16).

Political and social consequences

Articles found in the categories *political consequences* and *social consequences* are only taken up in articles that evaluate inequality as a problem. In articles addressing political consequences, the major concern is the instability and erosion of democratic structures driven by rising inequality. Two processes frequently highlighted in such contributions are (1) the increasing concentration of political and economic power in the hands of a small elite with rising influence on political decisions and processes and (2) the risk that the legitimation of democratic structures might deteriorate (further) due to the inaction of democratic governments to reverse current trends of increasing inequality, which is said to play into the hands of the populist parties. However, even though such complex political currents and processes are addressed and discussed in a set of articles particularly in UK and Irish articles, the narratives usually fail to contextualise the problem in a national context and remain on a very abstract level.

That *social consequences* were not a prominent topic in the articles discussing inequality as problematic, came quite as a surprise. Nonetheless, rising poverty and demanding healthcare issues are discussed as a consequence of growing inequality – both topics that figured prominently (for example, in the popular work of Wilkinson and Pickett [2009]) and were vividly debated at the time of its publication.

Redistribution policies as market distortions

Piketty (2014) devotes part four of his book to reflections on the welfare state, redistribution policies and public debt. Regarding taxation, he proposes a more progressive tax regime with top income taxes of 80 per cent applicable to annual salaries from EUR 500,000. He also recommends a global wealth tax of 1 per cent or 2 per cent to tackle the threats posed by rentiers as the "enemy of democrac[ies]" (p. 422) or the "society of supermanagers" (p. 265) to modern democracies.

In our corpus, a first, yet significant observation is that redistribution policies are less frequently addressed compared to economic inequality topics (see Figure 12.1). The general (quite obvious) pattern, valid for all newspapers of the four countries of our analysis, is that the articles that reject the idea of inequality as a problem (*Sunday Times*, *FAZ* and *Die Presse*) are likewise hostile to the idea of increasing redistribution policies.

In our corpus, it is mostly taxes that are addressed in accordance with Piketty's well-known arguments that new forms of wealth taxation are an essential starting point for any effective strategy to reverse the trend towards economic inequality in recent decades. Articles expressing a negative stance towards Piketty's policy proposals frequently discuss redistribution measures such as taxation

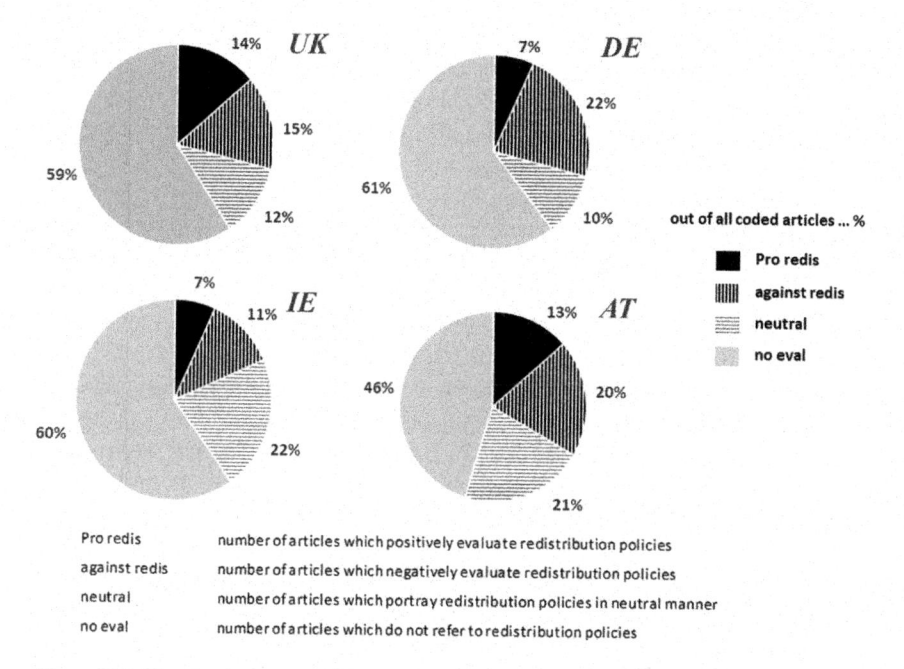

Figure 12.1 Number of newspaper articles by stance towards redistribution policies, 2014–2015.

of the rich/higher tax rates, in general, without further specifying the different forms of wealth and income taxation. Of all specific policies deprecated, wealth tax assumes a leading position in a majority of German articles. This signifies the strong opposition to wealth and inheritance taxation in the German-speaking countries. By contrast, income taxation is referred to only half as frequently.

Arguments in favour of Piketty's proposals and the (global) wealth tax are given priority, but they are referred to twice as often in UK articles. Inheritance taxation, in contrast, is exclusively picked up in the German articles and remains (almost) unmentioned in the English ones, while property taxation, on the other hand, is an Ireland-specific debate. Again, income taxation, with very few exceptions, assumes the status of a non-topic.

While the specific and complex national contexts of political and economic debates cannot be captured fully in this paper, we want to highlight a few contemporary national policy debates during the research period to contextualise the above. While the inheritance and gift tax was abolished in Austria in 2008 (Korom, 2017), there was some political discussion for a reintroduction in the relevant period. In Germany, we are confronted with a different situation: inheritance taxation does exist, but is, in fact, very low due to high amounts exempt from taxation for close relatives and corporate property (Bach and Thiemann, 2016; Korom, 2017). The high amounts exempt from taxation for the bequest of corporate property was ruled unlawful by the German Constitutional Court in

December 2014, a cause for contentious debates. Given the fact that both Austria and Germany range among the nations with the highest wealth concentrations, it is no wonder that wealth taxation has become part of public discourse, surprisingly though, it is presented as more of a threat than an option.

In Austria, the debate on a wage tax reform was ongoing at the time of the debates we have analysed (finally implemented in 2016), but a connection between Piketty's tax proposals for high incomes and an imminent wage tax reform was not made at all. A similar discussion was taking place in Ireland for a property tax, and the debate is present in the Irish media, albeit in the very few articles that deal with policies. For the UK, it seems puzzling that inheritance taxation is not picked up in any of the articles given the specific national context. Even though the UK taxes inheritance at a comparatively high rate, it grants large exemptions for close family members and, as a result, it raises very little revenue and applies to very few households (Atkinson, 2015; Wilson, 2018). Considering the example of the low corporate taxes in Ireland – a cause of major controversy both in Ireland and Europe – the absence of this topic in discussions on inequality (and public policy) has to be labelled as a significant silence.

We introduce another layer of analysis here in the form of three argumentative strategies. The first line of argument is grouped into what Vaara (2014) refers to as *inevitability*: texts proclaiming that redistribution policies are no good and not feasible, without any further explanation as to why this is the case. Piketty is characterised as a utopian, and his policy proposals are called "dutiful" (pflichtbewusst). The arguments come from a perceived realist perspective (which the authors themselves are claiming to take) because it is "inconceivable" that the introduction of a global wealth tax "will come to anything in the near future" (Priestland, 2014). Second and likewise, *prejudices* are introduced as soon as the subject of redistribution policies is addressed. Here, authors exert long-standing narratives and imaginaries to side line the debate over possible policies. That "high-tax policy" will "impoverish societies" might serve as an example as well as the idea that only enterprises stir innovation.

A further, third strategy can be termed *insinuation*. Frequent associations with Marx are construed in two different ways. German language articles present Piketty as the "New Marx" (even though he is highly critical of Marxist thought) and, thus, within the radical left of the political spectrum. Articles in English refer more specifically to the book C21 and its proposals which are referred to as "Marxian", "ideology-driven", "confiscatory" and "socialist utopia". Both strategies serve to undermine Piketty's credibility as a scientist and economist (and his work as a credible contribution to economic thought).

In all four countries and in all newspapers analysed, economic rationalisation features as an extensively applied strategy to de-legitimatise policies. Discursive strands making use of this strategy are constructing some form of causal relationship between the means (higher taxation on wealth and income) and a variety of negative effects (unemployment, low economic growth, etc.). This typically involves the explicit or implicit adaption of economic concepts such as the rational-choice theory (and neoclassical economics more broadly), often backed by quotes from experts. These classify redistribution policies as market distortions, as inefficient and entailing high costs for the economy and businesses. In order to lend more force to a rational argument, taxes are treated as personified agents (taxes kill) in active clauses, and a large array of metaphors are adduced to mark the immediate danger that emanates from them: taxes are a "burden" that squeeze citizens dry, "cause pain", "endanger life", are a "curse" and are sometimes placed in military, war-like semantic contexts. Furthermore, there is a strong tendency to present various social and economic actors as victims of state action, mostly companies and "the entrepreneur". Both groups are depicted as lacking agency in the face of an aggressive, overpowering and abusive state that subjects them to the risks of bankruptcy and capital flight.

While opponents of redistribution policies argue with negative impacts on growth and incentives, there are some positive arguments that mention enhancing stability, raising state revenues, boosting demand and restoring the meritocratic principle. However, even in pro-redistribution articles, we find a lot of neoliberal framing (taxes confiscate, need to be simplified) and little positive framing in the Keynesian sense, evident particularly in the German and UK articles. The latter argumentation is that state action to counteract market developments is necessary and useful (Keynesian), and a market correction is required to check the concentration of wealth. Still, the articles with a positive stance towards redistribution policies are fewer and their argumentation more defensive – policies are portrayed in an ambivalent way, highlighting both their positive and negative implications, albeit attesting more weight to the positive ones. Adjectives that semantically feed the opposite discourse, e.g. "kräftig besteuern" (to tax heavily), "der Staat kassiert" (the state seizes), evoking an image of pushing it too far.

The overall corpus of newspaper articles also ascribes a highly ambivalent role to the state. On the one hand, the state attributed with the capability to correct and mitigate inequality, contributing to a more equal society. On the other hand, a clearly neoclassic, neoliberal and sometimes even Hayekian state (the road to serfdom) is presented as "grossly inefficient", "dysfunctional" and state power as "abusive", with the "real problem" being debt, not inequality. The argument against redistribution policies is that less, not more state intervention is required, sometimes explicitly naming privatisation and private pension systems as necessities.

Given this portrayal of redistribution policies and the role of the state, economic prosperity is closely interconnected with entrepreneurialism. The question of what drives economic prosperity is often answered accordingly. The state reduces prosperity, while incentives and entrepreneurs drive it. Ordinary employees are not even mentioned, and politicians exclusively succeed in getting everything wrong. International agreements won't function, and even ordinary people just don't want (higher) taxes.

When public policies are referred to, or discussed, there is a high concentration of focus on taxes and regulation and less on the "investing" aspects of public policies, such as in schools, kindergartens, hospitals or infrastructure. We would like to point out again that we analysed a text corpus with a Piketty connection, and the relevant proposals in his book focus on tax policies, especially income, wealth and inheritance tax. Still, the articles ignore the fact that both the incentives for innovation and the re-distributional features of today's everyday life (health, general education, etc.) are based on regulation and public policies. These are an active counterpart to the forces of deregulated capitalism. As many scholars have stressed over the last decades (Galbraith, 1958; Mazzucato, 2015), it is exactly this mix of market forces and counteracting forces that provided for a system which manages to stabilise the economy and curb at least some of the rising social imbalances.

These different approaches may be taken to correspond quite closely to different underlying economic theories, assumptions and ideologies. Whereas neoclassical economics, for example, sees the role of the state in providing only a general frame for market economies, (Post-)Keynesian and other heterodox theories take a (critical) political economy approach, stressing the necessity of state intervention to curb the self-destroying tendencies of capitalism, without forgetting that state intervention can lead to contrary effects regarding inequality as well.

Conclusion

Our research has begun to close a gap in research on the mediated communication of economic topics. In the articles analysed, we can identify more significant and forceful statements on inequality than in a coverage of policy proposals. We are confronted with rather one-sided images and concepts: an overemphasis of meritocracy, strong discord over the economic consequences of inequality, an underestimation of the interconnectedness of political and economic spheres and a neglect of societal negotiations and power imbalances in society. The very conclusion on (further) redistribution policies is that they are mostly understood in terms of taxation, discussed and explained to a lesser extent than the general conviction that "something needs to be done" and are generally given highly negative attributions.

Throughout the corpus, numerous examples of significant silences (Huckin, 2002) are detected. In addition to an absent discussion about societal power relations, it also lacks acknowledgement that both the initialising of innovation and the redistribution features in modern societies (healthcare, general education, etc.) are based on regulation and public policies. They provide an active countervailing power to the forces of deregulated capitalism (Galbraith, 1964). It is exactly this mix of market and market-counteracting forces that provided for a system for stabilising the economy. Furthermore, the defensive articles that debate the issue within a historical perspective show a rather naïve faith in markets, which totally ignores the fact that the improvements for the non-wealthy over time were achieved by class struggles and (sometimes even militant) clashes of interest.

To summarise, the findings of this research identify a number of conceptual problems in the media coverage analysed, which may be referred to as biased simplifications: (1) an implicit justification and rationalisation of the (neo)liberal economic approach to the principles of individual work and merit, and of the centrality of the entrepreneur; (2) very restrained arguments regarding the positive role of public policies for economic development, stability and the welfare state and (3) a stark (though not total) opposition to new ideas for redistribution policies to counteract inequality. As far as substantial differences in the coverage between the different countries are observed, we find an extension of what Hallin and Mancini (2004) called a general trend, a transformation process of convergence and homogenisation between the different models of media systems.

Based on these results, we would need to question the media's normative function as a source of information and a watchdog. Being aware that such a seemingly irrevocable trend is not easily modified, we conclude with some suggestions that may be functional in bringing about changes.

1. Journalist's training and background

    In his article on media and the crisis, Joseph Stiglitz (2015) argued that economic topics were highly underrepresented in the media before the financial crisis and, therefore, journalists were not specifically trained to understand economics' nexuses. While, in the aftermath of the global financial crisis, the first argument is not valid any longer, the second still is. Therefore, training journalists in economics, providing a pluralist view, thus acknowledging that economic activities and policies do not necessarily benefit all, but involve a clash of interests, is of vital importance. It should not be disregarded that socialisation matters in how economic prerequisites are conceptualised and stories framed.

2. Ownership structures – Freeing media from commercial pressures

    The rather selective patterns of news media coverage are not surprising, given a commercial media system that is not only owned and controlled by wealthy elites but is also increasingly dependent on advertising and sponsorship. Thus, in our opinion, any appropriate programme of media reforms must be centred on the issues of new kinds of resources to support an alternative array of media institutions – characterised by organisational goals, institutional values and managerial ethics that are radically different to those of the mainstream.

3. Establishing a counter-public sphere

    As Habermas demanded, as early as in the 1960s, a counter-public sphere is a vital requirement for any political discourse and change (Habermas 1962). A variety of different and competing positions must be debated in a substantial way to produce constructive and productive discourse. As Galbraith (1964) argued, news media content needs a countervailing power to provide alternative and discursive tenors. With the digital revolution, the types of media where this can take place are manifold, but the message is still the same: that news, like education, is a public good and should be treated accordingly.

Notes

1 In this article, we use the term 'economic inequality' for income and wealth inequality. Furthermore, the term 'redistribution policies' is used to describe those policies which aim at reducing economic inequality.
2 For a review of the academic reception of Piketty's book, see also Theine and Grabner (2020).

3 The period also coincides with Piketty's C21 promotional tour to Ireland, the UK, Austria and Germany.
4 In the following, all very short citations in double quotes are taken from our empirical corpus. For the cause of readability, we refrain from citing all those.
5 "Geburt ist Glückssache und keine Leistung".

References

Acemoglu, D. and J. A. Robinson. (2015). The rise and decline of general laws of capitalism. *Journal of Economic Perspectives* 29(1), pp. 3–28.

Antonelli, G. and B. Rehbein. (2018). *Inequality in economics and sociology. New perspectives.* Oxon: Routledge.

Atkinson, A. B., T. Piketty, and E. Saez. (2011). Top incomes in the long run of history. *Journal of Economic Literature*, 49(1), pp. 3–71.

Atkinson, A. (2015). *Inequality: What can be done?* Cambridge, MA: Harvard University Press.

Bach, S. and A. Thiemann. (2016). Hohe Erbschaftswelle, niedriges Erbschaftsaufkommen. *DIW Wochenbericht* 3, pp. 63–71.

Bureau, van Dijk. *Orbis.* (2017). Accessed November 10, 2017. https://orbis.bvdinfo.com/

Esping-Andersen, G. (1990). *Three worlds of welfare capitalism.* Princeton, NJ: Princeton University Press.

Ferschli, B., D. Grabner, and H. Theine. (2019). *Zur politischen Ökonomie der Medien in Deutschland: Eine Analyse der Konzentrationstendenzen und Besitzverhältnisse.* ISW-Report Nr. 118, München: Institut für Sozial-Ökologische Wirtschaftsforschung.

Galbraith, J. K. (2012). *Inequality and instability: A study of the world economy just before the great crisis.* Oxford University Press.

Galbraith, J. K. (1964). *American capitalism: The concept of countervailing power.* Revised ed. London: Hamish Hamilton.

Galbraith, J. K. (1958). *The affluent society.* Boston, MA: Houghton-Mifflin.

Gandy, O. H. Jr. (2007). Minding the gap: Covering inequality in the NY Times and the Washington Post. *Paper presented at the IAMCR Section on Political Communication*, Paris.

Gimpelson, V. and D. Treisman. (2018). Misperceiving inequality. *Economics & Politics* 30(1), pp. 27–54.

Grisold, A. and P. Preston, eds. (2020). *Economic inequality and news media: Discourse, power, and redistribution.* Oxford/New York: Oxford University Press.

Habermas, J. (1971 [1962]). *Strukturwandel der Öffentlichkeit. Untersuchungen zu einer Kategorie der bürgerlichen Gesellschaft.* 5th ed, Neuwied/Berlin.

Hallin, D. C., and Mancini, P. (2004). *Comparing media systems: Three models of media and politics.* Cambridge: Cambridge University Press.

Homburg, S. (2014). Critical remarks on Piketty's "Capital in the Twenty-first Century". University of Hannover, Discussion Paper 530.

Huckin, T. (2002). Textual silence and the discourse of homelessness. *Discourse & Society* 13(3), pp. 347–372.

Jäger, S. (2015). *Kritische Diskursanalyse: Eine Einführung.* 6th ed. Münster: Unrast Verlag.

Jones, C. I. (2015). "Pareto and Piketty: The macroeconomics of top Income and wealth inequality". *Journal of Economic Perspectives* 29(1): 29–46.

Kapeller, J. (2014). "Die Rückkehr des Rentier". *Wirtschaft und Gesellschaft* 40(2): 329–346.

Korom, P. (2017). Erben [heirs], " in: *Handbuch Reichtum: Neue Erkenntnisse aus der Ungleichheitsforschung,* edited by Nikolaus Dimmel, Julia Hofmann, Martin Schenk and Martin, Schürz, pp. 244–254. Wien: Studienverlag.

Krugman, P. (2014). "Rich getting wealthier but inequality denial persists". *The Irish Times*, June 3.
Mazzucato, M. (2015). *The entrepreneurial state: Debunking public vs. private sector myths*. Vol. 1. Anthem Press.
Milanovic, B. (2014). "The return of "patrimonial capitalism": A review of Thomas Piketty's capital in the Twenty-First Century". *Journal of Economic Literature* 52(2): 519–534.
Monbiot, G. (2014). "The rich want us to believe their wealth is good for us all: As the justifications for gross inequality collapse, only the Green party is brave enough to take on the billionaires' boot boys", *The Guardian*, July 30: 29.
Peter A. H., and D. Soskice. (2001). *Varieties of capitalism: The institutional foundations of comparative advantage*, Oxford University Press, Oxford.
Pickett, K., and R. Wilkinson. (2009). *The spirit level: Why more equal societies almost always do better*, London: Allen Lane.
Piketty, T. (2011). "On the long-run evolution of inheritance: France 1820–2050". *The Quarterly Journal of Economics*, 126(3): 1071–1131.
Piketty, T., and G. Zucman. (2014). "Capital is back: Wealth-income ratios in rich countries 1700–2010", *The Quarterly Journal of Economics* 129(3): 1255–1310.
Piketty, T., and E. Saez. (2014). "Inequality in the long run". *Science*, 344(6186): 838–843.
Piketty, T. (2014). *Capital in the twenty-first century*. Oxford: Cambridge University Press.
Priestland, D. (2014). "Are we at a Piketty tipping point for the left? Unfortunately, history suggests not". *The Guardian*, May 7.
Rognlie, M. (2014). *A note on Piketty and diminishing returns to capital*. Retrieved from http://www.mit.edu/~mrognlie/piketty_diminishing_returns.pdf. [Last viewed 20.9.2016].
Schifferes, S. A., and R. Roberts. (2015). *The media and financial crises: Comparative and historical perspectives*, London: Routledge.
Schulz, J. (2014). "Erben ist ungerecht". *Süddeutsche Zeitung*, December 16: 17.
Smith, D. (2014). "Why has this frenchman got the world at his feet?" *The Sunday Times*, April 27: 16.
Stiglitz, J. E. (2015). "The media and the crisis. An information theoretic approach". In: Schifferes, S.A. and Roberts, R. eds. *The media and financial crises: Comparative and historical perspectives*. London: Routledge, 140–152.
Summers, L. (2014). "The inequality puzzle: Thomas Piketty's tour de force analysis doesn't get everything right, but it's certainly got us pondering the right questions". *Democracy Journal*, 33: 91–99.
Theine, H., and D. Grabner. (2020). "Trends in economic inequality and news mediascape". In: *Economic inequality and news media: Discourse, power, and redistribution*, edited by Andrea Grisold and Paschal Preston, Oxford/New York: Oxford University Press, 21–47.
Vaara, E. (2014). "Struggles over legitimacy in the Eurozone crisis: Discursive legitimation strategies and their ideological underpinnings". *Discourse & Society* 25(4): 500–518.
Van Dijk, T. A. (2004). From text grammar to critical discourse analysis. A brief academic biography. *Program of Discourse Studies*. Amsterdam: University of Amsterdam.
Wilson, T. (2018). *Inheritance tax on property: Everything you need to know about the 2017 changes to inheritance tax on your home, houses and property, and the rules and thresholds for the main residence nil-rate band in 2018/19*. WHICH, 2018. Accessed April 19. https://www.which.co.uk/money/tax/inheritance-tax/inheritance-tax-property-changes-asy688s1j5zj

13 The media and austerity

Mike Berry

Introduction

The 2008 Financial Crisis precipitated the worst global recession since the Great Depression. The initial response from policymakers was a revival of Keynesianism, as states across the world launched stimulus packages. However, the turn to Keynesianism was short-lived and by the middle of 2010, G20 finance ministers had endorsed a policy of fiscal consolidation as a response to a worldwide surge in sovereign debt (Giles and Oliver, 2010). This chapter uses a range of qualitative research on public perceptions and media narratives to show how the public came to accept the consequent sharps cuts to the welfare state that have widened inequality and restricted the life chances of significant sections of the population.

This turn to austerity has had major implications for inequality levels in the UK. Although as Clery (in this volume) notes, levels of poverty and income inequality did not rise between 2006 and 2018, this static aggregate picture masks the divergent fortunes of different groups of citizens. (Something Roberts and Grisold and Theine dissect in this volume.)

For whilst levels of pensioner poverty fell during this period – due, in part, to the 'triple lock' system – other groups, such as households with children, saw poverty rates increase. As a report from the EHCR (2017) demonstrated this was due to highly regressive changes to tax, welfare, social security and public spending, which hit certain groups – women, ethnic minorities, lone parents and families with disabled children – especially hard. As Beatty and Fothergill, (2014) have demonstrated, such policies also drove regional polarisation by widening the socioeconomic divisions between the most and least deprived areas of towns and cities and between richer and poorer parts of the country.

Austerity measures did not just reduce the spending power of disadvantaged groups, they also led to sharp cuts to social services, which are disproportionately used by poorer citizens. For instance, Dearden (2019) reported that, over three years, the average English council had reduced spending on services such as social clubs and youth workers by 40 per cent, with some places seeing falls of up to 91 per cent. Such cuts have had highly negative impacts with the All-Party Parliamentary Group (APPG) on Knife Crime finding that the areas suffering the largest cuts to youth spending also saw the largest increases in knife crime (Dearden, 2019).

DOI: 10.4324/9781003104476-17

Finally, austerity policies have led to a significant increase in wealth inequality (Financial Times, 2016; ONS, 2019) – something Carys Roberts discusses in her chapter. Although rarely receiving the same attention as income inequality, distribution of wealth is arguably as important. As Landy (2013, p. 12) argues wealth provides a store of financial resources available for 'improving life chances, providing further opportunities, securing prestige' and 'passing status along to one's family.' Furthermore, 'high levels of wealth can also buy influence, social capital and political power, in a way that high income alone cannot' (Landy, 2013, p. 13).

Despite the highly negative impact that austerity policies have had on social and economic inequalities, a substantial body of research has demonstrated that such policies were supported by media across a range of countries (e.g. Basu et al., 2018; Berry, 2015, 2016, 2018, 2019; Cawley, 2012; Schifferes and Knowles, 2015). For example, Cawley's (2012, p. 613) study of how the Irish press covered Ireland's budget deficit found reporting 'tended to amplify frames that favoured a broadly neoliberal response to the economic crisis: a reduced public sector and a smaller state'. Another strand of research has examined public attitudes towards balanced budgets and austerity. These have found publics are on the whole 'deficit adverse', but attitudes towards fiscal consolidation are mediated by ideology, education, social class, household income and trust in political elites (Afoko and Vockins, 2013; Blinder and Holtz-Eakin, 1983; Hansen, 1998; Hayo and Neumeier 2014; Stanley, 2014). However, only two studies have attempted to directly examine the relationship between media coverage and public attitudes towards austerity (Barnes and Hicks, 2018; Berry, 2019).

This paper unpacks this relationship using the British example of austerity. Britain has been selected for three reasons. Firstly, the UK instituted a particularly severe form of fiscal consolidation – especially between 2010 and 2015 (Krugman, 2015). Secondly, support for austerity in Britain has been remarkably resilient and has critically underpinned successive Conservative election successes (Ashcroft, 2010; Hunter, 2015). Thirdly, this consistent support for austerity policies appears to challenge a substantial body of academic research which finds governments struggle to reduce spending in the face of public opposition (Starke, 2006).

This chapter will next review polling on attitudes towards austerity. It will then examine qualitative research from focus groups, which unpack the beliefs and assumptions that underpin public attitudes. After this, the chapter will examine what studies tell us about media reporting of deficits and austerity. The chapter then considers how we should interpret the relationship between media frames and public attitudes before drawing some conclusions as to how media may have contributed to public acquiescence to austerity.

Public attitudes towards austerity in the UK

Between 2010 and 2015, YouGov ran a series of austerity themed tracker polls where they asked representative samples of the British population the same questions several times a month (Stanley, 2015). The research showed that, in every poll, more people thought cuts to public spending were necessary (rather than unnecessary) by a margin of between 20 per cent and 33 per cent. This was despite the fact people felt that the cuts were being carried out unfairly and too quickly. The research also found that, in every single poll, more people blamed Labour for the cuts than the Tory party – although the gap in blame between the two shrank from more than 30 per cent in 2010 to 6 per cent in 2015. Despite this narrowing, at no point during the five-year period did even a third of voters blame the Conservative party for the programme of cuts they designed and implemented.

Research also suggests that by 2018, 'austerity fatigue' had set in, with polling finding that two-thirds of all people – and even a slim majority of Conservative voters – thought public spending cuts had either gone 'a little too far' or 'much too far' (Singh, 2018).

To summarise then, until 2015, polling consistently showed that most people thought the austerity programme was unfair and carried out too quickly but also unavoidable. The medicine was seen as bitter but also necessary and those most responsible for the cuts were the Labour party. However, by 2015, austerity fatigue had set in and the consensus in favour of further cuts began to crumble.

Qualitative research allows us to unpack the structures of belief that underlie these attitudes. The remainder of this section will highlight the results of 16 focus groups conducted across the UK in 2009 (Berry, 2019), supplemented by the findings of later qualitative research (Afoko and Vockins, 2013; Stanley, 2014). In these studies, the deficit was widely seen to threaten a major economic crisis and was believed to be a result of historic Labour overspending. When asked which elements of public spending had contributed to the deficit, participants did not tend to highlight areas – that had seen major investment – such as health and education –, but instead pointed to issues such as bank bailouts, wars, immigration and welfare. Immigration, in particular, was regularly cited in groups of low income or older participants, where it was often the first factor that was identified. In one group, a participant spoke of immigrants 'taking all the money and bleeding it dry' (Low-income group, Glasgow). In another group, a participant spoke of how letting in more people meant that the 'books are not going to balance':

> We can't afford to keep them right there's people paying tax for 40 year and then there's somebody comes in here with a full family and they're getting the benefits, the same benefits that someone's been here for fifty year and then at some point the books are not going to balance. (Low income group, Glasgow)

It was also the case that welfare spending and the rise of a 'benefits culture' were widely seen as contributing to the rise in national debt.

RESPONDENT 1: I think this country's got into a benefits culture.
RESPONDENT 2: Yes definitely.

MODERATOR: And you see that as a big reason why the country owes so much money?
RESPONDENT 2: Yes.
RESPONDENT 1: Yeah. (Senior citizen's group, Surrey)

In another group, the deficit was seen as resulting from a mismatch between the 'paying' and the 'drawing' classes – a striking precursor to Coalition narratives of 'strivers and shirkers':

RESPONDENT 1: I think you have a huge disparity in that there a big problem in this country between those who will never leave the paying classes and those who will never leave the drawing classes and I think the younger generation particularly feel a civil war brewing because they spend all their lives going to work to pay for other people's children and quite sensibly decide they can't afford their own because they've got everybody else's to pay for. (Middle-class group, Coventry)

These views on welfare were supported by data from the British Social Attitudes Survey, which found a substantial hardening in attitudes towards those on benefits during New Labour's period in office. In 1997, only 28 per cent of the population agreed with the statement that 'benefits are too high and discourage work', but by 2008, this had risen to 61 per cent (Taylor-Gooby and Taylor, 2015). By 2011, Britain had the highest level of belief in the idea of 'welfare dependency' in a survey of 25 European countries, with 66 per cent of Britons agreeing that 'social benefits/services make people lazy' compared to 37 per cent of Norwegians and only 18 per cent of Greeks (Geiger, 2012).

Aside from immigration and welfare, other parts of public spending which were seen as having contributed to the deficit included public sector pensions, quangos, foreign aid and the EU. In one group, a respondent stated that the EU 'costs millions, trillions even' (Middle-class group, Warwickshire) and in another group:

RESPONDENT 1: We haven't mentioned the EU at all and an enormous amount of money goes into there. On the radio today they said it was going up by 60 per cent
MODERATOR: So you think the EU was a big element [in the rise in the deficit]?
RESPONDENT 1: It's a black hole.
RESPONDENT 2: It's a huge drain, isn't it?
MODERATOR: Is the EU a huge drain on the country?
RESPONDENT 1: Yes. (Middle-class group, Coventry)

What also came across strongly in several studies was a widespread perception that much of New Labour's extra public investment had been wasted (Afoko and Vockins, 2013; Berry, 2019; Stanley, 2014). One focus group participant said that the NHS under New Labour had seen 'some improvement but not a great deal' and that the money hadn't gone 'on what you want to see it go on: more beds, hospitals, more nurses, more doctors' (Low-income group, Glasgow). A common complaint was that the public sector now employed too many consultants or managers:

RESPONDENT 2: Julian don't you believe there's a lot of wastage? Look what they've done to the police, they've amalgamating areas into one, they could do with one HR, one personnel, one this one that.
RESPONDENT 1: What I'm saying is
RESPONDENT 2: And they could save a lot of money in all areas. They got an *overflow of managers*. (Middle-class group, Coventry)

Participants argued that the public sector was 'bloated', 'badly managed', 'wasteful' with many people employed in 'non-jobs'. In one group, a participant complained about the number of equal opportunities officers and argued that 'there must be thousands of people in local government who haven't really got a job' (Middle-class group, Warwickshire).

When participants were asked what could be done to reduce the deficit, they tended to point to proposals they had heard about in the media, or policies that addressed the issues they thought had caused the problem – such as immigration:

MODERATOR: What should be done to reduce the deficit?
RESPONDENT 1: They've got to stop all these immigrations coming in.
MODERATOR: Do you think that's a very big part of it?
RESPONDENT 1: I think that's a lot to do with it.
RESPONDENT 2: Yeah.
RESPONDENT 1: Yes I do.
MODERATOR: If you had to put an idea of the proportion of it what sort of proportion would it be.
RESPONDENT 2: I think it would be quite high
MODERATOR: Would it be a half, a quarter?
RESPONDENT 2: I would say three-quarters because I live in Thornton Heath and believe you me you go there now and honestly it's
RESPONDENT 1: Mmmm.
RESPONDENT 2: We're the odd one out. (Senior citizen group, Surrey)

A number of conclusions about public understanding of deficits and austerity can be drawn from these findings. Firstly, the operation of the economy is widely misunderstood. The public primarily sees government spending as analogous to a household budget or container where virtuous people – 'hard-working taxpayers' – are seen to put in whilst the feckless – welfare claimants and immigrants – drain the pot (Afoko and Vockins, 2013). The deficit crisis was, therefore, seen as having arisen from a situation where too few people were contributing and too many allowed to take out so that the 'money ran out'. Secondly, the public is significantly misinformed about the contours of public spending. Many issues that the public believed contributed significantly to the deficit were either incredibly small in the context of overall public spending –benefits paid to EU nationals, the Millennium Dome, plastic surgery on the NHS, MPs expenses – or were, like EU immigration, actually net contributors to the public purse (Vargas-Silva, 2017). These findings have been confirmed in a recent report by the Economics Statistics Centre of Excellence, which finds there is widespread public confusion about the operation of the economy, and the constituent elements of public expenditure (Runge and Hudson, 2020). Thirdly, support for austerity chimed with a widespread perception that the country had been living beyond its means and there had to be a reckoning. Respondents in both Berry's (2019) and Stanley's (2014) focus groups talked of the growth of a 'plastic society' where 'young people want everything now and they're not prepared to save for it' (Low-income group, Glasgow). But as Stanley (2014, p. 910) notes, such concerns over the real growth in household credit became conflated with perceptions of the public finances:

> The ambiguous nature of 'the UK's debt' allowed the middle-income participants to weave between different levels – personal, the state – with relative ease, seamlessly applying lessons from one and applying them to the other in a process of sense-making. It is also explicitly apparent when discussions of an everyday reliance on debt lead to comments such as: 'Politicians were doing same thing, borrowing money they couldn't afford'.

Such comparisons were particularly powerful because they resonated with deep-seated social beliefs that people had a moral responsibility to pay back debts and that 'one shouldn't live beyond one's means'. Fourthly, the widespread perception that much public spending was wasted – or worse, lavished on the undeserving – gave people the impression that significant cuts would fall on unpopular groups or could be made without impacting frontline services. Polling conducted in June 2009 found that 79 per cent of people agreed with the statement: 'making public services more efficient can save enough money to help cut government spending without damaging services the public receive' (Ipsos-Mori, 2009). This belief was also likely to have been influenced by the Conservatives' own messaging, which stressed that areas like the health service and education would be protected from cuts. In reality, although funding for the NHS did increase in real terms by 1.4 per cent per annum after 2010 – a fall from the average 3.7 per cent increase per year between 1948 and 2010 – it was nowhere near sufficient to cope with the accelerating demands of a rapidly ageing population (Leys, 2020).

This review of public beliefs and attitudes regarding austerity showed that the public believed that the rise in public deficit was caused by Labour overspending, and it threatened an economic crisis. Much of this perceived overspending was thought to have been wasted on non-productive public sector employment or support for the idle and feckless. Furthermore, the increase in EU immigration – particularly from the 2004 accession states – was also widely believed to have contributed to the deficit. To remedy these problems, the public believed that a period of austerity was both inevitable and necessary. If the media were significant in shaping such views, then reporting should have closely corresponded to audience beliefs. In the next section, we will examine this fit.

Reporting of deficits, austerity and underlying issues

The widespread public belief that the rise in the deficit threatened an economic crisis closely mirrors arguments that were dominant in the media from 2009 onwards. Research on press and broadcast coverage found that reporting presented a distorted and alarmist view of the public finances (Berry, 2019). Britain had entered the 2009 recession with an internationally and historically low level of public debt – most of which was long dated and held domestically. Writing in the newsletter of the Royal Economic Society, Neild (2010, 12) commented:

> Today's ratio of debt to GDP does not look abnormal, let alone alarming ... Our deficit – the one figure picked out by the Chancellor – is high, but our debt to GDP is average and our tax ratio is low. Our good corruption score indicates that we are capable of raising tax or cutting expenditure. And, it might be added, our history is outstandingly good. Few if any other countries have managed their national debt for 300 years without default. One would conclude that some action was needed, but not that there were any grounds for alarm.

However, in the British press, discussion of the deficit was infused with fear appeals and apocalyptic language. The scale of the deficit was 'horrifying' (*Guardian*, 23 April, 2009), 'terrifying' (*Daily Mail*, 20 February 2009), 'ruinous' (*Sun*, 26 March 2009) and had created 'a crisis...almost unprecedented outside wartime' (*Telegraph*, 23 April 2009). When international or historical comparisons were made, they were overwhelmingly negative and, at times, featured false information. For instance, in 2009, the UK's debt burden stood at 63.3 per cent of GDP, which was lower than Italy's 116.6 per cent or Greece's 128.7 per cent (Eurostat, 2014), but the *Mail*'s Peter Oborne claimed that:

> These latest official figures show that Britain's financial state is now far, far worse than countries such as Greece or Italy, which we have traditionally looked down upon and sneered at for their profligacy. Italy's indebtedness, though frightening, stands at little more than 100 per cent of GNP. Ours stands at twice that percentage and may well not be sustainable in the long term.
>
> (*Mail*, 20 February 2009)

Underlying the crisis narrative were six specific dangers which the rise in the deficit was said to have created: Britain might lose its AAA credit rating, foreign creditors may stop buying UK gilts, sterling could fall sharply, interest rates may rise making debt servicing very expensive, the IMF might be required to bail out Britain – and most seriously, the UK could go bankrupt:

> Whoever is in power must find urgent spending cuts of £50 BILLION ... Without such drastic surgery, Britain is going bust.
>
> (*Sun*, 6 July 2009)

> This is a time when Britain stands on the brink of bankruptcy, with the Government's debts expected to reach an unprecedented £1.5trillion.
>
> (*Mail*, 5 January 2009)

On the BBC too, many of these arguments were prominently featured and, at times, directly endorsed by journalists. A key reason for this was the dominance of a small range of elite political and economic sources who strongly supported balanced budgets and austerity. These included Conservative politicians, City analysts, the Bank of England, IMF, OECD and CBI. However, by far the most prominent non-political source on the BBC was the Institute for Fiscal Studies, who were treated as both the authoritative voice on fiscal analysis and a key definer of options for reducing the deficit. So, for instance, in one segment, a journalist referenced a report from the organisation which endorsed austerity:

> Well some economists have already warned there will have to be what they call two parliaments of pain before the public finances enter a healthier phase.
>
> (News at Ten, 10 June 2009)

The IFS occupies a unique space in BBC economic coverage. The former BBC economics editor Robert Peston has remarked that the thinktank is 'regarded as the ultimate authority ... basically, when the IFS has pronounced, there's no other argument. It is the word of God' (Akam, 2016). This deference to the thinktank has also been confirmed in academic research which demonstrates how journalists working in broadcast news and online construct the elevated authoritative status of the IFS using 'authority signalling' (Anstead and Chadwick, 2017; Chadwick et al., 2020). But this overreliance and deference to the IFS meant that economists, who doubted the existence of 'bond vigilantes' poised to dump government securities and push up interest rates, were rendered almost invisible in press and broadcast news (Koo, 2009; Krugman, 2009).

In terms of what had caused the crisis, public beliefs again correlated with media frames. Whilst Broadcasting tended to correctly identify the impact of the recession on tax revenues, some press reporting falsely linked the deficit to Labour spending:

> The extent of Gordon Brown's mishandling of the economy is now plain for all to see. He borrowed like a man possessed in the boom years when he should have been paying off debt.
>
> (*Express*, 22 July 2009)

...We ALL will have to foot the bill for Labour's years of showering the state with our money.

(*Sun*, 23 April 2009)

Furthermore, such narratives built on allegations of Labour profligacy which had become increasingly prominent since the turn of the millennia. A Nexis search of four right of centre national newspapers (*Daily Mail, Telegraph, Sun, Express*) using the search string 'public sector OR public spending AND bloated OR inefficien* OR waste*' showed an 800 per cent increase (from 50 to 450 per annum) in articles between 2000 and 2009. Below is a sample of headlines emphasising these themes:

> Brown reveals his other mistress – the wasteful, money-draining NHS.
>
> (*Telegraph*, 30 September 2003)

> £20BN RED TAPE AND PAY RISES SWALLOW UP MONEY FOR SERVICES: YOUR CASH GOES DOWN THE DRAIN.
>
> (*Express*, 26 April 2004)

> The Monster Devouring Britain: Despite the recession, the Guardian yesterday carried its biggest ever public sector advertising section for jobs. And guess what you'll be paying for them all.
>
> (*Mail*, 6 September 2001)

> THE WASTED BILLIONS WE ALL COULD SHARE.
>
> (*Sun*, 23 October 2003)

Effectively, much of the press attempted to delegitimise New Labour's extra public investment by arguing it had been wasted. This was because, as a former political editor of the *Sun* explained, they had doubts about its efficacy and it clashed with their preference for a low tax, small state:

INTERVIEWER: One of the key things we noticed in the period after 2001 when there was a very, very large increase in public spending, the reaction of a lot of the right-wing papers was to argue, effectively, that this extra spending was being wasted?

GEORGE PASCOE-WATSON: Yes.

INTERVIEWER: So that wasn't just a kind of coincidence, it was a deliberate strategy, you wanted to get that point of view across?

GEORGE PASCOE-WATSON: Yes, very much so. Our intellectual view had always been small government, minimal public spending, more *Sun* readers can keep more of the money they earn and in 2001 when they increased the health budget by whatever it was, £12 billion overnight, don't forget we also knew the background to that decision which was basically taken on the back of a cigarette packet. It hadn't been long plotted out and modelled (cited in Berry, 2019: 238–239).

The issue of 'gold-plated' public sector pensions and 'non-jobs' raised in numerous focus groups also mirrored their increased prominence in press accounts from 2002 (Berry, 2019). The same was true of welfare paid to EU migrants. A Nexis search of *Sun, Mail, Express* and *Telegraph* coverage using the keywords 'immigrant OR migrant OR asylum seeker AND benefits or welfare' saw a rise from 200 articles a year in 2000 to over 600 in 2008. Below are a selection of headlines from 2007, echoing arguments from the focus groups that migrants were a significant burden on the welfare state:

Immigrants who are a drain on the taxpayer.
(*Mail*, 1 October 2007)

Migrants 'putting billions on council tax'.
(*Mail*, 1 November 2007)

Immigrants with cancer 'could swamp the NHS'.
(*Mail*, 3 September 2007)

Benefits bill for migrants hits £125m; One in six East Europeans is claiming help from the state.
(*Mail*, 22 August 2007)

Schools are stretched to breaking point by immigrant children.
(*Mail*, 31 May 2007)

Hundreds have left my Romanian town. What for? British benefits; Special Report.
(*Mail*, 21 May 2007)

We can't cope with migrants, warn GPs.
(*Mail*, 27 April 2007)

Stop migrant benefit farce.
(*Sun*, 20 September 2007)

How you can fill your boots with British benefits.
(*Sun*, 15 September 2007)

TERRORISTS Free homes, healthcare and benefits.
(*Sun*, 11 July 2007)

There was also a close fit between focus group members' views on benefit claimants and the negative frames that have long dominated press coverage of welfare (e.g. Bagguley and Mann, 1992; Briant et al., 2011; Golding and Middleton, 1983; Misra et al., 2003; Morrison, 2019). Press accounts during this period were amplified by the rise in fictional and reality television representations of a feckless working class living on benefits (Skeggs and Wood, 2012). It is also notable that other issues seen as contributing to the deficit, such as quangos, foreign aid and the EU, had also been subject to a campaign of sustained negative media coverage over many years (Deacon and Monk, 2001; Anderson and Weymouth, 1999).

In terms of how to address the deficit, there was again a tight fit between media narratives and public beliefs. For instance, the widespread public belief that there was no alternative to sharp cuts in public spending, also dominated media accounts – whether, left or right leaning, press or broadcasting, tabloid or broadsheet:

> The deterioration in the public finances means the winner of the next general election – which has to take place by next summer – will have no choice but to slash public spending and hike taxes.
>
> (*Mail*, 22 July 2009)

> Cuts and tax rises: there is no other way.
>
> (Headline – *Telegraph*, 25 June 2009)

> We must freeze or even cut the cost of keeping six million state workers on the public payroll – or be abandoned by international creditors. There can be no sacred cows.
>
> (*Sun*, 6 July 2009)

> Labour is portraying the Tories as the old enemy of the public sector but it too will have to slash spending if by some miracle it hangs onto power.
>
> (*Guardian*, 19 June 2009)

> WE are heading for a new age of austerity. Whether Labour or the Tories win the next election, the country will be faced with making massive spending cuts. The reason is starkly simple. This year the Government will borrow £175billion – around £2868 for everyone in the UK.
>
> (*Mirror*, 3 July 2009)

> What will be cut, by how much and when? As the Government's coffers grow ever more empty, those are questions that can no longer be avoided.
>
> (*BBC1* News at Ten, 10 June 2009)

Finally, the lack of awareness in focus groups of alternatives to spending cuts reflected the almost complete absence of discussion of other options in the mass media. In this sense, the media limited the parameters of public debate by excluding alternatives to austerity.

How influence operates

This chapter has demonstrated a tight fit between how the public saw the deficit and the need for austerity – and how it was reported across the media.

Furthermore, in explaining their beliefs and attitudes, participants regularly pointed to things that they had read or seen in the media (Briant et al., 2011; Philo et al., 2019). Such findings are supported by experimental work which demonstrated that differential framings of the public finances could affect individuals' support for austerity (Barnes and Hick, 2018). The findings are further strengthened by data from the British Social Attitudes Survey, which shows that individuals who regularly consumed a deficit-adverse newspaper gave more priority to fiscal consolidation than those who read a newspaper which took a more relaxed attitude to the public finances (Barnes and Hick, 2018). When presented with such evidence, most social scientists argue that such correlations reflect patterns of 'selective exposure', where people seek out media which conforms to pre-existing political views so that media only have weak reinforcing effects on beliefs and opinions (e.g. Newton, 2019).

Putting aside the objection of where these 'pre-existing opinions' come from – if not partly from key socialisation agents such as the mass media – there are other problems with this argument. Firstly, as Gavin (2018, p. 830) notes, the evidence that individuals have developed partisan orientations and select media outlets based on such views in a pluralistic market is very thin. For instance, research shows that between 30 per cent and 50 per cent of the readership of national titles are aligned to a different political party than the one consistently supported by their newspaper of choice. Secondly, as Barnes and Hicks (2018, p. 342) argue,

> in order to selectively expose themselves to sympathetic information, individuals must know something both about their own views and about where to find these reflected in the media…but the new salience of fiscal balance as a political issue in British politics makes it less likely that deliberative selection is possible.

In fact, due to the media consensus in favour of austerity, there was little opportunity for consumers to 'selectively expose' themselves to an anti-austerity news outlet.

Another approach is to interpret the close fit between media frames and public attitudes in the light of the research literature on 'media effects'. One of the clearest findings on austerity coverage was the remarkable consensus across all media that the deficit had created an economic crisis and that cuts were unavoidable. According to the research literature, messages are particularly persuasive when they are consonant (Noelle-Neumann and Mathes, 1987). Research on both climate change and attitudes to the European Union has shown a preponderance of one-sided messages can be so powerful that they can overwhelm strong partisan attachments or cognitive selection mechanisms (Feldman et al., 2012; Peter, 2004).

Another important finding from the literature concerns the persuasive power of repetition. Messages become more persuasive the more they are repeated and this is even the case when the information is false – the so-called illusory truth effect – as long as the message appears credible and logical (Hasher et al., 1977;

Koch and Zerback, 2013). This is the case with the argument that Labour had 'maxed out the credit card' and so there would inevitably have to be cutbacks to 'balance the books'. This message was repeated many, many times by both the media and politicians and for much of the population the 'Swabian housewife' metaphor was easy to grasp and felt intuitively correct.

Research has also demonstrated that messages that evoke emotion – particularly anger – can positively affect retention, recall and may be particularly persuasive (Nabi, 1999; Tiedens and Linton, 2001). As we saw, the arguments that the deficit posed a major threat to macroeconomic stability were repetitive, consonant and infused with emotion. Furthermore, the thousands of negative media messages in the years leading up to the banking crisis, which focused on Labour waste, 'dole cheats' and immigrants, were again repetitive, consonant and likely to generate anger, through the activation and making salient of ingroup/outgroup cleavages (Tajfel and Turner, 2003). In this way, the constant focus on immigrants and welfare claimants, who are portrayed as getting preferential treatment, is likely to engender feelings of relative deprivation – an issue that the pollster James Morris (2017) has argued has been important in reducing support for Labour because 'Labour came to be seen as a party that put migrants before British citizens'. Relative deprivation was also central to press reports, which argued that those in the private sector were supporting a 'featherbedded' public sector living the high life at their expense:

> By the next election, we will be two distinct nations. One, a Britain of featherbedded bankers, public sector workers with lavish pensions and Afghan mothers-of-seven on £170,000 benefits. The other will be the nation of hardworking taxpayers, desperately worried about keeping their jobs, feeding their families and providing for their own old age, who will have to prop up the other lot.
> (*Mail*, 9 October 2008)

None of this is to say that the mass media were the only factor in generating public support for austerity, but the evidence in this chapter does suggest that the media played a significant role in the construction of public misunderstandings around the deficit, public spending, welfare and immigration, which underpinned support for austerity policies.

Conclusion

This concluding section will consider the various factors that had to come together to produce the public's acquiescence to austerity, and it sketches out how the media, politicians and public opinion were linked, in both the creation of this consensus and its eventual slow dissolution after 2015. To do this, I focus on the three periods in question: the years preceding the 2008 Financial Crisis, the period between 2009 and 2010 when debates around the public deficit peaked and finally, the period after 2015 when political and public support for continued austerity began to dissolve.

In the decade preceding the 2008 crash, the right of centre press played a key role in softening up public opinion for the eventual cuts to public spending that were to come after 2010. This was through a relentless process that delegitimatised New Labour's increases in public spending. This campaign was waged by all right-wing titles, both broadsheet and tabloid – even the News International newspapers, formally backing the Labour party (Berry, 2019). This process of delegitimisation helped shape a public climate that came to see much of Labour extra spending as being wasted (Berry, 2019). The press campaign was carried out independently of the Conservative party who, up to 2008, did not oppose Labour's extra public spending. During this period, press reporting is also likely to have contributed to the hardening in public attitudes towards those on benefits. As Duffy et al. (2013) note, it is difficult to find a straightforward correlational fit between the volume of negative press coverage and this shift in attitudes though, they argue, 'there may have been a cumulative effect, in which public opinion responded to years of coverage'. As Baumberg et al. (2012) note, this shift in public attitudes also coincided with a marked rise in press portrayals of benefits claimants, which stressed a lack of reciprocity and effort. Furthermore, this period saw a rise in precarity of employment and intensity of work – both of which may lead those in employment to become less tolerant of those portrayed as 'free riders' (Olsen et al., 2010; Standing, 2014).

During the key period between 2009 and 2010, when the public consensus in favour of austerity solidified, there was a confluence in the narratives being pushed by the press, broadcasting and political and economic elites. Through the projection of a series of uniform and consonant messages, these groups helped shape a public consensus that the rise in the deficit represented a fiscal crisis which necessitated sharp cuts to public spending. These messages worked because they resonated with the widely held public perception that the economy was like a container or household budget which could literally 'run out of money' (Afoko and Vockins, 2013; Berry, 2019). These messages also worked because the public has little understanding of the contours of public spending, the dynamic relationship between different economic phenomena – such as the multiplier – and the impact of indirect effects (Berry, 2019; Runge and Hudson, 2020). Finally, it is important to highlight the lack of strong counter-narratives to the austerity story in the public sphere at that time. Few in the economics profession were publicly challenging this narrative and significant figures, such as the Nobel prize winner Chris Pissarides, backed austerity (Berry, 2019). This was compounded by the fact that, in 2009, the Labour party was divided over the issue which prevented the creation of a clear and unified counter-narrative (Berry, 2019). Eventually, the group around Alistair Darling won the internal argument so that Labour ended up supporting – at least rhetorically – austerity after 2009 and crucially failed to contest the claim that its own overspending had created the crisis.

Although support for austerity did not begin to significantly erode before 2015, the years after the Great Financial Crisis saw concerns about poverty and inequality increase (BSA, 2019). However, this rise in concern was primarily concentrated in two groups – broadsheet readers and Labour supporters – which was likely to have been a consequence of the increased focus on inequality in left of centre and broadsheet newspapers (BSA, 2019). If parts of the press – likely in combination with nascent protest movements such as Occupy and UK Uncut – began to drive the issues of inequality and austerity up the public agenda after 2010, it was events post 2015 that really brought the issues to the forefront of public debate. Firstly, the election of Jeremy Corbyn as Labour leader shifted the party to a stance which unequivocally rejected austerity and pledged to reduce social and economic inequalities. Secondly, the Brexit result triggered an ongoing public debate about the parts of Britain 'left behind' by deindustrialisation. The argument that these regional inequalities needed to be 'levelled up' became a key rhetorical focus for first Theresa May and then her successor Boris Johnson. Thirdly, the coronavirus pandemic has illustrated with brutal clarity the health consequences of deep patterns of structural inequality, with both the economic and health costs borne heaviest by the poor and ethnic minorities (Conway, 2020).

As the pandemic subsides and attention inevitably turns to rebalancing the public finances, could public consent for austerity be re-engineered? Many of the necessary elements for it to happen seem again to be in place. The public is still vulnerable to 'balance the books' metaphors and public service media – despite complaints from leading economists – continues to use such misleading analogies (Ascari et al., 2020). Much of the press and the Conservative party would favour and campaign for such policies. Labour, currently pre-occupied with establishing its reputation for fiscal discipline, may not complain too loudly. This has to be set against public weariness of cuts to vital services and the desire of the Conservative party to hold onto the 'red wall' seats it gained in 2019. There is also the question of whether the national trauma of the pandemic will shift public attitudes in a more collectivist direction – as happened after World War II. Whatever happens, it is clear that the debate on inequality – both in politics and in the media – may well be entering a new phase.

References

Afoko, C. and D. Vockins. (2013). *Framing the Economy: The Austerity Story*, New Economics Foundation. Available from: https://neweconomics.org/uploads/files/a12416779f2dd4153c_2hm6ixryj.pdf

Akam, S. (2016, March 15). The British Umpire: How the IFS Became the Most Influential Voice in the Economic Debate. *Guardian*. Available at: https://www.theguardian.com/business/2016/mar/15/british-umpire-how-institute-fiscal-studies-became-most-influential-voice-in-uk-economic-debate.

Anderson, P. J. and T. Weymouth. (1999). *Insulting the Public? The British Press and the European Union*. London: Longman.

Anstead, N. and A. Chadwick. (2017). A Primary Definer Online: The Construction and Propagation of a Think Tank's Authority on Social Media. *Media, Culture & Society* 40, pp. 246–266.

Ascari G. et al. (2020). *Economists Urge BBC to Rethink 'Inappropriate' Reporting of UK Economy*. Available from: https://www.ippr.org/blog/economists-urge-bbc-rethink-inappropriate-reporting-uk-economy (Accessed 22 February 2021).

Ashcroft, M. (2010) *What Future for Labour?* Available at: http://lordashcroftpolls.com/2010/09/what-future-for-labour/

Bagguley, P. and K. Mann. (1992). Idle Thieving Bastards? Scholarly Representations of the 'Underclass'. Work, *Employment & Society*, 6(1), pp. 113–126.

Barnes L. and T. Hicks. (2018). Making Austerity Popular: The Media and Mass Attitudes toward Fiscal Policy. *American Journal of Political Science*, 62(2), pp. 340–354.

Basu, L., S. Schifferes, and S. Knowles. (2018). *The Media and Austerity: Comparative Perspectives*. London: Routledge.

Baumberg, B., K. Bell, and D. Gaffney. (2012). *Benefits Stigma in Britain*, Turn2Us. Available at: https://www.turn2us.org.uk/T2UWebsite/media/Documents/Benefits-Stigma-in-Britain.pdf

Beatty, C. and S. Fothergill. (2014). The Local and Regional Impact of the UK's Welfare Reforms. *Cambridge Journal of Regions, Economy and Society*, 7(1), pp. 63–79.

Berry, M. (2015). The UK Press and the Deficit Debate. *Sociology*, 50 (3), pp. 542–559.

Berry, M. (2016). No Alternative to Austerity: How BBC Broadcast News Reported the Deficit Debate. *Media, Culture and Society*, 38 (6), pp. 844–863.

Berry, M. (2018). Austerity, Media and the UK Public in L. Basu, S. Schiffers and S. Knowles (eds.), *The Media and Austerity: Comparative Perspectives*. London: Routledge.

Berry, M. (2019). *The Media, the Public and the Great Financial Crisis*. London: Palgrave-Macmillan.

Blinder, A. S. and D. Holtz-Eakin. (1983). *Public Opinion and the Balanced Budget*, Working Paper 1234, National Bureau of Economic Research.

Briant, E., N. Watson, and G. Philo. (2011). *Bad News for Disabled People: How the Newspapers Are Reporting Disability* (Project Report). Strathclyde Centre for Disability Research and Glasgow Media Unit Report for Inclusion London. Available at: http://eprints.gla.ac.uk/57499/1/57499.pdf

BSA. (2019). *Poverty and inequality: Have attitudes evolved in line with official trends or political and media discourse?* Available at: https://bsa.natcen.ac.uk/media/39288/6_bsa36_poverty-and-inequality.pdf (Accessed 11 July 2022).

Cawley, A. (2012). Sharing the Pain or Shouldering the Burden: News-Media Framing of the Public Sector and the Private Sector in Ireland during the Economic Crisis, 2008–2010. *Journalism Studies* 13(4), pp. 600–615.

Chadwick, A., D. McDowell-Naylor, A. P. Smith, E. Watts. (2020) Authority Signaling: How Relational Interactions between Journalists and Politicians Create Primary Definers in UK Broadcast News. *Journalism.* 21(7), pp. 896–914.

Conway, E. (2020). Coronavirus: We're All in This Together – But Some More Than Others. *Sky News*, 4 May. Available at: https://news.sky.com/story/coronavirus-were-all-in-this-together-but-some-more-than-others-11981917

Deacon, D. and W. Monk (2001). New Managerialism' in the News: Media Coverage of Quangos in Britain. *Journal of Public Affairs*, 1(2), pp. 153–166.

Dearden, L. (2019). Knife crime rise 'linked to youth service cuts', parliamentary report finds. *Independent*, 7 May. Available at: https://www.independent.co.uk/news/

uk/home-news/knife-crime-uk-stabbings-youth-service-cuts-government-austerity-a8901856.html
Duffy, B., S. Hall, D. O'Leary, and S. Pope. (2013). Generation Strains: A Demos and Ipsos MORI report on changing attitudes to welfare. Available at: https://www.demos.co.uk/files/Demos_Ipsos_Generation_Strains_web.pdf?1378677272 (Accessed 11 July 2022).
Equality and Human Rights Commission. (2017). Distributional Results for the Impact of Tax and Welfare Reforms between 2010–17, Modelled in the 2021/22 Tax Year. Available at: https://www.equalityhumanrights.com/sites/default/files/impact-of-tax-and-welfare-reforms-2010-2017-interim-report_0.pdf
Eurostat. (2014). *Government Debt as a Percentage of GDP.* Available at: https://tinyurl.com/yxa44avd
Feldman, L., E. W. Maibach, C. Roser-Renouf, and A. Leiserowitz. (2012). Climate on Cable: The Nature and Impact of Global Warming Coverage on Fox News, CNN, and MSNBC. *International Journal of Press/Politics*, 17(1), pp. 3–31.
Financial Times. (2016). *S&P: QE 'Exacerbates' Inequality.* Available at: https://www.ft.com/content/b4e604c8-b61a-362e-b741-a78f7009a569 (Accessed 11 July 2022).
Gavin, N. T. (2018). Media Definitely Matter: Brexit, Immigration, Climate Change and Beyond. *The British Journal of Politics and International Relations*, 20(4), pp. 827–845.
Geiger, B. B. (2012). *The Positive and Negative Consequences of the Welfare State.* Available at: https://inequalitiesblog.wordpress.com/2012/10/25/the-positive-and-negative-consequences-of-the-welfare-state/
Giles, C. and C. Oliver. (2010). G20 drops support for fiscal stimulus. *Financial Times*, 6 June.
Golding, P. and S. Middleton. (1983). *Images of Welfare: Press and Public Attitude to Poverty.* London: Blackwell.
Hansen, J. M. (1998). Individuals, Institutions, and Public Preferences over Public Finance. *American Political Science Review*, 92(3), pp. 513–531.
Hasher, L., D. Goldstein, and T. Toppino. (1977). Frequency and the Conference of Referential Validity. *Journal of Verbal Learning and Verbal Behavior.* 16 (1), pp. 107–112.
Hayo, B. and F. Neumeier. (2014). Political Leaders' Socioeconomic Background and Fiscal Performance in Germany. *European Journal of Political Economy*, 34, pp. 184–205.
Hunter, P. (2015) *Red Alert: Why Labour Lost and What Needs to Change.* Smith Institute. Available from: https://smithinstitutethinktank.files.wordpress.com/2015/07/red-alert-why-labour-lost-and-what-needs-to-change.pdf
Ipsos-Mori. (2009). *Public Spending Index – June 2009.* Available from: https://www.ipsos.com/sites/default/files/migrations/en-uk/files/Assets/Docs/poll-public-spending-charts-june-2009.pdf
Koch, T. and T. Zerback. (2013). Helpful or Harmful? How Frequent Repetition Affects Perceived Statement Credibility, *Journal of Communication*, 63(6), pp. 993–1010.
Koo, R. C. (2009). *The Holy Grail of Macroeconomics– Lessons from Japan's Great Recession.* London: John Wiley.
Krugman, P. (2009). *Invisible Bond Vigilantes.* Available from: http://krugman.blogs.nytimes.com/2009/11/19/invisible-bond-vigilantes/
Krugman, P. (2015). The Austerity Delusion, *Guardian*, 29 April.
Landy, B. (2013). A Tale of Two Recoveries: Wealth Inequality after the Great Recession. Available at: https://tcf.org/content/commentary/a-tale-of-two-recoveries-wealth-inequality-after-the-great-recession/?agreed=1

Leys, C. (2020). How a Decade of Austerity Brought the NHS to its Knees. *Tribune*. Available at: https://tribunemag.co.uk/2020/07/how-a-decade-of-austerity-brought-the-nhs-to-its-knees

Morris, J. (2017). Working-Class Desertion of Labour Started before Corbyn. *Guardian*, 25 February. Available at: https://www.theguardian.com/commentisfree/2017/feb/25/wings-labour-blame-electoral-collapse (Accessed 11 July 2022).

Morrison, J. (2019). *Scroungers: Moral Panics and Media Myths*. London: Zed Books.

Misra, J., S. Moller, and M. Karides. (2003). Envisioning Dependency: Changing Media Depictions of Welfare in the 20th Century. *Social Problems*, 50(4), pp. 482–504.

Nabi, R. (1999). A Cognitive Functional Model for the Effects of Discrete Negative Emotions on Information Processing, Attitude Change and Recall. *Communication Theory*, 9, pp. 292–320.

Neild, R. (2010). The National Debt in Perspective. *Newsletter of the Royal Economic Society* February.

Newton, K. (2019). *Surprising News*. London: Lynne Reiner Publishers.

Noelle-Neumann, E. and R. Mathes. (1987). The Event as Event and the Event as News: The Significance of Consonance for Media Effects Research. *European Journal of Communication*, 2(4), 391–414.

Office for National Statistics. (2019). Total Wealth in Great Britain: April 2016 to March 2018. Available at: https://www.ons.gov.uk/peoplepopulationandcommunity/personalandhouseholdfinances/incomeandwealth/bulletins/totalwealthingreatbritain/april2016tomarch2018#trends-in-total-wealth-inequality-in-great-britain

Olsen, K. M., A. L. Kalleberg, and T. Nesheim. (2010). Perceived Job Quality in the United States, Great Britain, Norway and West Germany, 1989–2005. *European Journal of Industrial Relations*, 16(3), 221–240.

Peter, J. (2004). Our long Return to the Concept of Powerful Mass media – A Cross-National Comparative Investigation of the Effects of Consonant Media Coverage. *International Journal of Public Opinion Research*, 16(2), pp. 144–168.

Philo, G., Briant, E. L. and P. Donald. (2013). *Bad News for Refugees*. London: Pluto Press.

Runge, J. and N. Hudson. (2020). *Public Understanding of Economics and Economic Statistics*. ESCoE Occasional Paper 03. Available at: https://escoe-website.s3.amazonaws.com/wp-content/uploads/2020/11/26140838/ESCoE-OP03-Public-Understanding-of-Economics-and-Economic-Statistics-V1.pdf (Accessed 11 July 2022).

Schifferes, S. and S. Knowles. (2015). *The Media and Financial Crises: Comparative and Historical Perspectives*. London: Routledge.

Singh, M. (2018). Poll Shows Even Tory Voters Feel Austerity Has Gone Too Far, *Financial Times*, 2 May. Available at: https://www.ft.com/content/c8d95118-4a42-11e8-8c77-ff51caedcde6

Skeggs, B. and H. Wood. (2012). *Reacting to Reality Television: Performance, Audience and Value*. Abingdon/New York: Routledge.

Standing, G. (2014). *The Precariat: The New Dangerous Class*. London: Bloomsbury.

Stanley, L. (2014). 'We're Reaping What We Sowed': Everyday Crisis Narratives and Acquiescence to the Age of Austerity. *New Political Economy*, 19(6), pp. 895–917.

Stanley, L. (2015). What Six Public Opinion Graphs Tell Us About Austerity. Available from: http://speri.dept.shef.ac.uk/2015/07/08/public-opinion-graphs-austerity/ (Accessed 22 February 2021).

Starke, P. (2006). The Politics of Welfare State Retrenchment: A Literature Review. *Social Policy and Administration*, 40(1), pp. 104–120.

Tajfel, H. and J. Turner. (2003). The Social Identity Theory of Intergroup Behaviour. In J. Jost, and J. Sidanius (eds.), *Political Psychology: Key Readings in Social Psychology*, New York: Psychology Press.

Taylor-Gooby, P. and E. Taylor. (2015). Benefits and Welfare: Long-Term Trends or Short-Term Reactions? *British Social Attitudes*, 32.

Tiedens, L. and S. Linton. (2001). Judgment under Emotional Certainty and Uncertainty: The Effects of Specific Emotions on Information Processing. *Journal of Personality and Social Psychology*, 81(6), pp. 973–988.

Vargas-Silva, C. (2017). *The Fiscal Impact of Immigration in the UK*. Available at: http://www.migrationobservatory.ox.ac.uk/resources/briefings/the-fiscalimpact-of-immigration-in-the-uk/. (Accessed 10 July 2018).

14 Covid-19, inequality and the media

Steve Schifferes and Sophie Knowles

The coronavirus pandemic has had a devastating effect on the UK economy as well as on the health and well-being of the nation. The series of lockdowns, which began in March 2020, shut down large parts of the economy and caused the largest fall in economic activity since records began. Both the health consequences and the economic fall-out from the pandemic have fallen unevenly across the public, exacerbating existing inequalities and differentially affecting the poor, ethnic minorities and those in frontline jobs. Poverty and inequality both increased, and small businesses and the self-employed face an uncertain future.

The media have played a key role in mediating the understanding of the crisis, as politicians and the press alike wrestled to stay ahead of the evolving situation. But how well did it explain the long-term economic damage to individuals and families, and the resulting rise in inequality? And how did the coverage relate to and affect public attitudes, and what did the public think of the media's reporting?

To examine these questions, we rely on fresh data from a specially commissioned public opinion poll that was carried out at the height of the pandemic in December 2020. Using longitudinal data from previous polls, we explored how the pandemic has changed public attitudes. Our assumption was that, during this major crisis, the public would be paying particularly close attention to economic coverage and would be better placed to critically examine it, just as it proved in the 2008 global financial crisis (Schifferes, 2015).

Our broad conclusion is that the same serious public concerns about the media coverage of the economy, identified during the previous crisis, have not gone away. There is little public trust in journalists to convey the economic situation truthfully or accurately and a concern that journalists do not cover topics in a way the public can relate to. While our data show growing public concern with inequality and poverty, there is disagreement on how much the government should do to tackle it despite the unprecedented scale of state intervention during the pandemic. This raises questions about the failure of the media to encourage a broader public debate on the structural causes of inequality or on redistribution. This parallels our evaluation of coverage during the global financial crisis, where the media focused on scapegoating individuals rather than looking at the underlying structural factors which led to the crisis (Schifferes and Knowles, 2015).

DOI: 10.4324/9781003104476-18

Literature review

Trends in inequality and poverty in the UK since Covid-19

It is clear that the pandemic has accelerated growing economic inequality on a global scale (OECD, 2020; World Bank, 2020). In the UK, the pandemic has increased both inequality and poverty, trends which were already evident in the past decade. Many commentators suggest that as an uneven economic recovery begins, the better-off will be the main beneficiaries. The economic impact of the UK pandemic fell particularly hard on ethnic minorities, the poorest households, younger generations and the self-employed who suffered the biggest loss of income during the pandemic (Rowntree, 2021a). By April 2020, one in five ethnic minority households was behind with their bills, twice the number before the pandemic. This comes on top of stagnant median incomes during the previous decade, with falls for the lowest deciles due to cuts in benefits. During the same period, the incomes of the richest 1 per cent grew much sharply (IFS, 2021).

Wealth inequality, already much higher than income inequality, also increased as a result of the pandemic. The richer half of the population who were able to stay in full-time work increased their savings due to a fall in discretionary spending during the lockdown. Much of these savings are now going into house purchase, raising average house prices by 10 per cent and further increasing their wealth (Bank of England, 2020). Meanwhile, poorer households, who lost income rapidly, exhausted their savings and had to borrow in order to pay their bills (Resolution Foundation, 2021a). Young people have also been hard hit. They are twice as likely to be unemployed as older workers and suffer from more mental health problems. The pandemic has increased inter-generational wealth inequality, as rising house prices make it even more difficult for younger people to get on the housing ladder (Resolution Foundation, 2021b).

Like inequality, poverty increased rapidly during the pandemic, with 2 million more people forced to claim Universal Credit. It is estimated that the planned withdrawal of the £20 a week uplift in Universal Credit will push 300,00 children further down the social ladder, with 9 of every 30 children (31 per cent) living in poverty. The majority of the poor are now working, but in part-time, low-paid or insecure jobs, which have been particularly hard hit during the lockdown. Single parents, black and Asian minority groups, private renters and those in already deprived neighbourhoods were also more likely to suffer from the economic consequences of the pandemic (Rowntree, 2021b). The long-term health consequences of the pandemic have also impacted more severely on the disadvantaged. People in deprived neighbourhoods had a four-time greater chance of contracting the disease, while life expectancy in these areas dropped by nearly two years – an unprecedented fall (Health Foundation, 2021).

The media and Covid-19

To date, the most significant real-time research on media and the pandemic has been conducted by the Reuters Institute for the Study of Journalism (RISJ).

Their rolling panel study of media coverage of Covid-19 from April to August 2020 (Nielson and Fletcher, 2020) showed that the public was heavily relying on the mainstream media for Covid-19-related news and far less on social media. There was an increasing distrust of politicians, while experts were seen as the most reliable sources of information. And, one-third of the sample said that media coverage of the pandemic had made things worse. The survey also found significant fluctuations as to whether public concerns about the pandemic outweighed concerns about its economic consequences, with the latter growing in significance by the end of their research period.

A follow-up comparative study, using focus groups, examined how people accessed news and information about the pandemic in eight countries, including the UK. It found a good deal of scepticism about how trustworthy media reporting had been (Nielsen et al., 2021). High levels of scepticism were also found in the analysis of UK data from the annual Reuters Digital News Report (whose fieldwork was carried out in early 2021) (RISJ, 2021). The report showed that, although trust in the UK media had increased slightly, it was extremely low by international standards, while only 6 per cent trusted the news on social media. It also pointed out that most people who used online news, as opposed to social media, relied even more on mainstream news sources, especially the BBC, a trend we also found during the global financial crisis (Schifferes and Coulter, 2013).

Previous media coverage of inequality and poverty

There is a wide range of studies on how the media have covered poverty and inequality. Much of this research reveals that the media focus on poverty much more than inequality. Such coverage often focuses on negative stereotypes of the poor and rarely addresses the structural causes of poverty and inequality (Golding, 1982, Berry, 2019; Lugo-Ocando and Harkin, 2015). There is a distinction drawn in news coverage between those who are deserving of state support, and those who are not. Peter Golding's pioneering research (in this volume; and see Golding and Middleton 1982; McKendrick et al., 2008; BSAS 36, 2019) shows the persistence of media stereotyping of the working-age poor who are portrayed as feckless scroungers. (For a comparative international perspective, see Chase and Bantebya-Kyomuhendo, 2015).

Iyengar (1990) found that media frames that highlight poverty as caused by individual character and actions, rather than societal problems, are more likely to be associated with negative perceptions of low-income individuals. In contrast, representations of the rich are often more complex, more elaborate and more positive (Kendall, 2011; McCall, 2013).

There are also criticisms of the media coverage of inequality, and particularly its failure to address possible policy solutions. It has been suggested that economic inequality remains partially hidden in a 'media shadow' as the news media have failed systematically to provide a complete, accurate and meaningful picture required for the public to fully grasp the situation. Research shows the missed opportunities by news media to analyse the wider system of power, problems of media ownership and the possible range of public policy responses (Grisold and Theine, 2017, 2020; Grisold and Preston, 2020: Mijs in this volume).

Looking at support for economic retrenchment after the global financial crisis, Berry's focus group research (Berry, 2019) suggested that public support for austerity emanated primarily through media framing of the issue, especially on television news. Simon Wren-Lewis (2018) argues that one reason for this was that the media ignored the critical views of independent economists. However, the interaction between public beliefs, media coverage and political discourse is complex. Research on why the public supported the 'household analogy' found that the public already believed that governments, like individual households, should balance their books, even before it became the key mantra used to justify austerity in response to the global financial crisis (Barnes and Hicks, 2020).

Attitudes towards the rich are also critical in explaining why people might be reluctant to support redistribution, particularly the belief that the rich deserve what they get. There is an urgent need for further media research on the portrayal of the rich and to what extent it has reinforced popular stereotypes. Recent focus group work by the LSE suggested that many people have aspirational views of wanting to emulate the rich, while the lack of consensus on what level of income makes someone rich makes it more difficult to get broad public agreement on increasing taxes on higher earners (Davis et al., 2020), a finding which has historical parallels in survey research going back to the 1980s (Schifferes, 1986).

The public's belief in meritocracy may explain why increasing inequality is actually correlated with less support for redistribution (Accominotti and Tadmon 2020; Luttig, 2013). Low trust in government is an explanation provided by Mijs in this volume. He shows that providing more information about the extent of inequality did not necessarily translate into more support for government intervention, especially in those countries with low trust in government and a belief that corrupt public officials would personally gain from higher taxation.

Our findings: survey methodology

At the height of the pandemic, in December 2020, we commissioned YouGov to poll 1,700 members of the public on their attitudes towards the pandemic as part of a YouGov regular panel representative of the UK population. We sought to explore a range of media consumption patterns, public attitudes toward economic inequality, and last, how these factors impacted levels of satisfaction in economic reporting. In order to be able to report on how opinions might have changed over time, where possible we asked identical questions to those in previous surveys to establish trends. Among other sources, we built on our own 2011 public opinion survey of attitudes to the coverage of the financial crisis (Knowles and Schifferes, 2020; Schifferes, 2015). We also drew on longitudinal questions from the British Social Attitudes Survey (BSAS, 2018, 2019) as well as some other sources. The questionnaire covered four main areas: attitudes to the economy, attitudes to poverty and inequality, media consumption patterns, and attitudes to the media coverage of the economy.

Public attitudes towards the economy: survey evidence

Our research showed that the economic situation was of paramount concern to the public in December 2020, at the height of the second wave of the Covid-19 pandemic in the UK. An overwhelming 75 per cent of the population thought the economy was in bad or very bad shape, and less than one in twenty thought it was in good shape. The public even rated the pandemic's threat to the economy as greater than its threat to the nation's health. But when it came to evaluating their own personal situation, the position was reversed, with people more worried about their own health than their income. This difference may reflect the large number of workers (one-third of the workforce) whose wages at that point in time were being paid by the government through the furlough scheme. Nevertheless, the state of their personal finances was still a major worry for one in five.

The public was also in no doubt about the extent of poverty and inequality in the UK and believed that the pandemic would make it worse. Two-thirds said that there was quite a lot of poverty in Britain, and they overwhelmingly expected it to increase further as a result of the pandemic. Likewise, the public thought the gap between those on high incomes and those on low incomes was too large, and by six to one, they said that this gap would increase, rather than stay the same (Figure 14.1).

These views on poverty and inequality do not stem simply from the response to the current pandemic but represent an acceleration of a shift in public opinion that had already begun. The British Social Attitudes longitudinal survey reported that 55 per cent of respondents said there was quite a lot of poverty in 2018 (compared to 65 per cent in our poll), a figure that had already increased by 13 percentage points since 2006. Similarly, the percentage who said poverty will

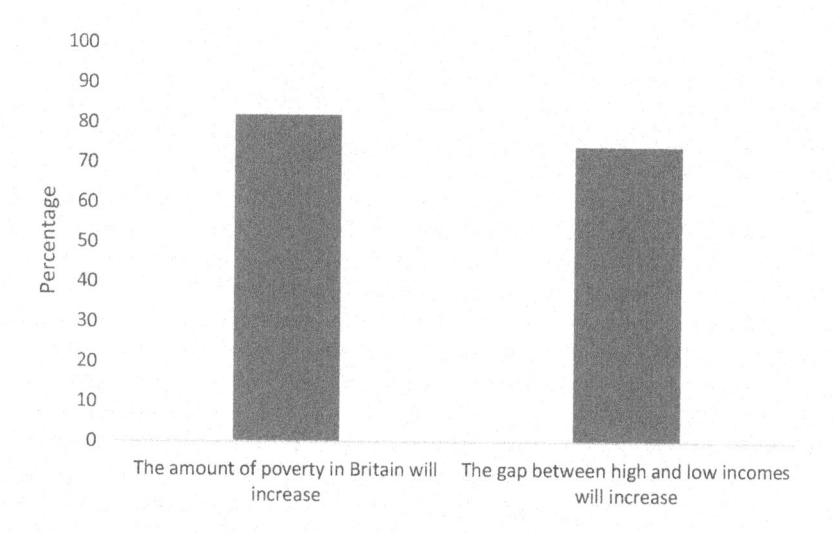

Figure 14.1 Percentage that think poverty and inequality will increase as a consequence of the pandemic.

increase in the next ten years rose by 18 percentage points over the same period (Clery, 2022). More research is needed to understand the causes of this shift. It may reflect increased dissatisfaction with austerity, and a shift in the Brexit political rhetoric towards seeing the government looking after the 'left-behinds', or the increased salience of poverty in the public discourse.

On more normative questions on inequality, however, opinion was more divided on whether such differences could be justified. Nevertheless, our results show a shift towards a more egalitarian perspective. In our survey, a majority, 55 per cent, agreed that for a society to be fair, the differences in people's living standards should be small. On the other hand, the public was evenly divided (33 per cent to 30 per cent) on the somewhat contradictory view that 'large differences in people's incomes are acceptable to properly reward differences in talents and efforts'.

Clearly, many people can agree with both these statements, suggesting there is considerable ambiguity in public attitudes to the rich. However, the longitudinal data suggest that there has been a significant reduction in those people to think large differences in people's incomes are justified. While the percentage agreeing with the first statement on fairness was only slightly greater than in 2016, there has been a sharp reduction in those who agree that large differences in income are justified to reward talent, down by 20 percentage points from 2016 (when 53 per cent agreed) and by 31 percentage points from 2008 (British Social Attitudes, 2018).

Looking at wealth rather than income, there are even stronger egalitarian trends. Three times as many respondents said that they would favour a more equal distribution of wealth even if the total amount was reduced, as opposed to those who said they would prefer more wealth even if it was more unequally distributed.

One factor in explaining this answer is that wealth distribution in the UK is far more unequal than the distribution of incomes, and wealth inequality has been rising fast, especially among the top 1 per cent, reinforced by a tax system that privileges wealth over income (IPPR, 2018). As we have seen, the pandemic has also increased wealth inequality through its effect on raising house prices. This is despite the fact that, for a very long time, most media coverage of wealth has mainly been within the personal finance pages of newspapers and on popular television programmes, which have glorified the house price boom and focused on how to increase your wealth through better investments (Schifferes, 2020) (Figure 14.2).

Taken together these findings suggest that public opinion has been moving in a more egalitarian direction since the pandemic despite the fact that many people can hold contradictory positions on these questions. A key question for further research is whether there has been a real and permanent shift in attitudes to wealth or whether there is still a strong reservoir of belief in meritocracy among many people who believe the rich are justly rewarded for their talents.

But when we look at the public attitudes towards addressing disparities of wealth and income, the evidence suggests that there is less appetite for concrete government action. A YouGov poll in 2014 asked a similar question and found that 56 per cent said they would favour a more equal distribution of wealth.

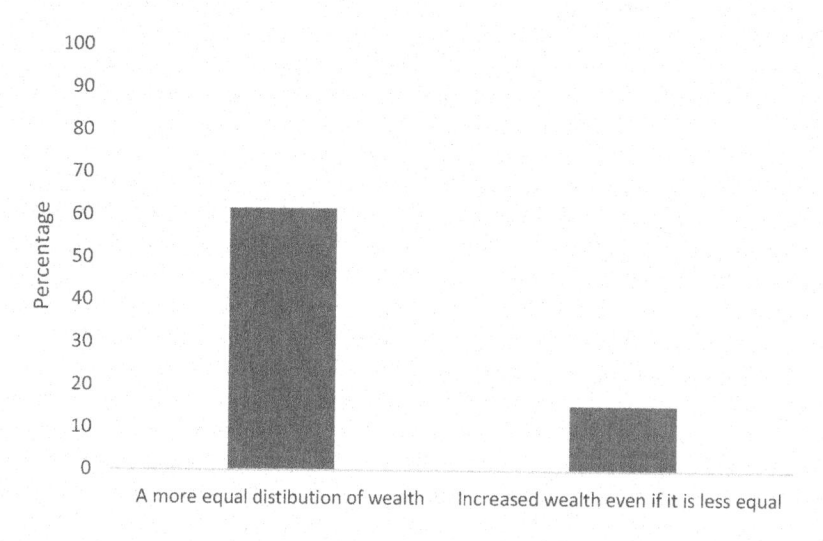

Figure 14.2 Percentage who want to see more equal distribution of wealth.

However, when they were asked specifically whether they would support high taxes to achieve this goal, only 45 per cent supported raising the highest rate of income tax to 60 per cent, and only 38 per cent supported raising taxes to 80 per cent for those on very high incomes (over £150,000) (YouGov, 2014).

Our own polling showed a similar division, using a broader measure of support for higher taxation which has been asked by the BSAS since 1983. Our respondents were evenly split on whether they would support higher taxes in order to spend more on health, education and social benefits, rather than keep the level the same. Equal numbers (40 per cent vs 42 per cent) wanted taxes to stay the same rather than rise although very few favoured tax cuts and cuts in services. Examining the trends that emerge from this long-running data set shows that support for increasing taxation is now rising but has still not reached the levels in the late 1990s and early 2000s during the early years of the Labour government. Compared to public views for most of the past decade when there was a two-to-one majority against increased spending and taxation, views are now evenly split, but nowhere near as favourable to supporting higher government as they were in the 1990s and early 2000s when two-thirds favoured this view. Our poll shows a broadly similar trend although slight retreat in support for government spending compared to 2018.

The BSAS suggests that changes in these attitudes could be seen as a 'thermostatic' reaction to correct a swing of government policy that people thought went too far. For example, the cuts of the Thatcher years were eventually followed by a desire for more public spending, while the higher government spending during the Labour government eventually led to a reduction in support for higher taxes to expand services, and disillusionment eventually set in after a decade of austerity. It may be that the huge government rescue package aimed at mitigating the effects of the pandemic may have made more people a bit more wary of further spending and worried about the large government deficit. This is certainly the media framing the current Chancellor wants to encourage despite his one-off increase in National Insurance taxes, but it remains to be seen whether he will be successful in the changed environment.

Another factor which may account for limited support for state intervention to tackle inequality is the lack of trust in government. When we measured trust in providing accurate information about the economic effects of the pandemic, politicians came lowest in our poll, with nearly one in ten respondents saying they were completely untrustworthy (on a scale of one to ten). The declining belief in the efficacy of government has been going on for a long time, ever since it was first studied in the 1950s (Almond and Verba, 1956), when more people in Britain trusted the government to do the right thing than in any of the other countries they studied. The decline in trust in politicians can be traced to tracking data from 1983 (IpsosMORI, 2011), which found that, by 2011, only one in five trusted politicians or government ministers to tell the truth. More recent data suggest that the trend has accelerated (YouGov, 2020). Our data suggest that the pandemic may have boosted mistrust even further.

The media and the economic crisis – trust in journalists

How well has the media reflected the public mood and helped mediate the debate? In this section, we look at public attitudes to media coverage of the economic effects of the pandemic. As our earlier poll in 2011 suggests, there may be a significant disconnect between public attitudes and the way these issues are traditionally portrayed in the media. Our key finding is the high degree of dissatisfaction with the media coverage of the economy, and a feeling of disconnect between journalists and the public.

During the pandemic, we found a high level of public engagement and concern about the economic issues, with 32 per cent following the news about the economy every day or several times a day, and 40 per cent several times a week or weekly. On the other hand, just 8 per cent of our sample say they are not interested in this kind of news. The percentage following the news closely are similar but slightly lower than in our 2011 poll, perhaps reflecting the fact that our 2011 survey was carried out at a moment when the euro crisis dominated the news agenda with the imminent collapse of the Greek economy (Figure 14.3).

Looking at how people consume the news, we find (in line with other research) that online news has become dominant although television news is still quite important especially among older viewers. It is newspaper readership that has declined most dramatically and particularly dramatically in regard to tabloid newspapers. Of course, much of the online news consumed has been from the websites of newspapers and television news organisations (RISJ, 2021). In contrast, our survey found a very limited engagement in social media as a source of economic news about the pandemic.

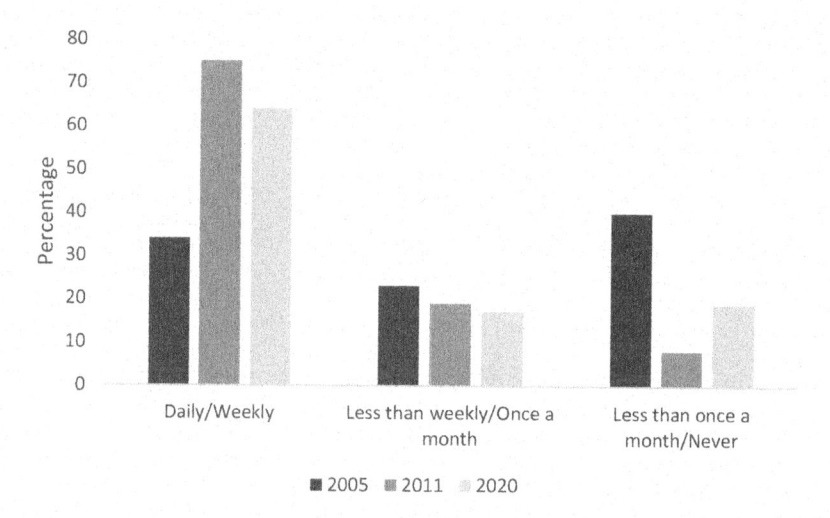

Figure 14.3 Frequency of accessing economic news, 2005–20.
Source: (2005) Baseline survey of financial capability, Table 7.5, p. 116; (2011) City/ICM poll, 2011.

But despite the intensity of their interest, the public was not satisfied with the coverage of the economy they received, and they were even more critical than we found in our 2011 survey. Only 2 per cent said they were very satisfied with the coverage, and 28 per cent fairly satisfied, compared with 35 per cent who were dissatisfied. In 2011, 52 per cent were satisfied and only 13 per cent were dissatisfied (Figure 14.4).

How can we explain this difference? One factor may be the relatively limited coverage given to the economy, compared to the health aspects of the pandemic. A survey we undertook using the Factiva database showed that two-thirds covered health issues, as opposed to one-third which focused on the economic impact of the crisis. This difference in coverage may partly be explained by the timing of our poll, which was carried out when the second wave of the pandemic was sweeping the country, and coverage of the health crisis overwhelming the NHS was salient.

Another factor may be that trust in media, in general, has declined substantially since 2011 (IpsosMORI 2011; YouGov 2020). However, when we compare trust in the media with trust in other institutions supplying information about the economy, we find a more mixed picture. Our survey showed a relatively high level of trust in news compared to other sources such as politicians or local government. One striking finding of the polling, which parallels some of the results of the Reuters Survey, is that the most trusted source of news on the economy were independent economists (Nielson and Fletcher, 2020). Further research is needed to examine why they were not used more frequently as sources of economic news, compared to the high profile and frequent appearances by public health professionals and scientists, who were also highly trusted by the public.

[Chart: Bar chart showing Percentage on y-axis (0-50) with categories on x-axis: Very satisfied, Fairly satisfied, Neither satisfied nor dissatisfied, Fairly dissatisfied, Very dissatisfied. Two series: GFC and Pandemic.]

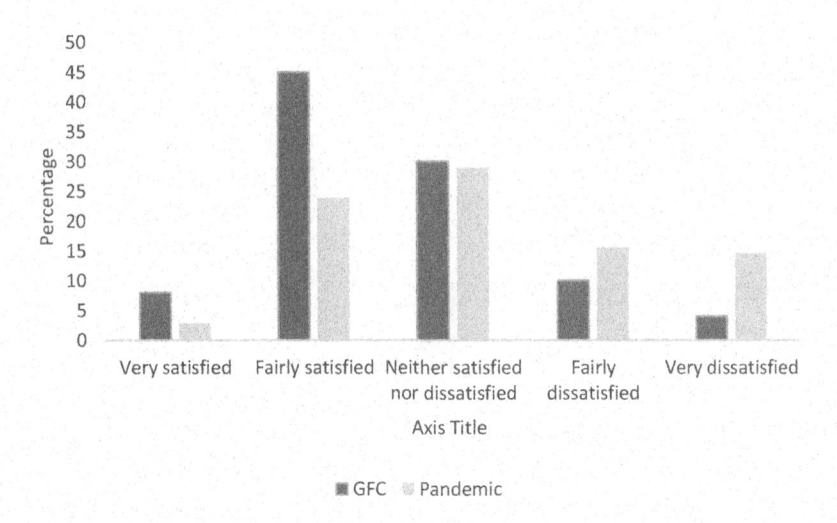

Figure 14.4 Public satisfaction with media coverage of economy during the pandemic, 2011 vs 2020.

It is also true that although the public does not trust the media, in general, they are more trusting in the sources they themselves actually use and, in particular, trust television journalists and journalists on upmarket newspapers far more than journalists in general (Toff et al., 2021; IpsosMORI, 2011; YouGov, 2020).

In order to understand the roots of the public's dissatisfaction, our poll also asked more detailed questions concerning specific aspects of the coverage of the economy (Figure 14.5).

a   Gave enough coverage to how developments affected me personally
b   Did a good job in explaining economic policies
c   Gave a fair and balanced picture of the state of the economy
d   Used too much jargon which I do not understand

A key finding is that nearly half of respondents said that journalists did not tell them enough about how the economic developments would affect them personally. In our 2011 poll, with slightly different wording, 68 per cent said they wanted more information about this aspect of the crisis, and 49 per cent criticised journalist's coverage of this issue. This could partly reflect the fact that much of the economic coverage of the pandemic focused on problems for businesses caused by the lockdown, and less on how individuals were coping with cuts in income.

Underlying this problem may be the disconnect between the world of journalists and that of the majority of the population. The Joseph Rowntree Foundation has suggested that, because of focus on one end of the spectrum or the other, an entire section of society – the working poor and lower middle class have been ignored, by the media, partly because reporters generally lack experience of

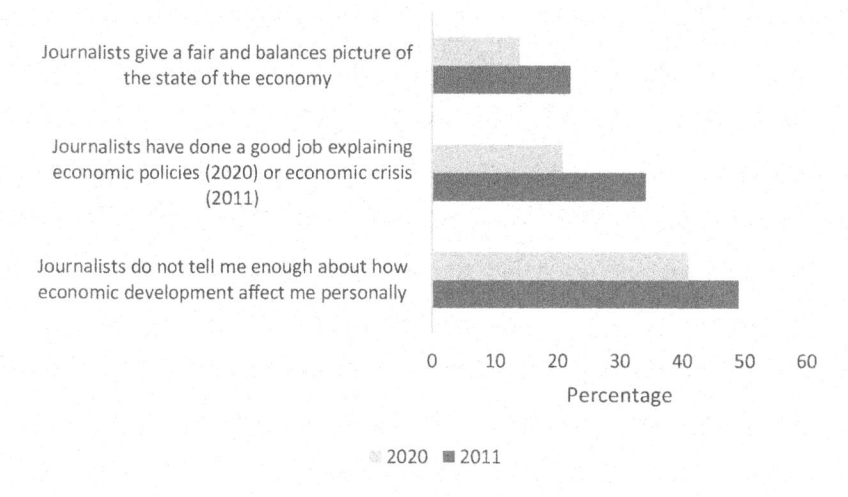

Figure 14.5 How well did journalists do covering the following? 2011–20.
Source: 2011: Schifferes (2015).

poverty and do not contact poor people in order to understand their experiences (Rowntree, 2020).

In addition, and even more striking, is that only 23 per cent said journalists had done a good job of explaining economic policies to the general public, compared to 34 per cent in our 2011 survey. It may be that this aspect of the coverage was puzzling because of the unprecedented nature of government intervention. It could also be that media coverage focused mainly on the immediate economic response, with little analysis of the long-term implications of this approach, other than within the existing media frame about the dangers of too much government borrowing. As government support is pulled back, it appears that much of the mainstream media will still be supporting the government's argument that we must now balance the books and limit public spending.

Regarding trust, it is striking that only 15 per cent felt that journalists gave a fair and balanced picture of the state of the economy, down from 22 per cent a decade before – another reflection, as we have seen, of the long-term decline in trust in journalists which have accelerated in the last decade. This cuts across other findings, both in our poll and by Reuters, showing some increased trust in the media as a source of information about the pandemic – although said coverage made things worse (Nielson, 2020). However, in interpreting these figures, we should note that the category 'journalist' has elicited negative views by the public for a very long time. It is also true that although the public does not trust the media, in general, they are more trusting in the sources they themselves actually use and, in particular, trust television journalists and journalists on upmarket newspapers far more than journalists, in general (Fletcher, 2020; Toff et al., 2021; IpsosMORI, 2011; YouGov, 2020).

The only area where there seems to have been a slight improvement compared to 2011 is in regard to economic jargon, where 28 per cent of respondents said this was a problem in our current poll, compared to 34 per cent in 2011. There may have been some recognition by news organisations in the intervening decade of the need to spell out economic terms in ways people can understand. But financial literacy remains weak across a wide swathe of the public (Schifferes and Knowles, 2015). When we dug deeper, asking people in our poll how well they understood key terms such as GDP and inflation, the results were less encouraging. More than half of our survey respondents were not sure they understood what GDP meant, and nearly half were not sure they understood government borrowing. People were most confident at understanding unemployment, but one-third were not sure about either interest rates or inflation.

These findings are backed up by recent focus group research by the Economic Statistics Centre of Excellence (ESCE, 2020). Their research found that a majority of the population had a very weak understanding of GDP and budget deficits and were not sure of the effects of either interest rates or inflation on the economy. It also pointed out that the experience of an economic crisis was a 'formative experience which seems to affect how much attention people pay to certain economic indicators and how they understand them'. It is clear that lack of financial literacy makes it harder to ensure that all sections of the community are able to engage in the economic debate. It is those most affected by the crisis – the poor, the young, and women – who often have a lower level of financial literacy and so are doubly disenfranchised (Schifferes, 2015; Knowles and Schifferes, 2020).

Conclusions

In the past decade, two huge economic crises have shaken the UK economy.

With the public showing intense interest in the scale of the economic damage and worrying about their own financial situation, these crises called out for detailed analysis and coverage which would enhance public understanding and facilitate a real debate on future economic policy. But in both cases, the media fell well short of public expectations in this regard. In the aftermath of the financial crisis, media coverage focused too much on scapegoating individual bankers and too little on reforming the financial system. During the pandemic, twice as many articles were published on the health crisis than the economic crisis despite the fact that our research showed that the public was more interested in the economic consequences of the pandemic. It also took a long time before the media (and official bodies) began to look at the inequalities produced by the pandemic (Public Health England, 2020; Racial Disparities Unit, 2021). It took a while for the media to challenge the government's mantra that 'we are all in this together', and even longer to move beyond covering the differential impact of Covid-19 on health outcomes rather than its widening and uneven economic effects, something that will be come into sharp contrast as the economic support packages wind down.

While we have focused on the public attitudes towards the economy and their view of the media, more research is urgently needed on the content of the pandemic-related economic coverage. This also needs to address the elements in journalism practice, including editorial decision-making, sourcing and the level of understanding of these issues (including inequality) among journalists themselves. This may help close the disturbing lack of public trust in the media which makes a more informed debate more difficult. More investigation into how news about the economy is understood and consumed by different groups, and how it can be improved, is also needed.

In a crisis, the media could play a crucial role as an agent of change, illuminating the key issues to ensure that we do not return to the failed policies of the past. Far too often, however, it has avoided addressing the long-term economic implications and policy choices. Failure to do so after the 2008 crisis contributed to a decade with stagnation in living standards and a sharp increase in wealth for those at the top. With the even greater challenges facing us in the next decade – including climate change, a rapidly ageing population and decreased economic prospects for the next generation – the importance of informed debate is more important than ever before.

References

Accominotti, F. and D. Tadmon (2020). *How the Reification of Merit Breeds Inequality: Theory and Experimental Evidence.* Working Paper (42). International Inequalities Institute, London School of Economics and Political Science, London.

Almond, G. and S. Verba (1956). *The Civic Culture: Political Attitudes and Democracy in Five Nations*, New York: Little Brown,

Bank of England. (2020). How Has Covid Affected Household Savings?, November, Bank Overground, https://www.bankofengland.co.uk/bank-overground/2020/how-has-covid-affected-household-savings

Barnes, L. and T. Hicks (2020). Are Policy Analogies Persuasive? The Household Budget Analogy and Public Support for Austerity', 29 March. Accessed at https://doi.org/10.31235/osf.io/7qa2b

Berry, M. (2019). *The Media, the Public and the Great Financial Crisis*, London: Palgrave-Macmillan.

British Social Attitudes 36. (2018). 'Poverty and Inequality' accessed at https://www.bsa.natcen.ac.uk/latest-report/british-social-attitudes-36/poverty-and-inequality.aspx

British Social Attitudes 37. (2019). 'Key Time Series: Public Attitudes in the Context of Covid-19 and Brexit,' accessed at https://www.bsa.natcen.ac.uk/latest-report/british-social-attitudes-37/key-time-series.aspx

Chase, E. and G. Bantebya-Kyomuhendo, editors. (2015). *Poverty and Shame: Global Experiences*, Oxford: Oxford University Press.

Davis, A., K. Hecht, T. Burchardt, I. Gough, D. Hirsch, K. Rowlingson and K. Summers. (2020). 'Living on Different Incomes in London: Can Public Consensus Identify a 'Riches Line'? *LSE*, CASE Report 127, February, accessed at https://sticerd.lse.ac.uk/dps/case/cr/casereport127.pdf

ESCE (Economic Statistics Centre of Excellence). (2020). *Public Understanding of Economics and Economic Statistics*, access at https://www.escoe.ac.uk/public-understanding-of-economics-and-economic-statistics/

Fletcher, R. (2020). *Trust Will Get Worse Before It Gets Better*, Oxford: Reuters Institute for the Study of Journalism, https://www.digitalnewsreport.org/publications/2020/trust-will-get-worse-gets-better/

Golding, Peter, and S. Middleton. (1982). *Images of Welfare: Press and Public Attitudes to Poverty*. Oxford: Martin Robinson.

Grisold, A. and H. Theine (2017). How come we know? The media coverage of economic inequality. *International Journal of Communication*, 11, pp. 4265–4284.

Grisold, A. and H. Theine (2020). Media and Economic Inequality. *Economic Inequality and News Media: Discourse, Power, and Redistribution*, Oxford University Press: London.

Grisold, A and P. Preston. (2020). *Economic Inequality and News Media: Discourse, Power and Redistribution*. Oxford: Oxford University Press.

Health Foundation (2021). *Unequal Pandemic, Fairer Recovery, the Covid-19 Impact Report*, accessed at https://www.health.org.uk/publications/reports/unequal-pandemic-fairer-recovery

IFS (Institute for Fiscal Studies) (2021). *Living Standards: Poverty and Inequality in the UK 2021*, July, accessed at https://ifs.org.uk/publications/15512\

IPPR (Institute for Public Policy Research) (2018), *A Wealth of Difference*, https://www.ippr.org/files/2018-10/cej-a-wealth-of-difference-sept18.pdf

IpsosMORI, Trust in Professions: Long Term Trends, Nov 2011 https://www.ipsos.com/ipsos-mori/en-uk/trust-professions-long-term-trends

Iyengar, S. (1990). Framing responsibility for political issues: The case of poverty. *Political Behaviour*, 12, pp. 19–40. https://doi.org/10.1007/BF00992330

Kendall, D. E. (2011). *Framing Class: Media Representations of Wealth and Poverty in America*, New York: Rowman & Littlefield.

Knowles, S. and S. Schiffres. (2020). Financial capability, the financial crisis, and trust in news media. *Journal of Applied Journalism & Media Studies*, 9(1), pp. 61–83.

Lugo-Ocando, J. and S. Harkin, editors (2015). *Media Discourses on Poverty in a Time of Austerity*. London: Rowman & Littlefield.

Luttig, M. (2013). The structure of inequality and Americans' attitude towards redistribution. *Public Opinion Quarterly*, 77(3), pp. 811–821.

McCall, L. (2013). *The Undeserving Rich: American Beliefs about Inequality, Opportunity and Redistribution*, Cambridge: Cambridge University Press

McKendrick, J., et al. (2008). *The Media, Poverty and Public Opinion in the UK*. New York: Joseph Rowntree Foundation

Nielson, R. K. and R Fletcher. (2020). *Most Say that News Media Have Helped Them to Respond to Cover, But One-Third Says News Coverage Has Made Crisis Worse*, Tenth Report of the UK Covid-19 News and Information Project, Oxford: Reuters Institute for the Study of Journalism, accessed https://reutersinstitute.politics.ox.ac.uk/most-uk-say-news-media-have-helped-them-respond-covid-19-third-say-news-coverage-has-made-crisis

Nielsen, R., A. Shultz, and R Fletcher. (2021). *An Ongoing Infodemic: How People in Eight Countries Access News and Information about Coronavirus*, Oxford: Reuters Institute for the Study of Journalism, accessed at https://reutersinstitute.politics.ox.ac.uk/ongoing-infodemic-how-people-eight-countries-access-news-and-information-about-coronavirus-year

OECD. (2020). *Building a Resilient Economy: How We Can Emerge Stronger from the Covid-19 Pandemic*, accessed at https://www.oecd.org/coronavirus/en/

Public Health England. (2020). *Disparities in the Risk and Outcomes of COVID-19*, accessed at https://assets.publishing.service.gov.uk/government/uploads/system/uploads/attachment_data/file/908434/Disparities_in_the_risk_and_outcomes_of_COVID_August_2020_update.pdf

Race Disparity Unit. (2021). *Second Report on the Progress to Address Covid-19 Health Inequalities*, accessed https://www.gov.uk/government/publications/second-quarterly-report-on-progress-to-address-covid-19-health-inequalities/second-quarterly-report-on-progress-to-address-covid-19-health-inequalities

Resolution Foundation. (2021a). *Living Standards Audit 2021*, July. https://www.resolutionfoundation.org/publications/the-living-standards-audit-2021/

Resolution Foundation. (2021b). *Stakes and Ladders*, June, https://www.resolutionfoundation.org/publications/stakes-and-ladders

RISJ (Reuters Institute for the Study of Journalism). (2021). *The Reuters Digital News Report 2021*, accessed at https://reutersinstitute.politics.ox.ac.uk/sites/default/files/2021-06/Digital_News_Report_2021re_FINAL.pdf

Rowntree (Joseph Rowntree Foundation). (2021a). UK *Poverty Report 2020–21*, Feb, accessed at https://www.jrf.org.uk/report/uk-poverty-2020-21

Rowntree (Joseph Rowntree Foundation). (2021b). *After a Decade of Deprivation We Need Policies that Prioritise Recovery for Families in Poverty*, https://www.jrf.org.uk/press/after-decade-deprivation-we-need-policies-prioritise-recovery-families-poverty

Schifferes, S. (1986). 'The Rich in Britain', *New Society*, 22 August, [8 page supplement produced by London Weekend Television reporting findings from its documentary series on the rich, *Fortune* (4 x 1 hr, tx 7–28 September 1986].

Schifferes, S. (2015). 'Why the Public Doesn't Trust the Business Press,' in Schifferes, S, and R Roberts, editors, *The Media and Financial Crises: Comparative and Historical Perspectives*, London: Routledge. pp. 153–168.

Schifferes, S. (2020). 'The Financial Press' in Conboy, M and Adrian Bingham, *The Edinburgh History of British and Irish Journalism in the 20th Century: Volume 3: Competition and Disruption 1900–2017*, Edinburgh: Edinburgh University Press. pp.189–210

Schifferes, S. and S Coulter. (2013). Downloading disaster: BBC news online coverage of the financial crisis. *Journalism*, 14 (2), pp. 228–252.

Schifferes, Steve, and S. Knowles. (2015). 'The British press and the first crisis of globalisation', in Schifferes, S, and R. Roberts, editors, *The Media and Financial Crises: Comparative and Historical Perspectives*. London: Routledge. pp. 42–58.

Toff, B., S. Badrinathan, C. Mont'Alverne, G.Arguedas, R. Fletcher, and R Nielson. (2021). *Overcoming Indifference: What Different Attitudes Towards News Tell Us About Building Trust*, Third Report: Trust in News Project, Oxford: Reuters Institute for the Study of Journalism, accessed at https://reutersinstitute.politics.ox.ac.uk/overcoming-indifference-what-attitudes-towards-news-tell-us-about-building-trust

World Bank (2020). *Poverty and Shared Prosperity 2020: Reversal of Fortunes*, accessed at https://www.worldbank.org/en/publication/poverty-and-shared-prosperity

Wren-Lewis, S. (2018). 'Mediamacro – why the news media ignores economic experts' in Basu, Laura, S Schifferes and S Knowles, editors, *The Media and Austerity: Comparative Perspectives*, London: Routledge

YouGov.(2014). *Voters Chose Greater Equality over Greater Weal*th, April, accessed at https://yougov.co.uk/topics/politics/articles-reports/2014/04/30/equality-more-important-wealth

YouGov. (2020). *Do People Trust Journalists?* March, https://yougov.co.uk/topics/politics/articles-reports/2020/03/26/trust-newspaper-journalists

15 Stuck in a feedback loop

Why more inequality leads to lower levels of concern[*]

Jonathan J.B. Mijs

Research describes the dramatic increase in income inequality in the West, in historical and comparative perspective (Atkinson, Piketty and Saez 2011; Piketty and Saez 2003). Despite the reality of increasing inequalities, however, the trend has not been accompanied by growing popular concern (Brooks and Manza 2013; Lübker 2007). Neither do citizens in more unequal societies express more concern about inequality than those in more egalitarian societies (Bucca 2016; Janmaat 2013; McCall 2013). How to make sense of this paradox?

Scholars have offered various explanations for citizens' lack of concern for the growing gap between the rich and poor. First, people are often misinformed about the actual state of inequality in their society. Specifically, evidence suggests that citizens greatly underestimate just how unequal a society they live in (Gimpelson and Treisman 2018; Norton and Ariely 2011; Osberg and Smeeding 2006). In other words, citizens may be unconcerned simply because they are unaware of the extent of inequality in their country.

A second line of scholarship suggests that living in an unequal society may actually make people more tolerant of inequality, as they get used to it and develop successful coping mechanisms (Bénabou and Tirole 2006; Trump 2017). In this chapter, I draw on both sets of insights to develop an alternative explanation for people's growing tolerance of inequality and their resistance to redistributing income and wealth: I argue that people increasingly believe that inequality is the outcome of a fair, meritocratic process where societal success simply reflects talent, ambition and hard work.

Figure 15.1 shows the trend in meritocratic beliefs in different countries in the 1987–2012 period for which we have comparative attitudinal data (Mijs 2018b). Indicated, for each country and time point, is the average score that citizens attributed to hard work in determining who gets ahead in society. A first thing to note is how strongly citizens, across the board, think success depends on hard work. With the exception of communist pre-1989 Poland, a majority in each country and time period believes there is a meritocracy society. A second thing

---

[*] This chapter is adapted from 'The Paradox of Inequality: Income Inequality and Belief in Meritocracy go Hand in Hand,' published January 23, 2019 in *Socio-Economic Review* (Oxford University Press). doi: 10.1093/ser/mwy051.

DOI: 10.4324/9781003104476-19

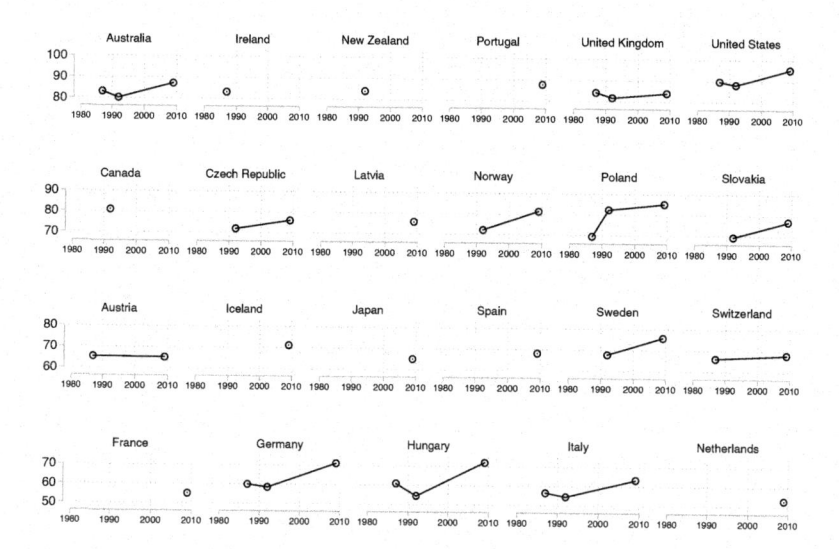

Figure 15.1 Belief in meritocracy across countries over time.
Source: Author's calculations from International Social Survey Program (2014).
Note: Indicated on the vertical axis is the approximate percentage of citizens, for each country and period, who believes that who gets ahead in society is decided by hard work.

to note is that the percentage of people who does has gone up in almost every country since the late 1980s. The West is marked by a striking convergence in citizens' views of success: in the most recent surveys, at least two-thirds of citizens in all countries—and as much as 95 per cent of Americans—attribute success to meritocratic factors.

In what follows I explore the relationship between country-level income inequality and citizens' concerns and beliefs about inequality, drawing on pooled data from the International Social Survey Programme, covering 49,383 citizens in 23 countries, over a 25-year period. In the first step of the analysis, I draw on between-country differences and changes within countries over time to describe how citizens in more unequal societies are more likely to explain success in terms of meritocratic factors and less likely to believe in structural inequality. This relationship is driven mainly by between-country differences, but I also find evidence that long-term changes in inequality are accompanied by a stronger belief in meritocracy, while belief in structural inequality remains stable.

In the second step of the analysis, I show that there is no statistical relationship between country-level income inequality and citizens' concerns about inequality. What explains people's concerns are their beliefs about the causes of inequality. I show that citizen's (individual-level) beliefs and popular (country-level) beliefs about inequality explain a large part of their concerns: people who believe inequality reflects hard work are much less concerned about inequality than citizens who see inequality as driven by structural forces such as a person's family wealth and connections.

In sum, income inequality is accompanied by popular beliefs that dampen citizens' concerns by legitimating the growing income gap as meritocratically deserved. I conclude by discussing implications for theory and research.

Background

Studies describe how people living among others of the same income level tend to hold meritocratic beliefs, while those living in more economically heterogeneous areas are more likely to think that success is determined by forces outside their control (Merolla, Hunt and Serpe 2011; Wu and Chou 2017). The latter can see what the former cannot: how life outcomes are shaped by money and resources.

Edmiston (2018:11) reports how in the absence of contact, his affluent interviewees displayed a "poor sociological imagination," whereas "[those] who had sustained interaction with, or experience of, structural constraints were much more likely to recognise the factors that might mitigate an individual's responsibility for their situation or actions." This finding may not be limited to people living in affluence. Research suggests that poor people tend to underestimate the extent of their poverty (Cruces, Perez-Truglia and Tetaz 2013) and, sometimes, blame themselves for their circumstances (McCoy and Major 2007). Shedd (2015) argues that such beliefs are situated in people's social environments. In her study of Chicago public school students, she finds that

> [their] perceptions of the world are indelibly shaped by their place in that world. (...) Youth of color attending segregated schools experience structural discrimination on a daily basis, but they lack the opportunity to make between-race comparisons on a daily basis. Students who cross boundaries, in other words, are more likely to see discrimination than those who do not make these journeys.
>
> (Shedd 2015:58)

These studies continue a line of research originating in the 1950s and 1960s, which describes how people's understanding of society draws on social comparison processes that are both limited and biased by their social context; people's perceptions and beliefs are "bounded by the private orbits in which they live" (Mills 1959:3). When making comparisons, people draw on a restrictive range of reference groups, namely, their co-workers, family and friends who tend to be socio-economically similar to them (Dawtry, Sutton and Sibley 2015). As Irwin (2018:204) puts it, "people read the world from their own situated position and extrapolate from their own experience." As a consequence, people underestimate social inequality (Mijs 2018a).

Growing levels of income inequality mean that experiences and interactions with people across income, wealth and racial fault lines are becoming more seldom. Research suggests that income inequality creates greater spatial and social distance between the wealthy and the poor, as they live their lives in different institutions: children grow up in poor or wealthy neighbourhoods, attend different (public or private) schools, find friends and romantic partners in their own circles and come to work in increasingly polarised labour markets (Massey and Tannen 2016; Owens 2016; Reardon and Bischoff 2011). Consequently, I argue, people on either side of the income divide are unable to see the breadth of the gap that separates their lives from those of others: as the gap grows larger, other people's lives fade out of view. Hence, large inequality paradoxically leads to insulate people from seeing the full extent of it. People underestimate the structural forces that make for inequality because they are increasingly unable to see it from their (isolated) position at the bottom or top of their (segregated) society. Without direct experiences, news reporting and statistics about (growing) inequality are not likely to change people's perspectives nor lead them to develop empathy for the plight of unseen others living across the income divide.

In sum, I hypothesise that citizens' consent to inequality can be explained by their belief that inequalities reflect the legitimate accomplishments of hard work rather than the operation of (unfair) structural forces beyond their control. Moreover, I posit that inequality creates the social conditions for its legitimation. The statistic of income inequality becomes economic reality when it affects affluent and poor people's wages and employment. It becomes social reality when it impacts the social and spatial environment in which the rich and poor lead their lives. Unequal societies are marked by greater social distance such that the rich and poor develop an understanding of society and their own place in it from a position of socio-economic insulation. As a result, people in more unequal societies underestimate the extent of inequality and the role of structural advantages or barriers that help or hurt them.

Methodology

Full details of my data, variables and analytical strategy are described in the article from which this chapter is adapted (Mijs 2019). Here, I summarise key methodological information.

Data. I draw on data from the International Social Survey Programme (ISSP), which is a cross-national survey started in the 1980s and grown since to span more than two decades and cover dozens of countries. My analyses cover three time periods: the first wave, 1987–88; the repeated survey in 1991–93 and the most recent data collected in 2008–12. Data for each country period are based on a representative survey of the adult population. Since my focus in this chapter is on Western countries undergoing comparable trends, I exclude non-European non-Western nations from the sample. Combining data for the three waves and accounting for missing data, I obtain a final sample of 49,383 in 23 countries and 43 country periods.

Dependent variables. I measure citizens' concerns about inequality as their response to the following question: "Income differences in [country] are too high." In measuring beliefs about inequality, I draw on a set of questions inviting survey participants to evaluate the relative importance of several meritocratic and non-meritocratic factors in determining life outcomes. The question reads as follows: "Please tick one box for each of [the following] to show how important you think it is for getting ahead in life..." (1) hard work, (2) having ambition, (3) having a good education, (4) coming from a wealthy family, (5) knowing the right people, (6) a person's race, (7) a person's religion and (8) being born a man or a woman. For each factor, people are asked to indicate, on a five-point scale, whether it is essential/very important/fairly important/not very important/not important at all. As with concerns about inequality, I multiply the five points to get a scale resembling percentages; ranging from 0 (not important at all) to 50 (fairly important) to 100 (essential).

In what follows my focus will be on the first factor—hard work. Hard work is arguably the most meritocratic part of Michael Young's equation, "Merit = Intelligence + Effort," for the simple fact that intelligence itself is conditioned by a non-meritocratic factor: who your parents happen to be (Mijs 2016). I prefer to look at the importance people attribute to hard work instead of a person's education or ambitions for the latter are reflective of that person's social background and family resources, as has been well described by social stratification research (Bozick et al. 2010). Unless otherwise noted, when I discuss meritocracy beliefs I am referring to citizens' belief in the importance of hard work relative to structural factors.

My measure of belief in structural inequality is based on responses indicating that a person thinks coming from a wealthy family or knowing the right people (factors four and five, respectively) is "very important" or "essential" for getting ahead in life. I look at these two rather than the full set of structural factors for two reasons. First, the cultural meaning of the other structural factors, referring to a person's race, religion and gender, is likely to vary considerably over time and between societies. As a result, citizens' evaluations of these factors may not be strictly comparable. Second, family wealth and connections are the only factors included in all survey waves, whereas the other categories are missing for some countries and years.

Independent variables. The level of income inequality is measured by taking the Gini coefficient of income inequality for each country period, drawn from Milanovic' (2013) *All the Ginis* data set. Models also include individual-level measures of people's position in society as proxies for their experiences with inequality. I consider to what extent people's concern and beliefs about inequality co-vary with their age, gender, education, employment status, social class and religion. I look at two measures of a person's social background, reflecting both their objective social position and a person's perception of their place in society.

Results

Explaining citizens' beliefs about inequality

In line with my theoretical expectations, I find a positive and statistically significant (p <. 001) relationship between income inequality and meritocratic beliefs: all else equal, citizens living in a country with a high level of income inequality like the US (Gini score of 44) have a stronger belief in meritocracy by about 12 points compared to those living in a more egalitarian society like Austria (Gini score of 23).

To visualise the interaction between country-level inequality and citizens' inequality beliefs by social class, I calculate and plot predictive margins (Figure 15.2). The upward lines in the left-side graph indicate the positive relationship between country-level income inequality and citizens' belief in meritocracy. The difference in citizens' beliefs, comparing the most egalitarian to the most unequal countries, is about 10 points. Whereas there is significant variation in beliefs by citizens' social class, the substantive differences are minimal; citizens across social classes hold strong beliefs in meritocracy. There are larger differences by social class in citizens' structuralist beliefs (right-side graph). Working-class citizens are much more likely to believe in structural inequality, and their beliefs are less affected by country-level income inequality. Lower and upper middle-class citizens are much less likely to believe in structural inequality when they live in more unequal societies, by as much as 20 points.

In sum, citizens in more unequal societies understand income inequality in meritocratic rather than structural terms, while people in more egalitarian countries see structural inequality. Statistically, these associations are driven almost entirely by relatively stable between-country differences rather than over-time

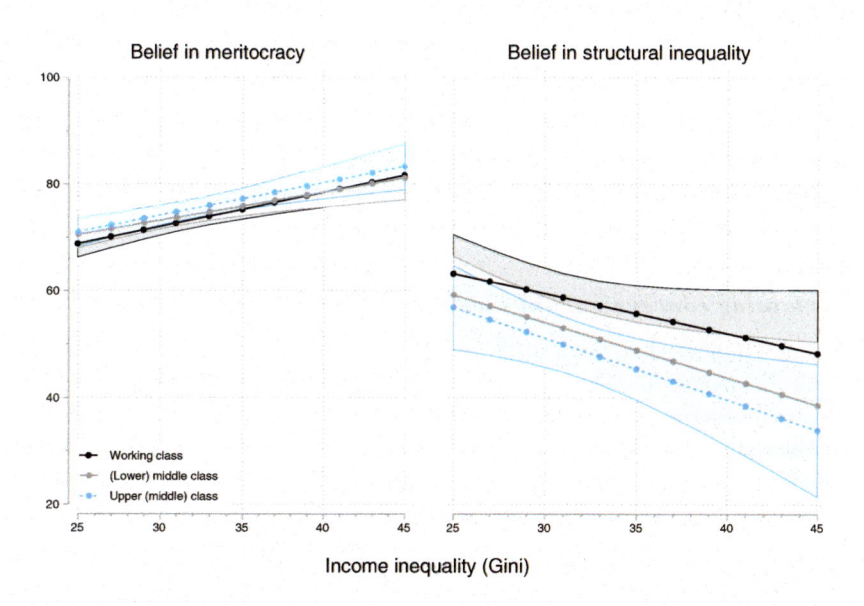

Figure 15.2 Citizens' inequality beliefs by social class and country-level income inequality.
Source: Author's calculations from ISSP (2014).
Note: Displayed are citizens' belief in meritocracy (left) and structural inequality (right), on the vertical axis, predicted by their social class and by the extent of country-level income inequality (horizontal axis).

changes in income inequality. In other words, knowing the level of income inequality in a country, relative to other countries, gives us purchase on their beliefs about inequality. Knowing how income inequality in a given society has changed between survey waves, however, does not help explain citizens' beliefs.

It may be that the over-time relationship is not as direct as implicitly assumed in the statistical models thus far. An alternative way to analyse the impact of changes in income inequality is to leverage the fact that individuals surveyed in the 1980s, 1990s and 2000s may have experienced a change in inequality in their lifetime. By comparing the level of income inequality in their country at the time they were interviewed with what it was when they reached adulthood, we have another means to study the potential impact of growing inequality. To do so, I group people in 5-year cohorts defined by the time they reached adulthood (i.e. 18 + survey year − age), and for each cohort, I document the corresponding Gini level of income inequality and country GDP per capita, as I did for each survey year (for methodological details, see Mijs 2018b). The range of cohorts is between those reaching adulthood in the 1950s to those who turned 18 in the 2010s.

Figure 15.3 shows the relationship between citizens' belief in meritocracy and the change in income inequality in their country, between the time they were 18 and the time they were interviewed. A positive number indicates growing inequality; a negative number indicates decreasing inequality. I find a small but non-significant relationship between changes in country-level income inequality and citizens' belief in structural inequality ($p > .10$) and a strong and statistically significant association with regard to citizens' belief in meritocracy ($p < .05$). Belief in meritocracy is an estimated 6 points higher for those who have witnessed the largest growth in income inequality, compared to those for whom the level of inequality in their society has remained stable, and 12 points higher compared to those who have experienced the sharpest decrease in inequality.

In the next section, I consider how differences in inequality beliefs impact citizens' concerns about inequality.

Explaining concerns about inequality

Having established an association between country-level inequality and beliefs about inequality, this section asks if (popular) beliefs about inequality explain citizens' concerns. I find that belief in meritocracy is negatively associated with concerns about inequality beliefs, as hypothesised. The relationship is driven both by individuals' beliefs ($p < .01$) and by popular belief in meritocracy ($p < .05$) as measured by the between-country difference in beliefs. I do not find a statistically significant relationship between citizens' concerns about inequality and over-time changes in popular belief in meritocracy.

Turning to consider the impact of citizens' structuralist beliefs about inequality, I find a positive association between citizens' concerns about inequality and their belief in the structural nature of inequality, both at the individual-level ($p < .001$) and when considering country-level beliefs ($p < .01$) and over-time change in beliefs ($p < 0.10$).

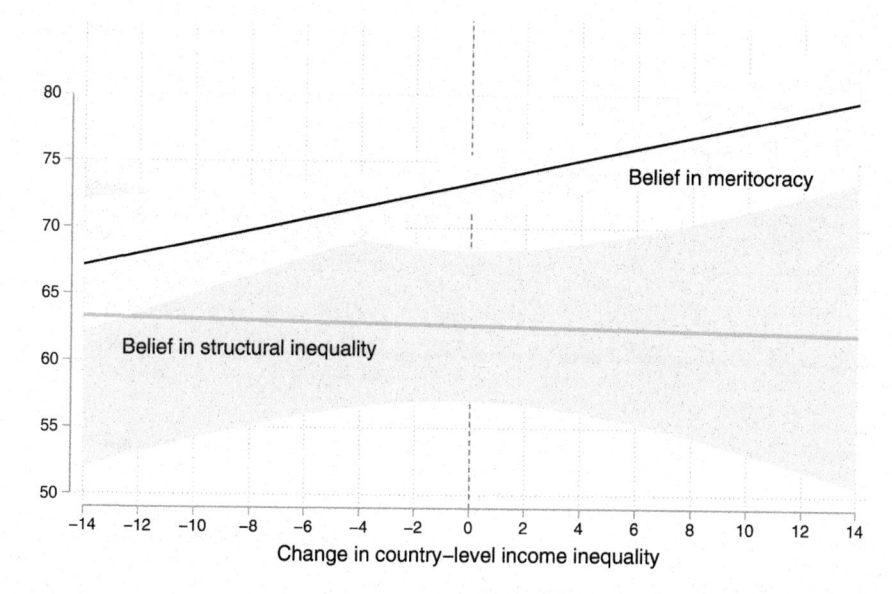

Figure 15.3 Citizens' inequality beliefs by change in income inequality experienced.
Source: Author's calculations from ISSP (2014).
Note: Displayed are citizens' belief in meritocracy (black line) and structural inequality (grey line), on the vertical axis, predicted by the change in country-level income inequality between the year a respondent turned 18 and the year they were surveyed (horizontal axis). A positive number indicates growing inequality, and a negative number indicates decreasing inequality, in units of the Gini coefficient of income inequality ranging from 0 (equality) to 100 (maximum inequality).

Last, I consider whether the relationship between citizens' inequality beliefs and their concerns about inequality differs by social class. I find significant interaction effects for country-average beliefs in structural inequality and meritocracy ($p < .001$). Country-level beliefs in structural inequality are a stronger predictor of middle-class citizens' concerns about inequality, as compared to working-class citizens. Conversely, country-level belief in meritocracy is an especially strong predictor of working-class citizens' concerns about inequality. I also find a significant interaction effect between citizens' social class and their belief in structural inequality ($p < .05$), but no significant effect when considering over-time change in country-level beliefs.

Figure 15.4 visualises the relationship between beliefs and concerns about inequality by social class. Citizens' concerns about inequality are generally much higher in countries where people believe that inequality reflects structural factors more than meritocratic factors, all else equal. The maximum difference in concerns ranges between 10 and 20 points, for lower and upper middle-class citizens. Working-class citizens' concerns, however, are unaffected by societal beliefs. Conversely, citizens are generally less concerned in countries where popular beliefs attribute inequality to hard work rather than structural forces. The

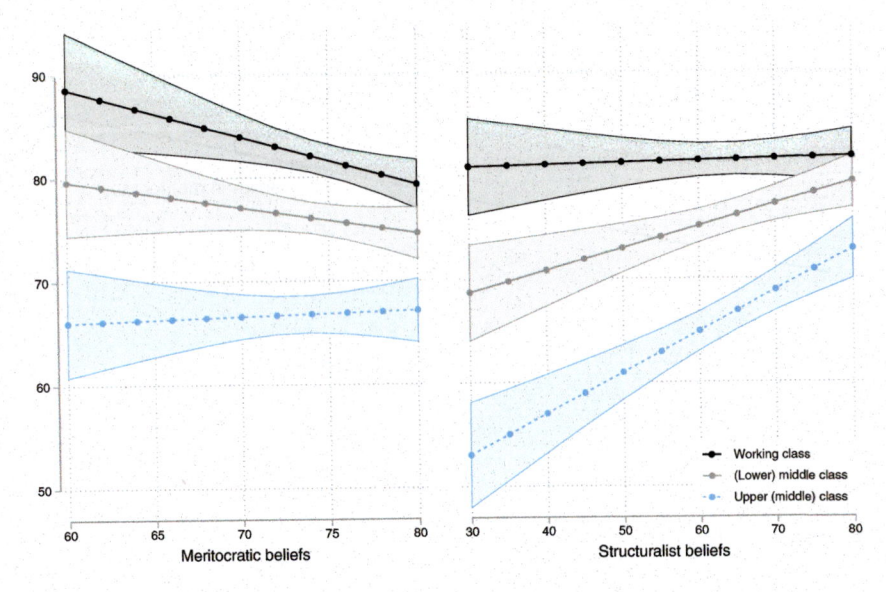

Figure 15.4 Citizens' concerns about inequality by social class and popular inequality beliefs.

Source: Author's calculations from ISSP (2014).

Note: Displayed on the vertical axis are citizens' concerns about inequality by social class, predicted by popular (country-level) beliefs in meritocracy (left) and structural inequality (right), on the horizontal axis.

difference in concerns is especially large for working-class citizens (10 points), smaller for lower middle-class citizens (about 5 points), and not significant for people in the upper middle class.

In sum, I have shown that citizens' concerns about inequality are strongly associated with their beliefs about the forces underlying income inequality. What fuels citizens' concerns about inequality is their belief that income inequality reflects structural processes that benefit some people, while putting others at a disadvantage. Conversely, belief in meritocracy dampens citizens' concerns. My findings suggest that concerns are driven both by people's own beliefs about inequality and by popular beliefs in a given country and time period.

Conclusions

Scholars and politicians have been puzzled by the lack of popular concern about the rising level of income inequality across the West. In this article, I provide an explanation by theorising, and empirically describing, a relationship between actual inequality and beliefs about inequality. I argue that what explains citizens' consent to inequality is their conviction that poverty and wealth are the outcomes of a fair meritocratic process. Citizens' meritocracy beliefs are solidified by the fact that people are unable to see the full extent of inequality in their society nor develop an awareness of the structural processes shaping unequal life outcomes. The reason for people's inability to see what separates them from their fellow citizens is that the lives of the rich and poor are increasingly divided between separate institutions: people live in neighbourhoods, go to schools and pick romantic partners and friends that fit their education and income level (Massey and Tannen 2016; Musterd 2005; Reardon and Bischoff 2011). Housing segregation, school stratification and social homogamy mean that one's chances of getting to know someone from a different socio-economic background, let alone developing an understanding of another person's privilege or plight, are slim. These then are the processes that produce the paradox we face, where citizens of some of the world's most unequal societies think of their country as the paragon of meritocracy (Bucca 2016; McCall 2013; Whyte 2011).

In this article, I show that citizens across the West have become more convinced that theirs is a meritocratic society. While countries have grown more unequal since the 1980s, nowhere have citizens lost faith in meritocracy. In fact, the empirical record suggests that belief in meritocracy in the Western world has never been as strong as it is today. Analysing variation between countries, I find that citizens in unequal societies more strongly believe that meritocratic factors are at the root of societal success, while giving less thought to structural, non-meritocratic, forces. Closely examining the variable pattern of growing inequality across the West does not give me much purchase on citizens' changing beliefs about inequality, but a cohort analysis, tracing citizens' beliefs and the trend in inequality they have experienced in their lifetime, reveals that growing inequality goes together with a strengthening of citizens' meritocratic beliefs. Citizens' beliefs about inequality, in turn, explain whether or not they express concern about inequality in their society.

These findings suggest paths for future work, theory and the politics of inequality. With regard to theorising about income inequality, my findings suggest that we may want to pay more attention to the role of experiences in reinforcing inequality (Dawtry et al. 2015; Edmiston 2018; Massey and Tannen 2016; Merolla, Hunt, and Serpe 2011; Mijs 2018a). Looking at politics and policy preferences through an experiential lens helps understand when and why rising inequality does not lead to popular concern. The analysis presented in this paper suggests that country-level inequality conditions people's experiences, but future research needs to explore different contexts that matter. A particularly interesting question is how national-level inequality translates into or interacts with inequality at the neighbourhood level and in social networks.

A necessary starting point for understanding the politics of inequality is to disentangle the relationship between experiences, beliefs and preferences. Publics in unequal societies may find themselves stuck in a feedback loop, where more inequality paradoxically leads them to experience less of it—and care less about it. Breaking that loop requires taking seriously people's beliefs and lived experiences, and designing social policy to bring the two in closer alignment. Until then, there is nothing surprising about the fact that people in highly unequal societies approach politics from the highly skewed vantage point of their own experiences.

References

Atkinson, Anthony B., Thomas Piketty, and Emmanuel Saez. 2011. "Top Incomes in the Long Run of History." *Journal of Economic Literature* 49(1):3–71. doi: 10.1257/jel.49.1.3.

Bénabou, Roland, and Jean Tirole. 2006. "Belief in a Just World and Redistributive Politics." *The Quarterly Journal of Economics* 121(2):699–746. doi: 10.1162/qjec.2006.121.2.699.

Bozick, Robert, Karl Alexander, Doris Entwisle, Susan Dauber, and Kerri Kerr. 2010. "Framing the Future: Revisiting the Place of Educational Expectations in Status Attainment." *Social Forces* 88(5):2027–2052. doi: 10.1353/sof.2010.0033.

Brooks, Clem, and Jeff Manza. 2013. "A Broken Public? Americans' Responses to the Great Recession." *American Sociological Review* 78(5):727–748. doi: 10.1177/0003122413498255.

Bucca, Mauricio. 2016. "Merit and Blame in Unequal Societies: Explaining Latin Americans' Beliefs about Wealth and Poverty." *Research in Social Stratification and Mobility* 44(-1):98–112. doi: 10.1016/j.rssm.2016.02.005.

Cruces, Guillermo, Ricardo Perez-Truglia, and Martin Tetaz. 2013. "Biased Perceptions of Income Distribution and Preferences for Redistribution: Evidence from a Survey Experiment." *Journal of Public Economics* 98(1):100–112. doi: 10.1016/j.jpubeco.2012.10.009.

Dawtry, Rael J., Robbie M. Sutton, and Chris G. Sibley. 2015. "Why Wealthier People Think People Are Wealthier, and Why It Matters: From Social Sampling to Attitudes to Redistribution." *Psychological Science* 26(9):1389–1400. doi: 10.1177/0956797615586560.

Edmiston, Daniel. 2018. "The Poor 'Sociological Imagination' of the Rich: Explaining Attitudinal Divergence towards Welfare, Inequality, and Redistribution." *Social Policy & Administration* 53(1):1–15. doi: 10.1111/spol.12366.

Gimpelson, Vladimir, and Daniel Treisman. 2018. "Misperceiving Inequality." *Economics & Politics* 30(1):27–54. doi: 10.1111/ecpo.12103.

Irwin, Sarah. 2018. "Lay Perceptions of Inequality and Social Structure." *Sociology* 52(2):211–227. doi: 10.1177/0038038516661264.

ISSP Research Group. 2014. *International Social Survey Programme: Social Inequality I-IV - ISSP 1987–1992–1999–2009*. Cologne: GESIS Data Archive.

Janmaat, Jan Germen. 2013. "Subjective Inequality: A Review of International Comparative Studies on People's Views about Inequality." *European Journal of Sociology* 54(3):357–389.

Lübker, Malte. 2007. "Inequality and the Demand for Redistribution: Are the Assumptions of the New Growth Theory Valid?" *Socio-Economic Review* 5(1):117–148. doi: 10.1093/ser/mwl002.

Massey, Douglas S., and Jonathan Tannen. 2016. "Segregation, Race, and the Social Worlds of Rich and Poor." Pp. 13–34 in *The Dynamics of Opportunity in America. Evidence and Perspectives*, edited by I. Kirsch and H. Braun. Dordrecht: Springer.

McCall, Leslie. 2013. *The Undeserving Rich. American Beliefs about Inequality, Opportunity, and Redistribution*. New York: Cambridge University Press.

McCoy, Shannon K., and Brenda Major. 2007. "Priming Meritocracy and the Psychological Justification of Inequality." *Journal of Experimental Social Psychology* 43(3):341–351. doi: 10.1016/j.jesp.2006.04.009.

Merolla, David M., Matthew O. Hunt, and Richard T. Serpe. 2011. "Concentrated Disadvantage and Beliefs about the Causes of Poverty: A Multi-Level Analysis." *Sociological Perspectives* (54):205–228.

Mijs, Jonathan J. B. 2016. "The Unfulfillable Promise of Meritocracy: Three Lessons and Their Implications for Justice in Education." *Social Justice Research* 29(1):14–34. doi: 10.1007/s11211-014-0228-0.

Mijs, Jonathan J. B. 2018a. "Inequality Is a Problem of Inference: How People Solve the Social Puzzle of Unequal Outcomes." *Societies* 8(3):64. doi: 10.3390/soc8030064.

Mijs, Jonathan J. B. 2018b. "Visualizing Belief in Meritocracy, 1930–2010." *Socius* 4(1).

Mijs, Jonathan J. B. 2019. "The Paradox of Inequality: Income Inequality and Belief in Meritocracy Go Hand in Hand." *Socio-Economic Review* (in press). doi: 10.1093/ser/mwy051.

Milanovic, Branko. 2013. *All the Ginis Dataset.* Washington, D.C.: World Bank Group.

Mills, C. Wright. 1959. *The Sociological Imagination.* London: Oxford University Press.

Musterd, Sako. 2005. "Social and Ethnic Segregation in Europe: Levels, Causes, and Effects." *Journal of Urban Affairs* 27(3):331–348. doi: 10.1111/j.0735-2166.2005.00239.x.

Norton, Michael I., and Dan Ariely. 2011. "Building a Better America—One Wealth Quintile at a Time." *Perspectives on Psychological Science* 6(1):9–12. doi: 10.1177/1745691610393524.

Osberg, Lars, and Timothy Smeeding. 2006. "'Fair' Inequality? Attitudes toward Pay Differentials: The United States in Comparative Perspective." *American Sociological Review* 71(3):450–473. doi: 10.1177/000312240607100305.

Owens, Ann. 2016. "Inequality in Children's Contexts Income Segregation of Households with and without Children." *American Sociological Review* 81(3):549–74. doi: 10.1177/0003122416642430.

Piketty, Thomas, and Emmanuel Saez. 2003. "Income Inequality in the United States, 1913–1998." *The Quarterly Journal of Economics* 118(1):1–41. doi: 10.1162/00335530360535135.

Reardon, Sean F., and Kendra Bischoff. 2011. "Income Inequality and Income Segregation." *American Journal of Sociology* 116(4):1092–1153. doi: 10.1086/657114.

Shedd, Carla. 2015. *Unequal City. Race, Schools, and Perceptions of Injustice.* New York: Russell Sage Foundation.

Trump, Kris-Stella. 2017. "Income Inequality Influences Perceptions of Legitimate Income Differences." *British Journal of Political Science* 48(4):929–952. doi: 10.1017/S0007123416000326.

Whyte, Martin. 2011. "Myth of the Social Volcano: Popular Responses to Rising Inequality in China." in *The People's Republic of China at 60.* Cambridge, MA: Harvard University Asia Center.

Wu, Alfred M., and Kee-Lee Chou. 2017. "Public Attitudes towards Income Redistribution: Evidence from Hong Kong." *Social Policy & Administration* 51(5):738–754. doi: 10.1111/spol.12192.

Index

absolute levels of wealth 30, 34
Administration of Unemployment Insurance in Britain 115
Afghanistan 146
African 24, 26, 33, 55, 63, 151
age 2–3, 18–19, 25, 31–33, 35, 42, 44, 171, 173, 230, 232
agency 30, 60, 151, 154, 160, 187
agenda 66, 81, 101, 126–28, 149
agenda-setting approach 137
agenda-setting approach to social problems 137
agenda-setting function of mass media 149
Age of Austerity 95, 134, 209
Algorithms 63
Al Jazeera 156
All-Party Parliamentary Group *See* APPG
Amartya Sen 120
Amazon 130
APPG (All-Party Parliamentary Group) 31, 39, 192
Asian 55–59, 212
assets 27, 29, 31, 34–35, 37–38, 40, 51, 58, 63, 68, 71–72; financial 13, 17, 69
attitudes to poverty 5, 171
attitudes to poverty and inequality 165, 168, 170, 172, 174, 214
attitudes to social mobility 42
attitudes to tax 38
audiences 118, 128–29, 134, 154, 209
austerity xvi–xvii, 5, 7, 90, 95–96, 126–27, 129, 131–34, 160, 192–209, 214, 216–17, 223–25
Australia 89, 152, 227
Austria xvi, xviii, 72, 75–76, 176, 178–81, 185–86, 190, 227, 231

Bangladeshi 24, 33, 62–63
Bank 36–37, 39–40, 104, 116, 126, 199, 212, 223
Bank of England 36–37, 104, 199, 212

BBC 89, 93–94, 119, 121–27, 132–33, 151, 155–56, 158, 199, 207, 213
benefits 4–5, 12, 27–28, 34, 36, 62, 87–93, 96–97, 100, 102–3, 127, 129, 194–95, 201–2, 204–5
Biden, Joe 55
billionaires 68, 71, 191
Blair, Tony 123, 125
BLM Movement 61
Bourdieu 71, 80, 100, 114
Breadline Britain xvi–xvii, 7, 93, 117, 120–23, 128–29, 131–33
Brexit 12, 27, 31, 44, 88, 206, 216
British newspapers 98, 101, 132, 142, 174
British Social Attitudes Survey 5, 111–12, 115, 165–67, 170–72, 174, 195, 203, 214
British tabloids 115, 160
Broadcasting Act 121
broadcasting regulation 126
broadsheet 169–74, 202, 205
Brown, Gordon 199
BSA 91, 206–7
budget deficits 222
budget, household 196, 205
Buenos Aires 160
Bush Jr. 146
business cycles 136, 145
Business Live 52

Cairncross 133
Cameron, David 45
Canada 227
Cape Times 151–52, 155–56
capital gains tax 34–35, 38
capitalism 77, 177, 188, 190–91
Caribbean 24, 55, 56, 63–64
Chancellor 38, 198
Chartered Institute of Public Finance and Accountancy (CIPFA) 93, 95
Chernobyl 141

Child Poverty Action Group 127, 132
Child Poverty Commission 45–46
children 3, 49–52, 58, 89–90, 117, 120, 128–30, 134, 212, 228, 237
China 237
Chomsky 112, 115
CIPFA (Chartered Institute of Public Finance and Accountancy) 93, 95
classes 43, 47, 51, 58, 64, 68, 71–72, 75, 77–80, 195, 202, 231, 234
Clegg, Nick 45
climate 126, 208
Clinton, Bill 143
CNN 151–52, 155–56, 208
Coalition 11–12, 74, 80, 107–8
Commission on Race and Ethnic Disparities 62
Commonwealth 59
Communications Act 123, 132
community 2, 59, 65, 132, 174, 222
Conservative Party 45, 51, 91, 107–8, 119, 121, 128, 194, 205–6
consumers 34, 59, 72, 128, 130, 172, 203
Corbyn, Jeremy 129, 206
coronavirus 56, 66, 175, 207
cost-of-living crisis 7
COVID 39, 213–25
Covid-19 38, 54–55, 58, 66–67, 130, 132, 211–13, 222–24
credit, universal 92, 129, 212
crunch, credit 141–42, 147

Daily Express 87–88
Daily Mail 65, 88, 110, 118, 127, 132, 198, 200
Daily Star 87–88
Daily Telegraph 100, 110
Darling, Alistair 205
Deaton Review 3
debt 31, 37, 41, 118, 125, 166, 187, 197–99; household 31, 81; national 126, 194, 198, 209; public 105, 107–8, 184, 198
deficit 126, 193–99, 202–5, 207
deindustrialisation 206
Democracy 114, 223
Democrats 146
Department for Education 49, 52
Department for Work and Pensions *See* DWP
Disability Discrimination Act 25
discourses xvi, 45, 47, 51, 59, 100, 113, 115, 178–79, 190–91, 224
discrimination 55–56, 60–61, 64–65, 152, 228

disparities 2–3, 55, 62–63, 152, 155, 195, 224
distribution 12, 14–16, 18, 20, 22–23, 26, 30, 40, 69–70, 74, 79
diversity 50, 101, 122
Downing Street 121
DWP (Department for Work and Pensions) 13, 27–28, 62, 65, 89, 91, 167, 175

economic crisis 13, 26, 90, 98, 154, 193, 197–98, 203, 207, 218, 221–22
economics xvi–xviii, 27, 39–41, 49, 81, 149, 176, 183, 189–91, 223, 236–37
Economics Statistics Centre of Excellence 197
Economist, The 101
economists 101, 146, 177, 182, 186, 199, 206–7
education 2–3, 47, 49–53, 58, 61, 63–64, 66, 172–74, 189, 193–94, 197, 230, 235–36
Education Endowment Foundation 49, 52–53
elite 43–44, 151, 199
Engels 72, 80
England 7, 15, 21, 32–33, 36–37, 39–40, 48, 53, 66, 104, 116
entrepreneurs 31, 39, 44, 123, 187–88
Equalities & Human Rights Commission 61
equality 8, 46–47, 54, 56, 58, 61, 63–64, 135, 182–83, 233
ethics 40, 96
Europe 52, 72, 79–80, 94, 96, 115, 147–48, 178, 186, 237
European Union 129, 178, 203, 206

Facebook 89
First World War 29, 105
Fiscal Studies 7, 52, 131–32, 199, 224
foodbanks 129
Foucault 57, 65
Fox News 126, 208
framing 100, 102, 116, 129, 137, 148, 157, 182, 206, 236
France 73–75, 81, 107, 115, 191, 227

Galbraith 176, 188–90
GDP 34, 105, 107–8, 198, 208, 222
gender 3, 14, 152, 230
Germany 1, 6, 72–75, 107, 177–81, 185–6, 227
global financial crisis xvi–xvii, 98–99, 189, 211, 213–14

Global South 151, 154
Google News 152, 155–57, 159
government policy 29, 90, 100, 217
government spending 105, 126–27, 196–97, 217
Great Britain 29, 41, 67, 209
Great Recession 99, 105, 114, 208, 236
Greece 75, 198
growth 14, 16–21, 23, 26, 33–34, 36, 44, 50, 123–25, 127, 147, 183, 187
Guardian 38–39, 65–66, 96–97, 131–32, 134, 141–44, 151–52, 156, 158–59, 178–81, 191, 198, 200, 202, 208–9
Gulf War 137, 141–42, 147

Habermas, Jürgen 189–90
Haldane, Andy 37, 40
Hall, Stuart 59
HFCS (Household Finance and Consumption Survey) 69, 73, 75–76
HMRC 91
homelessness 86, 125, 129, 165–66, 172, 190
Hong Kong 237
Household Finance and Consumption Survey (HFCS) 69, 73, 75–76
household incomes 12, 15, 20, 24, 131, 193
housing 24, 30, 36, 41, 46, 48–51, 53, 55–56, 59, 61, 177–78
Huffington Post 134

Iceland 227
Institute for Fiscal Studies (IFS) 199, 212
International Monetary Fund (IMF) 1, 37, 198, 199
Immigration 113, 195–97, 204
Income inequality 3, 11, 26, 29, 63, 71, 85, 136–48, 166, 193, 212, 226–35
India 1, 21
Indian Times 151, 155–56, 158
Ireland 20, 72, 75, 176, 178–80, 182, 185–86, 227
Irish Times 178–81
Italy 75, 198, 227
ITV xvi, 4, 118–123, 128–129

Japan 123, 227
Jobs 3, 37–38, 42, 47–50, 57–60, 94, 113, 158, 183, 196, 200–201, 204, 212
Johnson, Boris 44, 45, 61–62
Joseph Rowntree Foundation (JRF) 93, 118, 112

Keynes 177–78, 187, 188, 192

Labour Force Survey (LFS) 13, 57
labour market 3, 33, 37, 55, 57–58, 61, 63, 65, 74, 229
Low-income 37, 57, 89, 194, 196, 213
Lehman Brothers 125

Malthus 4, 99–101, 104–5, 111, 113–14
Mandelson, Peter 123, 143
Marx 71, 186
meritocracy 45–46, 135, 176, 182, 188, 214, 216, 226, 230–35
Miliband, Ed. 38
Murdoch, Rupert 122, 181

Narratives 45, 56, 59–60, 64–65, 68, 79, 98, 100–1, 113–14, 154, 184, 186, 192, 195, 200, 202, 205
Nationalism 113
National Centre for Social Research 90, 91, 95, 174
National Union of Journalists 94
Neoliberal 176–78, 187, 193
Netflix 130
Netherlands 72, 75, 227
New York Times 145, 151
NHS 54–55, 195, 197, 200–201, 219
Northern Rock 125

Obama 6, 65, 146, 158
Occupy Wall Street 146–47
OECD 1, 7, 11, 43, 47–49, 69, 135, 199, 212
Office for National Statistics (ONS) 12, 60, 94–95
Osborne, George 5, 91
Oxfam 153

Piketty, Thomas 5, 33, 35, 57, 68–69, 158, 176–77, 179, 182, 184–87, 189, 226
power 30–31, 34, 47, 49, 51, 64, 68–71, 80, 85, 93, 95, 100, 105, 111, 119, 123, 146, 150, 203, 192–93, 199, 202, 213

Qatar 152
Quangos 195, 202

Race Disparity Unit (RDU) 57, 62
Reaganism 136
Reuters Institute for the Study of Journalism 212
Rishi Sunak 45

Royal Economic Society 198
Runnymede Trust 63

social classes 33, 46, 68, 71–72, 74, 76, 79
social mobility 2, 3, 42–43, 45–51, 117–18, 168, 182
Social Mobility Commission 43, 46
South Africa 151–52
Stereotypes 1, 6, 59, 90, 102, 213–14
Stiglitz, Joseph 2, 55, 125, 189
Sunday Times 178–82

tabloid 90, 127–28, 160, 170–74, 202, 205, 218
Telegraph 100, 110, 118, 142, 198, 201–2
Thatcher, Margaret 11, 45, 48, 119, 121–22, 127, 135, 145, 178, 217
Theresa May 38, 45, 62, 206
Truss, Liz 45

underrepresented 51, 189
undeserving 86–87, 91, 125, 197
unemployment 4, 49, 57, 74, 91, 99–113, 119–20, 129, 147, 186, 222
Union 110, 120, 141, 157

vulnerable 118, 120, 154, 206

Wall Street Journal 138, 142, 145
Watchdog 150–51, 189
Welfare Reform Act 46, 90
Windrush Scandal 64
Working class xxii, 42, 202, 231, 234
World Bank 1, 212
World War II 206

YouGov 193, 214
Youth 192, 228